Working Order

Working Order

Workplace Industrial Relations over Two Decades

Eric Batstone

Basil Blackwell

First published 1984

Basil Blackwell Publisher Ltd
108 Cowley Road, Oxford OX4 1JF, UK

Basil Blackwell Inc.
432 Park Avenue South, Suite 1505,
New York, NY 10016, USA

British Library Cataloguing in Publication Data

Batstone, Eric
    Working order.
    1. Industrial relations—Great Britain—
    History—20th century
    I. Title
    331'.0941   HD8391

    ISBN 0-631-13751-3

Library of Congress Cataloging in Publication Data

Batstone, Eric.
    Working order.

    Bibliography: p. 344.
    Includes index.
    1. Industrial relations—Great Britain. I. Title.
    HD8391.B38   1984   331'.0941   84-12489
    ISBN 0-631-13751-3

Typeset by Pioneer, East Sussex.
Printed in Great Britain

Contents

Preface

This book, like Topsy, 'just grow'd'. It developed out of a series of seminars, conference papers and lectures given over the last five years or so in the United Kingdom, other parts of Europe, and Japan. At that stage most of my data related to the period up to 1978, which seemed sadly dated by the time I had the opportunity to revise the various papers and shape them into a coherent whole. There was remarkably little reliable or systematic data on the current industrial relations situation to supplement the earlier studies. Fortunately, a small grant from the Research Committee of the Department of Social and Administrative Studies at the University of Oxford permitted me to bring a good deal of the material up to date through a postal survey which forms the basis of Part II. In addition, the final chapter affords an international perspective. The work on Japan discussed there derives from my cooperation with Professor Totsuka and his colleagues at the University of Tokyo. The research on which the discussion is based was made possible by a Fellowship from the Japan Society for the Promotion of Science.

Many people have played a part in the creation of this book and I am grateful to them. Comments made at various seminars have often been useful. Clearly the work draws heavily upon my time at the Industrial Relations Research Unit at Warwick University: to my colleagues and friends there I owe a particular debt (although it should not be assumed that they would agree with the arguments presented here). In addition, I have gained a great deal of stimulus and support from my present colleagues and students, in particular from the Industrial Sociology Group at Nuffield College. David Deaton of the Industrial Relations Research Unit and Ken MacDonald of Oxford have given more specific advice and aid on the technical aspects of the survey analysis in Part II.

Trude Hickey, Margaret Bridgland and Brenda Dry have endured my scarcely legible drafts with goodwill and humour and managed to produce a more polished version. Helen Dore and Nicola Harris bravely and meticulously undertook the heavy burden of copy-editing. To all of them I owe a particular debt. Finally, my family have once more made a great contribution: my parents indexed the book; Toni has given both concrete help and moral support, while Tom and Peter have endured the process of research and writing once more with understanding and good spirit.

1 Introduction

Over the last two decades the 'problem' of workplace relations has been widely debated. In the 1960s commentators became increasingly concerned about the declining competitive position of the British economy: while there had been a trend in this direction since before the turn of the century, concern became widespread only when countries such as France and Germany actually overtook Britain in the international league of economic performance. A number of factors were cited as directly contributing to the sorry state of the British economy, but a particularly important cause was widely believed to be the pattern of industrial relations and, relatedly, the nature of work organization. Since the mid-1960s, therefore, the 'reform' of workplace industrial relations has become an important issue.

Three main strands of argument can be identified. The first held that trade unions had achieved an 'excessive' degree of power which they wielded 'irresponsibly' and to the detriment of consumers and the workers they were meant to represent. It was considered necessary both to check and to channel union power and, among other things, the law was deemed to have an important role in this respect. This approach to the 'problem' of industrial relations led to the 1971 Industrial Relations Act and guides the actual and proposed legislation of the present Conservative Government. An important aspect of monetarism — at least in practice if not in theory — is the reduction of union power through weakening the position of workers on the labour market.

At the other extreme, radical writers have argued that if a 'problem' of industrial relations existed it concerned neither economic performance nor the 'excessive' power of trade unions. Rather the problem lay in the structures of inequality which characterized society and which inevitably led to fundamental conflicts of interest. One could only, therefore, achieve 'order' in industry — and society — if fundamental structural changes occurred giving fuller recognition to the interests of workers. There was, of course, a considerable divergence of views as to precisely what structural changes were required: that is, what were the sufficient as well as the necessary conditions for 'order'.

Between these two extremes stood what has become widely known as the 'pluralist' or 'liberal pluralist' view, which held that in fact no fundamental problem of the balance of power within industry existed — workers and their unions were neither excessively nor insufficiently powerful. And while there did exist a significant conflict of interest between employer and employee, there were other 'cross-cutting' conflicts as well. Hence the employment relationship did not constitute such a fundamental and pervasive source of division as radical writers suggested, and, under certain conditions, it was possible to arrive at compromise between the interests of employers and employees. The way in which 'order' could be achieved, therefore, lay in the development of institutional arrangements which reflected the location of power and facilitated the development of coherent and explicit agreements between the parties. While the state could play a role in fostering and encouraging these developments and while it might also be necessary to operate incomes policies, the law, it was argued, had a limited role to play in the reconstruction of industrial order.

For much of the 1970s it seemed as if employers adopted the pluralist perspective, at a practical if not a philosophical level. At any rate, in the case of manual workers in manufacturing — on whom the debate largely focused — and in much of the public sector there were significant attempts to change institutional arrangements. These trends did not appear to be checked, and indeed were often encouraged, by legislation such as the 1971 Act and by other state initiatives including incomes policies. However, despite the continuing debates surrounding the 'problem' of industrial relations and the effects of what is often known as 'reformism' there has been remarkably little in the way of systematic attempts to assess what exactly happened to workplace industrial relations in the decade from the late 1960s. This is in itself a serious gap: it is that much greater because without an understanding of developments within that period we can scarcely hope to understand what is currently happening in the context of massive unemployment. Indeed, discussions of the current state of industrial relations appear to be largely based on the experience of companies which are likely to be exceptional in some sense or on 'intuition' and *a priori* theorizing which pay scant attention to the realities of industrial relations.

This book attempts to help fill this gap. In Part I it seeks to gather the available evidence and to assess both the scale and significance of workplace reform up until the late 1970s. Part II attempts to assess what is happening to workplace industrial relations in manufacturing at the present time, focusing almost exclusively on developments at the level of the company and workplace. This approach has been adopted for two main reasons: first, developments at national level have been widely (if rather unsatisfactorily) discussed and have often served to highlight the importance of the workplace level, and second, the study of workplace industrial relations is a sufficiently wide undertaking without extending it still further. However, this is not to deny the significance of the more general political atmosphere nor, more specifically, the importance of industrial relations legislation or incomes policies. Indeed, both will be referred to in the course of the book, while in the Conclusion the relationship between the workplace and broader factors will be considered.

Parts I and II broadly follow the same pattern. The structure and strategy of management is considered first, and then the organization of shop stewards. An attempt is made to assess the effects of particular substantive strategies upon workplace industrial relations. Before turning to these themes, however, it is necessary initially to chart in some detail the different perspectives which have been adopted in analysing workplace industrial relations, and reformism in particular, for these serve to structure much of the subsequent discussion. Following a well-established tradition, it is useful to start by considering what is widely seen to be the major statement of the liberal pluralist position — the Report of the Royal Commission on Trade Unions and Employers' Associations published in 1968, and commonly referred to as the Donovan Commission.

FRAMES OF REFERENCE AND REFORM

Donovan and the Liberal Pluralist Perspective

It would be wrong to suggest that reformism in British industrial relations followed from the proposals of the Donovan Commission. Indeed, as subsequent chapters will argue, it is open to question how far management espoused its philosophy. But the Report has become central to the academic discussion of industrial relations in Britain and, in Turner's terms, may be seen as 'leading people boldly in the direction they appear to be going anyway' (1968, p. 359).

In addition, it has to be remembered that the Donovan Report was a political rather than an academic document. Key members of the Commission were keen to prevent attempts to deal with industrial relations primarily through legal means, so that much of the Report is a critique of the unitarist approach. Nevertheless, within its overall argument there does exist a fairly coherent statement of the liberal pluralist position. In view of the fact that there has often been considerable disagreement over 'what Donovan really said' it seems sensible to outline its argument at some length. (I do not accept the view that the Report should only be seen as a critique of legal measures, since it does outline an alternative and it is against that alternative that legal regulation is assessed.)

The Donovan Commission, which reported in 1968, identified as 'the central defect in British industrial relations . . . the disorder in factory and workshop relations and pay structures promoted by the conflict between the formal and informal systems' (p. 262). The key feature of the 'formal system' — 'the official institutions' — was the industry-wide collective agreement. The 'informal system' had developed through 'the actual behaviour of trade unions and employers' associations, of managers, shop stewards and workers' (p. 261). Conflict between the two systems arose because, on the one hand, 'the informal system undermines the regulative effect of industry-wide agreements' while the formal system prevents 'the informal system from developing into an orderly and effective method of regulation' (p. 36). The Commission argued that this pattern of industrial relations was in need of reform because of its 'disadvantages':

> the tendency of extreme decentralization and self-government to degenerate into indecision and anarchy; the propensity to breed inefficiency; and the reluctance to change. All these characteristics become more damaging as they develop, as the rate of technical progress increases and as the need for economic growth becomes more urgent. (p. 262)

Workplace bargaining was, in Flanders' phrase, 'largely informal, largely fragmented, largely autonomous'. It was autonomous because external bargaining procedures could not respond to it; hence the role of the formal system continued to diminish, 'and with it the control of trade unions and employers' associations' (p. 18). It was fragmented because 'it is conducted in such a way that different groups in the works get different concessions at different times', and it was informal 'because of the predominance of unwritten understandings and of custom and practice' (p. 18). Management had done little to counter these developments. This, the Commission argued, was in part attributable to their attachment to their associations, and hence industry-level agreements, which would be weakened by comprehensive factory agreements.

Moreover, payment systems (notably payment by results) and the ways they were applied (the infrequent use of work study and the proliferation of additional payments) worked against plant-wide coherence. Higher levels of management seemed unaware of issues such as the distribution and purposes of overtime, while personnel managers — where they existed — were necessarily engaged in 'fighting fires' arising from 'disorderly pay structures and uncoordinated, personnel practices' which derived from traditional practices. At the same time, shop stewards — whose influence derived directly from the work group and indirectly from full employment — played an important role: but they could do little to impose order for 'trouble is thrust upon them' (p. 28). Moreover, the stewards' role — and hence disorder — was encouraged by managements' preference for dealing with them rather than full-time officials because stewards had an 'intimate knowledge of the circumstances of the case' (p. 28). Certain features of the unions also encouraged the tendency towards the rise of the shop steward. Multi-unionism and the structure of union government often meant that there was a hiatus between workplace realities and union officials' knowledge of them, so that union leaders might be 'out of touch'. Not only could this mean that stewards and workers opposed agreements made at industry level, but also union officials could play little significant part in disputes on issues not covered by industry agreements, particularly given full employment and the structure of the unions such that 'the seat of power has almost always been close to the members' (p. 32).

'Informal' arrangements were satisfactory to most of the 'participants', according to Donovan. Their attractions were that they were 'comfortable', they were flexible since rules and procedures could be circumvented, and they constituted 'a very high degree of self-government in industry' (p. 33). However, these comfortable arrangements meant that industrial relations were disorderly. Fractional shop-floor bargaining resulted in 'competitive sectional wage adjustments and chaotic pay structures'; these, along with the importance of unwritten understandings and custom and practice, helped to explain the growth of 'unofficial and unconstitutional strikes and other forms of workshop pressure'.

The Commission focused upon two aspects of the inefficient use of manpower: 'restrictive practices' and the problems of training. The latter were seen to be associated with the craft tradition and the Commission argued that obstacles to the employment of dilutees should be removed and the role of industrial training boards should be supported. On the former, the Commission argued that the 'formal system' was 'especially ill-fitted to accomplish improvements in the use of manpower'. For 'restrictions' were normally enforced by work groups, and industry-level bargaining could 'rarely exercise effective control over the methods of work employed in individual factories'. Moreover, the formal system assumed that working arrangements were a matter of managerial prerogative, while in practice there was informal and fragmented bargaining. In this environment, 'work group restrictive practices are likely to thrive, and yet any attempt to negotiate relaxation runs counter to the formal assumptions of the system' (p. 79).

The Commission rejected the possibility of 'forcing the informal system to comply with the assumptions of the formal system' on the grounds that 'reality cannot be forced to comply with pretences' (p. 36). It was necessary 'to introduce greater order into factory and workshop relations':

> What is required is effective and orderly collective bargaining over such issues as the control of incentive schemes, the regulation of hours worked, the use of job evaluation, work practices and the linking of changes in pay to changes in performance, facilities for shop stewards and disciplinary rules and appeals. (p. 40)

Industry-wide agreements could not 'meet the bill' because employers would not be prepared to delegate such responsibilities to their associations, and, in any case, the diversity of corporate characteristics precluded any effective 'outside' control over such detailed issues.

The Commission argued that 'factory-wide agreements can however provide the remedy'. Agreements of this kind could 'cover matters which industry-wide agreements must omit'. Factory agreements could deal with methods of production, the distribution of overtime, methods of timing jobs and conversion factors, wage differentials and actual rates of pay. They could set out grievance procedures which were consistent with other features of the organization. These could deal with such matters as work practices, discipline and redundancy. And factory agreements — according to the Commission — 'can cover the rights and obligations of shop stewards within the factory' (p. 41).

An important feature of the Commission's recommendations concerned the extension of collective bargaining and the fuller recognition of union and steward rights within the workplace. Essentially it rejected legal 'solutions' to the perceived problems of industrial relations beyond providing support to the philosophy of pluralism. Indeed, much of the Report is devoted to the need for firmer worker and union rights but a rejection of other 'legalistic' prescriptions.

The Commission emphasized two aspects of factory agreements. The first was essentially procedural, the argument being that 'the boards of companies' should 'review industrial relations, with particular objectives in mind'. These objectives were: to develop jointly with the unions 'comprehensive and authoritative collective bargaining machinery' and grievance procedures; to reach joint agreements concerning the position of shop stewards, covering such issues as their election, number and constituencies, credentials, access to members and other stewards in the plant, responsibilities of senior stewards, stewards' pay and facilities for training; management should also reach agreements on redundancy, disciplinary procedures and means to discuss and thereby promote safety (p. 45).

On more substantive matters, the Commission placed great emphasis upon explicit negotiation of, and formal agreement on, working practices. Drawing upon the experience of productivity bargaining, it recommended 'formal negotiation of work practices' — 'matters previously covered by "custom and practice" are for the first time made the subject of collective bargaining':

> a genuine productivity agreement offers solutions to many of the typical problems of industrial relations. It raises standards of supervision and of managerial planning and control. It closes the gap between rates of pay and actual earnings. It permits negotiation on performance. It enables demarcation difficulties to be eliminated or reduced. It concentrates decisions at the level of the company or factory. It formalizes and regulates the position of the shop steward. (p. 84)

The Commission was fully aware of the implications of its proposals for management and unions. In the case of the former, as noted above, it emphasized the need for top management — indeed, boards of directors — to develop conscious and coherent policies. Similarly, it recommended not only union initiatives to resolve problems of multi-unionism, but also to establish constitutionally the rights and responsibilities of stewards: thereby, it was claimed, they could both operate more effectively and at the same time be made more responsible to the union.

It is also worth noting, however, that the Commission was relatively realistic concerning the practicability of its proposals. It noted that factory agreements were no automatic guarantee of 'order': agreements may not cover all issues, the system could be manipulated, procedures 'can be by-passed, telescoped or ignored':

> Fragmented bargaining and informal workshop understandings

can flourish under a factory agreement as they can in its absence. All that is claimed for a factory agreement is that it is a means for the effective regulation of industrial relations within the factory where managers choose to use it for that purpose . . . No agreement can do a manager's job for him. A factory agreement however, can assist competent managers. . . If Britain is to shift to factory agreements the change must be accomplished by boards of directors. (p. 41)

But in addition, boards and managers 'cannot accomplish the reform by themselves. They need the cooperation of the trade unions, which must sign the agreements and take their share of responsibility under them.' In short, it identified a mutually supportive interaction between management reform initiatives, union support and formal factory agreements: it equally recognized a number of conditions which underlay the feasibility of such a 'virtuous circle'.

The proposals of the Donovan Commission have been outlined at some length because — particularly in recent years — they have been subject to a variety of interpretations, which will be outlined and assessed below. First, however, it is useful to consider the philosophy underlying the Donovan Report. As is indicated by the fact that a number of its members felt it necessary to sign 'Supplementary Notes', there was not a consensus upon the nature of reform. There was, however, a dominant perspective which, following Turner, became labelled as the Oxford school of industrial relations (a term no longer — if ever — applicable).

As commentators have been at pains to note, it is quite wrong to believe that this group agrees on all points — indeed, it is clear from their writings that they diverge significantly. They did, however, share — at least at that time — certain key tenets. Fundamental to these was the belief that — at least up to a point — divergent interests in society and in industry were legitimate and, indeed, a lynch-pin of freedom. Given the legitimacy — and the power — of different groups, legal moves to suppress industrial relations 'problems' were both immoral and likely to be ineffective. A process of bargaining could achieve some form of orderly compromise: institutions of joint regulation meant a 'place in the sun' for groups both substantively and procedurally and therefore gave them vested interests in the existing structure of industrial relations: hence liberal pluralists accepted as valid the thesis of the institutionalization of industrial conflict.

The logic of this liberal pluralist argument did not, however, assume that procedural or substantive arrangements were immutable. Indeed, alterations in the broader structure of society and industry meant that new groups could emerge and 'demand attention', and that the balance of power could change. The essence of the Donovan Commission's case was that such changes had occurred and that they required changes in institutional arrangements.

While the Donovan Report has been criticized for a tendency to confuse description and explanation, Fox and Flanders did attempt to develop a more theoretical account of the Donovan case. They argued that there had always been pressures towards 'disorder in industrial relations arising from the inter-action between normative aspirations and prevailing norms' (1970, p. 253). Groups sought to change the procedural norms or the substantive norms: disorder could also arise from 'an absence of regulation about certain issues on which one group at least has normative aspirations'. What was distinctive in the late 1960s was the addition of a further factor which they termed 'inflationary fragmentation'. Fragmentation involved 'a contraction in the size of the units of regulation, often accompanied by a shift from bilateral to virtually unilateral regulation'. They continued:

> . . . the ensuing disorder results, not from manifest conflict over procedural norms as such, but from the substantive consequences of the breaking up of larger units of regulation into a number of smaller and unintegrated units . . . this structural change is usually uncontested; the party on whom it is imposed being unable or unwilling to resist. (p. 253)

Fragmentation could be of different kinds — deflationary or inflationary. The former, consisting of 'an increase in autonomy at the establishment level' (p. 264) occurred in the inter-war period. But, unlike the 'inflationary fragmentation' of the late 1960s, deflationary fragmentation did not involve greater power for the work group but rather for the employer, who imposed inferior conditions: 'latent conflict was extensive, but the disadvantaged groups lacked the power to make it manifest' (p. 265). Hence, according to Fox and Flanders, it did not result in 'disorder'. But with inflationary fragmentation, the relative power of work groups increases, so that widespread 'disorder' develops.

It was necessary, in this view, to reconstruct normative order if cumulative disorder was to be prevented. If this were not done, there could develop 'responses which would be tantamount to a decision that Britain could no longer support its present extreme degree of pluralism' so that 'a measure of authoritarian state regulation must take over from an anarchic drift resulting from fragmenting regulation' (p. 268). Fox and Flanders continue:

> The first and most basic step towards the accomplishment of this task was identified with great force by the Donovan Report. The construction of agreed normative systems covering the company or plant is of crucial significance. Its importance derives from the fact that the company or plant is the only unit of regulation which can integrate the diverse and often conflicting normative aspirations of the various work groups . . . order at this level is basic and necessary to order at any other level. (pp. 269–70)

They went on to point out that Donovan — contrary to the interpretations of some commentators — recognized the need to integrate company bargaining with industry and national bargaining: the latter were crucial to prevent disorder arising from differences between plant agreements.

Another important feature of the Fox and Flanders argument — again developing themes in Donovan — is that, while agreement on substantive issues was important this

> can never be enough by itself to maintain order, for rapid change requires frequent adjustments in these substantive relations. If agreement extends only to the substantive relations themselves there is a danger of a new rigidity being established, with a consequent threat of disorder whenever those relations have to undergo change. What is, in a sense, more fundamental is building up agreement on procedural norms on how substantive relations are to be regulated which provide for flexibility and change in those relations when necessary. (pp. 273–4)

They recognized, as did Donovan, that the endeavour to develop a system seen as legitimate could not be certain of success: it was crucial that there be 'a forceful articulation of common norms by an authoritative source'. But, even so, 'the search may prove fruitless: proof can only be furnished, however, by the persistent breakdown of sustained efforts, not by an easy acceptance of the self-fulfilling prophecies of failure' (p. 274).

This pluralist approach was criticized from a variety of perspectives both at the time and subsequently. Moreover, a number of those closely associated with Donovan, or its approach, have subsequently either sought to reinterpret Donovan or modify its analysis. Within an essentially pluralist tradition, much of the criticism at the time focused upon such points as the lack of analytical or explanatory bite in the Donovan Report: its empiricism and historicism; the failure to take sufficient account of economic analysis; what some saw as the need for sanctions if agreements were not conformed to; its *de facto* concentration on the private sector; and, finally, the fear that an emphasis on factory agreements would militate against national-level policies such as incomes policies (e.g. *BJIR*, 1968). Many criticisms of this kind came from those who largely adopted a pluralist perspective. Later pluralist accounts will be briefly considered below. First, let us consider the arguments put forward from rather different perspectives — the unitarist, and the radical.

The Unitarist Critique

The essential features of a unitarist approach to industrial relations have been widely discussed and need little repetition here. Briefly, conflict is not seen as a necessary or legitimate feature of industrial relations. Rather, a commonality of interests exists, for the wages of the worker depend upon the profitability of the enterprise, and this, in turn, depends upon the whims of the sovereign consumer. It is only when competition, at least in major sectors, operates that optimal welfare is to be achieved. Within the enterprise, therefore, the entrepreneur has to be able to adjust operations speedily and flexibly to the dictates of the market; and it is the skill of the entrepreneur which permits the company to survive and prosper in the face of competition. Two points follow from this: first, the achievement of optimal welfare requires that workers should not be able to obstruct the workings of the market; second, they should defer to the wisdom and skills of those who provide their livelihood — the entrepreneurs.

There are, of course, a variety of other sources of justification for the authority of the entrepreneur, and the exact style of the entrepreneur may vary, but he does in effect play the role of father to the workforce. In extreme forms, a unitary perspective denies the need for, and the legitimacy of, collective organization on the part of employees. In other cases, a role for trade unionism is recognized, subject to certain conditions: essentially these centre upon the need for unions to act 'responsibly', so as not to endanger the operation of the market or the exercise of entrepreneurial skills.

Proponents of the unitary perspective agreed with Donovan that serious problems in British industrial relations existed in the late 1960s.

But they disagreed with the view that the fundamental problem lay in the institutions of collective bargaining as such. While these might require some modification, the fundamental problem was that trade unionists failed to abide by the collective agreements that they signed. The solution was to adopt measures which would both reduce the excessive power of the trade unions and encourage a sense of 'responsibility' in them. The primary means envisaged to achieve these ends was the law: the extent of existing union immunities must be narrowed so as to prevent strikes that are 'neither necessary to support legitimate claims nor desirable in the national interest' (1968, p. 30). In addition, it was necessary to ensure that irresponsible and subversive groups did not foment strikes and this was to be achieved by restricting immunity to the 'authorized' agents of properly constituted and suitably 'registered' unions. Finally, it was necessary to have available a range of sanctions, in the form of fines, in order to ensure that unions acted within the law.

From this perspective, Donovan was fatally mistaken on a number of key elements in its analysis. Not only was it wrong to place such great emphasis upon the reform of institutional arrangements, but its proposals to use the law primarily to bolster union rights and to encourage recognition of shop stewards within the plant would mean that those very groups who were the fundamental cause of 'problems' in British industry would have their power strengthened. Far from resolving problems, therefore, Donovan would exacerbate them: what was required was a reduction in, and not an extension of, the workplace power of trade unions.

Hence unitarists were far more convinced of both the efficacy of the law in industrial relations and the legitimacy of such legislation than were pluralists. From a unitary perspective industrial action was primarily to be attributed to groups which were either misguided or subversive. For the reality was that worker welfare depended upon employers and was therefore not in basic conflict with employer interests: thus many strikes were both unnecessary and ill-advised. Moreover, action by such misguided groups endangered the interests of all: workers themselves, employers, consumers and the nation.

The Radical Critique

The radical analysis is based upon the view that 'industrial relations' cannot be adequately analysed in isolation from the larger social structure. The actors in industry derive their interests, attitudes and resources in large part from that broader social structure. Society, it is argued, is characterized by fundamental inequalities and consequently by deep divisions and conflicts of interest. From this perspective, room for any constructive form of integrative bargaining in industry is strictly limited because of this all-pervasive conflict of interests.

The exact prescriptions of radical writers for the improvement of industrial relations vary widely: in essence, one can differentiate between Marxian and non-Marxian prescriptions. But they do share a common core: namely, that a precondition of 'order' is a major transformation in the social structure — the eradication or reduction of structured inequalities. For some — the radical pluralists — there is a deep-seated attachment to the goals aimed at by other pluralists: but, they argue, they cannot be achieved by the relatively marginal reforms proposed by Donovan.

The radical critique of Donovan claimed that the pluralist analysis assumes an equality of power; this is seen to be both factually inaccurate and to lead to misguided prescriptions. For this assumption means that workers' interests are defined in a misleading superficial manner; as a result the possibilities of meaningful compromise are exaggerated, the requirement that workers should abide by agreements is mistaken and Donovan's proposals turn out to be essentially managerialist. These points require rather fuller development.

According to the radical critique, the fundamental flaw in the pluralist analysis — the assumption of an equality of power — derives from over-emphasis of the manifest expression of bargaining power and the failure to take account of the significance of the 'hidden faces of power' — the mobilization of bias involved in institutions and structures and the ability to create and promulgate an ideology supportive of the powerful. Consequently, the pluralist analysis adopts an extremely superficial view of workers' interests: they are inferred from behaviour which is shaped by the differential distribution of power. The pluralist analysis does not, therefore, operate from a realistic set of fundamental assumptions: if it were not for the existing structure of power, then workers would espouse quite different interests. In the current context, their 'real' interests are inextricably entwined with the eradication or transformation of the existing social structure.

The pluralist analysis requires that workers conform to agreements which have been jointly made. Radical critics claim that pluralists see this in large part as a moral requirement following from bargaining between equal partners. For the radical, however, it follows from the inequality of power that agreements are signed by unions under duress. Accordingly, unions and workers cannot be expected to abide by agreements.

Having rejected these two tenets of the Donovan argument, radical writers go on to claim the pluralist case is basically managerialist, in practice if not in intention:

> for there are signs that where the objectives of efficient and effective management conflict with the objectives of would-be self-determining work groups, pluralist concern tends to be directed towards finding ways by which the latter can be contained within a regulative framework that promotes and maintains the former. (Fox, 1973, p. 213)

The pluralist approach, it is argued, rests upon the assumption 'that there is broad basic agreement' over the organization of industry, the fundamental distribution of power and control, and the broad objectives of industry. Hence workers who reject such perspectives are labelled by pluralists as 'social undesirables' and thus pluralists are in fact 'performing the function of supporting and justifying the existing order' (Fox, 1973, p. 221). Against this, radical writers such as Goldthorpe (1977) argue that it is not clear why workers should see as problematical such opportunities as they have to ensure overtime, exploit payment systems or enjoy a degree of 'leisure in work'. In other words, they may have little reason to concern themselves with the 'disorderly' consequences of their behaviour. Goldthorpe recognizes that union bureaucracies may have an interest in 'order', but they may be constrained from pursuing it because of the democratic structure of unions and their inability to control work groups.

Radicals have also criticized the way in which pluralists assume an identity of interest between unions and workers: hence they focus upon an essentially administrative issue of union government rather than upon union democracy — that is, the question of how far union leaders do indeed represent the interests of their members (for example, Hyman, 1975, pp. 64ff). Once this question is raised, then it follows that an ability to formulate comprehensive agreements acceptable to management and union leaders may not in fact be legitimate or acceptable to the shop floor.

Given these criticisms it might be expected that radical writers would be unanimous in their belief that the Donovan proposals would be ineffective. But this is not the case. For, broadly and crudely, there exists a considerable difference of view between what have been termed the radical pluralists and those who adopt a more Marxian approach.

The former have argued that reform was unlikely to achieve its goals. Fox, for example, has pointed to the failures of such reformist strategies as productivity bargaining. He claims that productivity agreements essentially constituted a 'low trust' approach on the part of management towards workers while expecting a 'high-trust' response on their part. In fact, in his view, workers tended to respond in kind, so that reformism was likely to achieve limited success (1974). Similarly, Goldthorpe held that the issues proposed for workplace bargaining could as easily lead to greater conflict as compromise, and that this could 'set strict limits to the extent to which reform is possible' (1977, p. 211); this was all the more likely given the satisfaction of participants with the 'current' pattern of industrial relations. Hence, he argued, pluralists 'have paid far too little attention to the matter of compliance with norms':

> Unless the norms implicit in the new regulative arrangements were ones to which the mass of those regulated felt some degree of moral commitment — which, on the evidence, would scarcely seem likely — then the acceptance that the reformed institutions could command would be of no more than a pragmatic, provisional kind; that is to say, these arrangements would in turn be exposed to distortion and 'decay' as they were found to conflict with the values and interests of those subject to them, and 'order' would once again become problematical. (1977, pp. 213—14)

In short, 'liberal reformism must be regarded as assuming precisely that which it seeks to create' (1977, p. 214).

While radical pluralists question the efficacy of reform, many more Marxian writers believed that reformism would be, and indeed has been, successful in terms of achieving managerial goals. This argument starts from a reinterpretation of the aims of reform: since the scope for accommodation between employer and worker interests is strictly limited, the aim of reform was — in reality — the furtherance of managerial goals. These focused on the reassertion of managerial control and increased efficiency and profitability. If this course of action was to be successful, then the interest of workers, in terms of the wage—effort bargain, job control, job security and so on, would necessarily be less fully met.

Having revealed the 'true' aim of reformism — an 'employers' offensive' — Marxian writers go on to claim that management have been successful in their endeavours. This fundamental success was due to a number of factors, including the broader structure of power in society which militated against the development of an awareness of their 'real' interests among workers. But, in addition, particular significance was attached to the changes in institutional arrangements and shop steward organization associated with reform. Hence the adoption of 'reformist' strategies involved the development of a more 'bureaucratic' form of steward organization. This served to centralize power among a key group of senior stewards, particularly those who received full time status and facilities from management. Such stewards became isolated from the shop-floor and dependent upon management; they consequently developed a managerialist perspective and acted as a managerial police force, exerting control 'over' rather than 'for' their members. This bureaucratic and managerialist steward elite were prepared to accept and promote 'orderly' industrial relations. They favoured the 'rationalization' of payment systems and were prepared to negotiate productivity agreements. Accordingly, they were instrumental in removing shop-floor controls which were fundamental to the defence and promotion of worker interests. At the same time, this new steward 'elite' became integrated into the official union structure, through sitting on such bodies as national executive committees and through union training courses. In this way, steward organizations were incorporated into management and became subjected to greater influence and control on the part of incorporated national union leaders. The basic conditions for 'corporatist' arrangements at national level therefore developed through the mirroring of those arrangements at plant level and through the development of national control mechanisms over the formerly autonomous and contestary actions of shop steward organizations.

Subsequent Pluralist Analyses

In the years since the publication of the Donovan Report, a number of pluralist writers have been critical of the Donovan approach, or have sought to redefine it. It has already been noted that a number of pluralists — outside of the 'Oxford school' — criticized the Report on a number of grounds: its approach to the analysis of industrial relations, its presumed failure to develop strong linkages between the plant and the national level, and — in some cases — the optimism demonstrated in its rejection of legal supports for the observance of agreements. But in subsequent years, a number of those closely involved with the thinking of Donovan have also reassessed its approach.

The most notable case is, of course, that of Fox who subsequently voiced doubts as to whether a liberal pluralist approach for an academic analysis of industrial relations was valid. McCarthy (the Research Director of the Donovan Commission), in a book co-authored by Ellis, was also critical of the Donovan analysis, basically on the grounds that it did not pursue the logic of its case sufficiently (this was explained in terms of its primary aim of challenging the unitary — or traditionalist —

approach with its emphasis upon legislative solutions). More specifically, McCarthy and Ellis argued that Donovan conceived of reform as 'a single major break with the past, rather than a continuous process of adaptation and change' (1973, p. 82). But the latter, they claimed, was a more realistic perspective, given the changing nature of product markets, managerial strategies and so on, and the fact that 'workers themselves develop new demands and aspirations, which the existing bargaining system is not equipped to deal with' (p. 83). Second, drawing upon empirical studies, McCarthy and Ellis argued that Donovan 'under-estimated the legitimate conflict' that could arise in the process of attempting to reform industrial relations: Donovan 'is written as if men of good will on both sides are more or less bound to discern the ideal bargaining structure once it is pointed out to them by the Commissioners. Of course, this is not the case' (pp. 84—5). Third, McCarthy and Ellis claimed that the Donovan analysis was really applicable only to certain sectors of industry, where there was a conflict between the 'formal' and 'informal' systems. Fourth, they argued Donovan had tended to isolate industrial relations from the wider society: 'it is time to . . . emphasize how far the industrial relations system is what sociologists would term a "sub-system". This means that it can be crucially affected by economic, social and political events that are beyond the control of those who sit round the bargaining table' (p. 195). Hence the successful implementation of reform strategies required that government policies, in particular, be supportive: such policies included a more active manpower policy, improved training, a greater emphasis upon stimulating employment in development districts, and incomes policies possibly associated with statutory price controls. 'Finally, the ideas of social planning and industrial democracy, that inform and underlie the notion of manage-ment by agreement, are related to more general aims and aspirations that extend beyond the workplace' (p. 198). McCarthy and Ellis's primary emphasis was upon 'management by agreement', involving a more continuous process of collective bargaining over an extended range of issues such that claims to 'managerial prerogative' ceased.

More recently, Clegg — a key member of the Donovan Commission — has discussed the Commission's analysis (1979). He focuses initially upon the distinction between 'formal' and 'informal' arrangements, the former being defined by Donovan in terms of the existence of written agreements. But, according to Clegg, 'by itself, writing a rule down does not necessarily formalize it' and, after citing the existence of 'authorita-tive' but unwritten agreements, he states that 'the crucial test of the formality of a rule is its authority. If it has been either authorized by the relevant signatures or hallowed by time, then it is a formal rule' (pp. 233—4); and later he stresses that 'most sociologists and students of industrial relations' use the term 'institution' to cover both formal and informal organizations (p. 450). Hence it is not surprising that 'there is. . . no clear division between formal and informal rules' (p. 234) so that even under formalized bargaining arrangements informality 'continues to thrive'. While Clegg recognizes that Donovan was over-simple in its consideration of formality, he goes on to argue that:

> The Donovan Commission's objection to the state of plant bargaining at that time, therefore, was its doubtful legitimacy and furtive character. They proposed formalization because they believed that open acknowledgement of the extent of joint regulation in the plant by all concerned would lead to a much-needed rationalization of the whole process of collective bargaining. (p. 237)

Clegg accepts that formalization was likely to lead to 'more rather than fewer conflicts between informal practices and agreed rules' and that 'old practices might continue to operate in breach of the agreements or that new practices would develop in conflict with them'. 'The Donovan Commission may therefore have had too simple-minded a view of legitimacy in industrial relations' (p. 238).

But, in Clegg's view, the necessary revisions of the Donovan anlaysis which are required do:

> not destroy their argument or render their recommendations worthless. The contrast which they drew between the formal and informal systems remains a useful if crude approximation to the state of collective bargaining in manufacturing at that time; formalization roughly along the lines of their proposals has led to substantial changes in collective bargaining, especially in manufacturing; and the effect of these changes might be judged, at least from some points of view, to have been predominantly beneficial. What the revision does entail is that there is no simple choice between formal and informal systems of bargaining. All collective bargaining systems are a mixture of the two. A system which relies heavily on informality is apt to encourage the growth of procedures and arrangements of doubtful legitimacy — at least from the point of view of senior managers, employers' associations, and unions outside the plant. A system which emphasizes and extends formality risks conflict between the formal rules and practices. (pp. 239—40)

Drawing upon Clegg's account (or reinterpretation) of Donovan, Sisson and Brown (1983) have discussed developments in the private sector. On pay bargaining, they point to changes in the nature of payment systems which effect greater rationality and central control, and the rise of single-employer bargaining in the case of larger establishments. In contrast to the formalization of bargaining over 'market relations' (pay) they claim that little formalization has occurred over 'managerial relations' (the organization of work): 'the scope of collective bargaining over managerial relations appears as hazy as it ever was' (p. 149). This, in their view, is because both managements and shop stewards have an interest in the continuation of informality:

> From management's point of view there are advantages in not making managerial relations the subject of formal agreements. The reasons which McCarthy gave to the Donovan Commission for management's reluctance to legitimize informal procedures have a general validity . . . (pp. 151—2)

Accordingly, they argue that formal productivity bargaining did not become more widespread in part because managements 'found that there were other, and less risky, ways of securing the benefits of productivity bargaining. For example, the reforms in . . . methods of payment . . . often proved the key to greater flexibility in the use of labour: group incentive schemes and simplified pay structures usually make it possible for individual workers to be moved from task to task without loss of earnings' (p. 149). More generally, they argue that an emphasis upon collective bargaining as essentially a process of joint regulation is 'both too restrictive and too idealized':

> In its basic form collective bargaining is a pressure group activity in which management and workers struggle to impose their views without any rules or agreements emerging. Management and governments may try to institutionalize the process in order to avoid anarchy and uncertainty . . . [But] underlying it there is a tacit agreement to disagree, an acceptance that there are areas where joint regulation is unwelcome. But that does not mean that it can be described as unilateral regulation. Management's actions are shaped by its expectations of what workers' reactions will be. (pp. 152—3)

A PRELIMINARY COMMENT ON COMPETING PERSPECTIVES

The preceding sections have outlined the various perspectives from which the analysis of workplace industrial relations has been undertaken. This is necessary because it has often been postulated that those, for example, who criticize the liberal—pluralist approach have in fact misinterpreted it. Careful attention, therefore, has been given to drawing up a summary of the various perspectives and supporting this with quotations and references. Hopefully, this gives us a reliable series of accounts on which to base an assessment of the competing views.

The main points of difference between the various perspectives centre upon three broad, but interrelated, issues: the proper focus of analysis and the distribution of power; the nature and role of formal agreements and the conditions for order; and the nature of interests. Each of these will be considered in turn.

Power

While careful to note the 'plurality of pluralisms', radical critics have consistently held that the liberal pluralist approach is fatally flawed by its assumption of an equality of power between employer and employee. However, it is striking that Hyman, in attempting to provide evidence for this contention, is unable to quote statements by British industrial relations pluralists which unequivocally indicate such a belief (1978). For these writers tend to talk about shifts in the balance of power, but to say that power has shifted in favour of workers is not necessarily to claim that workers have an equality of power. Moreover, Clegg, in his defence of pluralism, denies that he assumes an equality of power.

It is true, however, that pluralists place primary emphasis upon 'bargaining power', and this does mean that they tend to isolate industrial relations as a relatively discrete subject for analysis (although McCarthy and Ellis, for example, do recognize the dangers of such an approach, see p. 17). Furthermore, Clegg does maintain that in some situations it is not immediately evident where the balance of bargaining power lies. But this does not appear exceptional: radicals may also claim that, at least in certain circumstances, bargaining power is fairly evenly balanced. What they would want to argue is that it is insufficient to confine analysis to such manifest expressions of power.

The radical criticsm, therefore, really focuses upon how far it is possible to operate on the assumption of an institutional and real isolation of industrial conflict. Again, this argument cannot be pushed too far, for liberal pluralists are acutely aware of the way in which 'political' and 'industrial relations' issues overlap. Moreover, it is not the case that liberal pluralists assume an equality of power in society: it would be more accurate to say that, broadly speaking, they would prefer to see the continuation of the existing structure of inequality than to embark upon moves to greater equality which they fear might end up in dictatorship and poverty. In other words, they place a high value upon liberal principles and a presumed technical expertise on the part of management and are therefore prepared to accept a degree of inequality (Clegg, 1975, p. 316). This assumption of legitimate inequalities is demonstrated in a good deal of liberal pluralist writing. For example, it is to be seen in the argument of the Donovan Commission that it was management's responsibility to drive through reform: this argument would be illogical if it was believed that an equality of power existed. Similarly, Clegg's definition of industrial democracy in terms of trade unions acting as a permanent opposition, never able to become a 'government', is only comprehensible if a degree of inequality is accepted as legitimate and desirable. In this respect, the liberal pluralist position can be located midway between the radical and unitarist positions. (The virtues of a broader social anlaysis are taken up in the Conclusion.)

Order and the Role of Formal Agreements

Radical writers go on from their claim that an equality of power does not exist between capital and labour to argue that there is no moral compulsion upon workers to conform to agreements since they are signed 'under duress'. This view poses two problems: first, the exact significance of the notion of 'moral compulsion' for a sociological analysis, and, second, whether or not conformity does depend upon an equality of power. Both of these contentions are open to doubt.

It is true that Clegg's argument seems somewhat confused on the question of the morality of conformity to agreements. But what does appear to be true is that he would not wish to support such conformity solely or perhaps even primarily on the basis of morality. It is also a question of enlightened self-interest: if unions do not abide by the agreements they have made, then there may be little incentive for employers to respect union rights. This argument is consistent with the power dimensions underlying liberal pluralism: 'any group with the resources to make life difficult for others, even if only by repeated demands for attention, *is* likely to achieve some concessions' (p. 309). Moreover, it follows from this 'interest' argument that there may equally be occasions when unions (and employers) will not conform to agreements. Hence, according to Clegg, compromise cannot be the overriding priority of pluralism for, if it were, it would deny its own rationale: 'it can only give moral authority to the rules of compromise if it allows for the validity of other moral values which may clash with these rules' (p. 311).

The second question posed above concerned the exact significance of the notion of 'moral compulsion'. This appears largely to be an evaluative statement: but such statements are not solely to be found among liberal pluralists. For the implication of the radical argument is that under particular conditions unions would be morally required to abide by agreements. But, more fundamentally, there is a problem of where such moral arguments fit into an analytical discussion: academics may sit on the side-line and shout 'morality' but there is no immediate way in which this affects behaviour or improves insight. The more relevant question for an academic is under what conditions actors will abide by the canons of such morality. The radical replies, 'under conditions of equality'; the liberal pluralist argues in terms of recognition of interests and institutional arrangements which facilitate accommodation and the growth of strong bargaining relationships. The radicals' case, however, is less than satisfactory: 'moral' action may as easily reflect a highly unequal distribution of power as an equality of power: equality of power may be neither a necessary nor sufficient condition for 'moral' conduct under particular conditions. The sorts of variables pointed to by the liberal pluralist may play an essential role even where equality exists.

The question of rule-conformity is intimately linked to the more general question of 'order' and the extent to which enduring compromises can be achieved within the existing structure of society. Radicals have consistently claimed that the liberal pluralists have exaggerated the extent to which this is possible. In fact, even the Donovan Commission recognized that workplace reform would not automatically lead to order, and more recent writings by liberal—pluralists have argued that the introduction and operation of formal, written agreements is rather more complex than was initially envisaged. Hence, as noted previously, McCarthy and Ellis were led to argue the need for a continual process of bargaining and for broader structural changes (in the form of government action) to facilitate 'order' within the workplace. In this respect, the gap between liberal and radical pluralists is now considerably less than once appeared to be the case.

Along with this recognition of the difficulties of achieving order, a number of liberal pluralist writers have made explicit reference to the possible bias in the very concept — 'what appears to be legitimate may depend upon where you are standing' (Clegg, 1979, p. 238). However, the extent to which he incorporates this point into his subsequent analysis is somewhat limited. This is to be seen most clearly in his discussion of formal agreements.

Clegg recognizes that there are problems in distinguishing between formal and informal agreements as initially discussed by Donovan. According to him, the 'authority' of a rule is crucial, and accordingly rules may be authoritative even if they are not written down. But he then goes on to argue that a rule is authoritative or 'formal' (according to the revised definition) when it 'has been either authorized by the relevant signatures or hallowed by time' (pp. 233—4). If we take this version at face value then there are a number of interesting implications: Donovan involved the replacement of one set of formal rules (custom and practice) by another set (written and signed agreements): long-standing unwritten agreements are formal and authoritative and so are freshly signed agreements, but new, unsigned agreements only achieve the status of formality or authority when they have become 'hallowed by time'. In addition to these oddities, the use of this new definition increases the probability of major conflicts between formal rules.

The central problem with Clegg's account is that he does not pursue sufficiently systematically his recognition of the competing conceptions of order and the differential attribution of authority. What the Donovan Commission was concerned with was the 'furtive' nature of much custom and practice — in other words, agreements were legitimate only in the eyes of particular work groups and their immediate supervisors. The Commission wanted to see agreements which were both more 'rational' and legitimate in the eyes of higher management and union officials as well as workers and foremen. It underestimated the extent to which such agreements, authoritative in the eyes of senior management and possibly union officials, might be attributed little legitimacy by work groups and supervisors. Clegg now recognizes this point, but instead of asking how one can achieve agreements which have legitimacy in the eyes of all groups he confuses matters further through redefining 'formality'. A key sociological problem is therefore evaded by a confusing redefinition.

Another liberal pluralist anlaysis has focused upon the notion of 'trust' as a central precondition for effective workplace reform. Purcell seeks to investigate the conditions under which 'trust' can be developed between key negotiators (1981). But this approach confronts many of the weaknesses of the traditional Donovan analysis. For the 'problems' of workplace industrial relations rest in large part upon the fact that even where trust exists between negotiators, they may be constrained by those they represent; and, equally importantly, trust between negotiators does not guarantee that similar relationships will exist between work groups and management, or that interests can be accommodated. Purcell's argument is therefore close to a prescription for oligarchy and ignores the instability of such arrangements.

Sisson and Brown have attempted to move beyond a series of rather sterile definitional discussions to infer some type of logic in what they claim to be management strategy in the private sector. However, their argument that management has successfully formalized pay issues but not work organization issues presents a number of problems. First, formal payment systems based on job evaluation cannot be simply separated from work organization issues. Job evaluation requires the drawing-up of job descriptions and therefore necessarily involves some formalization of work. Second, Sisson and Brown pay scant attention to the ways in which 'formality' and 'informality' may interplay in the case of payment systems, 'decaying' the logic of pay differentials. Third, in so far as 'formality' can be maintained in terms of pay structure, it may intensify 'informal' pressures concerning work organization. These themes are developed more fully in later chapters.

More fundamentally, while Sisson and Brown draw upon the work of both Clegg and McCarthy with approval, they misinterpret it. Drawing upon McCarthy's discussion of the advantages and disadvantages of formality (1966), they claim that management has good reason not to formalize work organization issues. Formalism makes it more difficult to withdraw concessions; formal agreements might be exploited by stewards in the future; further concessions might be demanded; and management would not be prepared publicly to indicate the concessions they in fact make to workers. But McCarthy put forward these arguments not in the context of work organization but of procedural issues. In discussing substantive matters, the weight of his argument was that greater formality would serve management rather than worker interests: formal agreements would limit the scope for the reinterpretation of old agreements, they would constrain steward exploitation of tacit agreements and limit the range of negotiable issues (see also Marsh, 1966, p. vii).

Sisson and Brown might wish to assert that their misinterpretation of McCarthy does not invalidate the thrust of their argument. This may be so in principle. But in practice things look rather different. In particular, it is not clear why arguments which apply to pay do not relate to work organization especially since in practice the two are so intimately related. Under particular circumstances at any rate, management may enjoy distinct advantages in not formalizing payment systems (see Leijsne, 1980). Similarly, if management are able to enforce tight, formal systems in relation to pay, why cannot they do so in relation to working practices?

Or, conversely, if workers can win concessions on work organization, why cannot they do so on payment systems? In short, does formality necessarily shift the balance of advantage and why should it do so to differing degrees and in different directions across different kinds of issues?

Despite these problems, however, it is clear that many liberal—pluralists are now more aware of the limitations of workplace reform than they appeared to be in the late 1960s. In this respect, they again seem to have shifted more towards the views of such radical pluralists as Fox and Goldthorpe who have long argued that the effects of workplace reform and formalism would be more problematical than Donovan had envisaged. The only people who now appear to be convinced of the efficacy of formal agreements (possibly backed by legislation) are unitarists and more Marxian writers. The latter case is particularly ironic in view of their concerted criticism of the liberal pluralist perspective. In part, however, their position rests upon a fundamentally different interpretation of what Donovan was 'really all about'.

The Question of Interests

Despite some convergence in the views of radical and liberal pluralists, there still exist important differences between their perspectives on reform. These centre around the nature of interests and their compatibility. Flanders, and others associated with the Donovan case, argued that their proposals meant an extension of union influence and interests. The development of plant level agreements was seen to involve an extension of the range of issues which management would discuss and negotiate with the unions. In this way both management and unions would achieve greater control — that is, in the oft-quoted phrase 'management can only regain control by sharing it.' This theme of the extension of joint regulation subsequently became more strongly emphasized (as, for example, in Daniel and MacIntosh, 1972, pp. 81—2; McCarthy and Ellis, 1973). These later writers, however, also stressed that Donovan had tended to see negotiations as 'one-off' affairs, whereas they envisaged a continuous process of bargaining.

Critics of reform differed as to its effects. Unitarists were convinced that it would lead to an unacceptable extension of union influence, with no guarantee — indeed little likelihood — of any greater degree of consensus or cooperation. Radical pluralists, far from believing that reform would lead to excessive union and worker influence, maintained that it would not give sufficient weight to these interests and would fail for this reason. Other radicals, however, claimed that reformism militated against worker interests but would succeed. This was deemed to be so for procedural and substantive reasons: opportunities for shop-floor bargaining and control would be reduced and shaped by rules biased in management's favour; wage improvements associated with reform would rapidly disappear and would in any event be paid for by increased effort on the part of workers themselves: reforms such as productivity bargaining meant 'the restoration or enhancement of management authority' (Topham, 1969).

These different perspectives on the impact of reform reflect differences in the definition of employer, union and employee interests and in views concerning whose interests were promoted in the pre-reform era.

Put at its most simple, uinitarists believe that workers' interests are compatible with, and dependent upon, the achievement of employers' interests. If the latter are endangered — as with reform — then so are the former. For the liberal pluralist the interests of employer and employee do conflict, but this does not preclude some form of accommodation. This can be achieved in two related ways. First, it was argued that in the pre-reform era the pursuit of sectional interests within work groups (and within management) was often counter-productive for the achievement of their aims. Second, it was claimed that both sides in industry could better defend and promote their interests by reaching clear compromises than by engaging in an uncertain and continual process of guerilla warfare. Radical writers rejected this view (although to varying degrees), maintaining that the type of accommodation outlined by the liberal pluralist would serve merely to confirm, if not exacerbate, the existing structure of inequality. The implication for some radicals was that workers could better pursue their interest through a continuation of fractional bargaining than through reform. As will be argued in subsequent chapters, this thesis — that workers did in fact achieve significant gains in this way and could gain more in the future through this system — is open to question.

The compatibility of interests clearly depends largely upon what exactly those interests are. For the unitarist workers' interests appear to lie in continued employment and reasonable wage levels, along with the protection of individual rights, particularly in society more generally. But since these depend upon the continued viability of the employer in the marketplace it follows that these interests should not be pursued beyond 'what the market will bear'; otherwise, far from achieving their goals, workers will lose out.

The liberal pluralist gives some recognition to these arguments, but would claim that in the real world the achievement of the goals of the employer also depends upon a recognition of worker interests. However, the exact nature of worker interests tends to be somewhat unclear in some respects. For example, at times the Donovan Report conflates worker and union interests, taking it for granted that unions do represent workers, while at other times it distinguishes between the two: it notes, for example, that unions have particular institutional interests, while it also differentiates sharply between union and worker approaches to 'restrictive practices'. Writers such as Goldthorpe have accused Donovan of focusing upon the institutional interests of trade unions at the expense of recognizing the distinctive interests of workers (1974).

Liberal pluralists at the same time tend to see worker interests as essentially self-evident and unproblematical. Donovan, for example, sees them to lie in job security and wage stability, basing his view on the actions of unions and workers. But, as noted previously, radical writers argue that such inferences are illegitimate since action is shaped by the larger structure of power and the nature of union organization. Accordingly, radicals argue, the analysis of workers' interests cannot be confined to a study of their attitudes and behaviour within the industrial relations context or even the existing structure of society. Workers' real interests can only be determined in situations where they have a real freedom of choice (see, for example, Lukes, 1974). This argument has considerable validity, but it does confront two major difficulties. First, the attribution of interests becomes a very hypothetical activity (Batstone *et al.* 1977), with the risk that the analyst imposes his/her own views as to the 'true' interests of workers (Martin, 1980). Second, situations of 'real freedom of choice' rarely occur, so that the identification of 'true' interests involves ignoring key elements of the real social situation of workers: accordingly, it is difficult to use this notion of 'real' interests in an analysis of concrete situations. For the existing structure of power may mean that in many situations workers would be well-advised to pursue their 'immediate' rather than their 'real' interests.

However, the result of this radical process of thought is to emphasize that workers' interests lie primarily in the removal of the existing structure of inequality or the capitalist system. Hence there exists a basic incompatibility of interest between capital and labour. Compromises therefore cannot promote the 'real' interests of labour, and can only lead to illusory and transitory gains for workers. They can achieve real and lasting advantages only if they are won in the face of employer opposition — 'through struggle'.

These differences of view over workers' interests are intimately related to approaches to union government and democracy. (The significance of the use of these two terms has been emphasized by Hyman, 1975, pp. 64ff.) The pluralist tradition places relatively little emphasis upon concepts of democracy, (see, for example, Undy *et al.,* 1981); for if workers' interests are defined in the relatively simple, static and self-evident way noted above, then problems of policy formulation are likely to be seen in terms of developing technically efficient administrative procedures rather than in terms of the formulation and working out of goals. Since industrial relations concerns a limited conflict between groups whose interests are self-evident, attention is focused upon the maintenance of order within the union as a prerequisite of goal achievement. Clegg, for example, devotes relatively little space in his textbook to the question of union democracy; and while recognizing a variety of obstacles to member influence, as suggested by a simple theory of union government based upon union rule books, he derides the view that there are no checks upon union leaders (see especially 1970, p. 92).

The Donovan Commission spent some time on the question of union government. For example, as noted above, it was concerned to ensure a constitutional position for shop stewards which would both provide them with certain rights within the union and, thereby, permit and clarify the larger union's authority over stewards. In other words, Donovan was concerned with the integration of the steward into the larger formal union structure. But the extent to which union leaders were — or should be — responsive to member demands received little attention (for a critique of this position see Goldthorpe, 1975).

In criticizing this sort of approach, members of the radical school express a great deal of concern over questions of union democracy. For it is argued that notions of union efficiency can only be related to union goals and that these should be democratically determined. But radical writers equally tend to conflate goals and government, for they argue that union leaders are oligarchical and are therefore able to adopt incorporating policies in the name of the union. Democracy, they claim, must be defined in terms of an active member-involvement which challenges the position and policies of this incorporated union leadership; in other words, democracy means that radical and class-oriented policies are adopted. Radicals point to those occasions when rank-and-file activity has been associated with militant demands to support this contention. More directly, Hyman has argued that

> the goal of union democracy acquires significance only within a more radical conception of the objectives (at least potential) of unionism: as a basis for collective struggle *against* as well as *within* capitalism, as an agency which ultimately can be effective only as a means of collective *mobilization* of the working class. (1979, p. 63)

The implicit logic of such an argument appears to be as follows. Democracy can be seen to exist only when the members of a union are in a position to determine union policies and significantly affect their life chances. Their interests can be objectively defined, and it follows, therefore, that democracy can be seen to exist only where members choose to pursue those objective interests. If those objective interests are not reflected in union policy, then no real freedom of choice exists — that is, union democracy does not exist. Such limitations upon the freedom of choice may reflect particular features of union structure and control as well as 'external' factors such as capitalist hegemony. The proper role of a union leader can therefore be seen, according to this view, to be the raising of consciousness such that workers are able to identify real choices, and thereby bring on to the union agenda issues which were previously defined as 'givens'.

In other words, both pluralists and radicals tend to define democracy in terms of the goals pursued: both presume to define what members' interests are. Now, to a degree it is quite proper and reasonable to emphasize the constraints which exist upon the freedom of choice; and it would be sociologically naive to ignore the way in which workers' attitudes may be shaped. Indeed, both radicals and pluralists are inclined to emphasize the importance of 'educating' union members. But it is a theme which has to be treated with considerable caution precisely because it can easily lead to an attempt to impose perspectives upon trade unions. And this may be especially problematical, and indeed paradoxical, for the radical. For unlike the pluralist, the radical not only stresses the importance of objective workers' interests outside of the current economic and social structure, he also emphasizes the inequality of power existing within that structure. Even if, therefore, one accepts the radical notion of objective interest, it may not be rational directly and uncompromisingly to pursue such an interest because of the superior power of the capitalist.

This point has, of course, been a matter of considerable discussion within the left: it is perhaps best seen in the debate between Hyman and members of the Institute for Workers' Control over industrial democracy (Hyman, 1974: Barratt-Brown *et al.*, 1975). It is certainly a major difficulty in the development of a truly socialist strategy. But the important point for our present purposes is that the preceding argument suggests that a straight and simple association of democracy and uncompromising class action is extremely problematical. In practice one nevertheless finds an emphasis in many radical writings upon notions of struggle and the seizing of control as essential features and manifestations of union democracy, even when any gains are of an extremely sectional nature. And, conversely, there is a failure to recognize the gains which might be achieved through 'incorporation' without necessarily compromising future freedom of action.

Moreover, the radical school confronts a number of paradoxes in assessing union structure and strategy. National union leaders who do not accept the wishes of the membership and pursue moderate union policies can be seen as undemocratic. But what about situations in which union leaders, adopting broadly similar approaches to membership wishes, pursue radical policies? Such a situation is far less rare than much of the literature would suggest: it was a common feature in the early years of the general unions in particular. It has been far from uncommon in more recent years in a number of unions — particularly those dominated by a left-wing leadership, and in a number of white-collar and public sector unions.

The answers to this question could vary: the union leadership could be seen to be acting democratically in the sense that it is (a) pursuing workers' objective interests; (b) educating the membership so that it becomes aware of the full range of choice; or (c) it might be argued that union leaders can only really adopt radical policies if they are accepted by a majority, for they require mass mobilization. The first of these arguments has already been touched upon. The third point is subject to the same criticisms that the left have put forward against broadly similar arguments by liberal pluralists — if failure to conform to union instructions, deriving from an undemocartic decision-making process, can lead to disciplinary action resulting in a loss of employment, then members' freedom of choice may be significantly limited.

The second argument therefore would seem the most credible. But the implication is that unions should not adopt radical policies until an educated membership agrees with them. But this, in turn, raises a further series of problems: is it likely that a membership, unaware of its true interests, will elect a class-oriented leader? What chance has a union leadership got of educating its membership in the face of the forces of capitalist hegemony? and so on. (It is, of course, open to question how far a capitalist hegemony does exist,; and, if it does, the extent to which it does not contain major contradictions is even more open to question — see Abercrombie *et al.,* 1980). These themes have been highlighted by Mothé's discussion of the doctrinaire *militant* in France, in which he highlights the problems of isolation, introversion, inactivity and ideological nit-picking which such union activists confront (1973, especially pp. 129—43).

If problems exist in relation to the identification of worker and union interests, the same is true of management interests. But, in fact, these have received relatively little attention. All the competing perspectives tend to assume that management is concerned with profitability and/or efficiency. Some radicals operate upon an extraordinarily crude and reified conception of 'capital' (for example, Hyman, 1975). While there is some recognition that lower levels of management may have somewhat different priorities, or that the pressures upon them and their particular responsibilities may lead them to adopt courses of action which are less than optimal from the viewpoint of higher management, these themes are rarely systematically pursued. The notion, for example, that reform might work against the interests of foremen is rarely noted. And there is no reason to assume that reformism might not similarly militate against the interests of other, specialist, groups within management: in short, the diversity of interests and the importance of 'micropolitics' within management receive scant attention on the part of any of the perspectives outlined above.

And yet this would seem to be vital. The survey evidence collected for the Donovan Commission (Government Social Survey, 1968) indicated that many managers were quite content with the pattern of 'informal' industrial relations current at the time. Why this was so received little attention. And given this fact, it was not evident why managers might be induced to adopt the philosophy and prescriptions of the Donovan Commission. The latter's emphasis upon the power of 'education' would seem a little naive, particularly in the absence of any serious analysis of management.

Since the late 1960s there has been a widespread recognition of the need to investigate more thoroughly the structure and strategy of management in a wide range of related disciplines. However, there have in the last decade been far more cases of repetition of this prescription than of actually pursuing it (for an exception, see Batstone *et al.,* 1984). Much of the literature — notably in the labour process tradition — operates from over-simple deductions from a model of capitalist exploitation and the conspiratorial competence of management (and the idiocy of workers). This contrasts with the model of management within Donovan which suggests a lack of coherence in management practice at the same time as it assumes that such coherence can easily be introduced once management is aware of alternatives.

Interestingly, one of the best analyses of management's approach to labour relations was undertaken by a liberal pluralist, Flanders, in a section entitled 'Roots of Managerial Irresponsibility'. He argued that top management in Britain preferred 'to have as little as possible to do with labour relations' which were 'looked upon . . . as a nuisance, a disturbance diverting their energies away from what they regard as the more important aspects of their work' (1964, p. 251). In addition, he maintained that the growth of personnel management was less a reflection of a change of attitude than 'part of a general trend towards increasing specialization' (p. 252). This led to problems of managerial strategy since the labour practices promulgated by the personnel function were not coordinated with the *de facto* policies of line management — 'unresolved confusion over the role of personnel management can produce a compromise that gets the worst of all worlds' (p. 254). These points suggest that the model of management adopted in the debate on reformism has indeed been over simple.

CONCLUSIONS

In this introductory chapter the main approaches to the analysis of workplace industrial relations and its reform have been outlined, and key themes have been highlighted which will structure subsequent chapters. In addition, it has been argued that the debate between competing perspectives has on occasion misinterpreted the arguments criticized and that each of the dominant frames of reference — at least as they have been developed up until now — confronts serious analytical and empirical problems. These may be seen to derive in part from the way in which much of the debate has evolved. In some cases the priority appears to have been to 'expose' and criticize the underlying assumptions of any particular analysis: the ability thereby to label it is seen in some mysterious way to mean that it can contain no insights of any value. Along with this, major conclusions have often been drawn from the skimpiest of data. At the other extreme, there has been a tendency to ignore conceptual issues, and to engage too rapidly in inferring phenomena from less than adequate data. The aim of this book is to initiate a process in which there is a fuller and more careful integration of conceptual and empirical argument, but the very weaknesses which have just been noted mean that this is necessarily a 'second-best' task. However, it is a task which is necessary in order to understand what has happened to workplace industrial relations over the last twenty years.

PART I
The Decade after Donovan

2 Management and the Reform of Labour Relations

As chapter 1 showed, the Donovan Commission's proposals for reform placed considerable emphasis upon the role of management. If reform was to be introduced, management had to be the catalyst: it had to take the initiative in introducing formal bargaining at plant or company level; it had to develop proposals and plans for a fuller recognition of shop steward organization, for changes in payment systems and for new working practices. If such ideas were to be developed and successfully implemented, then important changes had also to occur within management itself. Industrial relations considerations had to play a more central role in management thinking, and management had to ensure that day-to-day decisions on industrial relations were consistent with overall policy; this meant that greater control had to be exerted over the actions of supervisors.

In this chapter we attempt to assess how far such developments did occur within management in the decade from 1968. However, such changes as were implemented may not be primarily or directly attributable to management's espousal of the rationale of reformism. Indeed, it is possible to conceive of a number of different kinds of pressure which led to changes in management's approach to labour relations. It is useful briefly to list these possibilities here; in the remainder of this chapter an attempt is made to explain the degree and nature of the changes which occurred in terms of the significance of these different kinds of pressure.

The first factor which may have led management to change its approach to industrial relations is simply the espousal of the rationale of reformism, even when there were not immediate industrial relations 'problems' or union pressures. Such an approach might be compared with the adoption of 'welfarism' by some employers in Britain around the turn of the century. The adoption of such a new philosophy on the part of management would suggest — at least in this instance — a changed conception of the nature of labour relations and a new model of the nature and legitimacy of worker and union interests. We will call this the 'reformist rationale'.

The second possible stimulus to the adoption of reformism derives from the realities of industrial relations: management confronts continual pressure from unions and workers and is forced to take greater account of their demands. If the first pressure to reformism is principled, this second pressure is pragmatic. It may, of course, lead to a fuller acceptance over time of the philosophy of reformism; but, equally, where reforms have been introduced on pragmatic grounds, there may be a retreat from reformism if and when worker pressure declines or when other considerations become important for key groups of managers (see, for example, Fox, 1974). We will call this factor 'union pressure'.

The third type of pressure which may lead to reforms in industrial relations may involve even less commitment to the rationale of reformism. This derives from government pressures, notably in the form of industrial relations legislation and incomes policies. If companies, for example, wish to protect themselves from legal proceedings, then they may be induced to develop formal procedures and to appoint specialists in the niceties of the law. Similarly, if incomes policies permit pay increases above the legal norm where they are associated with greater productivity, then there may be an incentive for management to engage in 'mock' productivity deals. In other words, in such cases there may be the outward appearance of reform but very little in real or substantive terms. We will call this factor 'external pressure'.

The fourth and final type of factor which may lead to reforms in labour relations is managerial change more generally. For example, in the late sixties there was a wave of mergers in British industry. Attempts to integrate merged companies and to develop control systems were associated with an increased division of labour within management: new specialist functions were introduced or expanded. From this perspective, an explanation of industrial relations reform is to be sought not in industrial relations as such but in the organization more generally. An increase in personnel specialists, for example, is to be accounted for in terms broadly comparable with those which would explain a simultaneous growth in accounting specialists in the firm (see, for example, Flanders, 1964). In this instance, reformism is best seen as a feature of developments in managerial control systems: industrial relations is, therefore, likely to be subordinated to managerial priorities rather than becoming one of those priorities in its own right. We will term this factor the 'organizational rationale'.

In practice, of course, these four factors may intermingle: one may develop out of the other. For example, the 'organizational rationale' may explain the appointment of personnel specialists but the latter may subsequently be able to introduce policies based upon the 'reformist rationale'. However, the extent to which they are able to do so is likely to be fairly limited: as a good deal of evidence suggests (for example, Elliott and Elliott, 1976), the extent to which technical specialists are able to shift the priorities of management tends to be limited. This is particularly likely when the area of specialism is one in which most managers believe they have expertise: such is the case with personnel management.

Furthermore, it is not necessarily true that a single factor explains all the features of management's approach to labour relations. It has been widely argued, for example, that 'external pressures' explain the introduction of productivity bargaining in the late 1960s; at the same time, it is quite conceivable that management was paying more attention to industrial relations considerations in the formulation of its general plans because of union pressures and the experience of industrial action 'sabotaging' previous investment plans.

In pursuing these themes, a number of areas of management structure and strategy are considered in this chapter. According to some perspectives, at any rate, the appointment of personnel specialists indicates a more conscious approach to labour relations on the part of management. A related question is how far labour relations considerations impinge upon management decision-making: for the logic of reformism was that industrial relations should play a more prominent and explicit role in the formulation of management policy. Another theme in the reformist rationale is that management should exert greater control over its industrial relations and the actions of lower levels of management. These themes are discussed in the next section of this chapter. The second section considers the key theme of reformism — the ways in which management attempted to change its relationships with shop stewards and to introduce substantive reforms. The final section considers the wider implications of the findings.

Much of the data presented in this chapter derives from an Industrial Relations Research Unit (IRRU) survey of workplace industrial relations. It consisted of 970 interviews with the person responsible for industrial relations in manufacturing establishments with fifty or more full-time employees. The sample was stratified to ensure that a sufficient number of large plants were included. The discussion below employs weighted data to make the results representative of manufacturing as a whole. The fieldwork was carried out between November 1977 and January 1978. The overall findings of the survey were published in *The Changing*

Contours of British Industrial Relations (Brown, 1981). It should also be noted that in the subsequent discussion the terms 'personnel' and 'industrial relations' manager are used interchangeably. In the questionnaire reference was made to a 'specialist personnel and industrial relations function' above the level of the establishment, and to 'personnel and/or industrial relations' responsibilities at establishment and board levels.

THE INTERNAL ORGANIZATION AND OPERATION OF MANAGEMENT

The Existence of Personnel Specialists

At the turn of the century personnel managers of any kind were relatively rare. They increased in number in the First World War and by 1918 the membership of the Central Association of Welfare Workers was 600 (Niven, 1967, p. 52). It has been estimated that by the beginning of the Second World War there were 1,800 personnel specialists, defined as persons with jobs and qualifications which made them eligible to join the Institute of Personnel Management. Largely due to government support, this number had grown to about 5,000 by 1945, but there was little subsequent increase until the sixties. Over that decade, numbers further increased to about 13,500 (Crichton, 1969, p. 192), and by the late seventies the number of specialists was about 20,000 — four times what it had been twenty years earlier.

A similar picture of the growth of the personnel function is obtained from surveys of companies and establishments. The IRRU survey found that in nearly a third (30 per cent) of the establishments surveyed there was a specialist personnel director, and in slightly more than a third (38 per cent) there was a board member who was specifically responsible for personnel as well as other matters. This was more than twice the number of medium-sized and large companies having a member with personnel responsibilities found in a survey in 1972 (BIM, 1972, p. 20; see also Marsh, 1971). Similarly, 71 per cent of establishments which were subsidiaries of larger companies in the IRRU survey had a specialist personnel function above the level of the establishment; comparison of the survey with Marsh's late sixties survey of engineering companies again suggests a considerable growth at this level (Marsh, 1971, p. 124). Finally, the IRRU survey found that in 46 per cent of establishments there was a personnel specialist. Comparison of the engineering plants studied with those in Marsh's survey suggests that it is at this level that there has been least growth. It is possible, however, that this is a distinctive feature of the engineering industry. To the extent that it does not have broader relevance, it suggests that recent developments in the personnel function have been focused upon the higher levels of company organization.

There was a tendency for the existence of the different personnel specialisms to be interrelated: in 72 per cent of establishments covered by a specialist industrial relations director there was also a specialist industrial relations manager at plant level. Where there was no specific industrial relations responsibility at board level, specialist industrial relations managers existed in only 39 per cent of establishments. Such managers were to be found least frequently where industrial relations constituted merely one of a variety of responsibilities of a director — in only 31 per cent of establishments.

In the case of subsidiary establishments, there was an especially strong tendency for their companies, if they had specialist industrial relations directors, also to have an industrial relations function at some level above the establishment. This was so in 91 per cent of cases. By contrast, such a function was found in the case of only 42 per cent of establishments with no industrial relations director at company level and in 60 per cent of those where the industrial relations director had other responsibilities as well.

As establishments grew in size there was a greater tendency for personnel specialists of all three kinds to exist. Only 21 per cent of establishments employing between 50 and 99 full-time employees had a local personnel specialist while, at the other extreme, 95 per cent of those with more than 1,000 workers employed such a specialist. Similarly, while 19 per cent of the smallest establishments had a specialist industrial relations director, 70 per cent of the largest establishments had such a board member. However, directors who had industrial relations as one of a number of responsibilities were more common in the smaller establishments — nearly half of the smallest size category had such a director, compared with less than one in five of the largest establishments. Finally, as subsidiaries grew in size there was a greater probability that there existed an industrial relations function at a higher level within the company. This was true of 57 per cent of the smallest subsidiaries compared with 86 per cent of the largest. It is probable that the existence of such a specialist function was even more strongly related to the size of the company as a whole, but the data necessary to assess this view are not available (see, however, Deaton, 1983).

The size effect (confirmed by the analysis of the data by Beaumont and Deaton, 1980) could, however, be consistent with any of the four kinds of pressure previously noted. It could, for example, be the case that large firms were particularly susceptible to the 'reformist rationale'. One explanation for this might be the existence of a more professional management, less committed to notions of managerial prerogative. For reasons which will subsequently become evident, it is unlikely that the reformist rationale was the key factor in the rise of personnel specialists in many companies. We will therefore focus first upon seeking to assess the relative significance of 'union pressure' and the 'organizational rationale' as explanations of the existence of personnel specialists.

The 'size effect' in and of itself gives little clue as to which is the more important. For, on the one hand, size clearly highlights the problem of internal management control, thereby encouraging a managerial division of labour. On the other hand, various indications of union strength and industrial conflict are also associated with size of establishment (Brown, 1981, pp. 53, 65, 87).

The IRRU survey permits the use of two indicators of the 'organizational rationale' which are relatively independent of the size effect or various aspects of union organization. The first of these is whether or not the establishment is a subsidiary of a larger company. If personnel specialists are more common in subsidiary establishments than they are in single-plant companies, then the organization thesis receives some support. This is indeed the case: while 61 per cent of subsidiaries had a personnel specialist, only 25 per cent of single independent establishments had a local industrial relations specialist (the tendency for subsidiaries to be slightly larger than independent establishments is insufficient to account for the size of this difference).

A second indicator with which to test the organization thesis is whether or not the company is British-owned. For, again, ownership is not significantly related to features of union organization and activity. If significant differences exist between foreign and British-owned companies, therefore, this again suggests that the organization thesis (and possibly the reformist rationale) is relevant. The survey indicates that there were indeed significant differences by ownership in the frequency with which personnel specialists were found at plant level. While over three-quarters of foreign-owned establishments had local personnel specialists, only 43 per cent of British-owned establishments did.

Unfortunately, the IRRU survey data do not permit any assessment of the extent to which the existence of personnel specialists is associated with other features of specialization. However, other studies — notably by Turner *et al.* (1977) and Gill *et al.* (1978) — suggest that personnel specialists can be seen as a symptom of the more general bureaucratization of management, thereby giving further support to the organization thesis.

Turning to the 'union pressure' thesis, a variety of indicators of union power and pressure are available from the IRRU survey. These include union density, union recognition, various features of steward organization and the experience of industrial action. All of these are associated with the existence of personnel specialists, and the associations are statistically significant. But the interpretation of these relationships requires great caution. For union organization can be seen as one element in the more general bureaucratization of a company. Hence those features of trade unionism which are generally seen to be most susceptible to managerial influence (see chapter 3) — recognition of non-manual unions, the existence of full-time stewards and regular meetings of shop stewards — are those which are most strongly associated with the existence of personnel specialists.

Only one indicator of 'union pressure' is available which can be seen as being significantly independent of factors subsumed under the 'organizational rationale' — industrial action. If personnel specialists are more common where the establishment has experienced strike action, then this may be seen as giving some support to the 'union pressure' thesis (although, as is argued below, the actions of personnel specialists may lead to industrial action). The IRRU survey did find an association between the experience of strike action and the existence of personnel specialists. But the variation was not very great — only 17 per cent as far as local specialists were concerned (38 per cent compared with 55 per cent), 14 per cent for specialist directors (23 per cent compared with 37 per cent), and only 8 per cent for a higher level of function in the case of subsidiaries (69 per cent and 77 per cent). These variations were much weaker than those found by ownership and whether or not the establishment was part of a larger company.

Using the same survey data, Beaumont and Deaton sought to assess the extent to which the existence of personnel specialists could be explained by union power. Focusing upon the existence of a specialist personnel director, and using discriminant analysis, they concluded that the evidence provided 'substantial empirical support' for their thesis 'that the presence of personnel management within the senior management hierarchy represented an organizational response to the presence of union power' (1980, p. 210). While I would not wish totally to discount this view, the preceding argument suggests that they have failed to take account of the 'organization thesis'. This is particularly ironic on two counts: first, they claim to be employing a contingency approach but then go on to treat 'multi-establishments' (that is, organizations in which a plant is a subsidiary) as 'one of our control variables' (p. 209). Second, and relatedly, their own analysis indicated that the two indicators of the organization thesis had considerably greater explanatory power than their indicators of union power. Hence their standardized coefficients for 'foreign-owned' and for 'multi-establishment' were -0.296 and -0.586 respectively (prior to their incorporation of an industry dimension into the analysis — its inclusion does not substantially alter the points made here). These compared with coefficients of -0.127 for industrial action, -0.256 for union density and -0.214 for multi-unionism. Thus even if we ignore the fact that union density is to some degree subject to managerial influence, the analysis of Beaumont and Deaton indicates the relatively greater importance of the 'organization' as against the 'union pressure' or, as they term it, the 'union power', thesis.

The view that the growth of personnel management owes more to the general nature of company organization than to union pressures of a kind specific to the company is further supported by the views of respondents. They were asked whether there had been any changes in the position of the industrial relations function over the last five years. A negligible number (0.1 per cent) said it had become less important and only 18 per cent said there had been no change. When the remaining 80 per cent or so were asked to explain the increased importance of the function, reasons relating to 'company policy' were almost twice as common as those relating to the increasing power or demands of the unions (24 per cent as compared with 13 per cent). However, more important than either of these factors was increased legislation: this was put forward as an explanation by well over half of those who perceived a greater role for the personnel function (see Watson, 1977, p. 28). This, as suggested earlier, might be seen as an 'external pressure' for the existence of personnel specialists. But some caution is necessary in attributing too much weight to this 'explanation'. For, first, well under 1 per cent said that no industrial relations function had existed five years previously: in other words, while the increase in legislation might explain greater importance it does not explain the existence of the function (it might also be suggested that if legislation is a major factor it merely indicates the marginality of the personnel function). Second, and relatedly, increased legislation was often only one of a variety of factors mentioned. Third, the view that legislation had led to a greater role for the personnel function was associated with many of the features already considered — size, and indicators of both the organization and the union pressure theses. In short, the differential impact of legislation appears to be due to the variables already considered.

Analysis of the IRRU survey data, therefore, indicates that while 'union pressure' may partially explain the existence of personnel management, the organization thesis has greater explanatory power. In addition, 'external pressures' appear to play a role in fostering the rise of the personnel specialist.

The Centrality of Labour Relations for Management Policy

A crucial theme in prescriptions for industrial relations reform was that management should take greater account of labour relations considerations in the formulation of policy. Hence the 'reformist rationale' would suggest that industrial relations would be relatively central in management deliberations, even when there was no clear threat of disruption of plans by workers and unions. The 'organizational' thesis, on the other hand, would suggest that since the rise of personnel specialists was part of a wider trend towards specialization within management, there would be relatively little tendency for labour relations to figure more strongly in management thinking at least outside of traditional industrial relations issues. From this perspective, union pressure is likely to account for greater attention being paid to labour relations factors.

In the IRRU survey we asked respondents how influential they thought 'personnel and industrial relations considerations are in formulating policy and making decisions in this organization' on a number of issues. The areas they were asked about were fixed capital investment decisions, major changes in production methods, wages and conditions of employment and decisions to make employees redundant. These issues were selected so as to give insights into what might be termed traditional industrial relations issues on the one hand, and more central managerial issues on the other. Respondents were offered four response categories: 'play the central role', 'heavily involved', 'consulted' or 'not involved at all'. In order to simplify the discussion, responses have been scored so that replies in which personnel and industrial relations (P & IR) considerations 'play the central role' are weighted by three and, at the other extreme, the percentage of replies in which they are 'not involved at all' is scored nought. Accordingly, if all respondents stated that such considerations were central, the total score would be 300; if all said they played no role at all the score would be zero.

As one moves from 'traditional' industrial relations into mainstream management decisions and policies, the importance of P & IR considerations declines. In decisions on 'wages and conditions of employment' the overall score was 178, indicating that P & IR considerations were more or less 'heavily involved'. On redundancy, the overall score was marginally lower — 169.2. 'Major changes in production methods' impinge directly upon the labour force but are also central to corporate endeavour; the overall score on this issue falls to 128.8, that is, P & IR considerations tend only to be 'consulted'. 'Fixed capital investments' are even more central to the pursuit of profit — the score falls to 84.6.

This overall pattern of decision-making provides some initial support for the view that managements did not take the rationale of reformism very far. Labour relations factors did not impinge to any significant degree upon management decisions on capital investment and major changes in production methods: on the former, two-fifths of respondents said that P & IR considerations were not involved at all. The findings of Hickson and Mallory support this picture (1981, pp. 47—60). It is important to keep the marginality of labour relations in mind when considering variations in their role.

Wages and conditions

Wages and conditions are, of course, the classic issue of industrial relations. It is not surprising, therefore, that P & IR considerations should be relatively important in management discussions in this area. It might equally be expected that personnel specialists would make such considerations even more central. The strongest relationship found was with such specialists at establishment level (reflecting, no doubt, the importance of plant bargaining — see below). As table 2.1a shows, local personnel managers were associated with an increase in the score of 58.3. As the table also indicates, a slightly stronger relationship was found with a more 'direct' organization variable, ownership. Both these relationships were weaker than those found with various aspects of steward organization: the existence of full-time stewards was associated with an increase in score of 90.3 over establishments where no stewards existed. Similarly, the score was 215.2 where there were regular meetings of shop stewards, compared with 139.5 where stewards had no meetings.

More complex tabulations indicate that, for example, where regular steward meetings were held the existence of local personnel specialists had no independent impact. On the other hand, where no such regular meetings were held local personnel specialists were associated with an increase in score of about thirty points — a relatively small figure. It seems reasonable to conclude, then, that steward organization was the major factor in explaining the centrality of P & IR considerations in the determination of wages and conditions of employment. Even here, the independent impact of personnel specialists was limited.

Redundancy

As in the case of decisions on wages and conditions of employment, the importance of P & IR considerations in decisions to make employees

TABLE 2.1 SCORES FOR CENTRALITY OF P & IR CONSIDERATIONS BY
'ORGANIZATIONAL' AND 'UNION PRESSURE' VARIABLES

(a) Policies and decisions on wages and conditions	
existence of personnel specialist at establishment level	+ 58.3
foreign-owned establishments (cf. British owned)	+ 67.1
existence of regular steward meetings	+ 75.7
existence of full-time shop stewards	+ 90.3
(b) Policies and decisions on redundancy	
existence of specialist personnel director	+ 83.0
establishment is a subsidiary	+ 67.4
existence of regular steward meetings	+ 72.0
existence of full-time shop stewards	+ 84.1
(c) Policies and decisions on major changes in production methods	
existence of specialist personnel director	+ 24.1
establishment is a subsidiary	− 4.0
experience of strike action for more than one day	+ 39.4
existence of full-time shop stewards	+ 46.1
(d) Policies and decisions on capital investment	
existence of specialist personnel director	+ 22.8
establishment is a subsidiary	+ 19.5
experience of strike action for more than one day	+ 53.8
existence of regular steward meetings	+ 30.6

redundant varied by industry and technology. But these relationships were only half as strong as with size, which appeared to be the real factor underlying these variations. Hence the score rises from 138.7 for the 50−99 size group to 238.6 for the 1,000 or more employees group.

Turning to the crucial question of the relative impact of worker organization and personnel specialists, fairly strong relationships existed between the importance of personnel and industrial relations considerations and the two aspects of steward organization. The score was 220.5 where there were full-time stewards but only 136.4 where no stewards existed. Similarly, in establishments where stewards held no meetings the score was 132.3, but reached 204.3 where regular steward meetings were held (table 2.1b).

Some of the relationships between features of personnel management and the centrality of P & IR considerations in redundancy decisions were stronger than in wages and conditions of employment decisions. The existence of a specialist industrial relations director gave a score of 219.6, compared with only 136.6 where no board member had responsibility for industrial relations. Subsidiary establishments scored more highly than independent ones, but within the former the existence of a specialist function at a higher level accounted for only about forty additional points. Finally, the existence of an industrial relations specialist at establishment level appeared to have relatively little impact on the centrality of considerations which such specialists formally represent; where no such specialists were found the score was 173.0, compared with 200.0 where there was an industrial relations specialist at establishment level.

We now need to try and assess the independent impact of these two sets of factors. In the area of wages and conditions of employment, it was noted that steward organization appeared to be a good deal more important than the existence of personnel specialists. But in redundancy decisions, more complex tabulations suggest that the latter played as great an independent role as steward organization, each accounting for about half the total variation noted. In other words, the highest score is found where, for example, stewards held regular meetings and there was a specialist industrial relations function; where either of these was 'missing', the score fell, and the lowest score was found where neither existed.

Major changes in production methods

As we move from 'traditional' industrial relations areas into more 'mainstream' management decisions and policies the importance of P & IR considerations declines. Moreover, there is no clear size effect. This is the case, for example, with decisions on major changes in production methods. On this issue personnel specialists appeared to have relatively little impact. The strongest relationship was with the most senior level of the personnel function (reflecting the centrality of such decisions for management). But even in this case, the existence of a specialist industrial relations director was associated with only a small increase in the score as compared with establishments where no director had specific responsibility for industrial relations — 140.2 compared with 116.1 (table 2.1c).

As for aspects of union power, the experience of industrial action appeared to be important for this issue. Where there had been no strikes, the score was 119.4; where strikes had lasted for more than a day, the score was 158.8. This variation is comparable with those by degrees of steward organization: for example, the existence of full-time shop stewards was associated with an increased score of 46.1 points compared with establishments where there were no stewards. Both variations are stronger than those associated with the existence of personnel specialists.

Capital investment decisions

The significance of industrial action is even greater when we turn to capital investment decisions. Establishments where no strikes had occurred scored only 68.3 compared with 117.6 where strikes had occurred (and 122.1 where these lasted for a day or more). This is a considerably stronger relationship than that found for the existence of steward meetings. Where no such meetings were held the score was 64.4; this rose to 95.0 where meetings of this kind were held regularly (the existence of full-time stewards led to an increase of only 16.5). One possible explanation for this contrast with traditional industrial relations issues relates to procedures. In areas such as wages, established procedures exist for negotiation and, therefore, conflict is more institutionalized. But capital investment decisions are seen primarily as an issue for management alone so that collective procedures for determining the central considerations (as distinct from minor details of implementation) tend not to exist. As a consequence, the threat of industrial action becomes of greater significance and, in plants which have experienced such action in the past, is likely to be taken more fully into account.

If this argument is correct, one corollary might be that the impact of personnel specialists would be greater, since they are in a position to point out the importance of taking into account possible worker reactions which could adversely affect the profitability of capital investments. But in fact the existence of industrial relations specialists at establishment level was associated with virtually no greater role for P & IR considerations; the score was 84.6 where they existed and 84.4 where they did not. The same pattern was found as far as subsidiaries with an industrial relations function at a higher level are concerned: where such existed the score was 80.6, but it was 80.9 when no such function existed. The only variation found was by the existence of an industrial relations director; whether such a director had other responsibilities or not seemed to make little difference, the score in both situations being about 91. But where no board member had a specific responsibility for industrial relations, the score falls to 68.2. Even this variation is relatively small.

Overall, therefore, it appears that experience of industrial action is the crucial factor in explaining the centrality of personnel and industrial relations considerations in fixed capital investment decisions. The existence at board level of someone with specific responsibility for industrial relations also has a minor effect which is largely independent of strike experience. But the importance of personnel specialists is much less than that of strike action.

In general terms, the findings of the survey support the view that features of union organization and power encourage management to be more aware of personnel and industrial relations considerations in the formulation of decisions. Moreover, as one moves away from traditional industrial relations issues to those traditionally defined as subjects of managerial prerogative, the sanction of strikes assumes greater significance. On all four issues investigated, the impact of personnel specialists was less than features of union power. Their influence, in terms of increasing attention paid to personnel and industrial relations considerations, diminished as one moved into issues more central to managerial endeavour. The only issue on which their influence appeared comparable with that of union power was redundancy. It may be that the personnel specialists' knowledge of the legal aspects of redundancy was of particular importance here.

The survey data therefore suggest that there is little support for the 'reformist rationale' thesis. The limited impact of personnel specialists is consistent with the organization thesis and indicates the importance of 'union pressure' factors, particularly outside the traditional ambit of 'industrial relations'.

The Structure of Management Control

The reform prescriptions for industrial relations placed considerable emphasis upon the need to ensure that lower levels of management did not sabotage policies formulated at plant or company level. It was, therefore, necessary to exert tighter control over supervisory staff. The organization thesis which we have put forward to explain the rise of personnel specialists would similarly suggest that an important feature of their role is control over other managers. Hence one would expect that the degree of discretion afforded to other managers would be less where such specialists existed. Similarly, where workers were strongly organized — the union pressure thesis — it might be expected that this endeavour to reduce managerial discretion might be that much greater, although possibly less successful. For strong union organization tends to encourage sectional concessions; the pursuit of more 'rational' or 'rationalized' industrial relations policies would therefore suggest the need for tighter controls over what managers did in the face of these pressures. But the adoption of tighter controls does not mean that union pressures disappear; indeed, they may intensify so that the individual manager is forced to make concessions even when these are formally contrary to managerial rules of conduct.

In discussing controls over management we also need to recognize that various forms of union—management dealing may constitute important means for limiting the discretion of managers, and for exerting some form of overall corporate control. For example, the decision to bargain within the company rather than jointly with other employees indicates the desire to pursue specific corporate interests. Similarly, the decision to bargain above the level of the establishment indicates the wish to ensure some pattern of uniformity across plants within a multi-establishment company.

Accordingly, in this section we look first at bargaining levels and the degree of discretion which plants within multi-establishment companies had on a number of issues. We then go on to consider the extent to which the personnel function did actually appear to be able to maintain control.

Bargaining levels and discretion

In considering bargaining levels, it is useful to divide the discussion into two parts, looking first at whether the company engages in single- or multi-employer bargaining and then, in the case of the former, at whether bargaining occurs at the level of the plant or at some higher level.

On the first question, the reformist rationale, the organization and the union pressure theses would, we suggest, all point in the same direction, namely towards single-employer bargaining. Deaton and Beaumont, in their analysis of the IRRU survey, found no support for this interpretation of the union pressure thesis. They concentrated, however, upon management's assessment of the difficulty of replacing labour as an indication of the existence of powerful work groups (1980, pp. 209—10). Their other union variables — union density and multi-unionism — were associated with multi-, not single-employer bargaining. There was, however, a relationship between the experience of strike action and single-employer bargaining which could be interpreted as consistent with a 'union pressure' thesis (Brown, 1981, p. 87). But, as is argued below, the direction of causality in this relationship appears, at least in part, to be from bargaining level to strike action.

The organization thesis receives considerable support from the IRRU survey data. For ease of discussion we can look at the ratio of establishments where there was single-employer bargaining to those where multi-employer bargaining was the most important means of determining manual workers' pay. Where a personnel specialist existed at establishment level, this ratio was 2.6; where no such specialist existed, the ratio fell to 0.9. Similarly, more direct indicators of the organization thesis — whether or not the establishment is part of a larger company, and whether it is British- or foreign-owned — are quite strongly associated with single-employer bargaining.

Indeed, factors consistent with the organization thesis were found by Deaton and Beaumont to be the most strongly associated with single-employer bargaining (at least before their inclusion of a set of industry dummies). The standardized coefficients of their discriminant function were: foreign ownership 0.471; establishment size 0.437; and the existence of a senior specialist personnel manager 0.380.

When we turn to the level of single-employer bargaining in multi-plant companies, the organization thesis also receives support. Foreign-owned companies were more likely than British-owned to engage in bargaining above the level of the establishment (Brown, 1981, p. 11). Moreover, the existence of a specialist industrial relations function above the establishment was associated with a centralization of bargaining. The ratio of 'above establishment' to establishment bargaining was 0.49 where a specialist existed, compared with only 0.15 where no such higher function was found. Deaton and Beaumont's analysis supports this picture of the relative importance of 'organization' factors (1980, p. 212), although they also found that labour costs tend to be associated with plant-level bargaining. There was also a tendency for above-establishment-level bargaining to be associated with industrial action, but the direction of causality here, as with single-employer bargaining, is open to a variety of interpretations.

The data on the degree of management discretion provide a similar picture. Respondents in subsidiary establishments were asked to assess the extent of local management discretion in the following areas: training policy, manual workers' pay, junior management pay, redundancies, dismissals and industrial relations matters generally. They were asked to rate the degree of discretion in terms of 'complete or almost complete freedom', 'considerable discretion within broadly defined rules', 'limited discretion within fairly detailed rules' and 'virtually no freedom'. For ease of exposition a scoring system comparable with that in the previous section is employed; that is, scores ranging from three for 'complete or almost complete freedom' to zero for 'virtually no freedom' are given. In addition, respondents were asked to assess changes in local management discretion over the last five years regarding pay and other terms and conditions.

As a preliminary to the more detailed discussion, it is useful to sketch briefly the overall situation concerning local management discretion. Local managements generally had a relatively high degree of discretion. This was particularly so in issues which were essentially individual, such as dismissal (263.0) and training (250.2), and in industrial relations matters generally (246.8). However, as issues became more collective in nature and had clearer financial and industrial relations implications the degree of local discretion tended to decline. Hence the score for local discretion in redundancy was only 192.0, more than seventy points below that for dismissal. Local discretion over manual workers' pay was 186.3, and even lower (178.3) for junior management pay.

As might be expected, the degree of local management discretion was associated with bargaining level. It was lowest where the most important bargaining level for manual workers was within the company but above the level of the establishment. This was true over all issues so that, compared with establishment-level bargaining, the score was about sixty points lower for junior management pay and for redundancy, about thirty points lower for dismissal and about forty points lower for 'industrial relations generally'. The relationship with other levels of bargaining was less consistent across issue areas, but generally speaking both multi-employer bargaining and 'no bargaining' were associated with relatively high levels of managerial discretion.

Relationships between the level of management discretion and indicators of union power were found, but were a good deal weaker than those with bargaining level. Hence the experience of strike action was associated with a lower level of local discretion over training (by thirty points) and the pay of both manual workers (by fifty points) and junior managers (by thirty points); the relationships were extremely weak in the other three areas. The existence of stewards was associated with lower local discretion over training (by forty points) and manual workers' pay (by sixty points) but the relationship was thereafter negligible. The impact of steward meetings was somewhat confusing, for in many instances local discretion was marginally lower where such meetings were occasional than where they were regular. But where stewards held meetings there was less local discretion over training, manual workers' and junior managers' pay, redundancy, and to some degree over the other two issues. However, it is also worth noting that where establishments used technologies which were particularly susceptible to disruption due to worker action — process, mass and large batch production — the level of discretion on crucial collective issues such as pay and redundancy was a good deal lower — by about sixty points — than in other establishments.

While union power was associated with a lower level of discretion for local management, the existence of a specialist personnel function above establishment level tended to be more strongly associated with centralization, apart from dismissals and 'industrial relations generally'. Hence such a function was associated with a reduction in local management discretion over training of forty points, despite the fact that this is a relatively marginal issue. In the case of pay questions, the existence of such specialists above the level of the establishment was associated with a reduction of almost eighty points concerning manual workers and nearly ninety points for junior managers. Local discretion over redundancy fell from 242 to 161.3 where a higher-level industrial relations function existed. It seems, therefore, that the organization of management was of greater importance than worker organization in affecting the degree of local management discretion (and bargaining level). However, it should be remembered that management centralization is in part an attempt to prevent domestic collective worker organization and action from creating what, from higher management's point of view, would be chaotic situations within and between plants.

A broadly similar pattern was found for changes in local discretion. Respondents were asked whether such freedom 'has increased, stayed the same or decreased on matters of (a) pay, and (b) other terms and conditions of employment' in the last five years. In just over half of the establishments there had been no change in local discretion over the past five years. Where change had occurred, almost as many establishments had experienced a decrease (21 per cent) as an increase (22 per cent) in discretion over pay. But over other terms and conditions of employment there had been a somewhat stronger tendency towards an increase in local discretion, 25 per cent experiencing this compared with only 14 per cent having their discretion reduced. There was no clear pattern of changes in local discretion in those subsidiaries which had experienced a change in the importance of industrial relations over the last five years.

There was, however, a consistent tendency for stronger worker organization to be associated with a decline in local management discretion over both pay and other terms and conditions of employment. The experience of (relatively) lengthy strikes was associated with a net reduction of local discretion of 19 per cent over pay but only 8 per cent over other terms and conditions of employment. Similarly, regular steward meetings were associated with a net reduction in local discretion of 27 per cent over pay and 12 per cent over other terms and conditions. The impact of the existence of stewards was stronger on the latter: a net reduction of 26 per cent over pay and of 46 per cent over other terms and conditions of employment.

These relationships are broadly comparable with the impact of bargaining level. Overall, there had been an increase in local discretion in all establishments except those engaging in company bargaining above establishment level: for example, establishment level bargaining was associated with a net increase of local discretion over pay of 9 per cent, while company bargaining above establishment level was associated with a net decrease of local discretion over pay of over 25 per cent.

The impact of particular features of personnel management upon the discretion of plant management was generally greater than that of features of union organization. The effect of the existence of local P & IR specialists was small: it led to a net reduction of local discretion of about 10 per cent. A reduction of twice this figure was associated with the existence of a specialist industrial relations director. But both of these relationships were largely due to the impact of a specialist industrial relations function above the level of the establishment in the case of multi-plant companies. For such a function was associated with a 45 per cent reduction in local discretion over pay and a 32 per cent reduction over other terms and conditions.

The data suggest that reduced local discretion — in other words, management centralization — in industrial relations was primarily accounted for by the growth of personnel specialists above establishment level — a feature of the 'organizational rationale'. Such a pattern is likely to become more widespread for, as Brown and Terry (1978) indicate, company- as contrasted with plant-bargaining is increasing in importance. This is no doubt in part explained by the increasing complexity of company organization, particularly the greater number of plants owned by a single company (Prais, 1976), and is most marked in those establishments particularly dependent upon uninterrupted production runs. It would seem that centralization is a managerial attempt to avoid problems commonly assumed to exist in an 'informal' system of industrial relations (Donovan, 1968). In any event, it is clear that while worker organization — or union pressure — tends to be the more important factor in terms of fostering management consideration of the personnel and industrial relations aspects of decisions, personnel specialists, whose existence is primarily explained by an organizational rationale, tend to be more strongly associated with the procedural aspect of centralization and reduced local management discretion. But while this may be the aim of management organization, it is not necessarily the case that it succeeds.

Control structures and practice

It was noted above that while managements might attempt to centralize decisions, a variety of pressures impinge upon local managers which might induce them to try to by-pass and manipulate centrally determined rules and procedures. Case studies have indicated the importance of this tendency (for example, Batstone *et al.,* 1977; Terry, 1977; Purcell, 1981). In the survey we had to content ourselves with seeking to assess how far specialist industrial relations managers at establishment level were satisfied with the cooperation of local management more generally.

Control and coordination strategies are, of course, likely to be less effective in larger organizations. Hence, for example, while about 60 per cent of personnel specialists in smaller establishments were very satisfied that management generally took heed of industrial relations procedures, this figure fell to 52 per cent in establishments with more than 1,000 employees. The strongest effect of size concerned the passing on of relevant information; just over 60 per cent of those in plants with less than 200 staff said they were 'very satisfied', but only 46 per cent of those in the largest (1,000 plus employees) establishments expressed a similar view.

Union pressure served to reduce personnel managers' satisfaction with the behaviour of management generally. Where strikes of more than a day's duration had occurred, for example, 5 per cent fewer said they were very satisfied with the extent to which management took heed of industrial relations policies and procedures; 7 per cent fewer were happy over how far management sought advice; and 15 per cent fewer were very satisfied concerning the extent to which other managers passed on information. Features of steward organization were even more strongly related to personnel specialists' satisfaction: the existence of regular steward meetings led to a decline in the proportion of personnel specialists saying they were very satisfied with managerial behaviour over industrial relations policies and procedures of 11 per cent, of 13 per cent concerning seeking advice and of 20 per cent concerning seeking information (compared with situations where stewards held no meetings).

Satisfaction was not only related to indications of union pressure but also to the extent to which higher management sought to impose control over local management. The previous discussion suggests two forms of control — bargaining level and the existence of an industrial relations director. If we consider bargaining levels, it appears plausible to suggest that the strongest form of control is single-employer bargaining above establishment level. For in this case the scope for local discretion is small. Multi-employer bargaining, on the other hand, can be seen as involving relatively little control for two reasons. First, it suggests that the individual employer does not seek to shape industrial relations in the company to take account of its particular and unique features. Second, and relatedly, multi-employer agreements typically cover a limited range of issues and hence may be expected to give greater freedom to local managements. Establishment-level bargaining may be seen as intermediate between these two extremes as far as control is concerned (the findings concerning management discretion support this interpretation). We might, therefore, expect personnel managers to express greater satisfaction with the general behaviour of management where the control exerted through the level of bargaining is less.

The data broadly support this view. Where multi-employer bargaining exists, over two-thirds of personnel specialists claimed they were 'very satisfied' with the extent to which managers took heed of industrial relations policies and procedures; this figure fell to 61 per cent where bargaining was at establishment level and plummeted to 45 per cent where there was single-employer bargaining above the establishment. A similar pattern is found concerning satisfaction over management passing on information: 62 per cent expressed themselves very satisfied where multi-employer bargaining took place, 57 per cent where there was plant bargaining and only 45 per cent where there was corporate bargaining. Variations were, however, much less marked as far as managers seeking advice was concerned: with multi-employer bargaining, 65 per cent were very satisfied; the figure rose to 67 per cent where there was plant bargaining and then fell to 62 per cent with corporate bargaining.

It appears that when control through bargaining level is supplemented by greater weight accorded to the personnel function in the overall control structure of the company — as with the existence of an industrial relations director — the level of satisfaction expressed by personnel specialists tends to rise again. Hence 51 per cent expressed themselves very satisfied with the behaviour of management as far as industrial relations policies and procedures were concerned where there was no industrial relations director; where such a director existed, the proportion rose to 59 per cent. A similar pattern was found on the question of managers seeking advice. As far as passing on information was concerned, the existence of a specialist industrial relations director was associated with 65 per cent of personnel specialists expressing themselves 'very satisfied', while only 51 per cent did so where no one represented the function on the board.

The personnel manager at establishment level appears from the survey evidence to confront strong cross-cutting pressures, particularly in multi-plant firms and where there is single-employer bargaining but above the level of the establishment. For in such circumstances, union pressures tend to weaken his or her control over other local managers who are induced to make local deals. On the other hand, if the personnel function occupies a relatively powerful position within the corporate control structure — as indicated by the existence of an industrial relations director — he or she may be able to maintain greater control over colleagues at plant level. Here the contradictory forces of 'union pressure' and the 'organizational rationale' are particularly evident: this theme is taken up more fully in the final section of this chapter.

MANAGEMENT AND LABOUR REGULATION

The Personnel Function and Joint Regulation

The preceding discussion has indicated that a specialist personnel function can best be seen as a form of control over plant-level management, with relatively little impact upon the priorities embodied in management decisions. Personnel and industrial relations considerations become more central with greater union power. It seems reasonable to expect personnel specialists to have a similar effect on joint regulation, that is, procedurally rather than substantively.

In this section these themes, particularly that of substantive reforms, will be only briefly considered, for they are discussed at considerable length in subsequent chapters. In addition, as these later chapters show, it is questionable how far attempts at substantive rationalization have been successful. Given the diversity of industrial relations in Britain, this is perhaps not surprising; but it does also suggest that what may be 'rational' from management's viewpoint in one context may not be so in another.

From the questionnaire it is possible to take a number of indicators of the extent of formalization and 'rationalization'. These can be conveniently divided into a number of defined areas. The first of these concerns attempts to formalize procedures: here the relevant (available) indicators are the existence of a formal pay procedure, the existence of consultative and health and safety committees and changes in relations with stewards in terms of recognition or regularizing meetings. The second area concerns attempts to rationalize behaviour in some way in relation to specific substantive issues: the areas selected for consideration here are the existence of a formal training policy and the attempt to 'rationalize' the wage-effort bargain in the form of productivity schemes. In addition, other practices are briefly considered. Each of these areas will be considered in turn and the impact of the industrial relations specialists assessed.

The formalization of procedures

The vast majority of establishments had pay and conditions procedures. 'Union pressure' factors appeared to play some role in encouraging such procedures; in particular, union density, the existence of full-time stewards and past experience of strike action. 'Organizational' factors were also important: foreign-owned establishments and multi-plant establishments were both more likely to have various kinds of procedures (Brown, 1981, pp. 44—6). It is not surprising, therefore, that there was a tendency for the existence of industrial relations specialists to be associated with a greater likelihood of formal procedures existing. For example, where there was a specialist industrial relations director only 6 per cent of establishments had no formal procedure, compared with 18 per cent where no one at board level had any special responsibility for industrial relations matters. Where industrial relations specialists existed there was a greater probability that the procedure would allow for the possibility of outside intervention. This was the case in 50 per cent of establishments where a specialist industrial relations director existed, for example, compared with only 25 per cent where no director was responsible for industrial relations. This indicates the concern of the specialists to provide formal means for dealing with disputes to avoid the application of such sanctions as strikes.

A second feature of procedural formalization is the introduction of joint consultative committees. According to the IRRU survey, these existed in 42 per cent of establishments, and three-fifths of them had been introduced since 1973 (Brown, 1981, p. 76). In their analysis of the survey data, Beaumont and Deaton (1981) found that such committees were associated with single-employer bargaining, this being seen as an indication of the personnel orientation of management. In the terms used here, we would see this as a desire to control industrial relations. In addition, they found that multi-unionism was associated with the existence of joint consultation; Brown notes a tendency for such committees to exist 'where shop stewards were well-established' (1981, p. 76).

Consultative committees were also more common where industrial relations specialists existed, and this pattern was found for all types of industrial relations specialist investigated. So, for example, in 53 per cent of establishments where there were local industrial relations specialists there were also consultative committees, while only 33 per cent of establishments with no local industrial relations specialist had such bodies. Health and safety committees were widespread, reflecting the impact of legislation. Even so, there was still a slight tendency for these to be more common where industrial relations specialists existed. Where these were found at establishment level, in 78 per cent of cases there was also a health and safety committee, while this was so in only 53 per cent of other establishments.

The final aspect of formalization of procedures concerns changes in relations with stewards. Such changes had occurred in the last five years in 35 per cent of the establishments surveyed. The main changes identified by respondents were as follows (percentages are of all those identifying changes): union recognition for the first time (15 per cent); the introduction of regular meetings with stewards (26 per cent); the introduction of procedures (23 per cent); the introduction of stewards (8 per cent); the more general formalization of arrangements (26 per cent); an increase in the number of committees (23 per cent); and the recognition of additional unions (9 per cent). Somewhat surprisingly, perhaps, there was no greater tendency for such changes to occur (in the case of subsidiaries) where a specialist industrial relations function existed at a higher level. But when all establishments are considered, there was a clear tendency for the existence of industrial relations specialists at both local and board levels to be associated with moves towards formalization. For example, in 47 per cent of establishments where there was a local industrial relations specialist some changes in relations with stewards had occurred, while this was the case in only 24 per cent of other establishments. Moreover, this was true of every single type of change identified above.

The picture identified here in terms of formalization is therefore consistent with the expectations outlined above. A personnel function formalizes industrial relations within management and with the unions and other workers' representatives.

'Rationalizing' work organization

This question, as we noted earlier, has to be approached with some care. For present purposes, however, we can most conveniently confine ourselves to a consideration of a number of substantive changes which have been emphasized in the literature on industrial relations reform — training, productivity bargaining, the use of job evaluation and work study, and the removal of piece-work.

Plants which were parts of larger companies tended to have formal training policies, and the existence of a specialist industrial relations function above establishment level accounted for no significant variation: 62 per cent of establishments where such a function existed had a formal training policy, but so did 65 per cent of other subsidiary establishments. Once we controlled whether or not the establishment was a subsidiary, no variation in the existence of training policies was found according to whether there were local or board-level personnel specialists.

Slightly fewer than half of the establishments surveyed had recently introduced productivity schemes or were planning to do so. There was no tendency for such schemes to be more common where industrial relations specialists existed. It is possible that the relatively widespread introduction of such schemes reflected the nature of incomes policies at the time: it is, however, worth noting that White concludes, on the basis of survey data at about the same time, that productivity-linked payments schemes were 'clearly associated' with a variety of management policies including 'improving labour utilization' (1981, p. 108).

Forty-three per cent of establishments used job evaluation for manual workers which suggests a significant increase in its use between 1972 and 1977. Brown suggests that 'external pressures' in the form of the Equal Pay Act 'is likely to have stimulated the spread of the technique' (1981, p. 111). Job evaluation was clearly spreading from large to small establishments. In addition to being associated with single-employer bargaining, it was associated with both our 'organizational' factors — ownership and whether or not the establishment was part of a multi-plant company. (Job evaluation was more common where establishments were foreign-owned and where they were parts of larger companies.) The existence of personnel specialists was not associated with the use of job evaluation; while its significance is hard to assess, there was a tendency for job evaluation to be more common 'where the industrial relations function was reported to have grown in importance within management in recent years' (Brown, 1981, p. 113: the 1983 survey also found job evaluation was associated with personnel specialists).

Work study was rather more common than job evaluation: it was used in half of the establishments in the IRRU survey. Again, it was more common in multi-plant firms; ownership was also associated with the use of work study, although it was British- rather than foreign-owned establishments which were more likely to employ the technique. Again, no association was found between the existence of any kind of personnel specialist and work study, although it was more common where the role of the personnel function had recently increased.

Despite widespread criticisms of piece-work, it was still the rule in two-thirds of the establishments surveyed. It may be that, with the increasing use of work study and other techniques, payment by results was by 1978 becoming less closely associated with fragmented bargaining than it had been previously (for example, Lloyd, 1976 — but see chapter

4 below). Piece-work, however, is less prevalent in foreign-owned establishments. There was a slight tendency for piece-work to be less common where personnel specialists existed, although this appears to be primarily attributable to other factors (such as ownership).

In brief, the extent to which the existence of personnel specialists was associated with substantive reform appears to have been limited. In their dealings with unions, as in their dealings within management, personnel specialists seem to have made more a procedural than a substantive impact.

MANAGEMENT STRUCTURE AND LABOUR RELATIONS STRATEGY

The preceding sections have indicated, using the 1978 survey findings, that management's approach to labour relations was shaped by organizational factors, union pressures and external forces such as government action. Another key factor — as is shown in Part II — was the market position of the plant or company: the 1978 survey was not of a kind to permit analysis of this factor.

Government action in the shape of industrial relations legislation and incomes policies has had a significant effect. Industrial relations legislation has encouraged the formalization of procedures and, along with this, has served to increase the importance of the personnel function in many companies (see also Daniel and Stilgoe, 1978). Incomes policies were a significant catalyst for changes in payment systems and the introduction of such methods as productivity bargaining. How far these state initiatives, and the more general support of governments for workplace reform, led to any fundamental rethinking of corporate labour relations strategy is less clear; it seems probable that in this respect the state played only a marginal role.

Organizational pressures appear to have been especially important in stimulating the proliferation of personnel specialists within companies. This widespread introduction of a personnel function is best seen as part of a more general trend towards increasing division of labour at management level; this is consistent with the views of Flanders noted in chapter 1, and with Turner *et al.*'s findings (1977). Personnel specialists, in turn, were strongly associated with attempts to establish formal procedures and control systems. This was true in terms both of internal management arrangements and of management's dealings with trade unions. However, while organizational factors had a substantive impact on labour relations, the impact of personnel specialists was largely of a procedural nature.

Many factors are associated with substantive changes in management's approach to labour relations (see, for example, Brown, 1981 and Batstone *et al.,* 1984). One finding is, however, particularly striking: union pressure, rather than the existence of a personnel function, explained the extent to which management took account of personnel and industrial relations considerations in their deliberations, especially on issues relatively far removed from traditional bargaining areas. The extent to which a 'reformist rationale' developed within management in the decade after Donovan would, therefore, appear to be fairly limited. This conclusion is supported by Marsh. He found that the extent to which substantive issues had been formalized was limited, and that the personnel function was still subordinated to line management as far as day-to-day employee relations were concerned. Moreover, industrial relations matters were not very often considered at the top level within companies. Marsh concludes:

> There is no evidence of more than a moderate movement in the 'Donovan' direction of 'comprehensive and authoritative agree-ments' at plant and/or company levels, if by this is meant agreements which are both consolidated, wide-ranging in coverage and content and systematically policed and administered at lower levels. (1982, p. 162)

The obvious question arising is why managers, and personnel managers in particular, have failed to develop more coherent personnel and industrial relations policies. In seeking to answer this question we shall first look at the nature of personnel management and then at the more general pattern of British management.

Personnel Management

The main body of this chapter has laid considerable emphasis upon the growth of personnel management since the late 1960s. But, as Daniel and Millward point out (1983, pp. 126—7) it does not follow that personnel specialists are ubiquitous. Moreover, it is important to remember that the definition of 'personnel specialist' in the 1978 survey was a fairly loose one; where a tighter definition is used considerably fewer personnel specialists are to be found. Third, even where managers are formally graced with a 'personnel' label, it does not follow that they have always performed this function or that they have received special personnel training. This is not, however, to argue that either of these is necessarily a 'good' thing. What these points do suggest is that many 'personnel specialists' may demonstrate less commitment to specifically 'personnel' interests than might at first be assumed.

Even within 'professional' personnel management there has always been a tension between the notions of promoting worker welfare and of merely acting as the labour agents of general management. Hence personnel management in Britain stems from two very different traditions. The first of these derives from the introduction of welfare and charitable activity into the workplace pioneered towards the end of the nineteenth century. In some respects this philanthropic approach derived from paternalistic traditions dating back to the master—servant relationship. But it was largely associated with nonconformist entrepreneurs, some of whom became convinced that, not only was it their moral duty to place emphasis upon the welfare of those they employed, but also that the well-being of the labour force was a precondition of industrial efficiency. In this way they reversed the logic of *laissez-faire* which claimed that the well-being of workers could be achieved only if industry was efficient. Such a perspective achieved a wider — though largely temporary — influence during the First World War as a result of the activities of the Health of Munitions Workers Committee and associated bodies.

The second tradition in the development of personnel management sprang from employers' endeavours to deal with trade unionism. For much of the nineteenth century industrial relations specialists did not exist. The task of dealing with employment and wages issues was part of the foreman's or subcontractor's job, and these frequently operated a sponsorship system. But as employers' associations were built up to deal with the growth of trade unionism, the employers' representatives acquired expertise in the methods of collective bargaining. At the same time, clerks employed to maintain wages and employment records in the larger companies gradually assumed an advisory role in industrial relations as they became repositories of knowledge on agreements, precedents and procedures. This industrial relations tradition was radically different from that of the welfare pioneers. Frequently anti-union in origin (the welfare tradition's paternalistic overtones meant it also was ambivalent towards unions — see Crichton, 1968, p. 17 and Chapman, 1970), it was much more part of the traditional management approach, for it involved the attempt to further conventional corporate goals by controlling the workforce (the two traditions were further differentiated by the class and sex of their members).

The tensions between these two traditions are to be seen in the subsequent history of personnel management. It is often argued that the welfare tradition declined in the 1930s and was further weakened by the subsequent rise of the welfare state. But, it did have an influence upon British occupational psychology and thereby was a factor in limiting the adoption of pure Taylorist methods of scientific management (Merkle, 1980, pp. 208—42). But the tension between the two traditions is apparent as late as 1957, when the Institute of Personnel Management declared that 'personnel management aims to achieve both efficiency and justice, neither of which can be pursued successfully without the other'. The clash between 'welfare' and 'technicist' rationales in personnel management continued to be a major topic of debate (Miller and Coghill, 1964), being central to the personal problems and claims to 'professional' status of the personnel manager (see, for example, Watson, 1977; Crichton, 1968; Legge and Exley, 1975; Thomason, 1976). But by the early sixties, the technicist rationale was clearly winning. Hence the IPM had redefined the aims of personnel management as follows:

> Personnel management is that part of management which is concerned with people at work and with their relationships within an enterprise. Its aim is to bring together and develop into an effective organisation the men and women who make up an enterprise and, having regard for the well-being of the individual and of working groups, to enable them to make their best contribution to its success.

In fact, data other than that found in our survey suggest that the extent to which personnel managers successfully pursued goals other than business efficiency as conventionally defined is open to doubt. As Legge and Exley argue, 'in practice, of course, few personnel specialists are able to change dominant organizational values . . . and exert . . . control over their relationships with other groups in the organization' (1975, p. 62). In so far as personnel managers do achieve influence, it is often based on expertise in interpreting the law, or on new means of achieving managerial goals. Moreover, to gain a voice within the key management groups, the personnel manager is required to demonstrate the relevance of his skills to the existing organization and its priorities. In other words, goals have to be taken largely as given (particularly since doubts are frequently expressed about the uniqueness of personnel managers' claimed competence, for many managers see 'leadership' and 'ability to deal with people' as basic managerial skills) and the personnel manager becomes an expert in ensuring that labour 'problems' do not obstruct company endeavours. Thus, for example, one major company has as its major personnel objective:

to serve the profitability of the Company by preserving and extending the areas in which management can exercise its function of making operating decisions which affect efficiency, costs or competitive effectiveness.

In another company the aims and objectives of the personnel function indicate a concern with worker interests in their own right only in terms of ensuring 'opportunities to advance . . . careers' and promoting 'healthy relationships'. The meaning of the latter is not made clear, but it can perhaps be surmised from the 'overall aim': 'to develop methods and procedures best calculated to promote the most efficient organization and management of its manpower' (see also Marsh, 1982, pp. 238—42). This is not to say that personnel managers totally reject notions of worker welfare or social justice. Traditional welfare functions, particularly for individual workers, exist in many companies. But welfare considerations tend to be treated as secondary, or else no conflict is seen to exist between, for example, notions of efficiency and justice, as indicated by the Institute for Personnel Management statement quoted earlier. This view is clearly open to question.

Selection and training are shaped by *company* requirements, and only secondarily by the needs of employees. Often the notions of 'development' and 'education' (still defined largely from a corporate perspective) are reserved for management while workers are merely 'trained'. Increasingly, training is evaluated in cost-benefit terms, but from a company rather than a worker perspective. As a major personnel management textbook notes,

> This [modern] conception of the personnel management function aligns it closely with the general managerial control function, and with the stream of scientific personnel management and eliminates the old welfare and man in the middle conceptions of it. (Thomason, 1976, p. 20)

An interest in 'welfare' considerations is therefore largely a secondary one. Hence, despite much discussion of welfare aims, evidence such as that given in the McCarthy and Parker survey (1968), suggests that, if anything, personnel specialists demonstrate even less sympathy to the workforce and trade unions than do line managers.

Nevertheless, the role of personnel specialists requires that they maintain a link with workers and their representatives, and in this sense they may be seen as 'men in the middle'. But their origins and role require that they keep their primary allegiance clear (see Dryburgh, 1972), for they are essentially involved in a conflict situation. This problem of primary allegiance and the need to maintain credibility with unions can be seen as partially resolved in two ways. First, there is a tendency to stress common interests, albeit within a pluralist perspective. In other words, in situations which contain elements of both common and divergent interests, the tendency is to stress the former. This is to be seen in some of the features of formalization discussed above. It is also to be seen in the nature of 'behavioural science' espoused by personnel specialists.

The second means by which personnel specialists seek to resolve the dilemma and at the same time prove their significance for management is by means of procedural rather than substantive 'rationalization'. This has been shown very clearly in this chapter, and is a point noted by Watson:

> The personnel function increasingly finds itself utilizing one formally rational technique to counter problems created by the application of other techniques based on such criteria within general management. (1977, p. 57)

It is also consistent with an emphasis upon what Legge and Exley (1975, pp. 59ff) call 'conformist' rather than 'deviant' innovation, with an emphasis upon 'auditing' and 'stabilization' relationships in Sayles' terms (1964, pp. 83—111), as can be seen in studies of collective bargaining reform (Department of Employment, 1971). Hence Clegg's statement in 1972 still appears to be true, despite his concluding cautious optimism:

> The story of British Personnel Management is an impressive record of growth which could easily give an exaggerated impression of the part which personnel managers have played in developing the system of industrial relations in the United Kingdom. In fact, until recently, the effect has been narrowly limited. (p. 166)

Yet the procedural emphasis of personnel management does in fact appear to have had some impact. For personnel managers tended to encourage the growth of steward organizations, and possibly at the same time frustrate the expectations of stewards because of the tendency towards centralization. We saw earlier that a number of features of worker organization are quite strongly related to the existence of personnel specialists. While it is undoubtedly true that the existence of collective organization on the part of workers encouraged management to develop a specialist function to deal with it, it is also clear that, in the decade after 1968 especially, personnel managers often encouraged union organization and developed more formal arrangements for stewards. In other words, union organization and personnel managers tended to encourage each other's growth.

The same reciprocal relationship exists between personnel management and strikes and other forms of industrial action. In an establishment which experiences such sanctions, it is quite likely that a specialist function will be developed to try to reduce such 'problems'. But, equally, if personnel managers foster steward organization and centralize decisions, then they may well stimulate industrial action. Supporting this view is the fact that the existence of a specialist industrial relations function at a higher level in the company has been shown to be the major factor in reducing local management discretion over, for example, pay — and lower local discretion over manual workers' pay was associated with higher levels of industrial action. Hence, in plants where local management had almost complete freedom only 40 per cent had experienced any form of industrial action, while where local discretion was limited, 61 per cent had such an experience. Again, it might be argued that causality operates in both directions. But the evidence provides only very limited support for the view that management seeks to centralize decisions in the face of local strike action. Moreover, a number of studies have indicated that institutionalization is associated with increases in the level of strikes. Daniel's survey of wage determination in industry found that sanctions and threats of sanctions during negotiations were considerably higher where management approval of the offer was given by an individual or body outside of, rather than within, the establishment, although a major role for a (local) personnel function did not appear to be related either to (threatened) industrial action or the size of settlement, (1976, pp. 69 and 67). Similarly, Turner *et al.* put forward comparable arguments suggesting that the formalization of company bargaining procedures and of shop stewards' status was a factor encouraging labour conflict (1977).

The Nature of British Management

This failure of personnel management to impinge more forcefully upon corporate strategy clearly relates to the more general nature of management. In pursuing this theme, we need — very briefly — to consider the traditional patterns of British management and its labour relations strategy, and then to look more fully at the developments in management organization which occurred from the mid-sixties onwards — that is, the factors subsumed under the 'organizational rationale'.

It is beyond the scope of this book to discuss at length the history of British management and labour relations. What is crucial for our present purposes is that top management typically concerned itself with financial rather than production issues, and typically adopted a short-term perspective. In other words, a company tended to be viewed as a body of financial assets rather than as a set of production facilities. Such a perspective was fostered by a variety of factors: among these were the failure of the state to develop coherent and positive policies towards manufacturing and the infrastructural services it required, notably technical education (for example, Supple, 1975; Ahlström, 1980), the power of financial institutions (for example, Jessop, 1980), the nature of the class structure (for example, Wiener, 1982), and the 'inheritance' from early industrialization (for example, Hobsbawm, 1969).

This had two important implications. First, it meant that management structure and personnel demonstrated a variety of weaknesses. The technical qualifications and competence of top and middle levels of management tended to be limited. In addition, control structures were typically poorly developed. For example, the failure of companies to develop adequate management accounting techniques was noted by the Committee on Trade and Industry in the 1920s, again by the various working parties set up to consider industrial performance after the Second World War and yet again in the early 1960s. Even in the last of these periods a survey of engineering companies had found that 22 per cent used no established method of investment appraisal, and only 17 per cent used methods such as discounted cash flow (NEDC, 1965). Similarly, even as late as the early 1960s, large British companies were characterized by the less efficient forms of organization: the functionally organized, unitary form (U-form) or the holding company (H-form) rather than the multi-divisional structure (M-form) (Channon, 1973). The extent to which coherent policies and strategies relating to production matters could be pursued was therefore limited.

Second, this failure to develop coherent, efficient structures encouraged the abnegation of labour relations by top management. Since they had few coherent policies, it was unlikely that they would have any in this area. Moreover, the historical dependence of many companies upon the skills of relatively autonomous craftsmen, upon subcontracting and upon the all-powerful foreman meant that labour relations issues tended to be dealt with on, or close to, the shop floor. The decentralized structure of many British unions encouraged, and was encouraged by, this pattern of management (non-)decision-making. Such an approach to labour relations meant that there was little need for personnel managers. The failure of the state to play an active role in fostering some coherent pattern of labour relations — beyond reaffirming 'voluntarism' — served to encourage the tendencies inherent within companies and unions (and, of course, in large part reflected these tendencies — see Phelps-Brown, 1983).

However, it is widely accepted that many companies began to change their approach to labour relations from the late 1960s. The obvious question is why; the conventional answer is the growth of shop floor power with full employment. This was undoubtedly a factor, but its importance should not be over-emphasized, for three reasons: first, there is a danger of exaggerating the degree of shop floor power (see chapters 3 and 4); second, such an account fails to explain why 'reform' occurred when it did; third, the survey findings suggest that union pressure was not the primary factor leading to changes in management's labour relations 'strategy'.

At the beginning of this book it was suggested that the explanation lay in the more general state of the economy. In other words, the change cannot be explained by specifically industrial relations factors: rather, it has been brought about by moves of the state and of management which were aimed at improving economic performance. Thus in the 1960s the state began to move away from its arm's-length relationship with the economy, giving support to the reorganization and rationalization of industry (and part of this did involve industrial relations, for example incomes policy and legislation such as that on redundancy payments). The state therefore played some — albeit largely permissive — role in the dramatic increase in industrial concentration in the 1960s and early 1970s. Whereas in 1958 420 independent firms produced half of manufacturing output, by 1970 about 100 firms were responsible for this proportion (Prais, 1976). The 'organizational rationale' outlined in earlier sections is intimately related to this increased concentration of industry.

While views differ as to their exact significance, mergers clearly accounted for a major part, if not virtually all, of this increased concentration (Hannah and Kay, 1977; Aaronovitch and Sawyer, 1975). The merger wave — in some years expenditure on acquisitions exceeded gross domestic fixed capital formation (Cowling, 1982, p. 72) — was motivated primarily by the desire to reduce competition rather than to reap economies of scale (Newbould, 1970). Moreover, the fact that most mergers were financed by the issue of new stock, meant it was not the high-performing companies which were the major acquirers. It is not surprising, therefore, that post-merger profit performance was inferior to the pre-merger performance of the companies involved (Meeks, 1977 and, more generally, Williams, 1983).

The problems of profitability in these new, large companies were in part due to the serious difficulties of developing adequate systems of control: these, in turn, reflected the management micro-politics of the newly formed companies as well as the sheer scale and diversity of corporate activity. The typical large company now had an increased number of plants, each of which tended to be smaller than had been the case prior to the merger boom (Prais, 1976). An idea of the complexity and diversity of corporate activity can easily be gleaned by skimming through the pages of *Who Owns Whom.*

Managements attempted to resolve these problems of organization, and in doing so appear to have encouraged a new 'organization consciousness' which led to the reorganization of many other companies. By the early 1970s a majority of the largest firms had introduced multi-divisional structures (Chandler and Daems, 1974), and some evidence suggests that this innovation partially alleviated the problem of low profitability (Steer and Cable, 1978). However, it seems from such evidence as is available that, even when they adopt multi-divisional forms of organization, British companies tend to do so in a distinctive manner.

First, as Channon (1973) has noted, British companies did not fully espouse the logic of the multi-divisional structure. In some companies, for example, divisional managers still participated in strategic decision-making while general officers continued to be involved in operational decisions. Moreover, it would appear that British companies still relied upon traditionalism to achieve coordination and control; managements, in making decisions, used 'the formalities of standing committees in conformity with pre-existing customary procedures' (Mallory *et al.,* 1983; see also Jamieson, 1980). The similarities with decision-making in industrial relations both currently and in the past (Marsh, 1982) are evident.

Second, British companies tend to be more decentralized than German or French companies. Child and Keiser, for example, found that British managers tended to have greater autonomy than their German counterparts so that they were engaged in rather more problem-solving; their roles tended to be more formally defined by official documents such as job descriptions and organization charts (1979, pp. 262—5). Horovitz similarly emphasizes the level of decentralization in British companies and the use of 'bottom up' strategic and long-range planning.

This tendency towards greater decentralization is associated with a third distinctive feature of British management organization. Top management control here, compared with France and Germany, tends to be less frequent and detailed. Moreover, the key theme in British control structures tends to be financial, with less emphasis upon production, technical or operational considerations (Horovitz, 1980).

In formal terms, accountancy and financial control are the most important functions at board level. A BIM survey published in 1972 showed that the single most common special directorial responsibility in Britain was finance; another survey found that qualified accountants were the single most common 'academic' group represented on boards of directors. Salary levels similarly suggest the relative dominance of accountants in industry.

As noted earlier, even as late as the early 1960s management accounting was relatively underdeveloped in Britain. But things appear to have changed dramatically since then. Not only has the number of accountants increased (so that by the late 1970s there were over 400,000 qualified accountants in industry) but more sophisticated accounting techniques have also been introduced. Thus, by the late 1960s a survey found that 70 per cent of companies had a long-range financial plan covering three years or more. Five years earlier only 30 per cent of the surveyed companies had such plans. In addition, the proportion of companies employing a staff group or an organization specifically for long-range planning had risen over the past five years from 5 per cent to 25 per cent. It was also found that the number of firms using discounted cash flow techniques for evaluating capital plans had quadrupled in the last two years (Robertson, n.d., p. 10). A study undertaken for the Ministry of Technology in 1970 indicated that 70 per cent of companies used some systematic financial method for appraising investments (Hansard, 14 December 1970).

The increased importance of management accounting and financial control techniques had two important implications for the conduct of labour relations. The first was that, particularly given the relatively low emphasis upon non-financial factors, these controls were largely of a procedural nature and focused upon outcomes. If these kinds of control are the dominant feature of British companies, it is not surprising that labour relations should demonstrate similar characteristics.

Second, the nature of financial controls militates against the serious consideration of labour relations matters at top management level (for evidence of this see Marsh, 1982; Maitland, 1983; Jacobs, 1978). The major features of management accounting have been summarized as:

the use of short-term subjective assessments to prepare budgets and their combination into profit plans. The use of budgets for control; the evaluation, motivation and accountability of managers. (Tricker, 1967, p. 59)

The creation of profit or cost centres throughout the company, and the individual responsibility of managers for the achievement of targets, are directed at making 'managers at all levels become identified with the total activities of the business' by means of coordinated plans expressed in 'comparable financial terms'. In this way 'the strategic planning of the businessman can be linked with the utilization decisions of the manager' and 'resource utilization can be studied, performance standards set and incorporated into corporate plan' (Tricker, 1967, p. 75). While such budgetary control systems necessarily involve consideration of a wide variety of aspects of the enterprise, these are forced into a financial mould and oriented towards questions of profitability. The financial logic becomes more manifestly dominant. Moreover, the nature of such control systems is not merely to seek to motivate managers but also to highlight as possible problems only those factors embodied in the plan. 'Variances' from the plan tend to be seen as requiring action at the (possible) expense of other more significant issues. The problems involved in this have been noted from a management perspective (for example, Tricker, 1967, pp. 75–86; Hopwood, 1973); but more importantly, if the control system stresses financial criteria and effectively treats workers as commodities, then the underlying structure for management action is scarcely conducive to many worker interests or 'good' industrial relations. The accounting perspective generally fails even to treat workers as a factor of production to be combined with other factors to best advantage or as a resource to be optimally employed. Even attempts to put a value upon 'human resources' from the perspective of the company are rare.

While I do not wish to suggest that attempts at financial control are totally successful (see, for example, Batstone *et al.,* 1977), it is useful to look briefly at a specific case to see how particular priorities are built into plans and the way in which these structure corporate decision-making. The example comes from a large multi-national company. A simple analysis of a planning meeting, involving head office personnel and the key managers of one of the main divisions, demonstrates the nature of priorities as indicated by the frequency with which particular topics were mentioned. Of the subjects referred to, 42 per cent were of an immediately financial nature, notably profits (18 per cent of all references), cash flow, costs, prices, and levels of capital expenditure. The second most frequently raised subject concerned the problems of marketing; these accounted for 22 per cent of all subject references.

The priorities of the plan, then, are clear: conventional financial criteria whose major point of reference was the market. In addition, 15 per cent of references concerned the importance of the planning and accounting system as a means of integration and control.

The subject area least frequently referred to was the labour force (10 per cent of all references, even less than to technical questions). Moreover, workers were seen primarily as a problematical commodity, so that two-thirds of the references concerned overmanning, disputes and wage claims which might endanger levels of profitability. There were scarcely any references of a more 'humane' nature, and those there were focused largely on the need to improve amenities and working conditions in a few plants.

Similar priorities dominated in later top management meetings to review performance and determine policy. These followed the structure of the plan and attention focused upon the extent to which profit targets had been met and upon explanations for variances. In all, immediate financial considerations accounted for over half of all the issues touched upon, and the state of the market accounted for a further 16 per cent. Matters relating directly to the labour force were slightly more important than in the planning meeting, although the emphasis was upon the need to reduce the number of employees, shifts and hours worked. Again, two-thirds of the references to workers treated them as a cost.

This pattern of priorities was reflected not only in the general plans of the company but also in the structure of capital investment proposals. The focus was upon the estimated costs of projects, the timing of expenditure and the types of reason (such as cost reduction of preservation of markets) for the proposals. While a plethora of indices of forecast profitability were required, the only reference to workers was 'redundancy', which was included under the heading of 'savings' achieved through the proposals. However, the company was considerably more aware of its 'social responsibilities' than most and, accordingly, where major redundancies were envisaged, a separate set of data was required. This involved details of those to be made redundant, any problems expected in achieving the redundancies (due to union opposition) and the costs to the company. Even, then, in the context of investigating social aspects — which were treated separately from the cause of the redundancy itself — cost priorities figured significantly.

Accounting systems do not merely foster particular priorities and discriminate between issues; their very language often serves to obscure certain realities of action. In particular, once different terms are substituted for 'human being', the notion of 'labour' as a cost becomes easier; it then follows that 'working levels' can be reduced as simply as stock levels. Such camouflaging rhetoric is easy to find in managerial discussions and reports. For example, 'opportunities were being taken to reduce high cost operation' with no mention of associated redundancies, or 'the company's involvement in [a plant] was being reduced immediately'. The language facilitates the making of apparently logical connections — 'there has been a fall off in demand and working levels': in other words, it fosters the view that it is quite natural that short-time working should be introduced when there is a temporary fall in demand (cf. the notion of 'consistency rules', Glasgow University Media Group, 1976, pp. 21—6). Similar obfuscating language is common in investment proposals. For example, in one case putting men out of work was referred to as 'it will be possible to produce requirements' in a lower number of shifts. As one study noted, not only did all directors view workers as costs, but also 'what was striking was the conventionalism of exploitation, not the ruthlessness'. The directors were men who 'knew current norms and how to work within them' (Winkler, 1974, p. 199). The procedures and language of accounting systems help to explain such 'conventionalism'. The new importance of financial control techniques, therefore, serves to reaffirm the traditional, essentially unitarist, assumptions of top management (Fidler, 1981). They are scarcely conducive to the espousal of the 'reform rationale'. It is precisely these 'organizational' pressures which explain the rise, and the largely procedural role, of personnel management.

3 Reform and Union Democracy at Plant Level

A major feature of industrial relations reform was the establishment of plant or company bargaining. This would, it was argued, reconcile the divergences between formal industry-level bargaining and informal shop-floor or fractional bargaining. Integrative bargaining could facilitate the achievement of both worker and management goals. The development of plant bargaining had implications for shop steward organizations which were as great as, if not greater than the implications for management. In order to be able to bargain at plant level, management had to give both fuller and more formal recognition to stewards. At the same time, if bargaining was to occur at plant level, rather than in an *ad hoc* manner on the shop floor, steward organizations had to become more coordinated so that stewards could speak with one voice in negotiations with management.

Not only would single-employer bargaining require changes in the organization of stewards, it would also require the provision of facilities which would help stewards to develop policy and negotiate with management. Hence it was recommended that management should provide a variety of facilities for stewards: these included offices, time off and opportunities for meetings and negotiations, and the right of stewards to be trained in the skills considered necessary for their new role (Donovan, 1968, p. 45). Management might also encourage the closed shop and adopt check-off arrangements for union subscriptions, thereby providing union security.

Single-employer bargaining was seen as having implications for the way in which the larger unions treated stewards. Most obviously, full-time officials had to be prepared to accept a shift of influence from themselves to the stewards. But, in addition, the Donovan Commission recommended that union rules should more fully recognize the shop steward, detailing modes of election and tenure of office. Moreover, the Commission was keen that, on the one hand, the powers of the steward should be clearly specified (particularly in relation to agreements, the branch and the local full-time official), and, on the other, that union rules should not hinder the development of inter-union steward committees which were deemed essential for the formulation of a coherent union policy at plant or company level. Rules of these kinds, Donovan argued,

> will make it reasonable to expect stewards (and their members) to act constitutionally, since they will at last be able to perform their functions within the compass of the rules. They will help to create a situation in which trade unions could properly be expected to discipline the small minority of shop stewards who at times abuse their position. (1968, pp. 187—8)

The operation of these new forms of shop steward organization would facilitate the development of mutually agreed rules between management and unions. Reform would permit the stewards to act as before, but more fully, as 'an accepted, reasonable and even moderating influence' (Donovan, 1968, p. 29). Through the negotiation of factory agreements the steward would be able to promote the interests of workers but still become committed to changes in working practices which would promote efficiency.

The Donovan Commission's view differed in a number of ways from many subsequent prescriptions. First, it placed considerable emphasis upon the continuing role and importance of the full-time official and the larger union. Subsequent discussion frequently placed much greater emphasis upon the shop steward. Second, the Commission showed a fairly tough-minded approach. As we saw in chapter 1, it was aware of the difficulties which might confront plant bargaining. Later prescriptions — particularly for 'indirect' approaches to productivity bargaining — placed rather more emphasis upon changing the industrial relations climate and fostering a much more cooperative approach on the part of stewards. These later prescriptions, therefore, took the early notions of accommodation and transformed them from a somewhat 'negative' approach to a much more 'positive' one.

Again, as noted in chapter 1, radicals are extremely critical of the underlying logic of the reformist case; they reject the view that there is either a moral or 'enlightened self-interest' case for unions to conform to agreements — such behaviour is seen to be both against worker interests and a sign of union incorporation. Similarly, they support (albeit in a rather distinctive and partial manner) the importance of union 'democracy' rather than union 'government', emphasizing the need for unions to respond to workers' interests. Finally, and most fundamentally, they are critical of the conception of workers' interests embodied in the reformist case: they see workers' interests as lying in a dramatic transformation of society, so that any form of accommodation with employers necessarily constitutes — at least in the most extreme view — a diversion away from their real interests. Such themes have been more widely argued in recent years (see, for example, Herding, 1972; Piven and Cloward, 1977; Pfeffer, 1979).

Given their fundamental criticisms, we might expect radicals to argue that the reform strategy was doomed to failure. But they have not: over recent years a number of more radical writers have claimed that the Donovan strategy has achieved considerable success. Not only have employers engaged successfully in a major attack upon workers' job controls which obstruct greater efficiency, it is argued, but they have also successfully taken the steam out of stewards by incorporating them.

Such a thesis has been put forward most clearly by Hyman (1979) and more tentatively by Terry (1979). In effect, they see reformed shop steward organization as outlined above creating those conditions of incorporation which radicals have claimed existed in the case of full-time union officials. Shop steward organization becomes hierarchical and centralized, developing its own 'institutional interests', while senior stewards are isolated from the realities of shop-floor life both through their full-time status, the provision of facilities and their involvement in plant-level bargaining. They become tied into the 'liberal rhetoric', which favours a managerial rationale, and consequently are induced to act as a form of control over, rather than for, the workers they represent. At the same time, the fuller recognition of shop stewards in union constitutions is seen as exposing them to the influence of an incorporated union leadership.

This thesis, if correct, is of considerable significance. In the first place, it attaches an even greater importance to institutionalization of a procedural kind than do liberal pluralists who are normally seen as institutionalists *par excellence*. For whereas the liberal pluralists argue that through reform workers can and do promote their interests, this is denied by members of the radical school. Part of the explanation of this thesis would appear to lie in the fundamental problem which the radical analysis confronts: namely, if capitalism does systematically work against workers' interests, why is the level of manifest industrial (and political) conflict so low? Thesis of institutionalization and incorporation, along with other theories, for example, of capitalist hegemony, provide some form of explanation. However, if these are seen to be too effective, then the radical school confronts further problems over the possibility of any radical social transformation. Thus, while they recognize the efficacy of incorporation, radical writers point to its contradictions and the risk of its rupture.

Relatedly, the radical account of the 'bureaucratization of the rank-and-file' assumes even greater significance in the context of arguments concerning union incorporation more generally. For it was traditonally argued that an important check upon union incorporation at the national level was the existence of 'rank-and-file' challenge. In the pre-Donovan era (and for a while afterwards) the shop steward was frequently seen to be the very embodiment of this challenge (see, for example, Cliff, 1970). The incorporation of the steward was therefore doubly significant; according to the radical view, not only did it facilitate management ends within the workplace to the detriment of workers' interests, but also provided a new means of control over the membership by the national union leadership. Accordingly, that leadership could more confidently enter into 'corporatist' arrangements with governments which served further to obstruct workers' interests.

Reformists and some members of the radical school, then, agreed upon the probable efficacy of industrial relations reform as far as shop steward incorporation is concerned. The former emphasized the way in which reform permits an accommodation between the (presumed) interests of the two parties. The latter placed much greater emphasis upon the incorporating effects of procedural reform itself.

In this chapter we consider the effects of reformism upon shop steward organization. As noted in chapter 1, this raises the question of how one conceives of union government or union democracy. However, the problems are simplified because the relevant question is of a relative rather than an absolute kind: that is, how far did reform lead to changes in the nature of shop steward organization. Did it become more centralized? Did it become more cooperative with management? (The additional question of the implications of any such changes for workers' interests forms the theme of the next chapter.)

To investigate the questions posed we have to be clear about the kinds of data required to test the competing theses. First, we need a fairly clear idea of the nature of steward organization and goals prior to reform. Donovan and the radical critique both appear to agree that pre-reform stewards within a particular plant coordinated their activities to only a limited degree. But the two approaches do differ considerably over the perspectives and strategies adopted by stewards. Donovan saw stewards as 'lubricants rather than irritants', people of 'moderation' and 'responsibility'. By contrast, the radical tradition saw them as constituting a major challenge to managerial control. It is important, therefore, to develop a fairly clear picture of pre-reform shop steward organization.

In doing so, we will concentrate upon the various aspects emphasized by Hyman in his thesis of incorporation. These concern the existence of senior and full-time stewards and the degree of control they are able to exercise; the democratic mechanisms of steward organization and the way in which they operate in practice; the provision of facilities and other forms of management sponsorship, the basis of their provision and their significance and implications.

In order to assess the scale and nature of change we need to draw a similar picture for the post-reform period and compare it with the earlier period. At first sight, this would appear to be a relatively simple process. In practice it is considerably more difficult, for a number of reasons. The most important of these is that stewards organization became more widespread. An important thrust of arguments by Hyman (1979), Terry (1979) and Willman (1980) is that in a number of industries management actively sponsored steward organizations. That is, steward bodies developed not so much from worker struggles as from management initiatives. They argue that such managerially created steward bodies are less likely to control working practices and more likely to act as a managerial police force. It will be necessary to try to assess the validity of this argument in its own right. But in addition, the question arises whether it is right to compare such steward bodies with those which existed prior to reform and which radical writers — often incorrectly — see as the product of worker rather than management initiatives. Such an exercise may be useful in some contexts but it provides only a partial picture. In order to develop a broader assessment, and hence a more valid one, it seems necessary and desirable to see how far such managerially created steward bodies did actually provide a degree of worker control compared with the pre-reform period of no steward organization. One might go further and seek to assess what degree of control would be exerted by workers in the current situation if management had not created stewards. Would some form of steward organization have developed anyway? Would it have been able to survive and exert control? Similarly, one can ask how far managerially sponsored steward bodies did continue to act as a managerial police force (if they ever did) and how far they began to adopt a more independent approach. (The question of management-sponsored steward organizations is considered separately on pp. 105—18.)

In short, a simple comparison between the overall pattern of steward organization pre- and post-reform has to take account of the more limited coverage of shop stewards in the pre-reform era.

This chapter focuses upon the thesis of the 'bureaucratization of the rank-and-file'. The first section discusses the following: the growth in the number of stewards in the late 1960s and the 1970s; changes in shop steward organization, focusing particularly upon questions relating to formal hierarchy, the relations between stewards and members and indicators of oligarchy; it also includes a brief discussion of the significance of the provision of union and steward facilities, and it also looks briefly at the relationship between shop stewards and their unions more generally. The second section focuses upon what can be seen as a 'special case' of the bureaucratization thesis — namely, that 'management-sponsored' steward organizations have distinctive characteristics. The final section, summarizes the argument.

CHANGES IN SHOP STEWARD ORGANIZATION

Growth in Steward Numbers

It is clear that throughout the period 1945—68 there had been a steady growth in the number of shop stewards; this trend accelerated after 1968. However, it is not possible to give an accurate picture of how many plants had shop stewards in the 1960s: estimates using the 1966 workplace industrial relations survey (which sampled manufacturing plants with 150 or more workers and a small number of construction sites with fifty or more workers) suggest that even in these relatively large establishments, one-third had no shop stewards and about 10 per cent had only one shop steward (Government Social Survey, 1968). Moreover, it is clear that in much of manufacturing steward organization was either non-existent or played a very limited role (see, for example, Lerner *et al.,* 1969), while even in vehicles there is a danger of exaggerating its significance (Tolliday and Zeitlin, 1982). Among white-collar workers, in private services and in much of the public sector, as will be seen below, shop steward organization was even more rare.

Between 1947 and 1961 Marsh estimates that the number of stewards in engineering increased at almost twice the rate of union membership (1973, p. 58). TUC figures for 1959 and 1966 suggest some acceleration in this trend. McCarthy and Parker calculated that there were 175,000 stewards at the time of the Donovan Commission (1968, p. 15). Using similar methods of calculation, Clegg estimated that 'the total for 1978 must be more than 250,000' (1979, p. 52) — a growth of over 40 per cent in a decade. If unaccredited shop stewards are included, Clegg suggests that the figure 'may be over 300,000'. This dramatic growth in the decade after Donovan — four times that of union membership — derived from two types of development. The first of these was the spread of shop steward organization into areas where it did not previously exist; the second was an increase in steward density, both in 'traditional' and 'new' sectors. However, even by 1980 manual stewards existed in only 44 per cent of establishments, and non-manual stewards were even more rare (Daniel and Millward, 1983, pp. 34, 54).

The first type of expansion was most evident in parts of the public sector. In some areas — notably the civil service, the Post Office and the energy industries — some form of workplace representation has a long history. But in other parts — particularly local government, health and education — shop steward organization is of much more recent origin and is often associated with a considerable growth in union density. In local authorities and hospitals, for example, there were scarcely any stewards in 1970, and in 1971 there were only 9,500 manual stewards in local government. Between 1971 and 1977, stimulated by a variety of factors including local government reorganization and the introduction of incentive payments, NUPE claimed a more than five-fold increase in the number of its stewards, reaching a figure of 10,000 (Somerton, 1977). By 1981, it had 'around 23,000' stewards (Eaton and Gill, 1981, p. 248).

In private non-manufacturing there has also been a significant growth of shop steward organization. Hawes and Smith, in a survey of 671 establishments employing fifty or more people in private non-manufacturing, conclude that 'in 1980 there may have been as many as 20,000 manual stewards and up to 10,000 non-manual stewards in office'. Further, they argue, 'it seems likely that there must have been a substantial growth in local union activity over the 1970s' (1981, p. 268). It seems likely that much of this growth occurred in establishments where there had been no stewards in the 1960s: in over a fifth of cases unions had been recognized for manual workers only in the last five years, and this was true in a third of cases for non-manual workers. If we double these proportions — which does not seen unreasonable — in order to get a picture of growth over the 1970s, then the spread of union recognition, which tends to be a precondition of steward organization, in private non-manufacturing is striking.

Steward organization spread among non-manual workers not only in the service sector, but also in manufacturing. This was partly due to the relatively rapid growth of union membership among white-collar workers, and partly to managements being prepared to extend union recognition from manual to non-manual unions. However, in 1978 in manufacturing establishments with more than fifty full-time employees, there were non-manual stewards in only just over a third of cases (Brown, 1981, p. 53).

It is difficult to obtain a precise estimate of the spread of manual shop stewards in manufacturing. One means of estimating it, however, is to examine union recognition, for this is closely related to the existence of stewards. Indeed, this relationship — consistent with reform — has become closer. Thus in 1966 the Government Social Survey found that in 82 per cent of establishments which recognized manual unions stewards existed (1968, p. 74), while in 1978 the IRRU survey found that stewards were present in 97 per cent of establishments which recognized unions (Brown, 1981, p. 52). Moreover, a very crude comparison between the 1972 and 1978 surveys suggests that, while in the earlier year manual stewards existed in 82 per cent of private manufacturing establishments, the figure for roughly similarly sized plants had grown to just over 90 per cent in 1978. Working back to a figure for the mid-1960s (on the basis of Clegg's figures — 1979, pp. 51—2) suggests that stewards may have existed in just over 70 per cent of plants at that time. In other words, on these extremely crude estimates, it would appear that stewards existed in 20 per cent more manufacturing establishments in 1978 than they did in 1966. As noted earlier, it is difficult to identify accurately the industries in which this growth has occurred: one cannot use steward replies from the 1966 survey as the basis of a comparison since the sample was confined to only six unions. The conventional wisdom (for example, Terry. 1983, p. 68) is that growth occurred largely outside of the metal-handling sector. While this is probably so, a comparison of foremen's response to the 1966 survey (which are broken down by sector in the published findings) and the IRRU survey suggests that there is a danger of exaggerating this pattern.

The second factor leading to an increase in the number of shop stewards is that there are more per union member. The 1966 survey gave an average figure of sixty for the constituency of a manual shop steward (Government Social Survey, 1968). The IRRU survey gave a figure of thirty-one members for 1978 (1981, p. 62) while Daniel and Millward found the number was twenty-nine in 1980 (1983, p. 34). Brown suggests that the IRRU survey may exaggerate steward density: but the difference in comparison with his earlier survey of GMWU stewards (Brown *et al.,* 1978) may be due to the latter's inclusion of the public sector and the tendency for GMWU constituencies to be larger than those of other unions. Certainly, the reduction in size of steward constituencies accords with other studies (for example, Batstone *et al.,* 1977; M. Barratt Brown, cited in Clegg, 1979, p. 52). In fact, three factors are likely to be important in greater overall steward density: first, the tendency for the number of stewards to increase over time where steward organization exists; second, steward organization has become more common in smaller establishments where their constituencies tend to be smaller (Daniel and Millward, 1983, p. 34), and third, the growth of steward organization among non-manual workers where, again, constituencies tend to be smaller (Brown, 1981, p. 62). Against this pattern, steward density tends to be lower among manual workers in much of the public sector (Clegg *et al.,* 1961, p. 49): however, there have been widespread redundancies in such sectors as mining and the railways, so that the relative importance of these low steward density sectors has fallen.

In sum, the number of shop stewards may well have increased by 50 per cent or more between 1966 and the late 1970s. While much of this growth occurred in 'virgin' territory, the increase in steward density in more 'traditional' situations also appears to be of considerable importance.

Shop Steward Organization

A key theme in the 'bureaucratization of the rank-and-file' thesis concerns the centralization of control. It is argued that, whereas in the past stewards tended to operate as representatives of their individual constituencies, with reform they began to act as representatives of a collectivity of stewards. Three particular features of steward organization are emphasized in this context: the growth of senior stewards, the increase in the number of full-time stewards and the development of powerful steward committees, controlled by senior stewards.

It should be noted, however, that even writers such as Hyman do recognize that there might be potential advantages in certain developments of this kind. For the individual steward, operating in isolation from his colleagues, often acted in an excessively parochial manner. Such parochialism could obstruct the interests of other groups and at the same time preclude the pursuit of issues which required a collective response on the part of the workforce as a whole. Hyman and others try to differentiate between what they see as a desirable movement towards steward coordination, on the one hand, and the development of a form of hierarchical control by an incorporated steward leadership on the other.

We can assess the 'bureaucratization' thesis more readily if we begin by specifying more clearly the stages in the argument. First, it indicates a change in the nature of shop steward organization dating approximately from the time of Donovan. Here three possible scenarios can be identified and it is not always clear which is being referred to. The most simple would indicate that these 'bureaucratic' features rarely existed in the pre-Donovan era. Alternatively, the thesis can be interpreted as stating that where these characteristics were found 'pre-Donovan' they tended to be means of coordination, but since then they have become means of control. Finally, it might be argued that, while pre-Donovan steward organizations have continued to play a largely coordinating role, new steward organizations are typically of an oligarchic and incorporated nature. Hence, as noted in the introduction to this chapter, it is necessary to be explicit as to what is being compared with what: however, in practice detailed comparisons are rarely possible due to lack of data.

Second, the bureaucratization thesis assumes that particular formal characteristics of steward organization are associated with an increase in hierarchical control and a more cooperative approach towards management. We need to investigate how far this is indeed the case, and this in turn raises a number of questions. Coordination has to be differentiated from control: presumably Hyman and others would argue that where coordination exists the formulation of policy is a collective enterprise which involves not just an elite of stewards but all stewards and workers. However, a fuller analysis would require consideration not only of the process of formulating policy, but also its implementation. And here it is difficult to know how proponents of the bureaucratization thesis would differentiate between coordination and control. It is not clear, for example, whether they would argue that, in the name of democracy, individual stewards and work groups should be allowed to go against policies collectively formulated at plant level, with the risk of a resurgence of self-defeating sectionalism.

This raises the more general question of the kinds of evidence required to test theses of oligarchy and incorporation. Here the proponents of the bureaucratization thesis have been somewhat lax. They have failed to adduce systematic evidence, for example, showing that there has indeed been a concentration of bargaining at plant level and a decline in shop-floor bargaining; they have failed to take into account the implications of increased steward density; they have not discussed the evidence relating to member—steward relationships; they have also failed to consider such traditional indicators of oligarchy as tenure in office and contested elections. Nor have they bothered to look at all carefully at evidence of incorporation: what is the evidence on possible changes in steward attitudes and behaviour? Is there a lower propensity to strike action post-Donovan? Did stewards in the 1970s demonstrate a greater readiness to cooperate with management and did they show less concern

about members interests? Did they exert more control over the membership? There follows an attempt to answer these questions.

Formal hierarchical features

As we have seen, steward organization was less common pre-Donovan
than it was in the late 1970s. It is therefore likely that formal steward
bureaucracy existed in fewer plants. On the other hand, in many plants
where steward organization did exist in the early 1960s there was a fairly
long tradition of hierarchical steward organization. Where branch
organization was based upon the place of work, hierarchy among lay
negotiating officials has often been the norm for fifty years or more. In
some cases where the branch is based on the place of residence, lay
branch secretaries have traditionally played the role of senior stewards
across a number of plants. And, of course, where steward organization
was underdeveloped or weak, a high level of centralized control existed
in the form of full-time union officials. In the latter situation, the
introduction of senior stewards might well mean a decentralization of
control.

Even where the union branch is based upon place of residence,
steward organizations frequently have a long tradition of hierarchy. In
the AEU, for example, demands for the 'bureaucratization' of stewards
have a lengthy history (Jefferys, n. d.) and provision for senior stewards
was made as long ago as 1920. The resurgence of shop steward
organization in the Second World War, facilitated by war-time
regulations and the encouragement given to Joint Production
Committees (see, for example, Croucher, 1982; Inman, 1957), was also
of a 'bureaucratic' nature (Jefferys, 1979). It is not surprising, therefore,
to find that by the early 1960s in engineering 'about one steward in every
10 is a convener. It is not known how many of these are formally or
informally recognized by their employers as acting in this capacity of
"senior steward", but the number must be very high' (Marsh and Coker,
1973, p. 59). Similarly, studies such as those by Derber (1955) and
Melman (1958) and official enquiries (for example, Cameron, 1957) all
indicate the importance of steward hierarchies. At least in the 'classic'
home of shop steward organization — engineering — a degree of
hierarchy was common.

However, survey evidence suggests that hierarchy was not confined to
steward organization in engineering. Clegg *et al.* for example, found that
about 16 per cent of the stewards they studied were conveners (1961, p.
149; this figure excludes branch negotiators). The 1966 workplace survey

found that 22 per cent of their steward informants 'described themselves as senior stewards or conveners' and 55 per cent of plants with stewards had senior stewards (1988, pp. 16, 77); in the 1972 survey over half the senior managers said that a senior steward or convener existed in the plant (1974, p. 10).

Thus some degree of hierarchy has been common for many years. It may simply have become more common recently (Brown *et al.*, 1978, p. 144). In 1978 the IRRU survey of manufacturing establishments employing fifty or more workers found that 74 per cent of those with stewards had recognized senior stewards (this was 55 per cent of all plants). The 1980 survey of all industries found that only 31 per cent of establishments had manual senior stewards or conveners — this was 52 per cent of those recognizing unions and 70 per cent of those with stewards (Daniel and Millward, 1983, p. 34). They were less common among non-manual workers.

The overall picture is complex. While there has been an increase in the number of manual steward organizations with senior stewards, this increase is not particularly dramatic and the majority of pre-Donovan steward organizations had them. If non-manual steward organizations are included in the analysis, then the increase in the proportion of steward bodies with senior stewards is even smaller.

However, the bureaucratization thesis argues that it is not merely the fact of the hierarchy but the fact that its top-most members are full-time which is significant. At one level it is not obvious why this should be so important. The proponents of the thesis would claim that by working at a machine or whatever, be it only for a few hours per week and be it only a 'mock' job, the convener keeps contact with the rank-and-file. But this argument assumes that continuing work experience is crucial to the playing of the representative role, even if the task undertaken is quite different to that done by the majority of those represented. It can equally be argued, however, that working 'on the tools' may make a convener less accessible to the majority of members and reduce his or her understanding of the nature of others' work experience.

For the present let us assume that the bureaucratization thesis is correct. We can then turn to the question of how common these full-time stewards are. Clegg *et al.* in the late 1950s found that 6 per cent of their sample of stewards said they spent more than an average of thirty working hours on union business and 4 per cent were virtually full-time. However, they felt that coveners were over represented in their sample, and made a tentative guess that 'the numbers giving half their time or more. . . might be as high as two thousand', certainly, in their view, 'there are far more of them than is often realized' (1961, pp. 180—1). In their engineering study first published in 1963, Marsh and Coker were unable to provide a reliable figure, but in their 1968—9 study they found that there were full-time senior stewards or conveners in 10 per cent of engineering establishments (1973, p. 124).

The 1966 workplace survey found that 1 per cent of the stewards interviewed claimed to be full-time (1968, p. 16) and that such full-timers existed in 4 per cent of establishments where unions were recognized (1968, p. 75). The 1973 CIR study found 5 per cent of stewards spent more than thirty hours per week on union business (1974, p. 18) compared with 3 per cent in the 1972 workplace survey (28 per cent of senior stewards): average time spent on union business was six hours for 'normal' stewards and twenty hours for senior stewards (1974, p. 12). Brown *et al.*'s GMWU survey indicated a higher number of full-time stewards in the mid-1970s, while in 1978 the IRRU survey found that full-timers existed in 12 per cent of manufacturing establishments where there were stewards. On the basis of these figures, Clegg suggests that over the decade up to 1978 the number of full-time stewards may have increased five-fold (1979, p. 52) — a rate of growth considerably in excess of that of stewards generally. However, despite this dramatic increase in numbers, only a minority of establishments have full-time stewards: Daniel and Millward found that in 1980 in industry generally only 3 per cent of establishments had manual full-timers (and only two-thirds of those employing 1,000 or more manual workers) : this was 5 per cent of those recognizing manual unions and less than 7 per cent of those with stewards (1983, p. 34). In addition, full-timers continued to be rare in non-manual steward organizations (1983, p. 54).

In sum, stewards who spent all or nearly all their time on union activities were by no means unknown in the pre-Donovan era. And while their number may have increased substantially since the late 1960s, by the late 1970s they were still to be found in only a small minority of establishments (although in a majority of very large plants). In other words, this aspect of steward bureaucracy is still the exception rather than the rule: and it is by no means self-evident that full-timers inevitably mean oligarchy and incorporation. They may be more available to members and thereby constitute a more democratic and a more efficient form of organization.

The third strand of the bureaucratization thesis contends that an important means by which full-time and senior stewards exert control is through shop steward committees, and that such bodies have become more common since the late 1960s. But such a growth of regular steward meetings is by no means clear from the available data. The 1966 workplace survey found that almost two-thirds of stewards claimed that meetings of stewards were held: 55 per cent said meetings of stewards from their own unions were held in the place of work and 47 per cent that stewards from different unions held joint meetings (1968, p. 22). Unfortunately, the published report does not give exact figures about the regularity of these meetings — possibly half were on a regular basis. By 1972 it was found that 59 per cent of stewards claimed that there were regular steward meetings at the establishment (Parker, 1974, p. 11): as in the 1966 survey, meetings of stewards from the same union were more common than multi-union meetings.

The IRRU survey found that in 1978 regular meetings of manual stewards were held in 37 per cent of manufacturing establishments (and 30 per cent in the case of non-manuals) where stewards existed (1981, p. 64: they were held 'occasionally' in a further 38 per cent). In 1980 Daniel and Millward found that there were single-union steward meetings in half of all establishments with stewards, and joint manual steward meetings in a third of those with two or more recognized unions (but in only 17 per cent of establishments were such meetings held by non-manual stewards — 1983, pp. 96—8). Only half of these joint shop steward bodies met once a month or more often in the case of manual stewards; only a third of joint non-manual bodies met this frequently.

The data from the various surveys are not, of course, strictly comparable. But the overall picture would appear to be as follows: a significant minority of shop steward organizations held regular meetings before the period of reform. While there was some increase in the proportion of bodies which held regular meetings between 1966 and the late 1970s, there is a risk of exaggerating this growth. Steward meetings have probably not increased dramatically in engineering, but do appear to have become a good deal more common in chemicals.

As in the case of the other aspects of steward bureaucracy, the exact significance of regular steward meetings is open to question. The bureaucratization thesis indicates that they constitute a means for senior stewards to ensure the compliance of other stewards. But it seems equally plausible to suggest that such meetings might provide an opportunity for rank-and-file stewards to impose checks upon senior stewards (see chapter 5).

Conversely, the bureaucratization thesis suggests that the absence of steward meetings is likely to increase steward autonomy. And yet, in such situations stewards might become heavily dependent upon the support of senior stewards and so become more effectively subordinated to them through personal debt relationships.

Stewards and their members

The thrust of the bureaucratization thesis is, of course, that the presumed formalization of shop steward organization has changed the nature of relationships between stewards and members: centralization has meant that stewards have become somewhat insulated from their members, so that they act as a control over rather than control for those they formally represent (see, for example, Cliff, 1971, p. 205). In fact, proponents of this thesis cite remarkably little evidence in support, and unfortunately there is relatively little data on which to assess such a view. Whereas the earlier surveys investigated steward—member relations in some detail, more recent surveys have all but ignored this issue.

The bureaucratization thesis is part of a larger ethos of 'workerism' or 'rank-and-filism' which assumes that the spontaneous actions of workers are to be applauded while those of formal worker organizations are to be condemned; pre-reform shop stewards were an expression of spontaneity. Or, to put the matter another way, the thesis accepts that there exists a tension between the 'movement' and 'organization' features of trade unions and believes that the former is the more valid. While accepting the high premium (apparently) placed upon democracy in this approach, I would wish to argue that the extent to which worker interests can be promoted without formal organization is limited and the extent to which stewards could ever be seen as simply part of the rank-and-file' is open to question (for a critique of rank-and-filism, see Zeitlin, 1982).

The earlier discussion suggests a number of reasons for doubting any widespread reduction in the influence of members on stewards. First, it has been noted that steward bureaucracy was relatively common prior to reform where stewards existed, which suggests that, if bureaucracy weakens member control, then such control was often already limited. Second, we have also seen that prior to reform fewer plants had shop stewards: in these cases workers were dependent upon employer goodwill, action by individuals or informal work groups, or full-time union officials. But in few such plants is it likely that workers achieved any significant degree of influence. Indeed, more generally there is a risk of exaggerating both the degree and significance of work group controls. While a good deal of literature stresses the way in which workers were able to exploit piece-work and custom and practice, it is now increasingly recognized that more commonly the latter worked in management's favour. Moreover, not only were a minority of workers paid on a piece-work basis prior to reform, but managements also achieved significant advantages from chaotic pay structures, particularly in not having to make concessions across the board. Third, it has been noted that steward density increased significantly after reform. In other words, it was likely that steward—member interaction became easier and stewards represented more specific worker interests. Moreover, a number of studies (for example, Batstone *et al.*, 1977) indicate that stewards with small constituencies are less able to adopt a leadership role.

Given the failure of recent surveys to investigate member—steward relations, we have to rely upon comparisons between the 1966 and 1973 workplace surveys for more direct and systematic evidence. It appears that along with the growth of steward bureaucracy there has also been an increase in steward—member meetings. In both years about two-fifths of stewards were able to hold meetings during breaks, but there appears to have been a growth in the proportion able to hold meetings during working time. In the 1966 survey about a third of stewards claimed that they could hold meetings of members in working time (1968, p. 24: according to foremen, the figure was 27 per cent). By 1973, 53 per cent of stewards and 56 per cent of foremen said meetings could be held in working time (see also Wilders and Parker, 1975, p. 15). This increase appears to be greater than the increase in steward meetings. It also casts doubt upon Terry's argument that 'there is little evidence of any increase in the use of mass or sectional meetings of workers and stewards as the normal forum of decision-making' (1983, p. 80). More than this, the bureaucratization thesis would suggest that such meetings had declined. Terry also claims that managements have encouraged the use of elections and ballots: such procedures may be subjected to a variety of very substantial criticisms, but — if managements have been successful in their endeavours — then the extent to which senior stewards can ride rough-shod over members' wishes is likely to be seriously constricted.

Further doubt is cast upon the bureaucratization thesis by stewards' assessments of their ability to 'get their members to see things their way when a particular dispute arose, and get them to do what they (the stewards) believed was right'. In 1966, 43 per cent of stewards claimed they could always do so, 17 per cent sometimes and 37 per cent said they could not. In 1973 only 15 per cent said they could always do so, 49 per cent said they 'usually' could and 34 per cent 'sometimes'. The addition of the code 'usually' clearly affects the responses: but even if one assumes that two-thirds of the stewards choosing 'usually', would have chosen 'always' in the absence of this option, the findings suggest no dramatic increase in 'excessive' steward control.

However, if bureaucratization produces steward oligarchy then it might be argued that the influence of 'manual' stewards over members is less important than that of senior stewards. By definition, increased and disproportinate power would reside in their hands. Yet the 1972 workplace survey found that senior stewards were only marginally more likely than other stewards to believe that they could 'always' or 'usually' persuade members (1974, p. 53); in 1973 even this variation had disappeared (1975, p. 63).

This picture of the limited influence of stewards is supported by further survey findings. In both the 1972 and 1973 surveys about three-quarters of employees said that the majority of members decided what action should be taken over any grievance or claim. And (in engineering) more employees thought that stewards did not try hard enough to get their own way with members than thought they endeavoured to do so 'too much' (1975, p. 63). This picture of the limited degree of steward leadership or domination is supported by more detailed studies (for example, Batstone *et al.,* 1977; Nicholson, 1976; Pedler, 1973).

Finally, comparisons between workplace surveys indicate no change in steward militancy (or lack of it) or the readiness of stewards to pursue member grievances. In only one set of responses does it appear that stewards have become more incorporated. In 1966, 70 per cent of employees claimed that their stewards took the workers' point of view (1968, p. 120); but in the 1970s this figure had fallen to about a quarter. This seems to be striking evidence of a distancing from the membership. However, on closer inspection it becomes apparent that the questions asked were significantly different. In the 1972 and 1973 surveys employees were presented with three options about stewards' approaches — they were asked whether stewards took managements', workers' or a fifty—fifty approach. But in 1966 they were not presented with the third option, simply being asked 'whose point of view does your shop steward take, the management's or the worker's?' (1968, p. 199). Identical questions were, however, asked of other groups, notably senior managers (the most comparable group across the surveys): relative to employees they tended to believe that stewards were more firmly committed to the workers' point of view, but their responses indicated no trend towards greater steward sympathy with management between 1966 and 1973 (1975, p. 96).

In short, although the available data are neither as reliable, nor do they cover as long a period as one would like, there is remarkably little support for the view that stewards have either become more distanced from their members or have assumed greater influence over them.

Other indicators of oligarchy

It was noted in the introduction to this chapter that proponents of the bureaucratization thesis had paid scant attention to a variety of conventional indicators of oligarchy. It is true that such indicators as contested elections and length of tenure of office confront a variety of problems: they may reflect member satisfaction as much as oligarchic control; elections and their results may be dismissed as 'bourgeois' deceits given the false consciousness of workers, and so on. They nevertheless do provide some further insight, albeit an insight which has to be treated with a degree of care.

If there has been an increase in steward oligarchy then one would expect that stewards would remain longer in office. Again, the evidence available does little to support the view that the degree of oligarchy has increased. In their 1958 survey, Clegg *et al,* found that stewards had held office for an average of seven years (1961, p. 162): the 1966 workplace survey found an average of six years, and that 36 per cent of stewards had held office for more than four years (Government Social Survey, 1968, p. 14).

In 1973 it was found that stewards averaged five years in office, and in 1977 Brown *et al.* found that 37 per cent of GMWU stewards had held office for over four years. These crude comparisons do not indicate any increase in tenure. Stricter comparisons are possible in the case of two unions — the NUGMW and the AEU. In the 1966 workplace survey it was found that 49 per cent of NUGMW stewards had represented their members for five or more years; in 1977 Brown *et al.*'s data indicate that only 37 per cent of GMWU stewards had been stewards for more than four years. While the latter figure may in part reflect the newness of steward organization in some sectors, the comparison gives no support to the contention that oligarchy was increasing (although Brown *et al.* found that management support of shop stewards did increase stability in office, as did the size of the shop steward body).

Similarly, the 1966 survey found that 30 per cent of AEU stewards had five or more years' experience; a survey by Barratt Brown *et al.* of AEU stewards in Sheffield in the 1970s found a slightly higher figure — 36 per cent (cited in Winch, 1981, p. 54). It might be suggested that this evidence supports a trend towards greater oligarchy. However, not only is the difference relatively small, but in addition the AEU in the Sheffield district has a strong militant tradition. In other words, the oligarchical trend, if such it be, is among a group of stewards who cannot easily be described as incorporated.

It might be argued that the rank-and-file steward is of limited significance in any consideration of oligarchy: what is crucial is the senior steward. High turnover among rank-and-file stewards might facilitate oligarchical control by long-serving senior stewards. On this argument, the crucial test of oligarchy is that senior stewards should have longer service than other stewards. Moreover, one might expect the difference in length of service to be considerable: for those electing senior stewards (be they members or other stewards) are likely to favour those who are well known and have a good deal of experience.

The 1972 and 1973 workplace surveys supply data about the different tenure periods of senior and rank-and-file stewards. Neither survey shows any tendency for senior stewards to have longer periods of service; the 1972 one, indeed, found that while 'normal' stewards averaged five years in office, senior stewards averaged only four (1975, pp. 17–18).

The second set of potential indicators of oligarchy concerns the way in which stewards achieved and maintained their positions. While the surveys and the questions asked are not directly comparable, it would not appear that there have been any major changes in the requirement to stand for election or in the (low) level of contested elections. In the 1966 survey, for example, four-fifths of stewards said they had technically to stand for re-election, although in practice less than two-thirds had done so (1968, p. 14). In 1980 Daniel and Millward found that about three-quarters of both ordinary and senior stewards (excluding 'sole representatives') had technically to stand for re-election and that in practice virtually all of them had done so (1983, p. 87). These findings suggest that the formal requirements of democratic practice are more fully conformed to now than they were prior to reform. Moreover, it would seem that the method of election might now more commonly be by show of hands than by ballot (something which radical writers generally applaud): in 1966, 'a show of hands was more than twice as frequent as a ballot', while for manual stewards in 1980 the former was nearly three times as common as the latter.

For the extent to which elections were contested, the problems of comparison are even greater. In 1966, 29 per cent of stewards said they had assumed the position in a contested election; marginally lower proportions said they were opposed in 1972 and 1973 (1975, p. 18). In 1980 steward respondents were asked, if there had been steward elections in the last year, whether 'two or more candidates stood for the same post on any occasion' and were given a range of response options. In the case of 'normal' stewards, about two-thirds said there had indeed been an election, and of these 41 per cent said that all or most elections had been contested — that is, about a quarter of all respondents (1983, p. 87). This would suggest — and one can put it no more strongly — that there has been no significant decline in competition for the post of shop steward.

In the 1972 and 1973 surveys it was also found that the competition for the post tended to be greater where the steward played a more active role. However, the 1972 and 1973 surveys found dramatically different responses concerning senior stewards' elections. Whereas a third said in 1972 that their initial election had been contested, only 9 per cent said this in 1973. This appears largely to be explained by the fact that in the 1973 survey many more senior stewards were found to have come to office in an unopposed election when the previous steward resigned (1975, p. 18). More generally, the earlier surveys indicate that less than 10 per cent of stewards first achieved their position by defeating the incumbent in an election.

The 1980 survey does provide some support for the oligarchy thesis as far as senior stewards are concerned, albeit in a somewhat confusing way. Senior stewards, respondents claimed, were no less likely technically or in practice to have to stand for re-election than other stewards, and the frequency of election was not significantly different. Nevertheless, 65 per cent of respondents said that elections had indeed taken place for ordinary stewards, but only 56 per cent said elections for the post of senior steward had taken place in the previous year (1983, p. 87). Another possible indication of senior steward oligarchy concerns their method of election, particularly in large steward organizations, for, in about two-thirds of the cases where there are more than twenty stewards, senior manual stewards are elected by the stewards rather than by the membership (1983, p. 90). Unfortunately, however, this does not give support to the bureaucratization thesis unless it can be shown that prior to reform senior stewards were more frequently elected by the membership. From the few pre-reform studies which deal with this question (such as Turner *et al.*, 1967), it seems that this was probably not the case.

Steward organization in action

The preceding sections have outlined at some length the available evidence concerning trends in the bureaucratization of steward organization, steward—member relations and some indicators of oligarchy. This evidence is less than ideal and it might quite rightly be argued, therefore, that it has to be handled with considerable caution. Yet it would be inadvisable to dismiss it out of hand: it is, after all, the best we have and there is a risk, if we ignore it and fail to produce more satisfactory evidence, that the analysis of steward organization becomes a worthless game of armchair theorizing or depends upon *ad hoc* information from even less reliable sources and of an even less reliable nature. However, it is useful to conclude this section with a brief consideration of case study data which seek to tap the realities rather than merely the formalities of steward organization.

Hyman cites two studies in support of his thesis of a bureaucratization of the rank-and-file since 1968. Both pieces of evidence in fact contradict his thesis. The first of these studies is that by Turner *et al.;* the fieldwork on which this work was based not only pre-dates Donovan but also had some influence on the thinking of the Commission. Moreover, this study is of particular significance since it involved the automobile industry, a sector in which stewards have normally been seen to be most militant and 'unincorporated'.

Turner *et al.* not only refer to shop stewards as 'the new establishment' but go on to point to the 'current complexity — almost formality' of organization (p. 206). One steward in twelve was a convener which 'already implies a considerable hierarchy among the stewards themselves' (p. 207), so that 'the workplace representative system is now an elaborate institution in its own right' (p. 208). Hence in numerous plants there were full-time senior stewards who enjoyed a variety of facilities. Turner *et al.* conclude that the shop stewards' organization had become a real union — and one with an almost similar degree of elaboration and complexity as the larger union. Because this organization was now the main agency for bargaining over actual working conditions (with what amounted to its own full-time negotiators) it had assumed, in relation to managements on the one hand and the rank-and-file on the other, many of the characteristics that the official unions had displayed under the earlier developments of national or industry-wide collective bargaining. The senior stewards, like the full-time union officials before them, were forced to assume the role of buffer between the employer and the operatives. Differences in the attitudes of individual stewards possibly had some effect, just as the differing attitudes of national union officials before them affected industrial relations in some measure. But, in general, the stewards' organization was under pressures that compelled it towards certain 'responsible' patterns of institutional behaviour —

'responsible' at least in the sense that its leaders were obliged to balance a variety of group interests against the particular sectional claims with which they were confronted, and to bear in mind the long-term desirability of maintaining good negotiating relationships with managements. In short, bureaucratization and a degree of 'incorporation' were already present in strong steward organizations prior to reform — and in the most 'militant' situations.

Hyman also refers to the work of Batstone *et al.* in support of his thesis that there has been a centralization of control in the hands of 'the small cadre of full-time or almost full-time stewards' (1979, p. 57). But this study also contradicts his thesis. For an Appendix discusses the historical development of steward organization in some detail and attempts to develop systematic measures of changes in the distribution of power within the shop steward body. The study did not find a process of increasing centralization, but the reverse. Both the power of the joint shop stewards' committee and of the conveners had declined steadily from the early 1950s to the 1970s, while sectional claims and strike action had increased (1977, pp. 281—8). Other studies also suggest that hierarchical control was significant prior to reform (for example, Goodman and Whittingham, 1973, p. 102; Higgs, 1969: Cliff, 1970, p. 205; Inman, 1957, p. 400; Melman, 1958; Clack, 1967, p. 31; Derber, 1955).

Stewards have typically sought to achieve at least some degree of coordination, and, relatedly, to prevent workers adopting individualistic and sectional courses of action. Brown made this point in his study of piece-work bargaining (1973), but it was also noted by previous writers. For example, Melman states:

> . . .in the history of the Standard union organization one of the important problems was to get shop stewards to see particular issues from the point of view of the workers' organization in the plant as a whole. In the interest of this same effort shop stewards have been frequently reminded by their senior stewards of the importance of frequent reporting to their constituent worker groups in order to get them to see their particular problems in relation to the rest of the plant. (1958, p. 24)

A similar theme is stressed throughout Beynon's study of the attempts to establish steward organization at Halewood, so that by 1968 the shop steward committee 'was in a position to establish a level of consistency in the job control exercised by each of its stewards on their section'

(1973, p. 142). Indeed, such attempts at coordination and control rested upon the need not only 'to represent the immediate wishes of their members' but also 'to provide a longer-term strategy that will protect the interests of those members' (Beynon, 1973, p. 206). If they are to achieve any coherent success, then, stewards must coordinate and that implies a degree of control. 'Internal discipline', as Melman puts it, is an inevitable companion of coordination.

Furthermore, it is at least plausible, as we have seen, to suggest that the influence of senior stewards declines where steward committees assume a major role and where bargaining is centralized. For where bargaining is fractionalized, the convener may become involved in many issues and frequently takes over the negotiations. He therefore has to confront the steward body as a whole less frequently, can build up personal debt relations with individual stewards and threaten sanctions on a more individualistic level. Certainly, a number of studies indicate the extent to which conveners or senior stewards become deeply involved in sectional bargaining, while Goodman and Whittingham note, on the basis of pre-Donovan evidence, that the growth of the senior steward role 'stimulates greater interest in their activities by the rank-and-file' (1973, p. 102).

One other point concerning centralization of control within steward organizations requires brief comment. Hyman refers to the exercise of sanctions as being a feature of new bureaucratized steward organizations (1979, p. 57). There were certainly isolated instances of manning-up strikers' jobs in the seventies but, equally, there were sympathetic strikes and demonstrations against senior stewards' decisions. Beyond impressionistic evidence, however, I know only one study over time which includes reference to sanctions which in this case appear to have been more widely used in the 1950s and 1960s than in the 1970s (Batstone *et al.*, 1977). In any event, it seems quite reasonable to argue that the need to use overt sanctions rather than persuasion leading to so-called 'voluntary' agreement (and 'persuasion' may often consist of threats of sanctions) is a demonstration of the loss of centralized control not only in itself but because it often requires resort to democratic bodies, including meetings of members.

It would, nevertheless, be absurd not to recognize the possibility of greater centralization of control within steward bodies. Certainly there are reactions against such control: Turner *et al.* identified (before-Donovan) the 'unofficial—unofficial' strikes which were not first approved by shop steward leaders. These appeared 'to be becoming the norm' in the car industry (1967, p. 223). But the extent to which such a norm continued in the 1970s is open to doubt: strikes in the car industry declined in frequency and increased in size even before the massive rise in unemployment, at least according to official statistics (see, for example, Hyman, 1977, p. 30). But this picture of a decline in the frequency of strikes is not supported by other accounts (for example, Edwardes, 1983). Even if we assume that the 'official' account is accurate, this 'fact' can be variously interpreted, as evidence of a more democratic trend so that 'unofficial—unofficial' strikes are less necessary, or of such centralized control that sectional action is precluded. The evidence of preceding sections casts severe doubt upon the latter interpretation (as does the alternative evidence, including Batstone *et al.,* 1977). Moreover, to argue the latter interpretation presents severe problems of a most fundamental nature for the 'bureaucratization' thesis, reflecting the inherent problems of 'rank-and-filism'. For if stewards are now able to 'control' workers this casts severe doubts upon how far militancy in the past was attributable to the radicalism of members. Conversely, if the 'inherent' militancy of members is still seen as important, how can a few incorporated senior stewards constrain it?

A further important source of data in this context concerns studies specifically devoted to the reform of collective bargaining. These are considered at some length in the next chapter: for the present the discussion will be confined to two sets of studies: those undertaken by the Department of Employment (D of E) and by Purcell. Neither, it has to be admitted, concern 'typical' situations: the Department of Employment studies can be seen as focusing upon 'classic' situations; Purcell's studies concern companies with severe industrial relations 'problems' so that the Commission for Industrial Relations became involved. Both reports, however, place considerable emphasis upon a centralization of power within steward organizations. The Department of Employment study, for example, points to the importance of 'senior lay officials' asssuming a 'stronger factory-wide coordinating role than in the past' (1971, p. 70), for they had 'to persuade the protesting members that it was in the interests of the membership as a whole that they should sacrifice their present position' (p. 84). Hence 'an important pre-requisite for successful plant bargaining. . . was the emergence on the trade union side of strong and capable senior officials who enjoyed the confidence of their members' (p. 85). Purcell similarly stresses 'the emergence of conveners with strong dominant personalities' so that there can be 'centralization of control' and 'continuity and quality of leadership' (1979, pp. 16—17).

Two points are significant here. First, such centralized leadership had existed for some time in a number of companies prior to reform (D of E, 1971, p. 54). Second, even if such centralization and the development of 'trust' relations are important for 'successful' reform, it does not follow that they inevitably occur where reform is implemented, nor that centralization exists in no other circumstances, nor that 'bureaucratization' guarantees centralization. It is not surprising, perhaps, that only two of the nine cases studied by Purcell in any way fit the model outlined by Hyman. More important still, Purcell's subsequent discussion (1981) of four of these case studies indicates that tight senior steward control tends to be short-lived. In none of these cases were conveners or senior stewards able to maintain their control when they were seeking to pursue management ends at the expense of workers' subjective interests.

An important factor in the claimed centralization of steward organization has been a set of managerial initiatives. These have not only taken the form of fuller recognition of stewards but also changes in payment systems and patterns of work organization. Sisson and Brown, for example, argued that a shift to job-evaluated plant-wide pay structures meant that 'the status of JSSC's and their leaderships has been further enhanced' (1978, p. 44). However, this argument is overly simple on a number of counts. First, plants with job evaluation sometimes operate more than one scheme and often also have payment by results, both of which may militate against centralization (see, for example, Daniel and Millward, 1983, pp. 204, 206): and, as is shown in Part II, job evaluation is not associated with a greater probability of there being a single bargaining unit for the plant as a whole (see also White, 1981). Second, as chapter 4 shows, changes in payment systems and agreements on labour flexibility may have only temporary centralizing effects. Stewards and workers soon learn to manipulate the new 'rules of the game' and thereby weaken such centralized control as once existed.

Finally, if there had been the degree of centralization suggested by the bureaucratization thesis, then convener bargaining would have increased at the expense of rank-and-file steward bargaining. But, as chapter 4 shows, there is little evidence to support this view: rather, all stewards have become increasingly involved in bargaining; this increased involvement has simply been marginally greater for senior stewards.

A note on management attitudes and shop steward facilities

The bureaucratization thesis places considerable emphasis on the dependence of shop stewards upon management for reform, and in particular for the provision of such facilities as offices, access to telephones, training, check-off and the closed shop. These are seen as an important part of the process of incorporation. However, this argument faces a number of problems.

First, the picture suggested by surveys of the pre-Donovan era is one of considerable management support for shop stewards. Clegg *et al.* for example, concluded that 'most firms enjoy good, even intimate relations with their stewards. . . one of the most important reasons for the great power and standing of stewards in many British industries is that management likes them to have it and has helped to give it to them' (1961, pp. 176—7). Scarcely any of the stewards they interviewed said management had imposed restrictions which seriously hampered them in carrying out their duties (1961, p. 75; cf. Brown *et al.*, 1978, p. 18). While some stewards said they knew of cases of victimization, stewards were on the whole likely to gain promotion (pp. 175—6, see also Government Social Survey, 1968, p. 37). Similarly, the various surveys indicate that most managers — a steady two-thirds or so — prefer to deal with stewards rather than full-time officials (Clegg *et al.*, 1961, p. 175; Government Social Survey 1968, p. 86; Parker, 1975, p. 49). In short, there is a long history of management support for stewards — it did not develop suddenly with reform.

Second, Hyman assumes that the provision of facilities is incorporating. But facilities are provided not only for senior stewards, but for all stewards — notably, the right to time off. If stewards cannot leave their jobs, it is more difficult for them to negotiate with management; if they do not have time off and a room for stewards' meetings, it is more difficult for them to develop common policies which overcome sectionalism and to share information essential for the formulation of strategy and tactics. More generally, access to telephones, reproduction facilities and so on may be important for communication with other stewards, members and the larger union.

Precisely for these reasons, stewards have traditionally fought for such facilities. In the nineteenth century miners demanded a full-time check-weighman; stewards in the First World War demanded rights and facilities; subsequently, in engineering, shop stewards' needs for time off were recognized (Marsh, 1973, p. 126). In the 1950s and early 1960s, both in the public sector and in more strongly organized plants, stewards enjoyed a variety of facilities (see, for example, Marsh, 1973; Melman, 1958; Derber, 1955; Turner *et al.*, 1967; Clack, 1967; Beynon, 1973; Higgs, 1969). The Cameron Report on Fords pointed out that the stewards had established their own office facilities outside the plant

(1958), something which presumably served to isolate them significantly from the membership.

Unfortunately, few systematic data are available concerning facilities for shop stewards. It seems likely that by the early 1970s they were more often able to hold meetings at the workplace and to negotiate with management above foreman level (Government Social Survey, 1968, p. 27; Parker, 1974, p. 39). In the early 1970s Marsh and Garcia found that a majority of conveners in engineering had the use of telephones, a fifth had secretarial help and just over one in ten had office facilities. However, it would seem that in other industries such facilities were relatively rare (CIR, 1971, pp. 32–3). It is clear, however, that facilities for senior stewards increased significantly in the 1970s: Daniel and Millward found that a majority of them had some access to telphones, office help and office facilities. But less than a third rated their facilities as 'very good' (1983. p. 43). If the provision of facilities is part of a management strategy of incorporation, then it would seem that managers should be a little more generous.

Third, to assume that the provision of facilities automatically ties stewards to management seems extraordinarily naive — union pressure can in itself be a factor inducing management to indulge in such generosity. A more plausible analysis might focus upon the questions of whether steward facilities are provided as of right or according to management discretion: in the latter case, as McCarthy argued some years ago (1962, p. 14), the position of stewards may be uncertain and management is able to sanction stewards. What probably is distinctive is that since the late 1960s, such scope for management favouritism has been reduced through more formal agreements or through resort to legal rights if necessary (Daniel and Millward, 1983, pp. 39–43).

Hyman also places considerable emphasis upon the growth of shop steward training as a means of integrating them, since courses focus upon 'negotiating expertise and orderly procedure rather than membership mobilization'. Certainly the amount of steward training has increased: in the decade up to 1975 provision for steward training more than quadrupled so that it was estimated that more than 17,000 students could be taught annually (TUC, 1975). By 1977/8 over 27,000 students attended TUC day-release courses, and in the following year the number rose to nearly 44,000 (TUC, 1979, p. 197). Over half the students were, however, on health and safety courses. Moreover, one has to take account of the increased number of stewards and their relatively high turnover. In 1966, less than a third of shop stewards had received any form of training specifically for their role (Government Social Survey,

1968, p. 15); the proportion had risen slightly to about two-fifths in the early 1970s (Parker, 1975, p. 27). In 1980, the proportion of stewards trained in the previous year was investigated, making comparison difficult. It was found that 27 per cent had undergone such training, although this might consist of only one day (1983, p. 36). This may not, however, indicate as great an increase in the proportion of 'trained' stewards as might at first be thought: a third of stewards change each year; and there appears to be no means of knowing from the survey what proportion of stewards having training in the previous year had had some form of training in previous years.

Three other points need to be taken into account. First, studies of the actual effects of training have often suggested that they are limited by the realities of workplace practice. Hyman's argument may, therefore, be seen as attributing an excessive role to what are typically relatively short courses. Second, the nature of training provision has changed significantly since the 1960s. In the past, with the partial exception of a few courses within the 'liberal education' tradition, a good deal of steward training was sponsored and controlled by management. Increasingly, however, steward training has come under the control of the unions (Daniel and Millward, 1983, p. 42). Third, the content, nature and goals of steward training courses have tended to change. While they cannot be described as schools for revolutionaries, they have increasingly moved away from teaching managerial techniques and so on towards a more critical approach which emphasizes themes of democracy and worker interests. Alongside this trend, there has been a shift from a formal teaching situation towards a more active debating role on the part of 'students' (for fuller discussion see Batstone, 1979). That is, even if stewards did receive more training in the 1970s than they had previously — and the extent to which this is true should not be exaggerated — it was probably less oriented towards a consensual approach to management than in the past.

Hyman also places some significance upon the spread of the closed shop under management sponsorship: that is, whereas once it was a source of union strength it is now seen as a source of union weakness. It does indeed appear to be the case that the closed shop became more common with reform: between 1962 and 1978 the coverage of the closed shop probably grew from about 25 per cent of manual workers to about 31—39 per cent in manufacturing (Brown, 1981, pp. 54—5). In 1980, Daniel and Millward — covering all sectors — found that 44 per cent of manual workers and 27 per cent of all workers were covered by the closed shop (1983, p. 61). That is, a minority of workers are in closed shops despite a significant increase.

It is true that, generally, managements support the closed shop where it exists and that closed shops tend to be post-entry. But neither of these facts necessarily means that they constitute a means of incorporation. The former may be a pragmatic response in the face of union pressure; the latter may reflect the spread of the practice from craft groups into less skilled groups where workers switch between quite different kinds of jobs. Hence it is not perhaps surprising that some employers and the government believe not only that the closed shop endangers individual liberty but also that it works against industrial harmony. Moreover, cross-tabulations from the IRRU survey show that strike action was almost twice as common where closed shops existed than where they did not.

Check-off — the deduction of union dues at source by employers — is similarly deemed to reduce steward and union independence. Certainly, the use of check-off has grown considerably: the IRRU survey found that a majority of private manufacturing establishments operated check-off, and that most agreements to this end had been introduced in the decade up to 1978 (1981, pp. 70, 73; Daniel and Millward (1983, p. 74) found that check-off was even more common in the public sector. However, its existence appears to be determined more by union policy than by management strategy. It is clearly of considerable administrative convenience to unions, and to the extent that it increases union funds, and so the ability to pay strikers among other things, then it increases the union's ability to challenge management.

Critics of check-off also argue that it militates against strong workplace organization because it reduces steward contacts with members. In fact there is little evidence to suggest that such contacts are limited (Parker, 1975, p. 51), particularly in view of increased steward density and improved steward facilities. Furthermore, chasing members for money can scarcely be seen as the best basis for a strong relationship between stewards and members (hence, perhaps the tradition in some unions of having dues collectors who are not stewards). In short, while both the closed shop and check-off may provide a degree of union security, it is far from evident that managements volunteer them in the absence of union pressure or that they lead to a more cooperative approach on the part of unions. Union security and the related 'collectivization' of the workforce may facilitate the pursuance of member interests and union goals which are contrary to management's interests.

Shop Stewards and the Larger Union

The bureaucratization thesis claims to identify a process of incorporation of stewards not only through management action, but also through that of unions. Hyman, for example, argues that there now exists 'a complex system of linkages between the relatively inactive membership on the shop or office floor and the top leadership in the TUC Economic Committee'. The General Secretary of the TUC might fervently wish that Hyman was right: I doubt, however, whether he would concur with this account.

This aspect of steward incorporation has recently been the subject of criticism by England. He makes four main points. First, the thesis ignores 'the variety of union constitutions and market environments': in some unions there are long traditions of such integration while in some industrial sectors shop steward organization has not yet developed in the manner envisaged by Hyman. Second, the thesis lacks historical perspective: the increase in shop-floor activity has led to a democratization of many unions, subverting traditional 'popular bossdoms'. Third, England argues, 'there is no evidence that [executive members] were either willing or able to use the disciplinary powers of the shop stewards committee to push [union] policy through'. Indeed, pressure was as likely to flow upwards as downwards. Fourth, if the *raison d'être* of the shop steward is to protect his or her own members' interests then this may obstruct incorporation at the level of the union nationally: 'even when shop stewards have been encouraged and sponsored from above by the official union machine they may behave autonomously and cause embarrassment to national leaders' (1981, pp. 27—8).

It is, none the less, true that in a number of unions stewards now receive more constitutional recognition and are represented on national negotiating committees; industrial conferences are also more common now than they were in the 1960s. Yet their significance is open to question. For example, fuller recognition in union rulebooks may simply provide stewards with a degree of legitimacy and protection which they did not previously have. Nor should the significance of industrial conferences be exaggerated, particularly in the context of the growth of single-employer bargaining (see, for example, 1981, pp. 8, 12). Thus, even between 1966 and 1973 the proportion of stewards who thought that full-time officials played a 'very important' role in local negotiations more than halved (1968, p. 21; 1975, p. 50). By 1980 manual senior stewards averaged only 2.5 meetings a year with their local full-time officials and less than half had contacted their national official or union head office in the previous year (Daniel and Millward, 1983, pp. 93, 95).

In both 1966 and 1973 only a quarter of shop stewards held another office in their unions (1968, p. 11; 1975, p. 18); but in the latter year nearly three-fifths of senior stewards did so. The different sampling methods of the 1980 survey make comparison difficult but Daniel and Millward found, for example, that only a third of senior stewards from the main manual union in establishments surveyed reported that they or other stewards held another union position — and then it was mainly membership of a branch committee (and in a fifth of establishments the branch covered only the workplace of the respondent). This level of union organization is scarcely renowned for its role in inducing stewards to conform to national policies.

If we turn to steward involvement at higher levels of the union, then a piece of simple arithmetic helps to put the bureaucratization thesis in perspective. There are many thousands of stewards and, in 1978, it is estimated there were over 5,000 full-timers. The number of seats on national executive committees and similar bodies of major unions which can be, let alone are, held by such stewards means that only a minority could possibly be integrated in the manner suggested by Hyman. Daniel and Millward hint that the number of stewards who were members of national and other bodies above branch or district level probably increased between 1966 and 1980 (1983, p. 91). But two points should be noted: the 1966 survey asked stewards about their own membership of other bodies while the 1980 survey asked senior stewards whether *any* steward in the establishment held such a position — one would therefore expect a much higher level of positive responses. Second, even if there were an increase, it is still the case that only a minority of establishments had a direct link with higher levels of the union — possibly as few as 10 per cent. And 'representatives on the top governing body of the union were mentioned by two per cent of primary manual respondents, six per cent of primary non-manual respondents and eight per cent of secondary non-manual respondents' (1983, p. 91). Such links, then, are not only rare generally but are to be found primarily in non-manual, and hence smaller, unions.

There is some evidence to suggest that a significant number of stewards are involved in industrial or company conferences organized by trade unions. In a survey of sixty-five unions in 1983 Marsh found that almost a third ran industrial conferences and about one-quarter held conferences for particular companies. However, the evidence from workplace surveys on this issue is rather complex. First, the question asked — which is normally interpreted as referring to combine committees — in the majority of cases may in fact refer to such official conferences. Hence in 1966, when a third of stewards said there were meetings of stewards from their own unions but different workplaces and a fifth said there were multi-union meetings of this kind, the majority of the meetings were organized by full-time officials (1968, p. 223). Second, there appears to be no steady trend: from the relatively high proportion found in 1966, the figure for so-called combines falls to less than 10 per cent in 1973 although the 1978 survey suggests that such meetings might have been as common as they were in 1966 (1981, p. 64). In 1980, single-employer meetings of stewards were found to exist in about two-fifths of plants, and multi-employer meetings in just over a tenth — exactly how many of these were 'true' combines and how many were official union conferences is unclear. However, the growth — and significance — of company and industrial conferences organized by the unions should not be exaggerated.

In short, there is remarkably little evidence to support the view that since reform a significant proportion of shop stewards have for the first time become more integrated into the larger union in such a way as to permit a higher degree of 'official' control over them. A more plausible thesis would seem to be that, within the general context of greater steward independence, such integration as has occurred has tended to impose greater checks upon the full-time official (see, for example, Undy *et al.,* 1981; Batstone *et al.,* 1984; and, more generally, see Pizzorno, 1978 and Sabel, 1982).

MANAGEMENT-SPONSORED SHOP STEWARD ORGANIZATIONS

In recent discussions of shop steward organization, considerable emphasis has been placed upon the significance of management sponsorship. Terry states, for example, that 'it is now possible to speak to [sic] the existence of "management sponsored" shop steward organizations in many areas of manufacturing industry and the public sector where, until recently, local organization was limited or non-existent' (1978, p. 6). He distinguishes between an engineering paradigm and other situations, but fails to specify exactly in what areas management-sponsored organizations are to be found. Hyman similarly argues that 'if shop stewards did not exist, they had to be invented', although he notes not only the role of the employers but also of national union leaderships in this process. Willman also distinguishes between 'independent' and 'management-sponsored' organizations, the latter being 'developed under the regime of direct or indirect managerial promotion' (1980, p. 43).

Management sponsorship is typically seen to be due to changes in ownership and management, and/or the introduction of new methods such as work study and new payment systems, or redundancy (Willman, 1980, p. 42; Terry, 1978, pp. 11ff). To achieve such changes, management believed it would be necessary or easier to have shop stewards with whom they could negotiate and thereby legitimate their activities.

In these situations, 'the basic outline of the steward organization is laid down in the same package that includes innovation in the collective bargaining machinery'. Important in this, according to Terry, is 'the recognition of senior stewards' and often these have achieved a position of clear domination, generally being 'involved at an early stage in all grievances or issues raised by the membership'. The skills senior stewards develop in this way make them appear irreplaceable. And this appearance may be further confirmed by adjustments in the electoral machinery, by management's 'judicious granting of certain kinds of physical facilities', by various forms of work organization and by management selectivity in their dealings with stewards (1978, pp. 9—10). Willman argues further that management-sponsored organizations will 'overwhelmingly' pursue policies 'which assist the rationalization of personnel administration' and will not 'seek to exert worker influence on the effort bargain (1980, p. 45). In other words, they will merely constitute an aid rather than a challenge to management.

In brief, a picture of management-sponsored steward organizations suggests that while, in formal terms, they may have a structure comparable with that of 'independent' organizations, this structure will be the product of managerial initiative, will be more centralized, and will serve to support rather than challenge managerial action. That is, management-sponsored organizations most clearly demonstrate a 'bureaucratization of the rank-and-file'.

The thesis that management-sponsored steward organization have distinctive characteristics is very difficult to assess for a number of reasons. First, it is not entirely clear exactly how we are to identify these organizations. In discussing the growth of shop stewards it was noted that it was extremely difficult at a general level to differentiate between situations where stewards had grown up for the first time and those where they had always existed. The problem is exacerbated by the fact that Terry notes that stewards may have previously existed even in management-sponsored organizations (1978, p. 5).

Second, if the thrust of post-Donovan reform was for managements more fully to recognize shop stewards, then this can be seen as a more general form of management-sponsorship which would presumably apply even where stewards had been in existence for a long period. Reference has already been made to evidence of the growth of shop stewards even in engineering. Management sponsorship, then, would appear to be a matter of degree.

Third, the 'reform of industrial relations', associated with productivity bargaining, job evaluation, changing payment systems, take-overs and a restructuring of management was common even in areas where 'independent' steward organizations had existed in the past. Moreover, such changes appear, from the available evidence, to be associated with the development of more formal steward organization even in these situations.

Fourth, Terry bases a good deal of his argument upon twenty-one case studies. In six of these however, a reason put forward for sponsoring steward organization was a strike, which 'was often associated with one of the other changes, such as redundancy or a changing payment system' (p. 11). In other words, there does appear to have been some challenge from the shop floor which induced management to engage in sponsorship. This fusion of sponsorship and worker pressure appears to apply more generally. Indeed it is precisely what one would expect: management in an ideal world might prefer not to have a union presence within the place of work, but once there are signs of worker pressure then they might well decide that it is better to routinize this pressure rather than ignore it, particularly if major changes are being contemplated. Hence Brown *et al.* found in their survey of GMWU stewards that a third said management had resisted their activities in the past but did not do so now (1978, p. 148).

Fifth, while management's recognition may have stimulated and facilitated steward organization, unions had often previously been trying to establish shop stewards. Certainly this is true in a number of white-collar unions; similarly, in the case of local government and the health service the initial impetus for steward organization — at least in the case of NUPE — was from the union itself. (Terry, 1983, recognizes this and the more general importance of worker initiatives.) Nor is it sufficient to see this, as does Hyman, as an attempt by the union hierarchy to incorporate and control shop stewards. Indeed, in a number of unions it was membership pressure — sometimes expressed by votes for key union positions — that led to this development. Further, as Undy *et al.*

show, even if the attempt was to control shop stewards the strategy often backfired (1981).

Sixth, the idea that management support is something new is simply wrong. While it may not have been formalized in the past to the extent that it was in the 1970s, many 'independent' steward organizations really developed during the Second World War under the sponsorship of government regulations. Moreover, as was noted earlier in this chapter, the majority of managers prior to reform actively supported shop stewards. Similarly, the 1972 and 1973 surveys indicated that less than a fifth of senior managers would object to a request for union recognition for manual workers; even for managerial and supervisory staff 'straight' objections occurred in only 35 per cent of cases (1974, p. 25).

Seventh, and most fundamentally, the thesis of management sponsorship isolates the analysis of shop steward organization and behaviour from the broader social and economic context in which it exists. As noted earlier in this chapter, a comparison between an idealized conception of militant steward organization among engineering craftsmen prior to Donovan and the realities of steward organization among part-time school cleaners in the 1970s is not particularly useful. It is necessary to recognize that the latter have less power and are inherently more difficult to organize; in addition the former have a long tradition of union power on which to draw. In other words, an analysis of 'sponsored' steward organizations has to pose and answer the question of why stewards did not previously develop autonomously; the answer is likely to relate to the inherent weakness of the workers concerned. And, given this fact, the more useful focus for analysis is the question of how far 'sponsored' steward organization has increased or reduced worker welfare relative to the previous situation.

These points, then, suggest that it is extremely difficult to differentiate between 'management-sponsored' and 'independent' steward organizations: pure types of each are probably to be found only rarely, and in most situations there is likely to be a combination of management initiative and worker/union pressure.

The problem is made that much greater because we simply do not have published studies of shop steward organizations which have clearly been 'management-sponsored' in some definite and clear manner; Terry makes use of some case study data, but they are not reported in a sufficiently detailed manner to permit a systematic assessment of this thesis. Willman produces no evidence whatsoever on 'management-sponsored' organizations. Perhaps the one study which comes close to this idea of 'management sponsorship' is Nichols and Beynon's study of

Chemco (1977). But even ignoring the problems of its methodology, the account does not appear to accord totally with the descriptions put forward by Terry and Willman; nor does it provide a clear picture of the nature of steward organizations; and, perhaps most importantly, it indicates that many workers are not constrained by incorporated stewards, that there are signs that they and some stewards aspire to a more aggressive approach to management, and that the major constraint is less the stewards than the bargaining of key issues above the level of the plant by full-time officials: such company-level bargaining — at least at the time of the study — was atypical and does not correspond to the descriptions of management-sponsored organizations typically put forward.

Given this lack of evidence, one alternative is to seek to identify those sectors in which management sponsorship of steward organization appears common and then see how far available data support the theses outlined at the beginning of this section. In the public sector, one can look at local government and the health service; in private manufacturing the identification of sectors is more difficult.

Private Manufacturing Industry

It is significant that Terry refers to the engineering 'paradigm' rather than to engineering specifically: he would presumably wish to include in this 'paradigm' the printing industry — or, at least, he would not wish to see management sponsorship as typical in this instance. We therefore have remarkably little to go on. One approach, however, is to try to identify industries where those features of steward and union organization frequently associated with management sponsorship are especially common and are relatively new. Brown suggests three features which are particularly dependent upon management support: the closed shop, check-off and full-time shop stewards (1981, pp. 57, 73, 120). As must be apparent from the discussion above I am less than convinced by these arguments; on some counts indeed, if we accept these features as indicators, engineering emerges as characterized by management sponsorship. This is, then, a very dubious exercise, but the temptation to perform it stems from the signal failure of the proponents of the sponsorship thesis to produce much evidence of their own. The result of the exercise (using the IRRU survey data) is to suggest that within private manufacturing, food, drink and tobacco, chemicals, clothing and textiles were the industries where management sponsorship was most common. This would largely conform to general opinion, and gains additional support from the fact that between 1966 and 1974 these were areas of considerable union growth.

From the IRRU survey it is possible to assess — again very crudely — how far our four industries demonstrate more strongly than private manufacturing industry generally the features of hierarchy and formalization. In looking at this evidence, however, we have to allow for a size effect, and therefore comparisons are made between the figure for the particular industry and the overall figure for manufacturing establishments in the size band into which the bulk of the industry falls.

One obvious indicator — the existence of full-time stewards — cannot strictly be used since it has been included as part of the definition. Another indication of hierarchy, however, is the existence of senior stewards; on this issue, only clothing showed a higher frequency than the average for the relevant size category. In terms of organizational complexity and coordination, three 'tests' are possible — the existence of regular steward meetings, regular inter-union steward meetings and the extent to which inter-union problems exist. (It should also be noted that only in textiles and clothing is the frequency of multi-unionism considerably lower than the figure for manufacturing industry generally; this can scarcely be attributed to recent management sponsorship rather than the historical development of union structures in these industries.)

Regular steward meetings were only markedly more common than might be expected in the case of chemicals; at the other extreme they were a good deal less common than might be expected in clothing. Inter-union meetings of stewards were much rarer in all four industries than the average for the relevant size categories. Inter-union problems did not exist in clothing (this may be explained in large part by the rarity of multi-unionism); only food, drink and tobacco accords with the expectation of fewer such problems where there was management sponsorship, while textiles had a scale of inter-union problems somewhat in excess of the average.

Management sponsorship might also be reflected in the nature of management—steward contacts; they might be expected to be established on a regular basis, to have recently been formalized and to demonstrate a more cooperative character. Regular meetings between management and stewards were only more common than expected in the case of chemicals, while in clothing they were much rarer than for the relevant overall size category. Recent formalization of management—steward relations was below the average for the relevant size category in chemicals, textiles and clothing, and in food, drink and tobacco was approximately the same as the overall figure for manufacturing. Consensual relations might be indicated by the existence of consultative bodies: in none of our four industry groups were these markedly more common than the overall figure for the relevant size category and in two of them — food, drink and tobacco, and clothing — such bodies were much rarer. However, in three of the four, new consultative bodies were a notable feature. If management sponsorship leads to incorporation it might be expected that consultative bodies were union-based: in all four industries this was less common than for manufacturing industry generally.

In short, from these extremely crude data, management sponsorship does not appear to lead to the features of steward organization that might be expected. Nor is there any clear and consistent pattern which would appear to fit all four industries, for example, fostering senior steward domination by encouraging senior stewards but avoiding steward committees which might challenge that domination; such a picture accords with the facts only in the case of clothing.

It should, once more, be stressed that these calculations are extremely crude. Moreover, many factors other than management sponsorship are likely to be relevant, while the exact form of sponsorship may itself vary considerably. However, it should also be pointed out that those who put forward the thesis of management sponsorship have not dealt with these possibilities; here we have been trying to 'test' those arguments they have put forward against the available data.

The third step, after identifying the relevant industries and after looking at features of steward organization, is to see how far management sponsorship is associated in our four industries with substantive features of management strategy typically seen as constituting part of the reform package. More specifically, we can consider the use of job evaluation and work study, the use of measured day work rather than piece-work, and the existence of various forms of productivity deal. Finally, if management sponsorship achieves its ends, then labour productivity should be higher (see chapter 4) and industrial action lower, than in other sectors, and the range of steward and union control should be limited.

According to the IRRU survey, the only one of our four industries in which job evaluation was employed more frequently than might be expected is clothing; in the other three industries job evaluation was less widely employed than in manufacturing industry generally in the comparable size category. In relation to work study and payment by results, the IRRU survey shows that two of our four industries used these more than would be expected, and two less. The picture, then, is inconclusive.

White's recent study of payment systems provides data on the use of measured day work and various forms of productivity scheme in food, drink and tobacco, chemicals and clothing as compared with mechanical and electrical engineering. Measured day work was rarer in our three 'management-sponsored' industries than in engineering (1981, p. 46). There was no clear tendency for any of these industries to be more likely to pay high rates to production workers to allow for productivity factors (pp. 82—3), nor to have self-financing productivity schemes (p. 86).

As was noted above, Willman in particular argues that management-sponsored steward organizations would have little, if any, control over effort. It is difficult to find published data with which to assess this thesis (although see chapter 4). Two recent surveys which did ask questions concerning the negotiation of work organization issues (Knight, 1979; Daniel and Millward, 1983) do not give sufficiently detailed breakdowns by industry. Storey, in his smaller survey, did investigate parts of two of our four industries, brewing and textiles, and asked questions concerning the negotiation of work organization and related issues. While he found that the number of issues negotiated in the 'sponsored' industries was lower, there was nevertheless a good deal of negotiation over such issues as manning (one reason why some issues, such as the scheduling of operations, were rarely negotiated was simply because in brewing and man-made fibres 'operations are more determined by the cycle of continuous process' — 1980, p. 138).

The lower level of worker/union control in these 'sponsored' industries is, however, largely to be explained by the factors which also explain why steward organization rarely existed in any developed form prior to the late 1960s. In their recent study, for example, Daniel and Millward (1983) emphasize the way in which the pattern of workplace industrial relations is affected by the proportion of women in the labour force. And, while a quarter of the labour force in production industries as a whole consists of women, it is considerably higher in three of the four industries under consideration here — food, drink and tobacco (40 per cent women), textiles (46 per cent) and clothing (76 per cent). Thus, according to the IRRU survey, collective sanctions are rarer in these industries than in manufacturing generally (although strike action is above the expected level in clothing and food, drink and tobacco).

The crucial question is how far 'sponsored' steward organization has affected worker interests. As chapter 4 shows at some length, on virtually all counts workers in our four 'sponsored' industries did better and demonstrated more militancy in the decade after 1968 than they had done before this date. It would seem, then, that such systematic data as

are available give little support to the idea that management sponsorship
has had widespread effects of the kind proposed in private manufacturing
industry.

The Public Sector

In sectors such as local government and hospitals there was, as has
already been noted, a dramatic growth of steward organization from the
late 1960s. Local government and the health services also seem to score
high on our indicators of management sponsorship of shop stewards and
union organization. In 1974, NUPE, for example, had 85 per cent of its
members on check-off. A few years later, Terry's small survey of GMWU
stewards in local government found that 54 per cent of check-off
arrangements had been introduced in the last three or four years (1982).
By that time the closed shop was relatively common — Terry found that
49 per cent of the manual workforce in smaller local authorities were
covered by the closed shop and 19 per cent in larger authorities. Terry
also found in his survey of GMWU stewards that about a third of local
authorities had a full-time shop steward — a figure three times that
found in the IRRU survey of private manufacturing industry. To the
extent that these are valid indicators of sponsorship, management in
local government and the health services appear to have engaged in a
good deal of it.

How has this affected the nature of shop steward organization?
According to Fryer *et al.*, in 1974 65 per cent of NUPE stewards were
not involved in any form of steward meeting, and by the later seventies
Terry found that for a third of GMWU stewards the branch still provided
the main opportunity to meet other stewards. Nevertheless, he did find
that regular steward meetings were held in 50 per cent of local
authorities. At first sight, this appears to indicate a more developed
pattern of organization than in private manufacturing. But when size of
employing organization is taken into account, the picture is rather
different: most local authorities employ over 1,000 workers. The great
majority of private manufacturing establishments of this size had regular
steward meetings. Inter-union meetings of stewards were also more rare
in local government. The same distinction applies to the position of
senior shop steward: Terry found that such a position existed in 70 per
cent of his local authorities; in large private manufacturing establishments the figure was 97 per cent. Hence, as Terry points out, 'there is
less evidence of the development of hierarchical steward organization in
local government than in private manufacturing. While steward

organization of a kind is universal, dominant senior stewards or convenors are less frequently found in local government' (p. 8).

How far have these changes been associated with an increased ability for management to introduce the changes it desires? The Commission on Industrial Relations investigation in the early seventies found that between January 1969 and mid-1971 changes in industrial relations practice were less common in local authorities than the rest of industry: productivity agreements were less common for manual workers (25 per cent as against 32 per cent); only 12 per cent of local authorities had introduced new wage systems compared with 31 per cent of other establishments; union recognition and new joint procedures were also less common. In sum, while nearly half of other establishments had introduced at least one of these changes, less than a third of local authorities had done so (CIR, 1973, pp. 45, 58).

By the late seventies, however, the picture had changed considerably. Two-thirds of managers in local authorities claimed they had put their relationship with shop stewards 'on a more formal basis', and joint consultation was widespread (broadly in line with large private manufacturing establishments). The use of work study appeared universal and had been used increasingly over the preceding five years. (Moreover, it is worth noting that the majority of work study schemes had been introduced at departmental level, suggesting the importance of stewards at this level — that is, steward activity of a sectional kind.) Finally, a majority of local government managers claimed to have reduced the work force in the previous two years.

The thrust in local authorities had not been towards measured day work but towards the introduction of bonus systems. In 1968, according to the *New Earnings Survey*, less than 3 per cent of full-time manual male workers and about 15 per cent of full-time manual female workers in local authorities received some form of bonus payment, although of minute proportions relative to total pay. By 1978, two-thirds of full-time manual male workers and 14 per cent of full-time female workers received such payments, and in the case of men these accounted for almost 14 per cent of total pay (at the same time, overtime pay had not declined in significance).

At first sight, then, it would appear that management was able to achieve its ends to a significant degree, by means of a somewhat partial form of shop steward organization. But more careful scrutiny raises doubts. First, as we have already seen, steward organization did not arise simply out of management's wishes; indeed, in contrast to his earlier arguments on the lay elite, Terry in his discussion of local government emphasizes the way in which the formalization of shop steward relations was an attempt to accommodate union militancy. Similarly, in their study of NUPE, Fryer *et al.* place a good deal of emphasis upon the way in which the experience of strike action encouraged steward activity and forced management to deal with stewards.

The extent to which management's industrial relations strategy met with success is also open to doubt. Terry found that 57 per cent of local authorities had experienced a strike of less than one day in the previous two years, 60 per cent a longer strike, 53 per cent an overtime ban and 47 per cent a work to rule. These rates were a good deal higher than those found in private manufacturing (Terry's data were collected prior to the industrial action of the winter of 1978/9).

A similar picture emerges from official strike statistics. The number of stoppages per 1,000 workers in Britain rose by 20 per cent overall between 1966—9 and 1970—3; in local government the figure rose by 22 per cent (although still lower in absolute terms than the national figure). In terms of days lost, the rate of increase in local government was approaching twice the national figure. Between 1970/3 and 1974/5, the overall number of stoppages in industry fell by 11 per cent; in local government it rose by 54.5 per cent. Over the same period, days lost per 1,000 workers fell considerably less in local government than in industry generally.

In addition, the means by which bonus systems were introduced provided for worker involvement in the decision, rather than decision by senior stewards. In the case of the National Health Service, at least, it also appears that reorganization and the introduction of bonus schemes encouraged a development of group and union consciousness (Manson, 1977, pp. 204ff). It is perhaps not surprising, therefore, that manning levels should have increased up to 1978, that labour costs grew faster than public expenditure as a whole, and that such indicators of productivity as are available (for example staffed beds and daily occupation of beds per worker in the NHS) fell over the period.

Finally, the Fryer *et al.* survey made some investigation of the issues raised by NUPE stewards with management (1978, p. 69). Such data have to be treated with caution since the authors do not tell us what questions they asked; caution is also necessary for other reasons. The survey was undertaken in 1974 when many stewards were new; in addition, female stewards in particular often represented dispersed and part-time workers; any comparison with Workplace Industrial Relations surveys should perhaps be confined to male stewards — 87 per cent of stewards in the 1973 WIR survey were male.

It is hard to tell whether the NUPE survey asked about a check-list of items or not, and whether it was asking about all issues ever discussed or was seeking to develop a picture of 'normal' issues. Moreover, given the newness of many of the stewards, their range of experience was likely to be limited. Table 3.1 gives data on broadly comparable issues; in the case of the WIR survey, the unbracketed figures relate to frequent negotiation with management or foremen, whichever is the larger, while the bracketed figure relates to issues ever settled by stewards. It can be seen that the conclusions reached will vary considerably depending which figure is taken: but on some issues, notably grading, working time and bonus problems, the NUPE stewards do not appear to be less active than the generality of stewards. On discipline and safety they appear somewhat less active when 'ever settled' responses are taken from the WIR survey. Moreover, it should be remembered that well over a third of the WIR stewards came from areas of traditional union strength, such as engineering. (Unfortunately, Daniel and Millward do not distinguish between central and local government, so a more up-to-date picture cannot be obtained from published sources.)

These comparisons are in themselves riddled with problems and we do not know how far such negotiation constituted a challenge to management. But to the extent that any conclusions can be drawn, and in view of the lack of alternative sources of data, it does not seem unreasonable to suggest that they give little support to the management sponsorship thesis. The picture emerges less clearly if women stewards are included; on the other hand, a good number of NUPE stewards operate in areas where groups of workers have considerable autonomy and in which immediate supervisors may be union members and often shop stewards (see, for example, Fryer *et al.*, 1978, pp. 171—2).

TABLE 3.1 ISSUES OVER WHICH STEWARDS REPORTED NEGOTIATIONS (%)

	NUPE local government	*NUPE hospitals ancillaries*	*WIR 1973*
Discipline	28	23	5(40)
Grading/job/evaluation	33	38	10(26)
Working time/stop-start times	31	41	6(29)
Bonus problems/bonus payments	40	29	14(33)
Safety	38	33	22(55)
Average	34	33	11(37)

The evidence available, then, does not appear to give much support to the thesis of management sponsorship within the public sector. Now it may be that this picture would change if fuller evidence were available; and it may be that in specific cases such management sponsorship does have the effects predicted by the thesis. Some of Terry's case studies appear to support this view, but he admits that these studies may not be typical. Moreover, he does not provide any firm evidence about the way in which dominant conveners exercise their power — how far they act as policemen for management; nor does he take account of the relative autonomy of many work groups or direct pressures by workers upon immediate supervisors in the dispersed work situations he discusses: nor does he relate convener dominance to the facts that steward density is high and steward coordination by conveners rather rare. More generally, Terry's discussion of shop stewards in local government emphasizes themes which are somewhat different from those he points up in his discussion of steward elites. In particular, he notes the way in which management strategy may be shaped by worker militancy.

Those who have promoted the thesis of management sponsorship themselves appear to be somewhat confused as to its significance. Terry, for example, argues that management would probably find it difficult to kill off the steward bodies it has helped to create and goes on:

> managements, as a result of their own actions, may increasingly come to be faced by collective reaction to their proposals, and herein lies the potential for substantial workplace organization, based in an understanding of the uses of collective action, and a solid organizational structure with which management are obliged to deal. (1978, p. 17)

Similarly, Willman demonstrates confusion. Not only does he cite the closed shop as both a feature of management sponsorship (p. 45) and a feature of worker influence on the effort bargain (p. 47); not only does he fail to grasp the purpose of Batstone *et al.*'s classification of stewards and to understand the relevance of notions of union principles to control; but he also recognizes at a number of points that sponsored organizations may achieve independence, and that the reverse may also happen. Indeed, he refers to militancy among such groups as health workers as an indication of this (p. 48). It is, therefore, difficult to see the significance of the distinction between 'sponsored' and 'independent' organizations; he really seems to be much more interested in the degree of control exerted by steward organizations. Management support may be one relevant factor, but it is only one among many, and may itself reflect worker and union pressure. To the extent that sponsorship does create militancy, then what appears to be of considerably greater interest than the thesis of management sponsorship is the broader question of industrial relations reform and the contradictions it embodies from a managerial perspective — that is, the main theme of this volume. (The tendency for workplace union organization to assume independence and a more conflictual approach is not confined to Britain — for example, Dubois (1976) has noted the same trend in France when managements, through relocation, have sought to avoid and evade union pressures.)

REFORMISM, MANAGEMENT STRATEGY AND SHOP STEWARD
ORGANIZATION

In this chapter, we have considered the available evidence relating to ideas about the impact of reformism upon shop steward organization. Both liberal pluralists and radicals have claimed that reformism would lead to a centralization of shop steward organization. The reformists argued this would promote workers' interests, even though direct day-to-day control over work organization would be reduced. This was so because stewards would play a role in determining the parameters within which management operated. On the other hand, radicals argued that the centralization of steward power would lead to a more sympathetic approach to management while the loss of day-to-day control over work would reduce the ability of stewards to promote workers' interests. Both schools of thought agreed that there would be — and was — a centralization of power within shop steward bodies and that this would facilitate the achievement of management goals.

In the course of the discussion we have concentrated upon a number of themes relating to this argument. First, it was shown that both reformists and radicals — at least in some cases — have relied upon a rather crude and inaccurate model of shop steward organization prior to Donovan. We put forward evidence to indicate that many features of 'bureaucracy' existed prior to 1968, particularly in the classic 'homes' of steward organization such as engineering.

Second, we argued that the extent to which there was an extension of 'bureaucratic' features has been exaggerated. Not only did many of these features often exist prior to 1968, but they were also far from ubiquitous by the late 1970s. Senior stewards may have existed in the vast majority of steward organizations, but they did so in most plants with stewards prior to 1968. There may have been a dramatic increase in the number of full-time stewards, but they still existed in a very small number of plants in 1978. Regular meetings of stewards were still relatively rare — it does not appear as if these were typical of shop steward organizations, and it is open to doubt how much more common they were in percentage terms by the late 1970s than they had been in the late 1960s.

There is a further point of significance here. What is striking is that no one has actually specified how far the various characteristics of steward organization coexist. In the IRRU survey, less than three-quarters of private manufacturing plants with more than fifty employees had any shop stewards. Three-quarters of the plants with stewards had senior stewards, that is, only just over half of all the plants surveyed. Of those plants with senior stewards, only just over two-fifths had regular steward meetings (although another two-fifths had them occasionally), that is, less than a quarter of all plants had both senior stewards *and* regular steward meetings. Twenty-eight per cent of plants with stewards but without senior stewards had regular steward meetings (and 37 per cent had them occasionally). Of those with regular steward meetings, only a quarter had full-time shop stewards, that is, only about 7 per cent of plants had regular steward meetings *and* full-time shop stewards. In other words, very few plants demonstrated all — or even two — of the characteristics of 'bureaucratized' shop steward organizations, although those that did certainly tended to account for a larger proportion of total employment. It is clear that there is a risk of exaggerating the scale and significance of bureaucratic changes in steward organizations since 1968.

We questioned not only the scale of change in shop steward organization, but also its significance in 'real' terms. It was stressed that one cannot simply 'read off' from formal structures the realities of the operation of shop steward organizations: many 'formal' developments in such organizations may have diverse consequences. Such evidence as exists suggests that there was an increase in steward density which was likely to be a significant counterweight to the slight relative — and not absolute — concentration of negotiating powers at the level of the senior stewards. Moreover, we suggested two other factors which need to be taken into account. First, if the growth of steward organization was at the expense of full-time official control, then it constitutes, in all probability, a significant increase in workplace control, for the senior steward is at least directly accountable to workers within the workplace. Second, particularly since all features of bureaucratization were rarely found, it is open to question how far they provided a firm base for oligarchic control.

In chapter 2 we argued that personnel management had played a primarily procedural role in industrial relations. Not only were personnel managers associated with the growth of corporate bargaining, but also with the development of various features of 'bureaucratic' dealings with shop stewards. This theme has been emphasized by Brown *et al.* (1978) in their discussion of NUGMW stewards. They found that various aspects of shop steward 'bureaucracy' were more likely to exist where management's approach was sympathetic; they also found that steward stability was higher in this situation. The IRRU survey supports this picture: senior stewards existed in over four-fifths of establishments with a personnel specialist but in only two-thirds of others; 20 per cent of plants with such a specialist had full-time stewards while only 3 per cent of other plants had them; and while over half the plants with personnel specialists had regular steward meetings, only 20 per cent of other plants did so. But, consistent with our argument in the previous chapter, and as the next chapter goes on to show at greater length, it is open to question how far these developments were associated with greater support for management. Not only, then, does the scale of change in the organization of shop stewards tend to be exaggerated, but also, as with management, and following from the nature of management change, these changes tend to constitute yet another case of 'plus ça change, plus c'est la même chose'.

Similarly, we have suggested that there are serious problems with the view that management-sponsored steward organizations are distinctive. There is little evidence to support the view that, in those sectors where management support was both significant and new during the 1970s, shop steward organizations were more bureaucratic or more sympathetic to management. It may be the case that they exerted less control over work organization than did older steward organizations: but this is precisely what one would expect. For if the workers concerned had had greater power, (be it from the production process, the labour or product market, or their own sense of solidarity) it is likely that steward organization would have existed in the past. In other words, an explanation for any 'weakness' which may exist relative to, say, engineering, has to rely primarily upon factors other than steward organization. Indeed, we have suggested that the creation of more developed forms of such organization was associated with an increase in steward power and more checks upon management prerogative. This can be attributed to a number of factors: the first is the counter-productive (from management's point of view) effects of management initiatives suggested in the previous chapter; second, there is a tendency, at least in earlier writings, to underplay the extent of union initiatives and worker pressures for the growth of steward organization; and, third, a variety of substantive factors associated with changes in payment systems and work organization, and with incomes policies, induced changes in worker, union and management practices. The IRRU survey is not of a kind which permits a careful assessment of these kinds of factor.

To sum up, this chapter has argued that theories of the 'bureaucratiza-tion of the rank-and-file' and of management sponsorship risk exaggerating the scale, nature and sources of change within shop steward organizations. Certainly changes have occurred, but few plants demon-strate all of the characteristics associated with 'full' bureaucracy. It is, of course, quite likely that some steward organizations were incorporated: that some new management-sponsored steward organizations acted as a police force for management. What has been argued here is that these arguments do not appear to apply in the majority of cases. Moreover, both arguments rely upon an inaccurate picture of shop steward organization prior to reform.

4 Reform, Economic Performance and Relative Gain

Industrial relations reform embodied two distinct, yet interrelated, strategies — the procedural and the substantive. The last two chapters have focused primarily upon the former. In this chapter attention is concentrated upon the substantive changes associated with industrial relations reform: more specifically, an attempt is made to trace how far, and in what ways, the 'frontier of control' was affected and how reforms affected the relative gains of workers and employers. However, in looking at substantive change, procedural elements of reform cannot be totally ignored, for they figure centrally in definitions of control. This term is crucial to the whole discussion of reformism, for it is the focus of the differing interpretations of its presumed success.

As noted in chapter 1, Flanders and others associated with the promotion of reform claimed that their proposals meant an extension of union influence. Plant- or company-level agreements extended the range of issues negotiated between management and unions and, the argument went, in this way both management and unions would achieve greater control — or, in the oft-quoted phrase, 'management can only regain control by sharing it'. This theme of the extension of joint regulation subsequently became even more strongly emphasized by writers such as Daniel and Macintosh (1972, pp. 81—2) and McCarthy and Ellis (1973): they stressed the need to extend negotiation over an even wider range of issues than initially proposed by Donovan, and to go beyond a simple belief in the possibility of 'one-off' negotiations.

On the other hand, many were sceptical of the reformist case. As noted in chapter 1, many managers rejected it precisely because they believed that reform involved an extension of union influence without any guarantee of increased cooperation or consensus (see, for example, Ogden, 1981; Fox, 1974). Many radicals not only argued that the procedural aspects of reform were aimed at steward incorporation, but also that many substantive proposals were contrary to workers' interests. Topham (1969), for example, pointed to what he saw as 'aggressive tactics on the part of management and the related fears of many stewards'. From this perspective, any wage improvements associated with reform would be both short-term and paid for by workers themselves; joint regulation by means such as productivity bargaining in fact involved 'the restoration or enhancement of management authority' and the limitation of steward activity.

These different interpretations rest ultimately upon differences of view as to the compatibility of worker and employer interests. This question has been discussed at some length in chapter 1 and need not be repeated here. But in addition to this, another question relates to the interpretation of the effects of substantive reforms: this concerns the way in which joint regulation would operate. With reform there was to be a distinction between the processes of rule-creation and rule-application. The reformist case was that union representatives would be involved in the creation of rules and thereby would have a wider range of influence. But in exchange for union involvement in what could be seen as the formulation of management policy, management would have greater freedom — within the parameters set by the agreements — in the day-to-day organization of work. That is, fractional bargaining would be reduced, and such shop-floor level negotiation as continued to take place would be structured by the jointly agreed rules. And, according to reformists, those rules would reflect and embody worker interests.

Against this, radical critics argued that those rules involved a buying out of worker and union influence and so were favourable to management. While workers would have greater need for shop-floor bargaining, the opportunity for it would be reduced. Moreover, if stewards were forced — or chose — to negotiate within the terms of the jointly agreed rules, then they would be working against the interests of their members and acting as a managerial police force (see, for example, Topham, 1969; Cliff, 1970; Hyman 1978). Such risks were that much greater because, particularly as stewards became more fully recognized by management, their institutional interests would diverge from those of workers (Goldthorpe, 1974).

What constitutes increased worker control from one perspective, then, is reduced worker control when viewed from the other. If control is non-zero-sum, then it follows that an increase in coordinated and jointly agreed control over the wage—work bargain is — at least potentially although not necessarily — in the interests of both management and the 'collective worker'. But if control is largely 'zero-sum', as radicals claim, then the question becomes much more complex: changes are likely to shift the balance of advantage in favour of one party rather than the other. But one cannot then assume that the shift is invariably in management's favour. This question requires more careful consideration.

First, while most control issues may be zero-sum, not all are (see, for example, Hyman and Elger, 1981). Further, there may be particular advantages from workers' perspectives in joint rather than unilateral control. For joint control as defined by the reformists may increase the possibility that control is exercised by all workers rather than being the privilege of a few: it would not simply be the most powerful who were able to impose a check upon management. Further, unilateral forms of worker regulation may be particularly susceptible to decline in the face of a concerted employer onslaught or of various changes in market conditions, organization or methods of production. Institutionalized arrangements may make worker influence rather more secure.

Second, there is a school of thought within the radical tradition which views any form of worker influence dependent upon governmental or employer support as a sham. Rarely, if ever, is evidence produced to support this contention — perhaps not surprisingly, for it often supports the contrary view. The growth of the shop steward movement, for example, in both world wars owed a good deal to various forms of external support. (This is not to say that all kinds of formal influence will inevitably work in workers' favour — such a view would be as excessively simplistic as its opposite.) Employer attempts to stem, or cut off, worker pressures by providing institutions of joint regulation do not necessarily mean that the influence workers achieve is not significant, or that it is less than they would otherwise gain. To argue that only controls won through 'struggle' are real and meaningful is to fly in the face of historical experience and to assume both worker stupidity and employer omniscience. In other words, it is quite possible that employer initiatives can provide a platform from which workers can achieve not only immediate and significant influence but also a base from which further control might be won in the future.

Third, and relatedly, many critics of reform appear excessively pessimistic — hence the view noted above that moves to joint regulation from worker and managerial unilateral control are both often seen to involve reductions in worker control. This could be so, but it is not clear why it should necessarily be the case. Why is it that workers should 'lose' when they move into issues previously controlled by management as well as when management moves into areas formerly unilaterally controlled by workers? That is, if a shift from managerial regulation to joint regulation means workers are tied by a managerial rationale, why should it not be the case that a shift from worker to joint regulation equally ties management by a worker rationale? Conversely, and, more obviously, if a move from unilateral worker control to joint regulation involves a reduction in worker control, why does a shift from managerial prerogative to negotiation with unions not involve a reduction in managerial control? C. Wright Mills argued that union leaders were ensnared by 'the liberal rhetoric' of compromise associated with collective bargaining; while employers might thereby seek to manipulate unions, it seems — at least at first sight — equally reasonable to argue that management was necessarily constrained by that 'liberal rhetoric', with its emphasis upon cooperation, 'reasonableness' and good will. Indeed, Mills himself appears to recognize this point for he states:

> . . . there are many hitches in union management cooperation. If the CIO ideologists are not careful, the managers of corporate property will select only the reasonable concessions that are offered . . . but they will reject labour's pretensions to a voice in production within the plants and in planning for the US political economy. (1948, pp. 120—1)

The obvious question is, what happens if the 'CIO ideologists' are careful? To argue that 'care' is a unique feature of management is scarcely a convincing sociological thesis.

Fourth, to assume that union and worker interests are totally divergent is as unacceptable as to assume that they are identical. It has generally been assumed by radicals — at least until recently — that the shop steward was the embodiment of member interests. The radical school of thought has now jumped to the opposite extreme. The last chapter focused upon this question, but it is useful to reiterate several points here. If an 'iron law of democracy' checks the 'iron law of oligarchy' in trade unions nationally, this may be expected to be even more true at plant level where stewards are subjected to strong member pressure, where issues have a direct and visible impact upon workers and where small groups of workers may more easily challenge decisions. Further, great care has to be taken in counterposing what are deemed to be worker interests and the institutional interests of unions or, even more, of shop steward organizations. For in important respects the two sets of interests overlap even if they are not identical: workers may be expected to have an interest in the maintenance of an organization geared to the pursuit of their demands and which does not have to be recreated on every issue. Conversely, it is dangerous to underestimate the extent to which the institutional interests of unions depend upon pursuing worker interests, notwithstanding various forms of provision for union security: the closed shop not only guarantees union membership, for example, but has been the basis of unilateral control by craft unions. The expressed interests of individual workers have often to be compromised for the sake of the majority and this generalized interest, and its maintenance, can be a major institutional interest of a union (see Batstone *et al.,* 1984 on the internal negotiation of order in unions). To recognize tensions, and partially and potentially divergent goals and interests, is very different to a blanket argument that union and worker interests are inevitably or generally opposed.

Fifth, the radical critics of reformism focus upon managerial intention and assume that reality conforms to it. In other words, little attention is paid to the extent to which management does in fact achieve its goals either in agreements reached or in the application of those agreements; relatedly, insufficient attention has been given to the conditions under which management succeeds or fails in these endeavours. (The reformists themselves have frequently failed to probe these questions.)

The answers to such questions are not likely to be simple. It is well known that managements have often failed to introduce proposed reforms (see, for example, Batstone *et al.,* 1978) and have been forced to make major concessions in formal agreements, permitting ongoing union/worker control (such as mutuality or *status quo* clauses). As will be discussed more fully below, managements frequently encounter severe constraints on the application of agreements even when these indicate wide scope for 'legitimate' unilateral action on their part. In short, the perspectives of both promoters and critics of reform often ignore the very features which are central to their arguments — the processes of negotiation of 'reform' agreements and of their application in practice (cf. McCarthy and Ellis, 1973, pp. 82—6). This is in spite of the fact that these processes have been central to the analyses which informed both the reform package and much of the radical tradition in Britain.

The discussion so far has served to highlight and assess differences of view about the implications of industrial relations reform for what we might loosely term the frontier of control. It is also crucial for an assessment of what has actually happened. For it suggests that analyses such as that of Storey (1980) are excessively simple and fail to support his blanket assertion that his work has revealed 'that the range of bargaining and unilateral worker control has undoubtedly *widened* in each of the industries surveyed during this decade' (p. 164). His contention is no more justified by his data than the opposite thesis which he roundly condemns. Any satisfactory analysis has to demonstrate some awareness of the complexity of control, a complexity which is greatly increased when changes have to be assessed over time and in the face of less than ideal data.

The present discussion, however, permits us to clarify what exactly was involved in the prescriptions for reform. Broadly speaking, the aim was to reduce worker control over day-to-day aspects of work by inducing workers' representatives to legitimize managerial freedom, largely in exchange for commitments relating to the presumed economistic priorities of workers and the institutional interests of unions. A number of implications follow. First, at least in the early and more mechanistic models of reform, one implication was that after an initial and dramatic surge in the intensity and range of bargaining, there would be an overall reduction in both. Later reformist prescriptions were less convinced of the likelihood of any subsequent decline in bargaining activity. Second, the reform package also sought to centralize plant bargaining; in other words, it might be expected — if reform were to achieve the aims set for it — that the bargaining activity of senior stewards should increase relative to that of other stewards. Third, there would be a dramatic decline in the significance of unilateral control. Fourth, the shift from unilateral to joint regulation would be more dramatic in the case of workers than of management. Fifth, to the extent that workers and stewards did negotiate over issues, their opportunities and arguments would be more agreement-oriented and rule-bound. Finally — and most centrally for management — an increase in its freedom would permit it to increase labour productivity. These are the themes under consideration in this chapter. The discussion turns first to changes in bargaining activity in the decade after 1968. Second, data concerning changes in labour productivity are discussed. In subsequent sections, more specific aspects of reform are considered: productivity bargaining and changes in payment systems. Then, after a brief consideration of job-based control, we turn to an assessment of the relative gains from reform in the seventies.

BARGAINING ACTIVITY

The logic of reform indicated, in its earliest form, only a temporary increase in bargaining activity and a subsequent decline. Later versions of the theory suggested that the range and amount of bargaining would continue at this higher level. But both versions proposed a centralization of bargaining. In this section we consider these questions.

In order to build up a general picture, we need to look at the survey data but this presents a number of problems. Ideally one would want to compare surveys undertaken before and after reform which asked identical questions of the same respondents. This is not possible: we have to make do with three sets of survey evidence, which are far from ideal.

The first set of surveys consists of the various workplace industrial relations surveys undertaken under official auspices. The first of these was undertaken for the Donovan Commission in 1966; subsequent surveys were undertaken in 1972 and 1973, although they used different sampling methods. These data provide some picture of the pre- and post-reform situation, although ideally one would like more recent and more comparable survey data.

One reason for the lack of comparable recent material is that in the seventies an interest developed in shop steward organization, collective bargaining and consultative procedures rather than the experience of individual stewards and managers; this meant that the studies which were undertaken sought either to build up a picture of the social situation of the steward or to focus upon the broad pattern of institutional arrangements. These studies are of limited relevance to our present concerns.

There are a few later studies which are relevant. The first of these was undertaken by Storey. He investigated the range of issues negotiated in just under 100 establishments in engineering, brewing, transport and textiles in 1971 and 1978. His work has the distinct advantage of permitting fairly confident and reliable comparisons over time; but even the earlier survey postdates the initial thrusts towards reform. Nevertheless, it is clear from his data that there was a continuing reform process in most of the plants he studied (1980, pp. 111–23), so that this problem is less great than might at first be supposed.

Three further surveys can be compared. In 1968 Clarke *et al.* undertook a survey of firms in the private sector of manufacturing, construction and transport which included questions on areas of negotiation. The time of this study broadly overlaps with the beginnings of widespread reform. More recently (1976) the Department of Employment commissioned a survey of medium to large manufacuring plants (Knight, 1979) which permits some crude comparisons with the Clarke *et al.* study. The main differences between the two studies are: the substantially lower response rate in the Clarke *et al.* survey; the Department of Employment survey excludes construction, transport and communication which made up about 12 per cent of the Clarke *et al.* survey; in the latter a third or more of the sampled firms employed fewer than 200 people, the minimum size of establishment for inclusion in the Department of Employment survey; there are also slight variations in the exact questions asked and which are considered here: Clarke *et al.* asked questions which, for some respondents, might be of a hypothetical nature rather than relating to actual practice. This could mean that the 1968 data exaggerates the range of bargaining at that time. The third survey — that of Daniel and Millward (1983) — can be compared with the study reported by Knight. In this section, each of these three sets of roughly comparable data will be considered in turn.

Both the 1966 and 1973 surveys investigated the extent to which stewards, managers and foremen negotiated a range of broadly comparable issues. The published data do not permit comparisons of the specific issues negotiated at industry level. They do, however, permit comparisons of the number of issues negotiated. At first sight, it would seem that the average number of issues ever negotiated by stewards fell; but this is in fact due to factors such as the inclusion of NUR representatives in the 1966 but not in the 1973 survey. Even so, while only a quarter of stewards negotiated eleven or more issues in 1966, 40 per cent did so in 1973. Similarly, if we consider stewards in metal-handling trades, about 40 per cent in 1966 said they personally discussed and even settled with management eleven or more issues investigated (these covered quite detailed areas relating to wages, working conditions, hours of work, discipline and employment issues; see the Government Social Survey, 1968, p. 31). The 1973 survey found that about 45 per cent of broadly comparable stewards did so.

When we turn our attention to foremen, a similar picture emerges. Overall the average number of issues ever negotiated by foremen in 1966 was seven of those listed; in 1973 it was eleven. In metal-handling, the increase was from eight to twelve; in the rest of manufacturing the increase was even more dramatic — from five to eleven. Expressed differently, in 1966 30 per cent of foremen in the metal-handling trades claimed to negotiate eleven or more issues; in 1973, 66 per cent in metal manufacture and 50 per cent in mechanical and instrument engineering claimed to do so. When 'low bargainers', negotiating six or fewer issues, are considered, the figure for metal-handling trades in 1966 is found to be 47 per cent. This declined to less than a third of foremen in the 1973 survey.

Finally, a comparison of the 1966 and 1973 surveys indicates that for managers the average number of issues ever negotiated fell from sixteen to eleven; this trend occurred in both metal-handling and in the rest of manufacturing. Similarly, 70 per cent of managers negotiated eleven or more issues in 1966; only 57 per cent did so in 1973. This trend was found in both metal-handling and the rest of manufacturing.

The 1972 and 1973 surveys asked respondents whether, since assuming their positions, the amount and range of their bargaining activity had increased. The resulting picture is one of greater activity. Only about 10 per cent of any category of respondent claimed either range or amount had fallen. The 1973 survey, for example, found that the *net* proportion of respondents claiming to have experienced an increase in their range of bargaining (in other words, those claiming an increase less those claiming a decrease) was 31 per cent for senior and lower managers, 12 per cent for foremen and 20 per cent for stewards. (The significance of the detailed variations are considered below. These figures also suggest a slight slowing down in the rate of increase relative to the 1972 survey.) Similarly, data on changes in the amount of bargaining activity also indicate an increase. Net increases of 38 per cent for senior managers, 40 per cent for stewards and 22 per cent for foremen were found.

In the early stages of reform, at least, the comparison of the workplace industrial relations surveys indicates a general increase in the amount of bargaining activity. Moreover, the increase in negotiation was common across all issue areas; hence, for example, over half the stewards claimed increases in bargaining over wage issues and working conditions, and between a quarter and a third over hours of work, discipline and employment. The fact that the largest increase in bargaining for *all* groups was over working conditions is of particular interest, for it is precisely in this area, covering such issues as allocation and pace of work, job transfers and manning, and new jobs and machinery, that one might have expected reduced activity, particularly for foremen, if reform had 'worked'. Similarly, the second largest increase for all groups was over wage issues, where again the reform package would lead one to expect the reverse (although in this case the number of foremen experiencing an increase was substantially smaller than for any other group).

A similar picture of an increase in negotiation in the early years of reform emerges from a comparison between the work of Clarke *et al.*

and that reported by Knight. Daniel and Millward's 1980 study suggested, at the least, subsequent stability. Comparisons can be made on four issues: redundancy, disciplinary procedures, new working methods and matters relating to capital. As was noted above, the surveys employed different sampling methods: some allowance can be made for differences in size of firm, however, since Clarke *et al.* in places provide data which permit estimates of the proportion of establishments with more than 500 or 1,000 employees where particular issues would be negotiated, making comparison with the Department of Employment survey more reliable.

The Clarke *et al.* survey found that just under a quarter of all the firms studied would negotiate 'to discharge workers no longer needed'. This figure rose to 45 per cent in the case of those employing more than 1,000 people (1972, pp. 88, 99—100). Eight years later, the Department of Employment survey found that 96 per cent of companies negotiated over redundancy (1979, p. 32). Daniel and Millward only present data concerning negotiations at establishment level: in manufacturing they found that 75 per cent of establishments negotiated redundancies (p. 199). This suggests a slight fall compared with the 1976 figure of 85 per cent, but may reflect the smaller size distribution of the 1980 survey (and perhaps a centralization of negotiations over redundancies).

A similar dramatic increase in bargaining is indicated by the data on disciplinary procedures. The 1968 survey found that 36 per cent of firms would negotiate on this issue, a figure which increased to 50 per cent for those employing over 500 people (pp. 90, 109). The 1976 survey found that 99 per cent of firms negotiated disciplinary procedures. In 1980 the vast majority of plants (83 per cent) had such procedures, the majority being introduced in the last ten years (1983, pp. 160, 164).

Clarke *et al.* also investigated how many firms would negotiate 'to introduce new working methods'. They found that 38 per cent of firms would do so (39 per cent of those with more than 500 staff, p. 88). The Department of Employment survey investigated the extent of negotiation over 'major changes in production methods', an issue which, compared with the Clarke *et al.* question, is of greater significance and includes elements traditionally more central to managerial prerogative. Nevertheless, the survey found that 86 per cent of companies negotiated on this issue, suggesting a significant increase in bargaining over the period between the two surveys. The Department of Employment survey found that in two-thirds of cases such major changes were negotiated at establishment level. In 1980 Daniel and Millward found that 72 per cent of establishments negotiated this question (1983, p. 199).

The fourth area involves an even cruder comparison. Clarke *et al.* asked if companies would negotiate over the raising of additional capital or over the allocation of 'profits between investment, dividends, reserves, etc.'. None would do so. The Department of Employment survey found that 11 per cent of companies negotiated over capital investment (32). The figure is low, and the Clarke *et al.* questions 'tighter' in the sense that they relate to issues which have a less direct and obvious impact on the shop floor. But the comparison is suggestive of a growth of bargaining. Even more strikingly, in 1980 24 per cent of establishments appear to have negotiated on capital investment, although the exact meaning of 'negotiation' may vary (stewards were only half as likely to say negotiations over this matter took place, 1983, pp. 199, 182).

Greater confidence can be placed in Storey's surveys — they cover the same population and employ the same questions for both 1971 and 1978. Storey sought to investigate not 'conventional bargaining items such as wages' but 'more marginal items found to be sensitively poised as areas of contention' as well as issues traditionally reserved to management decision (1980, p. 128). Hence he asked about issues such as speed and quality of work, manning, job content, investment policy, ownership and scheduling of operations — twenty-five issues in all. He found that in a third of establishments in 1971 eleven or more of these issues were negotiated at workplace level; by 1978 this figure had risen marginally to 36 per cent. At the other extreme, 30 per cent negotiated zero to six issues in 1971, this figure falling to 27 per cent in 1978. Moreover, most of the manager and steward respondents to Storey's questionnaire claimed that there had been an increase in the range of bargaining (while none claimed that it had declined). Hence 89 per cent of managers and 66 per cent of stewards expressed this view (1980, p. 131).

Storey's data, then, suggest some increase in the range of bargaining, rather than a decline. Indeed, when consideration is turned to specific issues it is found that in only one area is there any significant decline in negotiation: the number of plants where negotiation was reported over redundancy fell from 56 per cent in 1971 to 50 per cent in 1978. On the other hand, there are fifteen issues on which 5 per cent or more establishments reported negotiations in 1978 which did not in 1971. Moreover, a number of these issues are of major and direct relevance to day-to-day productive efficiency, for they include not only shifts and discipline, but also manning (+11 per cent), rest periods (+8 per cent), job content (+9 per cent), and transfers of employees (+5 per cent).

The surveys considered here, then, in the main indicate an increase in the range and amount of bargaining. The main exception is that the amount of negotiation over redundancies and discipline was lower in the 1980 survey than in Knight's study. (This seems largely attributable to the inclusion of smaller establishments in the 1980 study; and, even if there were a real decline, it is of interest that it should be in these areas rather than issues more directly relating to the organization of work.) The early reformist and radical arguments therefore receive little support. However, it might still be the case that bargaining has become more centralized, as these theses would argue. Doubt has already been raised over this trend towards centralization in chapter 3. And, unfortunately, surveys conducted in the late 1970s did not investigate the precise levels at which bargaining took place. We have, therefore, to rely upon data from the studies undertaken in the early 1970s, although in Part II evidence relating to 1983 is discussed.

The 1973 workplace survey indicates no clear and absolute move towards centralization, for both 'normal' (as distinct from senior) stewards and foremen showed net increases in bargaining activity. Indeed, on the union side there was no difference in the net increase in the range of bargaining for stewards and senior stewards, indicating that there had not even been a relative centralization (1975, p. 33). On the management side, however, similar questions indicated a process of relative centralization; for the net increase in range of bargaining for both senior and lower managers was about 30 per cent, compared with only 12 per cent for foremen (1975, pp. 33, 130). It would seem, then, that relative centralization on the management side occurred but without a corresponding change on the steward side, suggesting that 'normal' stewards were negotiating at higher levels of management; if this was so, then the control of senior stewards could be reduced (cf. Batstone *et al.,* 1977). This possibility gains some support from crude comparisons of responses to questions concerning ease of access for stewards to managers above the level of foremen: in 1966, 89 per cent said they had this right, compared with 96 per cent in 1973 (the comparisons are especially crude since the published data do not permit any controls by industry; if one could it is probable that the increase would be even higher). Further, it appears that stewards may seek to deal with managers rather than foremen since the former are seen to be more likely to accept union demands (1975, pp. 69—70).

This picture is confirmed on the management side as far as the amount of negotiating activity is concerned — a net increase of 38 per cent for senior managers and of only 22 per cent for foremen (1975, pp. 26, 129). The 1973 survey does not give details concerning senior and other stewards. The report of the 1972 survey, however, does suggest some relative centralization: for while 58 per cent of stewards as a whole claimed an increase in negotiating activity, 72 per cent of senior stewards did so (1974, pp. 25—6). These findings, then, give somewhat greater support for the view that a process of relative centralization occurred on the steward side: but, again, it should be stressed that this is not an absolute centralization.

The logic of centralization was that it should facilitate the efficient use of labour. It is, therefore, useful to try to assess how far this has been the case. In both the 1966 and 1973 workplace surveys foremen were asked whether they 'thought that the kind of work done by the people they supervised could be better organized and arranged'. In 1966, 41 per cent of all foremen, and 46 per cent of those in metal-handling, thought this was the case (p. 113), a figure which rose to 45 per cent overall and 60 per cent in engineering in 1973 (p. 92).

In the 1966 survey senior managers were asked a question relating even more directly to industrial relations, namely, whether the organization of work could be improved 'if they had been free to arrange their labour force as they wished'. Fifty-seven per cent of those in metal-handling thought this to be the case. The later workplace surveys did not ask this question, but Marsh *et al.* did do so in 1969 in a study of engineering. They found that the proportion of managers agreeing with this view had increased to 74 per cent (1971, p. 20). Both surveys asked the managers expressing this view how far they thought trade unions were a factor in preventing them from using labour more efficiently. It would seem that over the period 1966—9, unions in engineering had imposed greater controls on the use of labour: for, of the full sample of metal-handling/engineering managers just over a quarter saw the unions as playing a significant 'obstructive' role in 1966 compared with about a half in 1969 (1968, p. 90; 1971, pp. 20, 101).

These comparisons can be crudely updated by looking at Storey's work. He investigated the significance of unilateral worker control and custom and practice. In 1978, unilateral control existed on 12 per cent of issues in engineering (1980, p. 139). Moreover, 'the six decision areas which shop stewards most frequently claimed were subject to the control of the workers in their own establishment' were remarkably similar to those over which managers told Marsh *et al.* in 1969 that restrictions were particularly likely to arise — manning, overtime allocation, transfer of employees, demarcation, speed of work and rest periods (1980, p. 136; 1971, p. 21).

But even if fractional bargaining increased so that there was no absolute centralization, it might still be the case — as reformists and radicals claimed — that bargaining became more rule-oriented and, to the extent that rules operated in management's interests, there was therefore an increase in control. Three approaches to this question are possible: the first is an investigation of job-based control — this is undertaken in a later section as is the second, the consideration of productivity data. The third is a consideration of the extent of formalization and its significance relative to informality.

The 1972 and 1973 workplace surveys found that there had been a significant increase in the range of subjects covered by workplace agreements, although custom and practice still appeared significant (1975, pp. 40—2). However, as Parker noted in a review of the various surveys, 'whether or not the workplace procedures were written down, a network of informal practices and "short-cuts" was very common' (1975, p. 98). Moreover, the 1973 survey found that collective agreements rarely covered issues relating to working conditions: for example, in only just over 10 per cent of plants did they deal with work allocation, or pace of work or manning of machines (1975, p. 28).

In reporting the 1973 survey, Parker suggests that 'the ratio between individual bargaining and collective agreement [on an issue] is an indication of the stewards' involvement in local bargaining' (1975, p. 29). While there are good reasons for questioning the significance of such ratios, it was nevertheless decided to calculate them for both the 1972 and 1973 surveys (questions on the coverage of collective agreements were not asked in the 1966 survey). Averaging the ratios for each of the items within each broad issue area, the following results are obtained (data from p. 28):

wage issues 0.996 (increase of 29 per cent over 1972);
working conditions 2.526 (increase of 41 per cent over 1972);
hours of work 1.108 (increase of 23 per cent over 1972);
discipline 1.977 (increase of 14 per cent over 1972);
employment issues 1.393 (increase of 86 per cent over 1972).

Two points are particularly worthy of note here. First, there appears to have been a systematic increase in steward involvement; second, the degree of steward involvement is very high in issues relating to working conditions, such as labour allocation, pace and quality of work, manning, job transfers and new machinery — the very areas where managerial discretion was to be increased and steward influence reduced through reform. If Parker's argument is correct, local bargaining appears to have increased.

One other point is significant. The assumption implicit (or sometimes explicit) in a good deal of debate concerning industrial relations reform is that restrictions on managerial freedom derive largely from work-group pressure rather than from formal union policy. If this is so, then centralization and formalization will reduce such restrictions. However, Marsh *et al.*'s survey of engineering managers throws doubt upon this view (at least for the earliest years of reform). First, 96 per cent of those who believed there were restrictions on the efficient use of labour said that the union was a factor in these 'problems'. Moreover, it was union policy at district level that was seen as the major source of difficulties. Within the plant, half the managers believed that shop stewards were a source of restriction either exclusively (40 per cent) or along with informal groups (1971, pp. 101–3).

It seems probable that formalization increased substantially after 1973. According to Daniel and Millward, for example, four-fifths of establishments had, by 1980, formal procedures relating to discipline and dismissals and individual grievances; three-fifths had procedures for pay and conditions disputes. Moreover, the increase in the use of job evaluation and possibly work study would also indicate increased formality — the former, for example, requires the writing of formal job descriptions. However, as later sections in this chapter and Part II indicate, the extent and significance of formalization over work organization issues appears limited even in the late 1970s and 1980s.

For the present the evidence suggests that reform led to an increase in the range and intensity of bargaining. While it should be recognized that the extent to which managerial prerogative was 'invaded' is very limited, it is nevertheless the case that a wider range of issues became the subject of bargaining. Moreover — as far as one can tell from survey evidence — the process of reform did not lead to a reduction in fractional bargaining over job-control issues. There is some evidence that bargaining may have increased more at higher levels within the establishment than at lower levels, but this was relative rather than absolute. Similarly, the movements towards reform do not appear to have removed informal practices, including what might loosely be termed custom and practice and unilateral worker/union regulation. Indeed, if anything, the restrictions upon managerial freedom may have tightened.

It should be stressed that the nature of the available data is far from ideal for assessing these developments. Nevertheless, the evidence from the surveys is strikingly consistent on the matters considered. It indicates that the hopes of reformers and the fears of radicals were both confounded by experience. More qualitative data on job-based control, evidence concerning the impact of specific reforms and data on labour productivity provide further support for this contention.

LABOUR PRODUCTIVITY

Industrial relations reform was intended by Donovan to facilitate increased efficiency and productivity. The preceding section has considered what, then, are essentially intervening variables — changes in methods of bargaining and the level, range and amount of bargaining. In these areas it has been argued that, in the main, the extent to which reform led to greater managerial freedom in the use of labour was limited; indeed, if anything, management's freedom of manoeuvre was reduced. If this is so, then one would — at the most simple level — expect there to be no increase in the rate of growth of productivity. On the other hand, the promoters of reform and its radical critics would anticipate a faster growth of labour productivity. In this section an attempt is made to assess these differing views.

The 'problem' of British productivity is generally seen to be two-fold: first, since before the turn of the century the rate of productivity growth has consistently been below that of other countries; and second, as a result, the absolute level of productivity in Britain is now, and has been for some years, below that of its major competitors.

On the first point Maddison, for example, has shown that the average annual compound growth rate of GDP per man hour for sixteen countries has consistently been above the British figure since 1870 (1979, p. 195). On the second point, Britain's slower rate of productivity growth meant that by the 1970s levels of real product per head were lower in Britain than in the main European countries: 'by 1973 . . . they were 30 per cent ahead of the UK' (Jones, 1976, p. 84). Even if comparisons are made with the USA, where the rate of productivity growth has been relatively slow over the post-war period, it is still the case that the 'productivity gap' 'has not been removed but, if anything . . . may have widened'. In 1950 the ratio in favour of the USA was 2.7, in 1975 it was 2.85 and by 1978, it is estimated, it was 3.0 (Prais, 1980, p. 193).

Hence, since the late 1960s, the annual average percentage change in output per employee in the UK has actually declined. In 1963—8 it was +4.4 per cent; it fell to +2.9 per cent for 1968—73, and in 1973—9 it fell even further to +0.9 per cent. While it is true that the rate at which the productivity gap was increasing relative to the average for OECD countries slowed down in the 1970s (OECD, 1982) it is still the case that it was increasing. In manufacturing the US/UK ratio of productivity increased between 1968 and 1971 from 2.89 to 2.91, while the Germany/UK ratio rose from 1.35 to 1.52 (Smith *et al.,* 1982, p. 5). At first sight, then, the labour productivity data give little, if any, support to the view that industrial relations reform achieved the ends of its promoters.

Changes in labour productivity are not, of course, solely attributable to changes in working practices. Also important are factors which facilitate growth (including government policy), the nature and distribution of the labour force, capital intensity, the adoption of new methods of production and the level of industrial development. And, of course, the state of the world economy is also extremely important, along with such 'chance' factors as oil crises and the discovery of oil and gas resources. The analysis of labour productivity is therefore extremely complex, and it is beyond the scope of this volume to undertake any such analysis here. What can be done, however, is first to look at explanations of the British productivity record to see how far 'industrial relations' factors figure, and, second, to examine the question of the link between industrial relations and productivity more directly. The first task can only be undertaken briefly here. But it is clear that many theories which seek to explain the British productivity record do involve labour relations factors, either explicitly or implicitly.

It has often been argued that high rates of growth of productivity are to be found in less developed economies which are 'catching up' with the more developed. Thus the rapid growth rates of many West European countries would be explained in terms of their catching up with the USA, whose productivity growth rates have been lower. This rather mechanistic model may be questioned on a number of grounds. First, it is an economist's convergence thesis and is, therefore, susceptible to many of the criticisms applied to convergence theories more generally (see, for example, Goldthorpe, 1971). Second, this approach would suggest that, as Britain began to lag further behind other major countries in terms of absolute productivity levels after the late 1960s, its rate of productivity growth would accelerate (see, for example, Allsopp, 1979, p. 256). This applied only for a few years in the early 1970s; hence if the theory does have any inherent validity, a set of factors fairly specific to Britain would have to be adduced to explain this country's failure to conform to the model — British industrial relations might constitute one candidate for this role.

Another theory explains productivity growth in terms of labour supply. Kaldor and Verdoorn argued that high growth in output, and so productivity, could be explained by the ability to attract labour from less productive sectors, notably agriculture, to more productive ones (1966). However, not only has Kaldor himself modified his position (1975), but also recent experience both in Britain and elsewhere casts doubt upon the credibility of this thesis, at least for the last decade or so. Allsopp argues:

> In the manufacturing sector, where there did appear to be a good relationship between employment and output, and hence the possibility of the operation of a labour constraint, productivity accelerated in the second half of the 1960s as a result of the 'shake outs' of labour. This did not lead, however, to more rapid growth . . . The international cross-section evidence also suggests that there was little relationship between employment input and output for manufacturing in the late 1960s and early 1970s. (1979, p. 258)

The level of investment is frequently put forward to explain low productivity and productivity growth in Britain. Data on levels of capital investment do indeed provide some support for this view: as a proportion of GDP it is lower in Britain than in most of its competitors (for example, Brown and Sherriff, 1979; it should, however, be remembered that, if manning levels are higher in Britain, data relating to capital per worker will tend to exaggerate the picture — in other words, the figures will reflect not only levels of investment but also working practices). Two points also counsel caution. First, while capital investment may be lower, this does not appear to mean that British capital equipment is inferior in some sense (see, for example, Bacon and Eltis, 1974; Caves, 1980, p. 170). Second, and more importantly, 'observed differences in capital intensity . . . contribute nothing to explaining differences in relative productivity' (Caves, 1980, p. 171). Caves' study used a less than ideal measure of capital intensity, but Carrington and Edwards (1979) found that the productivity of UK investment between 1960 and 1976 tended to be lower than that for other countries; for example, it was less than half the German figure (1979). Nor, it seems, can this difference be explained primarily in terms of the concentration of investment in different industrial sectors for the period under consideration (Elliott and Hughes, 1976). One factor put forward to explain these differences in capital productivity has been industrial relations (see, for example, Jacobs *et al.,* 1978).

Some economists argue that productivity increases depend upon a growth of output. Wenban-Smith's recent analysis of productivity in individual industries provides some support for this view, but he notes that

> the relation is not equally strong in both directions; that is, of all

the manufacturing industries in which productivity growth improved, only half also increased their output growth. On the other hand, where output growth increased between the two periods, three-quarters of the industries also improved their productivity growth rates. (1981, p. 61)

There are also problems in identifying the exact direction of causality in these relationships: it is quite plausible to suggest that higher productivity is a factor in output growth, and that market pressures may be of such a kind as to increase labour productivity due to the demise of less efficient firms (this is noted by Wenban-Smith).

Low productivity (growth) in Britain has also been attributed to 'the balance of payments position, or the exchange rate and the development of exports' (Allsopp, 1979, p. 258). But, as Caves and Krause point out, recent British experience offers very limited support for this view (1980, pp. 8—9). They conclude that 'the argument that Britain's economic problems have been caused by its links with the rest of the world is unconvincing' (p. 10). The view that high import prices lead to inflation and hence lack of competitiveness, for example, introduces inflationary wage demands as a key factor in price rises; but if labour relations were not central, then 'low import prices should lead to low inflation, and this is not the case'. It follows that 'the real explanation [of inflation] lies in the behaviour of domestic labour markets rather than of import prices' (1980, p. 8).

The study of British economic performance by the Brookings Institution argues that policies of macro-economic management cannot be seen as a primary factor in low productivity and performance over the last two decades. Citing the findings of a study by teams of economists who sought to assess the impact of alternative policies in the period 1964 to 1977, they conclude that 'we cannot convict the managers of causing the disappointing economic performance through inept setting of the macro instruments' (1980, p. 11). Similarly, explanations in terms of the scale of government economic activity, taxation or the distribution of income do not stand up once comparisons are made with other countries (Phelps-Brown, 1977).

Clearly, many of the factors alluded to in the previous discussion play some role in an explanation of low productivity (growth) in Britain. Several of them, however, assume significance in part because of labour relations and other institutional factors. As the Brookings Institution study argues:

British labour has taken on a linchpin role among alleged adverse influences on inflation in the short-run and productivity in the long-run. (1980, p. 16)

The operation of the economy involves social processes and hence the pursuit by various interest groups of their own specific goals. That is, the relationships between economic indicators are created by the interaction of social groups. As Aaronovitch has recently stressed, one has to recognize 'the importance of class and institutional relationships in economic growth. Matters like investment and productivity have to be analysed not as things that have the ability by themselves to change the growth rate of economies (it is clear that they have not) but as part of a dynamic structure' (1981, p. 69).

Such a view, of course, underlay industrial relations reform. It is also reflected in many economists' attempts to explain low productivity (growth) in Britain. Having suggested that other sets of factors cannot — at least by themselves — provide a satisfactory explanation of this fact, we can now turn to the second task indicated at the beginning of this section — evidence concerning the impact of labour relations on productivity.

The view that labour relations has been an important factor in low productivity (growth) in British industry has long been commonly held: recently, it has been propounded with renewed vigour not only in government policy, but also in the works of a wide range of writers, for example Kahn-Freund (1979), and Kilpatrick and Lawson (1980). These writers emphasize patterns of behaviour which trace their origins to the nineteenth century (and hence can be seen as consistent with theories of institutional sclerosis; see, for example, Olson, 1982). Looking at more recent experience in various industries, Caves expressed productivity in each British industry as a ratio of productivity in its counterpart in the USA, and then sought to explain variations in the productivity shortfalls. He did this for the years 1963, 1967 and 1970/2. Hence his work covers the years surrounding our key date of reform. He found that there was no tendency for poorly performing British industries to catch up on their American counterparts: where productivity was low, the gap was increasing (pp. 176—7). This picture is supported by Elliott and Hughes' comparison of British and German industrial productivity (1976). Moreover, Caves found that productivity growth tended to be slower for industries concentrated in the older industrial regions even when 'technological opportunity' was (crudely) controlled for. He also found a negative, but not statistically significant, influence for 'labour disturbances'. Wragg and Robertson, however, found a stronger negative relationship between conflict and productivity for the period 1963 to

1973, and a weak negative relationship between productivity and the proportion of the industry's labour force covered by collective bargaining arrangements (1977; the utility of the indicator employed for the latter purpose is, however, open to question). Ball and Skeoch similarly found for 1973 that 'productivity declines as the proportion of the industry's workforce covered by collective agreements increases' (1981, p. 44).

Caves concludes his analysis in the following terms:

> the productivity performance in Britain, compared with those of other countries, varies significantly and persistently from industry to industry. Furthermore, no evidence was found that the laggard sectors are catching up — if anything the forces that make productivity low also make it grow slowly, and the low-productivity sectors are straying further from the pack. (p. 179)

In seeking to explain 'the traits that mark UK manufacturing industries for slow extinction' he points to

> those stuck with the heritage of divisive labour-management relations and located primarily in old industrial regions. My statistical evidence suggests that the difficulty lies not in union organisation and the presence of collective bargaining arrange-ments per se, but in long-standing attitudes of the workforce that sustain hostility to change and co-operation. (p. 179)

In addition, he argues that there is evidence to support the view that poor management is a factor in explaining low productivity (p. 180).

Prais investigated the 'productivity gaps' between British and German and American manufacturing industry up to the early 1970s. His conclusion was not dissimilar to that of Caves. He attributed Britain's poor relative performance primarily to 'the technical calibre of its workforce' and 'the social and legal system which governs the way its members work together' (1981, p. 272).

Similarly, in 1976 Pratten and Atkinson reviewed twenty-five industry studies of productivity over the years 1944 to 1975 and indicated that there was no evidence of any decline in 'overmanning and inefficiency'. Indeed, to the extent that any pattern can be identified, it would seem that 'management failures' may be of less importance, but 'labour restrictive practices' were imposing a growing constraint on higher productivity. A more recent review of industry studies also suggests the importance of worker and union controls in explaining low productivity (Taylor, 1982, pp. 79—98).

This is not to maintain that labour relations are the sole or even the primary cause of the British productivity gap. Smith *et al.*, for example, note that while 'labour force quality and industrial relations exert an influence on international performance', comparative capital intensity, scale of activity and rate of output growth are also relevant (1982). In a study of productivity levels in broadly comparable plants of multinational companies in the UK, Germany, France and North America, Pratten tried to assess the significance of labour factors. About a fifth of the inferior British performance relative to North America he attributed to strikes, major restrictive practices and other manning issues. Similar factors accounted for about a third of the difference between France and the UK, and almost half of the Germany—UK difference (1976, p. 61).

A number of studies, therefore, indicate that there are organizational and institutional factors other than 'direct' labour relations variables which are likely to be significant in explaining low productivity. Many of these are related to the kinds of factor highlighted in the discussion of management in chapter 2 — the qualifications of management and the priorities embedded in management structure. Two wider sets of theories or accounts of growth rates and performance are of relevance here. The first is the thesis put forward by Williams *et al.* (1983) that the relatively inferior performance of British manufacturing is attributable primarily to the 'institutional environment', and in particular the dominance of financial interests: these serve to divert corporate priorities away from physical productivity and complicate funding for long-term productive investment. However, their argument underplays the significance of industrial relations: for Britain to be behind 'less than a decade' (p. 37) is a great deal when the average annual growth in real value added in OECD countries between 1960 and 1980 was nearly 5 per cent and when British growth was still lower than that of other OECD countries. Rather, the argument which flows from this volume, and particularly chapter 2, is that these institutional weaknesses are intimately related to the pattern of industrial relations and the 'failures' of reform.

The second relevant type of argument is that which seeks to explain low productivity growth in terms of the nature of interest groups and the development of institutional sclerosis over time, as such groups are able to control the nature of development in their own interests (see, for example, Olson, 1982). While such theories confront numerous problems (see, for example, Mueller, 1983) they do appear to have some relevance: it has been noted in the preceding pages that a number of studies refer to 'longstanding' problems, while it has often been stressed that current 'problems' of industrial relations find their origins in the nineteenth century. The argument over the continued dominance of financial interests might also be incorporated into such a mould. And it follows from such arguments that it would be extremely difficult to introduce reform fully and efficiently if it endangered dominant interests. Our findings concerning the limited intrusion of the 'reformist' rationale into management thinking and the limited scale of change in sectional steward organizations would be consistent with such an institutional account. These themes are taken up more fully in chapter 9.

This section, however, has looked at 'explanations' of productivity and its growth which take little account of reform as such. Given the emphasis upon labour relations in such explanations, it is perhaps a rather sad comment that no studies have been published which cover recent years and specifically include an analysis of the impact of reform. It is, nevertheless, possible to build up a very crude picture — and, if nothing else, its very crudity might incite others to undertake a more serious analysis. The crudity derives both from the data themselves and the failure to control for other variables (although such weaknesses are far from unique to this discussion).

Using data from the *Monthly Digest of Statistics,* the *New Earnings Surveys* and the *Department of Employment Gazette,* it is possible to investigate how far the coverage of collective agreements is associated with changes in output per head for the period 1973—78 in twenty industries. If reform had been successful, then productivity should have grown more in those sectors where collective agreements were more common, and particularly where local agreements had been made (it should be noted that the *New Earnings Survey* lumps together 'company, district and local agreements', but district and local agreements — according to Brown (1981, p. 12) — cover less than 1 per cent of all manual workers in manufacturing). As for earlier periods, the results suggest that the greater the coverage of collective agreements, the lower the rate of productivity growth. No variation emerges when the coverage of local agreements (compared with other collective agreements) is considered but the relationship between collective agreements and low productivity growth is stronger for 1973—8 than for 1968—73. This suggests — and we can state the matter no more confidently — that collective agreements became a greater constraint on productivity and that local agreements had no effect upon performance.

If industrial relations reform entailed further union recognition, then it might be expected that union membership — particularly growth in membership — would be associated with higher productivity. The data on union density collected by Bain and Price (1980) up to 1974 permit an analysis of thirteen industries. There is a negative relationship between productivity growth in the period 1973—8 and union density in 1974. Change in union density between 1968 and 1974 had a weak, negative relationship with productivity growth.

Other analyses which are possible with available data are even more crude. The IRRU survey permits an investigation of eleven industrial sectors. Here only the strongest relationships, where no comparable official data exist, will be mentioned. The correlation between single-employer bargaining in 1977—8 and productivity growth between 1968 and 1978 is −0.2695; between regular meetings of stewards with management and productivity growth the correlation is −0.2682. Other relationships between aspects of procedural reform and productivity growth are much weaker: those suggesting a negative relationship include the coverage of the closed shop, the recognition of a multiplicity of unions and recognition of senior shop stewards. Those suggesting very weak but positive relationships include the existence of a specialist industrial relations director, regular steward meetings, the existence of a full-time shop steward, check-off and the increased formalization of industrial relations over the last five years. Turning to substantive reforms, a weak negative relationship was found between job evaluation and productivity growth. The strongest relationship of all, however, was that between productivity growth and work study, the coefficient being −0.6982.

It must, again, be emphasized that many other factors are likely to be more important than these reform variables in explaining productivity growth, and that the data are far from ideal. It is quite conceivable that, were these other factors included in the analysis, relationships between productivity growth and reform might become more positive. Hence great caution is required. But the overall conclusion indicated by these data is that reform was not associated with increased productivity growth rates. At the minimum, they suggest that reform has failed to match the aspirations of its promoters and the fears of its radical critics. This picture is supported by evidence concerning specific features of reform strategy, the subject of subsequent sections.

PRODUCTIVITY BARGAINING

The preceding sections have indicated that the process of reform rarely imposed severe limitations on the level and nature of bargaining and, if anything, was associated with a greater range and depth of bargaining.

In addition, evidence at the macro-level suggests that reform was not associated with an increase in productivity growth rates. In those areas where labour controls were in the past seen as imposing severe limitations upon company performance, the same was true in the seventies.

In this section we shift from a consideration of 'macro'-data to focus upon a key feature of reformist attempts to increase productivity, namely, productivity bargaining. The Donovan Commission placed considerable emphasis upon such bargaining and even more upon its underlying rationale — the linking of 'negotiations about pay' with 'considerations of efficiency' (1968, p. 85). This view was also reflected in a number of incomes policies in which increases above the pay limit were permitted if they were associated with greater productivity, while 'quangos' such as the National Board for Prices and Incomes were keen supporters of productivity agreements. Brown felt able to describe the productivity bargains of the late sixties as 'the first symptoms of a continuing revolution in British industrial relations', in the directions prescribed by Donovan (1974, p. 421). Similarly, McKersie and Hunter argued 'that productivity bargaining has been the vehicle which has given substance to plant-level negotiations. In other words, productivity bargaining has provided the focus and content which has made plant bargaining a reality' (1973, p. 339).

In the late sixties, there was a tremendous growth in productivity agreements. Over the years 1967 to 1969 more than 4,000 agreements, covering about a quarter of all those employed (Nightingale, 1980, pp. 319—20), were recorded. But in the early seventies it appears that productivity agreements, at least those explicitly labelled as such, became less common. Brown attributes this to earlier experience of productivity agreements during periods of incomes policy. It is commonly argued that a large number of 'fake' agreements were made under incomes policies in order to pay increases in excess of the legal maximum. This meant, in Brown's view, that the term 'productivity bargain' 'will never recover from the semantic degradations into which incomes policies have forced it' (1974, p. 421). Nevertheless, he argued, the underlying idea of negotiating changes in working practice continued so that 'to some extent . . . we are all productivity bargainers now' (1974, p. 421).

In the late seventies the notion of productivity bargaining reappeared, again stimulated by the particular form of incomes policies developed by the Labour Government, although it was called the 'SFPD' — the self-financing productivity deal. By 1978 a majority of firms had either actually introduced such schemes, or were planning to do so. White found in his survey of 401 firms that just over half had 'some type of self-financing productivity scheme' (1981, p. 81).

Over its somewhat chequered career, productivity bargaining has taken a wide variety of forms. The literature abounds with distinctions between different types of bargain and approach — the total as against the partial agreement, the productivity agreement as against a less specific efficiency agreement, the direct approach (focusing upon trading off increased skill and effort utilization for higher earnings) and the indirect approach (focusing upon a more integrative approach). In the more recent period of productivity deals the distinctions have become even more profuse.

Many of the distinctions, however, focus upon the central tension which underlies industrial relations reform more generally. On the one hand, there is the idea of the productivity agreement as the outcome of 'pressure bargaining', involving a straight exchange of changes in working practice for more money. On the other hand, emphasis is placed upon changes in organizational philosophy and approaches to labour relations which facilitate changes in working practice as a feature of everyday life, rather than as the occasional product of lengthy sessions at the bargaining table.

In practice, also, there appears to have been an uneasy tension between these two elements. Many of the early promoters of productivity bargaining were keen to emphasize that it consisted of much more than the buying and selling of working practices. But at the same time, they were aware of the very real risks that a focus upon 'organizational climate' might lead away from significant change in working practices. McKersie and Hunter, for example, proposed a 'midway' strategy which they termed 'mixed bargaining'.

It has often been argued, as we have seen, that the 'loop-hole' in incomes policies in the late sixties encouraged productivity agreements which, in form if not in substance, were of the 'direct' type, focusing even more than previous agreements upon direct increases in effort rather than, as in the earlier period, broader changes in organizational practice (see, for example, Nightingale, 1980). The National Board for Prices and Incomes then became more favourably inclined towards efficiency agreements which, it believed, permitted 'constantly rising levels of efficiency'; this could be achieved only with 'close and continuous cooperation between management and workers' (1969, p. 42). In the more recent period, agreements appear to have been both of the direct and indirect kind, (see, for example, White, 1981; IDS Reports 162 and 186).

In any event, despite the early optimism concerning productivity bargaining, assessments of the level of success fell steadily in the late sixties and early seventies. McKersie and Hunter, for example, pointed out:

> The NBPI estimated the proportion of soundly based agreements as 75 per cent in early 1969. Clegg estimated the proportion at 50 per cent in early 1971 and the EEF at 25 per cent by mid-1971. No doubt the passage of time has made more accurate appraisal possible and the earlier optimism and rhetoric has given way to more honest assessment of results. (1973, p. 54)

Assessment of the more recent spate of productivity agreements is more difficult: the Incomes Data Services studies cited earlier suggest the possibility — if not the probability — of 'fake' deals, but these surveys were not really of a kind to permit any real evaluation. Similarly, in his survey White was not able to make any clear assessment of the efficacy of productivity deals: but he did find that, while negotiated productivity rates were not linked significantly with turnover or absenteeism, they were associated with higher than average industrial disputes; self-financing productivity schemes facilitated recruitment and reduced turnover, but were also associated with a high incidence of industrial disputes (1981, pp. 127—8). Survey data, however, confront problems of identifying cause and effect.

One means of developing a picture of more recent experience is through the reports of the Price Commission and, to a lesser extent, the Monopolies Commission. These studies provide some detailed and 'hard' evidence concerning productivity schemes in sixteen companies (several studies have been made of some companies; studies considered here are Monopolies Commission, 1980, 1981a, b; Price Commission, 1978a, b, c; 1979a, b, c, d, e, f, g, h, i, j, k). The data indicate that there were clear and significant increases in productivity in only a quarter of the cases; moreover, in at least two of these 'successes', higher productivity seems largely attributable to major schemes of capital investment. A similar picture of the limited 'success' of productivity bargaining has recently been drawn by Clegg, who concluded that:

> the long run economic gains have not been large. It is not at all easy to discern any impact of productivity bargaining on the overall performance of the economy; and many of the companies which had negotiated apparently successful productivity deals in the sixties were again faced with problems of low performance and substantial over-manning during the seventies. (1979, p. 143)

How is one to explain this 'failure'? A common explanation, as already noted, is that productivity agreements failed precisely because they became a means of evading incomes policies. But this view may be questioned.

It is worth recalling, first, that the aim of the 'loop-holes' in incomes policies was precisely to encourage productivity agreements. The National Board for Prices and Incomes, indeed, expressed the view that pay increases based on productivity 'should displace pay settlements on grounds of "comparability" ' (1969, p. 43). To believe that such intentions are always reflected in practice would, of course, be naive. It is, none the less, worth remembering that the shape of the relevant incomes policies was such as to give management a distinctly favourable position in relation to the workforce: if workers wanted pay increases above the norm, then management could insist upon higher productivity. If management wished to raise wages — for example, to recruit labour — then it does not automatically follow that it would be prepared to throw away an opportunity to increase productivity at the same time. Consistent with this view is the fact that, even under incomes policies, productivity agreements appeared to involve significant changes in the 'intensity of labour and included "penalty clauses" and "managerial prerogative" clauses in later agreements' suggesting 'a tendency on the part of managers to accept [a] reversal to "management by fiat" ' (Nightingale, 1980, pp. 326—7). The argument, then, that incomes policies ruined productivity bargaining is not immediately self-evident. Furthermore, it can be argued that without the stimulus provided by incomes policies, productivity bargaining would scarcely have got off the ground.

McKersie and Hunter's study supports the view that incomes policies encouraged more hasty agreements, with the consequence that they focused upon direct means of increasing labour productivity. However, their study suggests equally that the impact of incomes policies in fostering a 'direct' as against an 'indirect' approach can be easily exaggerated. For, first, they argue that 'indirect' approaches have always been rare. Second, they did exist during incomes policies. Third, McKersie and Hunter point out that the indirect approach is not only a lengthy, but also a 'high risk' method. Fourth, and relatedly, they found that companies frequently switched from the indirect to the direct approach: as one of their informants put it, 'at some point we have to get down to the nitty-gritty job of using carrots and sticks' (1973, p. 312).

If 'genuine' productivity agreements fail to lead to higher productivity, then the incomes policy explanation is less credible. The near-evangelical promulgation of 'success stories' of productivity agreements a decade ago shows a remarkable similarity to the more recent spate of 'success stories' about autonomous work groups: both frequently expatiate in detail over the intention and the process of introduction, but then become vague and confuse aspiration with reality when it comes to assessing results.

At the same time, discussions of productivity bargaining frequently highlight the need for care, planning and training. This is quite proper and reasonable in the sense that most schemes for change have to be tailored to the specific situation. But when the vast majority of schemes end in failure and this is explained in terms of lack of preparation, lack of education or a basic misunderstanding of the philosophy of productivity bargaining, it seems reasonable to suggest that more fundamental problems exist. Similarly, success is often defined not in terms of higher levels of productivity, but improved relationships (see, for example, Daniel and Macintosh, 1973). It is worth asking what the purpose of such improved relationships would be: the answer for management is presumably higher productivity and yet, as the quotation from Clegg above indicates, this does not appear to have been the result.

The basic concept of a productivity agreement is that workers receive some form of recompense for improved productivity which is directly attributable to their efforts. Unless an extremely indirect approach is adopted, such agreements therefore rest upon the view that it is possible to make such an attribution. This may in reality be difficult for a number of reasons. The process of production may be such that it is difficult to attribute improved productivity to any particular group and so to determine 'proper' rewards; productivity may rise or fall due less to variations in effort than to technical manning requirements which preclude marginal changes in labour inputs in direct proportion to changes in output; problems of measurement of output may be significant in many cases; and so one might go on (see Batstone *et al.*, 1984). In short, there may often be severe problems in separating out the contribution of labour. This is perhaps seen most clearly in the case of new technology: it may require no greater effort or skill on the part of the workers and therefore one might argue that they should receive no payment for working with new technology. On the other hand, that technology may introduce new features into the work situation, and also produces nothing unless it is put into operation. The marginal analysis of neo-classical economics offers no solution here. In short, the very concept of productivity bargaining may often be extremely problematical.

Much of the literature on productivity bargaining identifies various stages in the process: these typically include planning, negotiation, implementation and operation, and maintenance. In looking at the dilemmas of productivity bargaining it is useful to consider these various stages in turn.

In planning schemes to improve productivity, great emphasis is placed by 'experts' upon careful analysis of the existing work situation and the exact means by which productivity can be improved (at least in those cases which involved the adoption of a direct approach). The lack of careful planning has often been seen as a factor in 'failures' in productivity bargaining. The obvious question is why such failures appear to be so common. One answer might concern the conflict between direct and indirect approaches; another, related, explanation might involve the very concept and applicability of productivity bargaining in a particular context.

The process of planning may be problematical. Typically, a relatively senior manager or group will be given the task of developing plans; they occupy a particular position within the structure of power and interest which constitutes the managerial hierarchy, and their specific responsibilities will tend to differentiate them from other managers. They may constitute a threat to the routines and interests of some managers (and, equally, a potential ally to others). Their position may, therefore, cut them off from particular sets of information and this fact may in turn foster in them a very different perspective from that of other managers. The result of such processes may be that they find it extremely difficult to develop a 'realistic' plan of action.

These processes of social isolation of the planners appear to be recognized, if only indirectly, in a number of studies which emphasize the importance of an 'educational' programme within management. In other words, the planners have to seek to win other managers to their perspective. This may well be difficult; a thoroughgoing productivity scheme may constitute a fundamental challenge to the traditional modes of operation within management (see chapter 2). Indeed this fact is often seen as one of its virtues (see, for example, Flanders, 1967; Donovan, 1968; McKersie and Hunter, 1973). But it is by no means certain that such a challenge will be successful: managers have vested interests in particular patterns of action; the policies contained within schemes for improved productivity may conflict with other priorities or endanger various modes of intra-managerial and management—worker accommodation. The controls which are necessary in a tight productivity scheme impinge upon management as much as upon workers. And, like workers, managers demonstrate considerable skill in the manipulation and evasion of controls (see, for example, Hopwood, 1974).

Hawkins has pointed to similar problems in the case of efficiency agreements. First, there is the problem of measuring improved efficiency deriving from 'greater flexibility in working practices on an informal, day-to-day basis' (1972, p. 187). Second, such day-to-day, almost *ad hoc* improvements in productivity depend importantly upon the foreman. But, as Hawkins points out, productivity bargaining, among other things, both reduced the power of supervisors and alienated them (see, more generally, Child and Partridge, 1982). Accordingly, it can be argued, there are likely to be severe problems in inducing them to play their vital role in raising productivity.

Between planning and implementation is the stage of negotiation; and here, again, various problems crop up frequently. First, and most obviously, union representatives may simply refuse to engage in productivity bargaining, or workers may refuse to accept proposals emanating from such bargaining. A number of studies refer to the failure of management to achieve union agreement to productivity deals (see, for example, Nightingale, 1980). In addition union representatives became less and less prepared to engage in such agreements: this was even true of the classic Fawley case (Flanders, 1964). Similarly, a number of writers have suggested that as productivity bargaining became more widespread, unions began to impose stricter conditions upon agreement (see, for example, Nightingale, 1980; Fox, 1974).

Even where agreement is finally reached, therefore, it may not accord with management's initial plans. Indeed, this frequently appears to be the case. The process of bargaining may mean that what was initially a fairly tightly conceived and direct approach on the part of management may result in an agreement which is really of an indirect nature. That is, instead of specifying in detail agreed changes in working practices the agreement merely states that, in exchange for higher wages, the union(s) will engage in discussions to achieve commensurate savings in labour costs (see, for example, Batstone *et al.,* 1984).

In practice, it is often difficult to assess the efficacy of such 'understandings' from management's point of view. There is no guarantee that changes in working practices will result; union representatives can often explain any failure to increase productivity in terms of managerial behaviour or technical and market factors, and hence absolve themselves of any 'blame'.

The obvious question, therefore, is why management should be prepared to make such agreements. One answer is that they really do believe that such agreements are useful. Managers, aware of the realities of power, may believe that such general commitments are better than nothing. For those negotiating agreements, such *claims* may be an important means of defending their own position within the micro-politics of management and/or of defending the position of the company more generally (see, for example, Batstone *et al.,* 1984).

Even where managements and unions sign agreements on, for example, labour flexibility there may be severe limitations upon managerial freedom of action. In particular, agreements frequently include mutuality or *status quo* clauses. The TGWU, for example, warned of management's attempt to increase its control, and recommended union resistance. It advised:

> every effort should be made to extend the subjects that shall be determined by mutual agreement between employers and employees through their trade unions.
>
> The policy is not one of a once-for-all bargain, but a continuous process of bargaining in which the union keeps open all its options to deal with the new circumstances and opportunities for gains for its members as and when they arise. It is equally important that every member understands this principle of mutuality and the objectives of employers in trying to buy it out. (Quoted in McKersie and Hunter, 1973, p. 331)

The TUC similarly recommended *status quo* clauses in its 1964 'Programme for Action', while in 1970 the CBI also advocated *status quo* provisions as a means of reducing disputes and encouraging observance of procedures ('Disputes Procedures', April 1970).

Certainly such checks upon managerial freedom have been a feature of many agreements. In the case of British Leyland, for example, management was forced to concede that 'proposed man assignments' and 'the applicable work and time standards' should be given 'to the workers concerned and to Union representatives' and that 'man assignments shall be mutually agreed'. Many other matters were similarly to be 'resolved domestically by mutual agreement' (Totsuka, 1981, p. 21).

Agreements relating to such matters as greater labour flexibility and mobility frequently included conditions which might permit negotiation over their application. One agreement on the utilization of manpower, for example, included at a number of points the phrase 'in appropriate circumstances' as well as a final paragraph stating that 'the method of implementing the principles will be the subject of local discussions and agreements on each works or site'. The Weekly Staff Agreement at ICI similarly emphasized local agreement, and labour flexibility was limited by the conditions that 'only the Signatury Unions in possession of the work can agree to any other trade or grade performing any of that work' and that 'each Signatory Union reserves the right as to whether or not to accept any particular work from any other trade or grade' (Roeber, 1975, pp. 327, 331).

The nature of agreements reached on productivity, therefore, may institute *de jure* rights for union representatives to negotiate over the implementation of an agreement. In some situations, therefore, productivity bargaining has extended and consolidated union power, and often shifted that power closer to the workforce (see, for example, Gallie, 1978; Hawkins, 1971, p. 25). Indeed, a number of writers have argued that greater participation was one of the key features of productivity bargaining (see, for example, Stettner, 1969, pp. 168—80). McKersie and Hunter point out that under traditional forms of consultation 'real' participation was usually confined to 'peripheral issues'. They continue:

> By contrast, productivity bargaining has brought participation into the centre of the picture in two respects. Participation has been a necessary pre-requisite as well as a resulting condition of productivity bargaining. (1973, p. 334)

It has sometimes been argued that such an extension of participation occurred only in the process of negotiating the agreement, when management discussed a wide range of issues with union representatives. But, the argument runs, once the agreement was signed, day-to-day negotiation was both reduced and more rule-oriented (see above); the rules shaping workplace behaviour are seen as being more managerially-oriented than was custom and practice.

The thrust of the preceding argument is to cast doubt upon these contentions. For mutuality and the conditional and qualifying statements relating to working practices in agreements may open up new possibilities for bargaining on a day-to-day basis. To the extent that these conditions exist and to the extent that the agreement covers areas not previously the subject of worker and union influence, then productivity agreements may expand fractional bargaining. Even where they cover areas previously the subject of custom and practice, they may provide a new legitimacy for worker influence and control.

Similarly, our argument casts doubt upon the significance of the view that such fractional bargaining is more rule-oriented *and* against worker interests. More specifically, three points follow from the argument. First, to the extent that rules emanating from an agreement provide for union influence in their application and reflect union interests in other ways, then rule-oriented bargaining might further promote workers' interests. In other words, we are questioning the view that rule-orientation is necessarily a managerial orientation. A good example of this is cited in one of Purcell's case studies. In one company he studied an agreement was successfully achieved which contained clauses concerning labour flexibility. But in a crisis that agreement had to be relaxed in order to achieve an efficient level of performance (1981, p. 178). In other words, the agreement appears to have imposed significant constraints upon labour flexibility.

Second, the clauses in productivity agreements may provide an opportunity for the intrusion of 'custom and practice' and a set of less formal agreements resulting from past fractional bargaining. Indeed, such arguments may be further strengthened by the way in which agreements frequently explicitly recognize unions' or workers' job property rights (as in the ICI agreement cited above).

In discussing the process of negotiation, we have moved inevitably into issues concerning the implementation of agreements. Here a number of points from the earlier discussion are relevant — the problems of measurement and planning; the differing interests within management; the bias in workers' favour which may be built into rules. But there are also other important elements.

First, companies typically operate in an uncertain environment. Plans may not in fact reflect the future accurately, so that when implemented they may create additional problems. Patterns of demand may be such as to create difficulties for implementing new working practices; new technical developments may have a similar effect. Given the nature of the actual agreements signed, changes in working practices may serve as obstructions to greater efficiency (see, for example, Price Commission, 1979, p. 29).

Second, workers and stewards may use the new rules as a check upon managerial freedom. We have already suggested that the nature of the agreed rules may contribute to this. But even those rules which apparently provide management with a good deal of freedom may in practice be used as a check upon its freedom. Hence, for example, Roeber notes that at ICI 'the very success of the agreement in laying down new ways of defining and assessing jobs' could result in 'new, complex demarcations', particularly where a 'tradition of teamwork and flexibility was broken down to be replaced by rigid job definition and demarcation' (1975, pp. 275–6). Nichols and Beynon similarly point to the way in which workers employed new formal job descriptions against the company, using them as a basis for refusing mobility or for demanding upgrading (1977, pp. 137–8, 144). Such possibilities appear to be particularly rife where conflicts exist between elements of an agreement, for example, job descriptions and requirements for mobility. They may be exacerbated by management's failure to realize the limitations of mobility imposed by specialist training (see, for example, Batstone *et al.,* 1984).

These problems may be exacerbated by the structure of authority implicit in a productivity agreement which formally prevents local accommodation between supervision and stewards (see, for example, Roeber, 1975, p. 275). Two broad courses of action are possible in this situation: compliance with the formal agreement or some form of fractional, 'informal' bargaining. It appears that both managers and workers often choose the latter course of action: in the case cited above from Nichols and Beynon's study, upgrading resulted. In some cases formal procedures and rulings are used as a threat by stewards and foremen to encourage informal deals (Purcell, 1981, p. 138). As a result, the aims of those managers who designed the productivity deal may be obstructed. Armstrong *et al.,* for example, cite cases where mobility was limited because of the way in which measured day work was introduced (p. 98) where only upgradings were used (and not downgrading, p. 102) and where elements of the control system simply fell into disuse (p. 104). Nor should these events appear particularly surprising. To the extent that differing interests exist within the workplace, one might expect that workers and managers would engage in the tactical invocation and interpretation of rules. Crozier, for example, has highlighted the way in which rules may be used as a check upon managerial discretion (1964).

Looking at the question from another angle, one could argue that productivity deals, like any other form of agreement, have to be incorporated into the pre-existing pattern of norms and understandings:

> The signing of a formal agreement is only a starting-point: case law has to be developed and this occurs through debates and disputes, which serve ultimately both to develop a consensus upon the interpretation of specific clauses, and a network of informal agreements and custom and practice which make the agreement meaningful in particular contexts. (Batstone *et al.,* 1978, pp. 52−3)

In this process, clauses in the new agreement may be subjected to considerable reinterpretation in order to make them consistent with practices and understandings that have greater legitimacy in the eyes of workers, stewards and local managers. As Eldridge and Cameron point out, at shop-floor level custom and practice may have a good deal more legitimacy than agreements signed at a higher level (1968).

It is, of course, possible that workers and stewards — and even local managers — seek to prevent the implementation of an agreement. Such cases are cited in a number of studies (for example, Purcell, 1981, pp. 119, 169; Armstrong, *et al.,* 1981, pp. 114, 131). Where workers are unable to achieve any form of mutually agreed solution, then accommodation may take other forms. They may engage in sabotage and skiving; may simply refuse management orders or may develop their own informal methods of working (see, for example, Nichols and Beynon, 1977, pp. 135, 137, 141; Nichols and Armstrong, 1975, pp. 66, 69, 72ff). Moreover, such attitudes may lead to a heightened bargaining awareness. Productivity deals, in any event, highlight the link between effort and reward. It does not seem unreasonable, therefore, that workers should become more concerned about the rewards they will receive before they undertake work. This can mean that stewards simply refuse to implement the agreement (see, for example, Purcell, 1981, p. 169) and/or that they refuse to agree to any new productivity deals (see, for example, the Price Commission, 1979, p. 35), or that they even withdraw from the existing agreements (Price Commission, 1978, p. 23). Heightened bargaining awareness may also mean that, blocked from bargaining in traditional areas, stewards and workers begin to exert pressures in new areas. Effort drift (Purcell, 1981, p. 120) or grade drift (Gill *et al.,* 1977) may result and create problems for management comparable with previous problems of wage drift. Workers may begin to demand additional payments for any work or effort beyond what is defined as 'normal' (see, for example, Armstrong *et al.,* 1981, pp. 114, 131).

Even in the case of Fawley, where a famous and apparently successful productivity agreement was signed (Flanders, 1964), such heightened bargaining awareness developed and created new problems for management. In reviewing the Fawley experience, Fox concludes:

we see [here] another example of how changes initiated by one side which were perceived by the other as being in a low-trust direction led to greater specificity, formality and inflexibility of rules and relations. Management's move to strengthen its control over the workgroups was countered by workgroup moves to contain and limit that enlargement of control by precise definitions and rigorous policing of the new frontiers. In applying that countering strategy, the workgroups showed that the degree of trust they felt towards the company was significantly less than management had supposed. (1974, pp. 130–1)

This, we would argue, is a common feature of productivity bargaining. It would, of course, be wrong to suggest that all productivity agreements have failed to achieve management's ends. The thrust of our argument, however, is that the rhetorics of productivity bargaining, in terms of some fuller recognition of worker interests and rights, may serve to shift the frontier of control in workers' favour. In this respect we are adopting a more critical perspective than that of McKersie and Hunter. Their study found that few productivity bargains actually improved productivity: they concluded that such agreements merely changed the form of industrial relations. We have argued that that change in form was often itself significant, for it encouraged, not the notions of cooperation and integrative bargaining favoured by McKersie and Hunter and others, but of low-trust strategies and bargaining awareness on the part of the workforce.

Certainly, studies of particular industries provide limited support for the view that productivity agreements have had a significant impact. The previous section and the literature cited at the beginning of this section support this view. But we may usefully conclude by discussing the evidence cited by Taylor in his recent review of union influence on industrial performance (1982). He refers to a study of shipbuilding which showed that in 1979 British yards were only half as efficient as the Japanese, and that over a third of the working day was non-productive (p. 146). In 1980 BSC stated that it had been unable to make agreements on flexibility 'stick'; problems of inefficiency were still rife in construction (p. 148). Labour productivity in engineering was 50 per cent higher in Germany than in Britain over the period 1973—5, and the EEF declared that 'inefficient practices' were still the greatest barrier to improved productivity (p. 149). Taylor also cites the Ryder report which listed in considerable detail the inferior productivity record of the British compared with other countries: in many areas, British productivity was only about half that of continental producers (CPRS, 1975, esp. pp. 87ff), despite the widespread introduction of productivity bargains.

We would conclude, therefore, that — at least under the economic and political conditions of the 1970s — productivity agreements generally failed to achieve the stated aims of reformists. As Nightingale has pointed out:

> In severe cases workers proved able to use the newly formulated rules *against* management. Alternatively, some developed 'informal' controls in ways unanticipated by managements. Nor were shop stewards invariably drawn into the insidious institutional web . . . a productivity bargain could have the opposite effect. In other cases, shop stewards became involved in a whole new range of disputes which arose from the new kinds of authority claimed by management and their supervisors. Moreover, the 'tightening-up' of supervision which accompanied many agreements tended to force

them into a new position of authority on behalf of their members rather than into a 'policing' role. (1980, p. 331)

However, the arguments outlined above assume certain features of the industrial scene. In particular, they assume considerable power and a conflict orientation on the part of workers, and a failure on the part of management (and government) to 'punch its weight'. Events in the late seventies — market pressures and government policies — may have changed this pattern. This is a theme which is taken up more fully in chapter 5.

PAYMENT SYSTEMS AND STRUCTURES

The Donovan Commission and subsequent reformists placed considerable emphasis upon the need to rationalize payment systems. In the late 1960s and early 1970s, for example, piece-work was frequently seen to be a major problem, leading to inequitable wage structures and obstructing the introduction of efficient working practices: measured day work was at that time widely recommended. More recently, as noted in chapter 1, it has been claimed that managements sought to exert centralized control over wages in such a way as to facilitate managements' production goals (Brown and Sisson, 1983; Purcell and Sisson, 1983). Hence, rather than developing formal negotiations over aspects of work organization, managements focused upon pay strategies. The extension of group-based incentives, for example, was seen as placing pay firmly in the arena of central, rather than shop-floor, negotiations; a move from payment by the piece to time-based incentives was claimed to obfuscate the link between effort and pay; the use of work study was thought to legitimate management decisions and reduce the scope for bargaining. Job evaluation was seen as having particular significance: it centralized pay bargaining, thereby reducing parochial wage increases; it meant that (with joint committees) stewards became the guardians of the job evaluation scheme; it reduced the number of occupational grades and fostered single-employer bargaining. In short, these developments facilitated coherent, centralized pay bargaining and provided a basis upon which management could reassert control over many aspects of the workplace without resort to formal bargaining. The overall logic of this argument has been questioned in chapter 1: here we will consider the evidence concerning these changes in payment systems. First, we look at the question of measured day work.

Measured Day Work

Measured day work (MDW) was strongly recommended in the late sixties as a means of reasserting managerial control and removing the many perceived problems associated with payment by results — (PBR) (see, for example, OME, 1973). Correspondingly, radical critics such as Cliff saw it as a means by which management regained control over the work process, reducing labour costs, enhancing the power of the foreman and restricting the role of the steward (1970, pp. 39ff).

Very often, it seems, neither hopes nor fears were realized. The Office of Manpower Economics study, for example, once its optimism and enthusiasm is cast aside, provides much evidence for this point of view. The reasons relate both to management and worker organization. On the management side, MDW was often introduced with little commitment on the part of management as a whole, and limited overall strategic thinking (1973, p. 24). The OME also found it difficult to reach many firm conclusions simply because very few firms had relevant data, a fact which casts doubt upon much of their work. In assessing the operation of MDW, it found that in some plants work-measurement was based on 'existing, and sometimes suspect, data' and occasionally 'measurement techniques were so weak and shop-floor bargaining carried to such a fine art that employees were able to secure a doubling of standard times. Experienced shop stewards may under MDW turn their attention to bargaining over effort and achieve degrees of control of work which management had not anticipated.' Further, there appeared, over time, to be an increase in queries over standards and 'slippage', facilitated, it seems, by the infrequency of managerial checks on standards; 'in only a few cases were systems used to the full, either to analyse failures, to meet targets or to undertake occasional manpower audits.' Although the OME was unable to reach firm conclusions on the effect of MDW on effort, it appeared that under particular conditions (such as irregular work flow and frequent changes in product or method) 'the wage drift of PBR might be replaced by effort drift under MDW'. Sanctions for worker under-performance were apparently rarely imposed; the OME's conclusion that this was due to the skill of supervisors is, however, open to doubt in view of their other conclusions concerning the dilemmas for foremen occasioned by the introduction of MDW. Further, the need for sanctions might well have been less because most managers did not immediately seek to impose fully revised performance standards. While some managers clearly achieved some of their aims, the OME itself casts doubts upon the validity of many managers' claims.

The lack of preparation of management in introducing MDW is indicated by, among other things, the conflicts of departmental interest which occurred and the frequent failure to realize that the supervisor, who had necessarily to play a key role in controlling effort and organizing production, would experience a change of role. At the same time, not only was there increased bargaining at plant level over 'formal' aspects of the agreement but also, because of greater 'effort awareness' on the part of workers and their stewards, foremen experienced more severe problems than they had in the past. Very often management simply lacked the organization to achieve its aspirations: a major precondition for improved effort was that supplies and work should be well organized. This was not the case in many firms and, particularly where workers had moved from PBR, they had little incentive to resolve these problems themselves (see, for example, IWC Motors Group, 1978, p. 14). Similarly, Conboy states that:

In practice, most failures to meet performance are because of management or production failures. One study of a rather sophisticated scheme showed that about four-fifths of failures to meet performance were directly due to shortcomings of this kind. (1976, p. 33)

A more recent survey also draws a picture of the problems of MDW for management (Lloyd, 1976). While the OME had forecast a continued dramatic shift to MDW, this British Institute of Management survey found that as many firms were moving away from, as into, MDW schemes. Moreover, management respondents often cast doubt upon the claimed advantages of this method of payment:

The problem of the incentive being taken for granted was rated higher than with other schemes. . . It is surprising perhaps that the two problems of new methods and machines being difficult to introduce and that the schemes are difficult to understand are mentioned at all by respondents, as measured daywork is often thought to be free of these drawbacks . . . effort/reward comparisons between jobs, such as those normally associated with PBR, are not necessarily absent from measured daywork. (Lloyd, 1976, pp. 32—3)

In overall terms the BIM survey found no greater managerial satisfaction with MDW than with other schemes surveyed, with only just over a third claiming MDW was 'very successful'.

The more recent survey of payment systems by White found that by the late seventies measured day work was fairly rare. Only 8 per cent of the plants surveyed used this system for production workers, and about 5 per cent for maintenance workers (1981, pp. 48, 52). While he found a number of plants were planning to introduce, or had recently introduced, MDW (p. 79), he argues that 'the added managerial sophistication and supervisory skill required for manning these systems appear to have prevented their wide adoption' (p. 10). Moreover, while MDW was associated with low turnover and absenteeism, it was also associated with 'a particularly high incidence of industrial disputes' (p. 127). Ogden, in his case study of reform in one company, found that the fear of conflict prevented the introduction of MDW in the first place — piece-workers opposed greater management control, and in addition managers feared that the removal of incentives would lead to a fall in output (1981, pp. 34—5; see also Batstone *et al.,* 1978 and IDS, 1981).

Clegg similarly casts doubt upon the successes of MDW. He points out that while it was associated in coalmining with a fall in disputes for a few years, this was not so in the docks and the car industry. In addition, 'All three industries experienced a marked fall in productivity during the early seventies' so that there was a shift back to PBR.

If, in fact, the operation of MDW provided some sense of stability of work along with greater earnings, and yet failed to increase managerial control, then the findings about employee satisfaction with MDW are easily understood. At the same time, 'MDW tended to be accompanied by a growth of union influence within a firm' and related changes in bargaining arrangements were seen to involve a shift in the balance of negotiating power in favour of the unions (OME, 1973, p. 40). While some stewards may have experienced difficulties with the change of payment system, and possibly some decline in their activities if there had been a movement away from PBR, there were compensating factors. First, stewards became more aware of the need to control the effort side of the bargain (Heath, 1969, pp. 194ff) and, at the same time, problems relating to 'effort bargaining no longer took place in a situation where disputes are directly resolved in connection with one particular individual' (OME, 1973, p. 41).

In addition, one has to take account of the less 'formal' activities of workers and their stewards. As McKersie and Hunter argued,

> if American experience is any guide (where measured day work has been used for several decades), workers will develop their own devices for controlling the effort bargain involved in measured day

work to the same extent as they have the wage bargain involved in traditional payment-by-results systems. (1973, p. 289)

This does, indeed, appear to have been so. In addition to the points noted above, the experience of MDW in coalmining and the car industry are illuminating on this point. For it was clear that, particularly where managements attempted to exploit the assumed potential of MDW, they met with resistance. Even if there was only a brief honeymoon when MDW was known as 'leisured day work', frequently management attempts to increase the pace of work failed. This, for example, was the conclusion reached by the Central Policy Review Staff (1975, p. 102) who pointed to the lack of sound management targets, overmanning and disputes over manning levels, a lack of incentive for workers to produce and an excess of untrained foremen. The sanctions workers applied included not only traditional patterns of bargaining and strike action, but also sabotage (for a lengthy account, see Brown, 1977). Beynon's study of steward organization at Fords similarly shows how, even in a new plant, stewards achieved a significant level of control over the organization of work (1973). And Edwards and Scullion found no reduction in industrial action following the introduction of MDW in one of the plants they studied (1982, pp. 235—7).

This is not the place to ponder upon the apparently frequent failure of management to achieve its ends. If 'failures of planning and control' appear to be so consistently found, this suggests that more basic factors are at work. Many of these relate to competing priorities and interests within management; others relate to the inherent weaknesses of bureaucratic control and planning. A more fundamental explanation may lie in the traditions of job control and direct democracy identified as key features of British trade unionism by Kahn-Freund (1979). For not only are there very real conflicts of interest so that reform through consensus may be impossible, but also the tradition and power which the nature of work organization, managerial inefficiencies and job skill gave workers, could be used to challenge and exploit formal systems developed by management. The attempt to reform industrial relations often stimulated fuller union involvement in what were traditionally areas of managerial autonomy but rarely permitted a comparable managerial intrusion or control at lower levels of the organization. In sum, managerial attempts to 'rationalize' work and industrial relations often served to increase rather than reduce steward and worker control. Nor is it entirely clear that managements were subsequently able to assert control after measured day work had been in operation for some time, as suggested by the Institute for Workers' Control (1978) — at least until unemployment reached massive proportions. For, first, much of the Institute for Workers' Control evidence is of an *ad hoc* kind and refers to managerial intent rather than achievement. Second, management's efforts to regain control were often associated not with an extension of Donovan-type reforms but with their removal. Third, these new attempts at exercising control frequently involved the reintroduction of incentives (including attendance bonuses).

Other Changes in Payment Systems

In chapter 2 we indicated that, while there are no relevant systematic data, it appears probable that over the decade from 1968 there was a growth in formal single-employer bargaining. But it does not follow that only one bargaining unit existed in a plant: indeed, the IRRU survey implicitly recognized this by inquiring about the last pay settlement 'made with any major group of manual workers'. In a recent survey, Moulding and Moynagh (1982) found that in plants where collective bargaining occurred, three in five negotiated with more than one group of workers. This partly reflected the tendency towards a variety of bargaining units among non-manual workers. But where bargaining with manual workers only was concerned, three-fifths of plants employing 1,000 or more workers negotiated with more than one group. Daniel and Millward found that in a majority of multi-union situations there was more than one bargaining unit for manual workers in 1980 (1983, p. 46). Thus, while fragmented bargaining may have declined, it has not by any means been eradicated. Indeed, even when bargaining over annual wage increases is confined to a single group, this does not preclude bargaining over money on a more day-to-day basis with small groups of workers (see, for example, Daniel, 1976, p. 32).

It is certainly true, as Sisson and Brown point out, that between 1973 and 1979 the importance of the bonus element in pay declined: for those male manual workers receiving PBR payments, the payments fell as a proportion of total earnings from 28.6 to 20.6 per cent. On the other hand, the proportion of male manual workers in receipt of PBR rose from 43.3 to 47.0 per cent (although in 1977 the figure was only 39.5 per cent). Over the period 1968 to 1979 the percentage of total earnings for all male manual workers in manufacturing from PBR fell from 15.7 to 9.7 per cent (White, 1981, p. 17).

It is not possible to trace trends in the relative use of individual and group incentives. In 1968 the National Board for Prices and Incomes suggested that group payment systems were not widely used 'except where it is impracticable to distinguish the individual worker's contribution' (1968, p. 5). But such situations were probably common. In the mid-seventies, Lloyd (1976, p. 30) found that 68 per cent of the establishments with incentive bonus schemes made group or departmental payments: crude calculations based on White's published data suggest that the figure could have risen to about three-quarters by 1979: but it should also be noted that it was common for establishments to have both individual *and* group bonuses — ignoring plant bonuses and piece-work, 44 per cent of establishments with group bonuses also used individual bonuses (1981, p. 65). Unfortunately, we do not know the relative importance of the different types of bonus in total earnings.

Moreover, it is questionable how far the apparent changes in payment systems are attributable to some coherent management strategy. White, for example, refers to 'the element of "fashion" in collective incentives' (1981, p. 140), while payment systems — or, more strictly, the multiplicity of payment systems in a single plant — indicates an *ad hoc* approach. This has been stimulated by government policy: it seems likely that the decline in the significance of incentives may in part be due to changes in employment distribution, but it is also in part attributable to the nature of incomes policies — it seems that companies often simply added on the wage norm as a supplement. Similarly, the dramatic growth of collective incentives reflected government pressures in favour of self-financing productivity schemes from 1977: not surprisingly, White found that managers often 'regarded their own schemes as expedients or stop-gaps, from which they expected no substantial benefits' (1981, p. 140). Bowey *et al.* similarly note that managements' main aim in introducing productivity incentive schemes 'was to increase earnings for employees' (1982, p. 41). Moreover, Lloyd found that managers believed there were a number of problems with collective incentives; these included high administrative costs, employees' difficulties in understanding the schemes, low quality output and 'some inflexibility of men, machines and methods' (1976, p. 31). White found that collective schemes, particularly plant-wide bonus schemes, were associated with a higher than average level of disputes (1981); a move towards collective incentives might be expected to facilitate collective action relative to individual incentives with considerable individual bargaining (Brown, 1973).

Two trends do, however, appear to be fairly consistent. The first of these is the extension of job evaluation; the second a wider use of work study. Brown, for example, suggests that the number of establishments using job evaluation increased by a half between 1972 and 1977; by 1978 43 per cent of manufacturing plants used it in relation to manual workers (1981, pp. 111—12). In 1980 Daniel and Millward found job evaluation in less than a quarter of the establishments they surveyed, which indicates its rarity in small plants (1983, pp. 204—7). Similarly, work study was done in half of the establishments surveyed in the IRRU study; its use had increased in a third of establishments (1981, p. 114), although Daniel and Millward found less work study — again reflecting the inclusion of smaller establishments (1983, p. 201). The key question, however, concerns the significance of the proliferation of these techniques.

It appears quite common for job evaluation to be employed for only part of the manual labour force. White, for example, found that a third of the plants he investigated in 1979 applied job evaluation to production workers, but only 22 per cent did so for maintenance workers (1981, pp. 46, 52). Even if we assume that all production or maintenance workers were covered by the scheme if one existed, and that all those establishments using job evaluation for maintenance workers also used it for production workers, then truly plant-wide schemes existed in only two-thirds of cases: in reality, the proportion could be a good deal lower. Its impact upon job grading may, therefore, be less than one might expect: in any event, no systematic data are available concerning trends in the number of occupational grades, though certainly the general impression is a trend towards a reduced number (but see Batstone *et al.*, 1984 who question the significance of such a trend). Moreover, job evaluation is frequently associated with various forms of incentive payment, which may be based on groups (or individuals) smaller than an occupational grade — indeed, in large plants this is generally the case (Daniel and Millward, 1983, p. 206). Differential bonuses may therefore upset the neat, rational pay structures deriving from job evaluation and may stimulate direct pressures for grade drift, particularly from those who receive smaller incentive payments.

Second, if job evaluation is to succeed its results have to be seen as legitimate. This rarely appears to be so. Willman, for example, found that while there was broad general agreement among workers on the relative worth of different jobs, the areas of disagreement were of particular significance since they focused on those work groups which were the most crucial to the question of relative wages (1981, p. 53; see also Clements, 1976). Little wonder, then, that (particularly in large plants) problems over wage differentials tended to occur that much more often where job evaluation existed (Daniel, 1976, p. 32). Indeed, to the extent that job evaluation highlights differentials, its extension may explain why Daniel found that 'differentials, job grading and comparability' were seen as issues giving rise to day-to-day claims (1976, p. 36). Unsurprisingly, therefore, the introduction of job evaluation was not associated with a reduction in the level of industrial disputes.

Job evaluation may entail the centralization of certain aspects of bargaining: the ranking of jobs has to be done centrally and claims for regrading may be handled by a central committee. But a sense of inequity on the part of certain groups of workers can still lead to sectional demands and pressures. These may in part be directed at, and handled by, a central body but aggrieved workers are quite likely to exercise sanctions against local management who may be induced to make concessions of various kinds. Where worker pressures exist, management has a number of alternatives. It may seek to maintain the 'integrity' of the job evaluation system, but this could incur heavy costs. In one plant studied by the author, such an approach by management led to a lengthy series of disputes over working practices and arrangements and, finally, to the withdrawal of key groups of workers from all joint industrial relations institutions. In other cases, production may suffer less from direct action by workers than from the workings of the labour market. Lupton and Gowler, for example, report one case where inability to recruit young workers to a low evaluated job led to production bottlenecks (1974, pp. 21—2). Purcell and Sisson similarly note that there may be problems of flexibility and adjusting to labour market forces (1983).

On the other hand, concessions to powerful groups automatically reduce the integrity of the scheme (the scale of this problem may be reduced by skilful selection and weighting of the criteria used in evaluation, but if this is done, then the 'rationality' of the system — other than in terms of formalizing tradition — may be limited; and in some cases it is not even possible to do this). Moreover, concessions of this kind may induce other workers to engage in similar moves to improve their grading. Hence grade drift may occur: Daniel found that upgrading was a means of increasing earnings in over two-fifths of the establishments he surveyed (1976, p. 32). If a work group is sufficiently powerful, it is likely to have its way, if only because a 'rational' structure of job grading is not the dominant priority of most managers: or, alternatively, the maintenance of the integrity of the job-evaluated structure may be at the expense of the integrity of other elements of the payment system. Moreover, it is worth noting in this context that one reason why job evaluation is less common among maintenance workers is the insistence of many craftsmen upon the 'craft rate'.

In other words, the very attractions of job evaluation — its integrity and coherence — may become serious problems, particularly given multi-unionism and a tradition of fractional organization and bargaining. Its legitimacy may be in question from the outset: and if its integrity and coherence are maintained, then serious problems may develop in other areas. The view that such difficulties can be reduced or eradicated through steward involvement in the introduction and operation of job evaluation, so that they become 'the guardians of the scheme', is similarly open to question. While it is true that job evaluation committees are frequently joint bodies, what is equally interesting is that conveners often choose not to sit on them, preferring to maintain their freedom of action. Moreover, in the previous chapter we have questioned how far stewards do act in a coordinated manner. If they do not, then the commitment of one or two steward representatives on a job evaluation committee to the scheme, may have limited influence over the actions of other stewards. Finally, as Willman (1981, p. 150) has pointed out, stewards will probably view job evaluation as a bargaining tool just as they do other payment systems.

Similar questions arise over the efficacy of work study. This, it will be recalled, has been thought to be associated with a reduction in the scope and fragmentation of bargaining while serving to legitimate management decisions, if only because it introduces consistency into performance standards. But all of these points are open to question. Batstone *et al.*, for example, found that a major focus of bargaining concerned work study times; these were associated with a high level of fractional bargaining, and as a consequence they were a major source of both inequity and disputes (Batstone *et al.*, 1977 and 1978). In another company, an internal study found that work study standards varied by as much as 150 per cent — scarcely a high level of consistency.

What is striking about work study is that it ties pay and effort issues closely together and may, therefore, be expected to encourage more bargaining; and in so far as it involves detailed consideration of the tasks of particular groups of workers, there is likely to be a tendency towards a greater role for individual stewards. The trend in the 1970s for the amount and range of bargaining by individual stewards to increase was noted in a previous section. Clegg similarly notes that bargaining pressures can lead work study engineers, ratefixers and supervisors to 'diverge further and further from the official conversion factor in order to win acceptance for new job values: and the clamour grows louder for older jobs to be retimed to yield earnings closer to the current "going rate" ' (1979, p. 135).

Similarly, it is not immediately evident why a change from payment by the piece to time-based schemes should have any dramatic effect. All this does is to interpose a further variable between output and pay. It is scarcely likely to delude either workers or stewards into thinking that there is no link between effort and pay. At the same time, it provides a further point for possible negotiation and pressure. Hence Bowey *et al.* found that incentive schemes based on time standards were more easily manipulated than other types of schemes (1983, p. 52).

In sum, we have posed a number of question-marks against the view that changes in payment systems and structures have led to dramatic changes in the nature and content of bargaining. In the first place, the extent to which management has adopted and implemented coherent pay policies is open to doubt, while the very profusion of competing pay principles in a single plant probably provides a host of contradictions which are fruitful ground for sectional bargaining. Second, as noted in chapter 1, it is not clear why managements — as Sisson and his colleagues argue — should seek formality over pay structures and steward organization, but maintain the traditional patterns of informality over production matters. For to the extent that managements insist upon maintaining the integrity of formal pay structures, they are in effect shifting the obvious means of worker accommodation into production matters. The net effect, therefore, may be to increase managements' need for an equivalent formality in this area — or, conversely, to decrease the formality of pay structures. Both appear to have happened quite frequently.

These points are perhaps best summed up by Clegg in his discussion of collectively agreed rules:

> where the agreement obliges them to accept work study, trade unionists will allow the work study engineers to carry out their investigations but query the results. If the agreement binds them to accept the findings of work study, they will not challenge the results themselves, but assert their right to negotiate over the new manning scales which management proposes to introduce on the basis of the findings. Should the agreement bind them to accept the manning scales proposed by management, they may accept them, but the managers may find to their disappointment that the output is less than they had expected, and that manning will have to be increased again if orders are to be met. (1979, p. 122)

One further point might be added: where shop steward organization is strong, it is open to question how often managements will be able to achieve formal agreements of this kind or to operate them effectively.

Finally, it is worth asking how far these changes in payment systems and structures derived their logic from organizational factors and particularly the development of financial control procedures, noted in chapter 2. Unfortunately, no systematic evidence is available on this question but, in some companies, at least it appears that the accounting function played an instrumental role in changing the methods by which pay was determined: frequently, the aim was to develop a coherent financial control system.

JOB-BASED CONTROL

If industrial relations reform was to be deemed successful, then the degree of worker control and influence over various aspects of their jobs should have been reduced, as management gained greater freedom to deploy labour and increase effort. But an attempt to assess changes in the degree of job-based control confronts two major problems. The first of these concerns data: job-based controls are particularly difficult to investigate at the best of times, but it is especially difficult to build up a general, reliable picture across a wide range of plants through the available surveys. Accordingly, we have to rely to a great extent upon case studies and the views of (hopefully) well-informed commentators.

The second problem is more fundamental — namely, identifying exactly what areas should be investigated under the heading of 'job-based control'. This term has been selected here because terms such as 'unilateral control' and 'custom and practice' are problematical for a number of reasons. By discussing these briefly, it is possible to come to a more satisfactory picture of what constitutes 'job-based control'.

It is frequently argued that the classic case of job control is the craftsman: the craft operates a system of unilateral control over a number of important areas such as recruitment, manning, methods of working and levels and styles of supervision. It is not the intention here to dispute these facts, except to note that no craft union does in fact have 100 per cent union density nationally among those undertaking tasks within its claimed job territory. Rather, the point at issue is the notion of 'unilateral' control. This is so for two reasons. First, the kinds of control which crafts operate frequently find their origins (if not their continuation) in managerial strategy. Craft autonomy involved a form of self-discipline on the part of workers which could be compatible with profitability (Hyman and Elger, 1981, pp. 118—19). Second, craft controls are bounded by, and intermingle with, a variety of jointly agreed and management-initiated rules and actions. Generally, management can choose who to recruit from within the craft and which workers should undertake which tasks within the specified job territory. Similarly, questions of training, quality of work and levels of pay — all crucial to the craft — are not the subject of exclusive and unilateral craft control.

Accordingly, it is dangerous to exaggerate the degree and significance of such controls. While it is true that managements have traditionally tailored their organization to accommodate craft controls, the latter are nevertheless importantly implicated within a broader set of rules which are not the sole creation of the craft.

Not dissimilar points are relevant to the question of 'custom and practice' (C & P), which is often seen in terms of workers (rather than stewards) exploiting managerial error in order to impose some form of control over their work (see, for example, Brown, 1973). First, as various studies indicate, C & P need not be solely or even primarily biased in workers' favour: indeed, both Batstone *et al.* (1977) and Armstrong *et al.* (1980) argue the reverse. Second, it is somewhat misleading to attribute the growth of C & P simply to managerial 'sins' of omission and commission: for such 'sins' reflect endeavours to achieve certain ends in the face of (possible) employee non-cooperation. Indeed, Brown talks of the growth of C & P largely in terms of fractional bargaining (and stewards may be intimately involved in this). Third, and relatedly, it is again necessary to locate C & P within the broader structure of the workplace and its rules of operation. At one level, C & P can be seen as the outcome of differences in power and interests. But at another level — and more specifically — it reflects and derives from the specific structure of rules and regulations within the workplace, be they jointly agreed or managerially determined. In this sense, therefore, C & P may be seen as a means by which rules are or are not applied to particular situations. This process may involve not only questions of invocation and interpretation of a specific rule or agreement, but also a choice between rules and norms which conflict in their application to an issue. From this perspective, C & P is often rule-oriented and thereby creates new sets of rules, albeit with somewhat localized legitimacy. Hence one should not see C & P as being too divorced from the larger structure of rules; accordingly, there is no *a priori* reason to assume that the fractional bargaining surrounding rule application (and hence the creation of new rules) should be the preserve of workers rather than stewards (see Batstone *et al.*, 1977).

The pressures towards the manipulation and evasion of rules derive from a variety of sources. Rules are invariably of a general kind so that a process of interpretation is required for their application and such interpretation may be the subject of disagreement. Managers and workers (and stewards) have varying interests which are reflected in debates over interpretation: some may have an interest in strict application, or in claiming that one rule should have priority over another. For example, workers may argue that their formal job descriptions preclude mobility to other jobs. Both parties may equally have an interest in the manipulation or evasion of formal rules: management may seek 'favours', for example, in order to 'get a rush job out'. The cost extracted by workers may be 'concessions' concerning the application of other sets of rules.

In other cases it may simply be difficult for management to enforce the rules. As Cressey and MacInnes have recently emphasized, most jobs require some discretionary behaviour on the part of workers (1982; see also Kusterer, 1980). Sometimes, moves towards the expansion of jobs — for example, job enrichment and autonomous work groups — may increase this discretionary content. Similarly, formal rights for management to utilize labour more flexibly may confront problems of supervision which preclude their application. Such factors, relating to the nature of the work process itself, provide important means by which workers can impose pressures for concessions on the part of foremen and management.

A good deal of literature points, moreover, to the interests which many workers have in achieving a degree of control over their jobs. This, after all, is the origin of craft control, a model subsequently developed and applied by some semi-skilled groups (see Zeitlin, 1981). Surveys similarly indicate the desire of workers to have more control over their immediate jobs (see, for example, Heller *et al.*, 1981; Brannen *et al.*, 1976), while case study data indicate the multiplicity of ways in which even unorganized or weakly organized workers adopt a variety of individual and collective strategies in order to achieve some degree of autonomy or control (see Marriott, 1973 for a review of much of the relevant evidence).

Given these pressures, there is little reason *a priori* to assume that the multiplication of jointly agreed rules at plant level associated with industrial relations reform should inevitably reduce job-based control. It is true that schemes such as productivity agreements often involve some form of commitment to greater labour flexibility (these issues have been discussed more fully above). But a number of comments are necessary here. First, we have noted that a substantial number of agreements in fact hedge flexibility around with a number of conditions. Important are conditions relating to negotiation over specific cases of flexibility, and the inclusion of mutuality or *status quo* clauses. Second, agreements often appear to conflict so that the probability of fractional bargaining is further increased. The conflict between job descriptions and flexibility was noted as one such possibility. Third, the discretion necessarily afforded to workers and the more general problems of managerial control afford unions modes of accommodation which may serve to increase worker autonomy and control. Recent case studies, notably by Nichols and Beynon (1977), Nichols and Armstrong (1976), Armstrong *et al.* (1981), and Purcell (1981), highlight various short-cuts adopted by workers, the 'informal' introduction of work rotation, 'effort drift', straight refusals to carry out tasks, and sabotage. Fourth, even jointly agreed rules may in practice be rejected by stewards and workers. Purcell's study highlights examples of this concerning conversion rates (1981, p. 119) and flexibility rulings (1981, p. 169). Fifth, agreements may in other ways impose limitations upon management. Hence, Purcell's discussion of a plant in which key stewards adopted a cooperative approach towards management shows that strict limitations were imposed upon various issues including levels of effort (1981). Sixth, joint agreements are likely more fully to reflect union and worker interests in terms both of what Armstrong *et al.* refer to as 'consensual principles of justification' such as consistency and fairness and of their 'resistance principles' concerning the effort bargain and property rights in jobs. To the extent that they do, they may open up opportunities for bargaining over issues of job-based control in areas where, very often, those notions did not previously exist (see, for example, Armstrong *et al.,* 1981, p. 108).

In short, industrial relations reform rarely constituted a fundamental challenge to the way in which work was organized. By seeking marginally to change working practices, it confirmed the notions of job territory and property rights which underlay so much of British industrial organization. So, for example, it is still the case that manning levels in Britain exceed those in France and Germany (see, for example, Dubois and Monjardet, 1978; Chemicals EDC, 1978). Marsden has highlighted the way in which apprenticeships in Britain involve the acquisition of skills within a particular 'job territory', while in Germany they reflect the particular and changing needs of the employer for skills. He suggests that this means that the employer is less able in Britain to use labour flexibly. Modes of job regulation and job training are therefore mutually reinforcing (1981). Moreover, such a distinctive British pattern can be found among non-craft groups (see, for example, Zeitlin, 1981; Kahn-Freund, 1979). To the extent that industrial relations reform modified these practices marginally they simultaneously reaffirmed them. Accordingly, far from removing job-based control, industrial relations reform may have led to a more explicit recognition and legitimation of job-based controls in the 1970s.

REFORM AND WORKER REWARDS

According to the radical critique of reformism, in the decade after 1968 the wage-effort bargain should have turned to the disadvantage of workers. That is, the level of effort, productivity and job loss, as well as profits, should have increased, while (the rate of growth of) earnings should have fallen. In addition, steward incorporation — or, for the reformist, the success of reformism — should have meant a decline in the level of strike activity.

The problem of assessing such hypotheses is that economic and political conditions do not remain constant. Moreover, these conditions are not unaffected by management and union action, as the earlier discussion of productivity indicates. It follows that such actions, by affecting broader conditions, can indirectly affect future gains and losses. For example, if workers successfully demand wage increases in excess of productivity, then — at least at some point — competitiveness is likely to decline. As a result, workers may be less able to achieve further wage increases and/or to maintain employment levels. That is, past success may work against future success. At the same time, other factors — government policies, oil crises, and so on — also affect the relative ease with which workers can pursue their interests. If, because of such factors, unemployment increases, then union strength may be weakened, and thus wage increases may become smaller and strike activity decline.

Some theories relevant to the present topic have already been discussed, notably changes in job control and levels of effort and productivity. Here we will concentrate upon official data, both for the economy or manufacturing as a whole and for six industries which provide a cross-section of manufacturing. Two of these — vehicles and shipbuilding — have long traditions of strong and militant shop steward organization; the others — textiles, clothing, food, drink and tobacco, and chemicals — have only recently developed 'sophisticated' forms of steward organization (see chapter 3).

The first means of gauging the impact of reformism is to take a zero-sum approach to the question of higher productivity. That is, we assume that any increase in the rate of growth of productivity involves an intensification of effort which is contrary to workers' interests. It is a particularly severe test both because of its assumptions and because it ignores technical progress. If, since Donovan, there was no increase in the rate of productivity growth, then the radical account of reformism is not supported.

In applying this test the ratio of the change in net output per head for the decade after 1968 compared with the previous decade is used. In all cases the ratios are less than 0.5, indicating that the rate of productivity growth was dramatically reduced in 1968—78 compared with the previous decrease. In the case of shipbuilding the ratio was only 0.28, and in textiles it was only 0.15.

It can, however, be objected that these findings reflect the decline in (the rate of growth of) output in the latter decade in all of our industries except shipbuilding. On the other hand, it can be countered, first, that over a decade it should have been possible to align labour and output so as to maintain productivity trends. Second, even if we control for market trends by comparing British productivity changes with those of other countries, the same picture of worsening performance emerges. The German/UK productivity ratio increased — that is, British performance worsened — over the period 1968—77: the ratio was 1.21 in food, 1.04 in chemicals, 1.29 in shipbuilding and vehicles, and 1.17 in textiles and clothing. Similarly, the US/UK ratios were as follows: food 1.12; chemicals 1.08; shipbuilding and vehicles 1.18; and textiles and clothing 1.03 (Smith *et al.,* 1982, pp. 65—6).

A second test of worker gains concerns the extent to which unions were able to maintain employment. This theme has recently been taken up by Hyman and Elger who argue — on the basis of the experience of British Rail, British Leyland, British Steel and Fleet Street — that the failure to prevent job losses is an indication of union weakness and incorporation (1981). This is an extremely tough test of union strength, for it suggests two ultimate possibilities: either that unions can maintain employment even if demand for the product or service has ceased to exist; or that the unions are able somehow to maintain demand. The former would be implausible in any society; the latter may be plausible under certain conditions but it is hardly news to say these scarcely exist in Britain.

A more 'reasonable' test — at least relative to a notion of incorporation — is whether or not unions were able to prevent employment falling at the same rate as output. On this test, the cases cited by Hyman and Elger suggest considerable union strength: for in three of the four cases cited by them and where data are easily available (the exception being Fleet Street), employment fell less than output between 1973 and 78 — the differences being 6 per cent (British Rail), 13 per cent (BSC) and 21 per cent (Leyland) (Pryke, 1981, p. 238). Martin's study of Fleet Street suggests a similar pattern, at least between 1970 and 1975 (1982).

If we apply this measure to the decades before and after 1968, the radical argument would lead us to expect that in the post-reform decade employment would fall more than output or increase less rapidly with greater output, than in the pre-reform decade. In fact, this hypothesis receives no support from the data.

Employment in our six industries, and in manufacturing as a whole, fell significantly over the period 1959—68 despite the fact that net real output increased in every case except shipbuilding. In the post-reform period, output fell in two of our industries and in textiles employment fell even faster than output (but only 2 per cent more than in the previous decade, when net real output had increased significantly). In the other industries, while net real output grew less rapidly post-reform, employment fell less than it had in the pre-reform decade. These data, therefore, fail to support the radical thesis: indeed, 'reformed' steward organizations appear to have been better able to defend their members' employment.

A third test of the impact of reformism concerns strike action. Both reformists and the radical critics suggested that strikes would decline on all dimensions. Official statistics indicate that the average number of strikes per year between 1969—78 as compared with 1963—8 increased by 20.6 per cent. In only one of our six industries — shipbuilding — did the official number fall (by 38.9 per cent), although in vehicles the number increased by only 3 per cent. However, both these industries kept their place in the top five for strike frequency (Smith *et al.*, 1978), so that these two cases can scarcely be described as evidence of a strong tendency towards steward incorporation. In our other four industries, with newly 'sophisticated' steward organizations, the increase in strike frequency was considerably above the national average: in food, drink and tobacco it was 95 per cent; in chemicals 51 per cent; in clothing 77 per cent; and in textiles 53 per cent.

Official statistics tend to underestimate the number of strikes. It is useful, therefore, to turn to a consideration of survey data. However, in addition to the fact that the various surveys are not strictly comparable, the questions asked are different. For example, the 1966 survey investigated strikes of all kinds since managers had assumed their present positions — an average of nine years for senior managers. Thirty per cent said they had experienced a strike (36 per cent in metal handling, 28 per cent in other manufacturing). In addition, nearly half of these said they had experienced only one strike (1968, p. 83). Hence the number experiencing strikes in the last two years would probably have been a good deal lower. In the 1972 and 1973 surveys managers were asked about their experience of strike action over the last two years. However, they were asked about national and non-national strikes separately. In 1973 (1972 figures in brackets), 40 (20) per cent of senior managers said they had experienced a national strike in the last two years; in addition, 18 (32) per cent said they had had a non-national strike in this period (1975, pp. 78, 144). Unfortunately, we do not know how far the two responses overlapped. But assuming there is not a total overlap, and given the longer time period investigated in the 1966 survey, it seems reasonable to conclude that there was probably a significant increase in strike activity. The 1978 IRRU found that 33 per cent of establishments had experienced a strike in the last two years (Brown, 1981, p. 84). Again, taking into account the different time periods investigated, this suggests a considerable increase over 1966. To the extent that surveys are comparable, then, they give little support to the incorporation thesis as far as strike frequency is concerned.

The official statistics are more reliable when we turn to the number of workers involved and 'days lost' in strikes. Here the evidence of greater 'militancy' is even more striking, as table 4.1 shows. It can be seen that the increases were dramatic, to say the least.

The evidence gives considerable support to the view that there was no increase in the tendency of shop steward organizations to become incorporated. Moreover, what is particularly striking is the way in which 'newly organized' (in the sense of 'sophisticated' shop steward organizations) sectors showed dramatic increases in strike propensity (and it should be noted, the figures used above have not allowed for reduced employment levels).

Furthermore, in the 1970s the sanctions adopted by workers, far from becoming more 'moderate', became more radical. In addition to the use

TABLE 4.1 WORKERS INVOLVED AND 'DAYS LOST' IN STRIKES

	Workers involved *(% change)* *annual average* *1969—78* *annual average* *1963—8*	*'Days lost'* *(% change)* *annual average* *1969—78* *annual average* *1963—8*
Food, drink and tobacco	+ 284.4	+ 992.7
Chemicals	+ 130.8	+ 295.5
Shipbuilding	+ 47.4	+ 139.5
Vehicles	+ 31.3	+ 234.4
Clothing	+ 276.9	+ 102.1
Textiles	+ 219.4	+ 233.3
All industries	+ 34.3	+ 277.4

of secondary and flying pickets, it has been estimated that in the 1970s 'over 300,000 workers have been involved in over 300 occupations' (Campaign Against a Criminal Trespass Law, 1979). In addition, workers formed combine committees to fight plant closures and considerable interest was shown in the development of alternative corporate plans by stewards (see, for example, Elliott and Wainwright, 1981). These initiatives are of especial interest since they were most commonly found in companies which had been at the forefront of 'reformism'. Hence factory occupations were most common in large plants which had 'reformed' industrial relations (TUSIU, 1976).

A fourth hypothesis deriving from the radical critique of reformism is that the wage—effort bargain would become increasingly unfavourable to workers. The effort and productivity aspects of this hypothesis have already been considered. We now need to look at the wages side. If the radical thesis is correct, then first, earnings would not have kept their value in real terms, and second, the growth of earnings would not have exceeded the growth of productivity and, possibly, would have been significantly below it. On both counts, earnings in the post-reform period would have been inferior to earnings prior to reform. Relatedly, the share of profits relative to wages should have increased post-reform.

It is important to remember that in the post-1968 period workers had to obtain substantially greater monetary increases in order even to maintain real earnings: in 1963—8, only an increase of 3 per cent per annum was necessary. In 1969—78, an increase of almost 12 per cent per annum was necessary. Nevertheless, real earnings increased more rapidly in the latter period in the economy as a whole, and in every one of our six industries, except shipbuilding. In shipbuilding, increases were very high in both periods — in 1969—78 the average real annual increase, for example, was 6.7 per cent compared with a national figure of only 4.6 per cent.

Not only did earnings tend to rise faster than inflation, they also increased in real terms faster than did productivity. This was true in both 1963—8 (except chemicals and textiles) and in 1969—78. In the latter period, however, the gap between productivity and real earnings increased: by 2.0 per cent overall; by 1.7 per cent in food, 3.6 per cent in chemicals, 2.7 per cent in vehicles, by 0.6 per cent in shipbuilding, and by over 2 per cent in clothing and textiles.

Moreover, the increase in real earnings took place at the expense of profits. Between 1963 and 1968 the average annual rate of return on trading assets (in pre-tax real terms, net of stock appreciation and capital consumption at replacement cost) was 10.75 per cent; between 1969 and 1978 this figure averaged only 7.4 per cent (Bank of England

Quarterly Bulletin, 1981, p. 228).

The best way, perhaps, of testing for incorporation is to look at the relative shares of income from employment and profits in gross domestic product (GDP). Between 1959 and 1968 the ratio of gross trading profit (after stock appreciation, prior to depreciation and including financial institutions) to income from employment was 21 per cent. Between 1969 and 1978, this ratio fell to 16 per cent. (Similar patterns are revealed using other profit figures: for example, if industrial and commercial gross trading profits and rents after depreciation and stock appreciation is used, the corresponding figures are 15.6 per cent and 12.7 per cent.)

In short, then, on virtually every indicator we have taken, there is little evidence to support the view that the greater sophistication of shop steward organization was associated with a more incorporated approach to management. This is true, with one or two exceptions, whether we look at productivity, employment levels as compared with changes in output, real wages (even allowing for productivity), levels of strike action or the relative shares of wages and profits. In short, while incorporation may have occurred in some cases, it does not appear to have been a common feature, at least relative to the pre-reform era, and up to the late seventies.

CONCLUSIONS

In this chapter we have focused upon the effects of reformism. It has been shown that reform did not lead to a reduction in shop-floor, or fractional, bargaining. Indeed, particularly when the increase in steward density is taken into account, such bargaining appears to have increased considerably. It may be, however, that the increase in bargaining was even more dramatic for individual senior stewards than for individual 'normal' stewards. Moreover, there are some signs that 'normal' stewards became increasingly able to bypass foremen and pursue sectional interests with higher levels of management. Formal agreements did not appear to have precluded 'informal' bargaining or agreements.

Second, evidence relating to labour productivity was considered. We argued that most accounts of Britain's productivity performance are either incomplete or involve — implicitly or explicitly — some recognition of the importance of labour relations factors. Moreover, using the scanty data available, it was tentatively suggested that reformism did not appear to be related to increased productivity. This picture was supported by a consideration of specific reform strategies — productivity bargaining and changes in payment systems. Finally, after pointing to the continued significance of job-based control, we turned to the evidence of worker rewards or losses from reformism. Compared with the pre-reform period, the data suggested fairly consistently that reformism had not in fact militated against workers' interests. Finally, the evidence on the shares of profits and income from employment indicated that employees had gained considerably more from reformism than employers.

A number of points do, however, require emphasis. First, much of the data used in this chapter is less than ideal for our purposes. Nevertheless, it does seem important to use what is available, rather than treat its less than ideal nature as an excuse for ignoring the susbtantive effects of reform or relying merely upon contentions founded upon even more partial data. Second, the preceding discussion should not be taken to imply that labour relations were the only — or even the dominant — factor in Britain's poor economic performance. As we have already seen, many factors figured in this. But it has equally to be remembered that the rationale of reformism was precisely that it should be able to prosper in adversity. Third, as was emphasized in chapter 2, the nature of management structure and strategy intermeshes closely with the pattern both of 'traditional' labour relations and the precise directions which reform took. In addition, the nature of management probably had an independent effect (see, for example, Prais, 1980; Caves, 1980). We return to this theme in chapter 9. Fourth, to the extent that managers, stewards and workers checked the logic of the market, then they were storing up problems for the future unless union pressures were to lead to some major structural changes which could satisfy both their interests and the demands of the international marketplace. Fifth, and relatedly, as in previous chapters, we have paid relatively scant attention to the political scene. Many of these themes are considered more fully in the final chapter.

PART II
Workplace Industrial Relations in 1983

5 Developments after 1978

Part I focused on the decade up to 1978, since this could be seen as the high point of what has been called reformism in workplace industrial relations. Moreover, the analysis so far has focused upon the workplace level. In fact, of course, many developments were occurring over the period at national level. Relationships fluctuated wildly between the state and the union movement: there were a number of 'political' strikes against industrial relations legislation and its effects; strike action was even instrumental in pulling down a government. At the other extreme the unions and the Labour Party — subsequently the government — committed themselves, in the form of the Social Contract, to a closer set of working relationships than had existed for over two decades. This led to an increase in industrial relations legislation and an environment in which national union leaders found a new, though tentative, national influence. Throughout the period there were many years in which incomes policies were in operation, some supported by the union movement and others opposed by it. And, of course, after the oil crisis in the early 1970s the international economy confronted growing problems.

These themes have only been touched upon in preceding chapters, for they have been written about voluminously elsewhere. They clearly did have some impact at workplace level, however. Most obviously, increasing economic problems were associated with some attempts at rationalization, and many aspects of this have been considered in chapter 4. The long-term trend of falling employment in manufacturing accelerated. And, as part of this process, redundancies multiplied. Incomes policies clearly had an effect upon wages, although this was not as dramatic as might have been expected: for some workers, wage norms under incomes policies led to wage increases which were larger than they would otherwise have received; for some, the 'let out' clauses meant incomes policies had little effect upon the level (as distinct from the specific form) of pay rises; and in many cases, a 'catching up' process followed the relaxation of incomes policies. In a number of instances, notably in the public sector, the operation of formal and informal incomes policies, along with attempts to change the criteria for pay determination, were the subject of lengthy disputes. Similarly, in the 1970s the volume of industrial relations legislation increased dramatically, some of it merely removing or reversing earlier legislation as the party in power changed. Generally speaking, the proliferation of laws has not had a major impact: equal pay legislation increased women's pay relative to men's, at least for a while, although possibly in large part because of the shape of incomes policies. But in the main it would appear that the impact of the law was to accelerate the very processes which we have been discussing so far — the formalization of industrial relations procedures and the extension and possibly the bureaucratization of shop steward organization (see chapter 2).

Moreover, developments at workplace level had a significant impact at national level in a number of ways. First, the Social Contract era, as noted above, brought union leaders a new-found influence which to a significant degree was associated both with their long-standing role within the Labour Party and with the readiness of the Labour Government to involve them. At the same time as national union leaders were playing an expanding role, the preceding chapters have shown that shop steward organization was becoming increasingly influential. The relationship between the national and local levels within the trade unions was an extremely delicate one for all concerned, particularly given the fact that the TUC leadership was dependent upon the support of individual national union leaders who, in turn and to varying degrees, were constrained by shop stewards and the rank-and-file membership.

A bifurcation of power within the trade unions had been developing for some years leading to a number of moves to renegotiate internal order and to allow more workplace bargaining. Developments in the 1970s further encouraged these trends, and shop stewards became more fully recognized in the formal machinery of the unions. As we saw in chapter 3, some commentators proclaimed that there was a move (and a successful one at that) to incorporate shop stewards by a two-pronged approach. The first was fuller recognition and the reform of industrial relations at the level of the workplace which, it was claimed, would foster a steward elite which would be sympathetic to management goals of rationalization and increased efficiency. The second was the fuller integration of shop stewards into the larger unions, thereby subjecting them to closer control by national leaders and making them the mouthpieces of the Social Contract philosophy rather than its opponents at shop-floor level. With this two-pronged approach, therefore, the realities of British union structure would become supportive of what many have termed the development of 'corporatist' arrangements in this country. While, if they had been successful, reformism and changes in union structure in this period may well have been mutually supportive, there is little evidence to suggest that they constituted part of a coherent, thought-out strategy on the part of those who were able to implement policies of this kind.

Indeed, potentially the most significant development in this respect concerned proposals for industrial democracy. These, in and of themselves, suggested the severe limitations of workplace reform. From the union side industrial democracy was seen as a means of overcoming the sectional nature of shop steward power: while unions might have significant influence at plant and national levels, they typically had little at what many saw to be the key level — that of the company. Moreover, board-room representation or planning agreements would provide a means whereby unions (and shop stewards) would be able to play a role in the more detailed planning which was envisaged for British industry. However, as is only too well known, in practice planning agreements scarcely got off the ground and the Bullock Committee's proposals for union-based 'parity' representation on the boards of large private companies received a cool response in most quarters. The changing patterns of influence within the Labour Government meant that such enthusiasm as there had been for worker directors waned; many union leaders — and even more strongly organized shop stewards — were suspicious, to say the least, of board-room representation; and management prepared to wage a concerted battle against the proposals.

Paradoxically, except in parts of the public sector (see Batstone, Ferner and Terry, 1983), it was management which took up the theme of industrial democracy. In many cases this was merely an attempt to take the initiative and to convince shop stewards that, if Bullock's proposals were made law, they would have little need of them. But the extent to which companies introduced union-based schemes of joint consultation in particular, and the fact that this trend continued even when it was clear that Bullock was politically a non-runner, suggests that another rationale developed. This stemmed from the recognition of the limitations of reformism. In effect, its logic had been that greater steward recognition and formalization would induce greater cooperation in the workplace. In the main, this was not happening. It would seem, therefore, that what management was trying to do was to create by new means the atmosphere of 'trust' which should have grown out of workplace reform. As subsequent sections of this book indicate, such an approach has continued up to the present. But the emphasis has shifted from 'democracy' to 'involvement', and the focus has widened from concentration on union representatives to include direct involvement of employees.

However, as chapter 3 showed, despite fuller integration into larger union structures and the introduction of new forms of 'involvement' at workplace level, shop stewards wielded their new-found influence to induce trade unions to withdraw from the Social Contract as it failed to match up to expectations. Unions became less and less prepared to accept tough incomes policies norms, as monetarist policies began to overwhelm the 'welfare' themes which had been central to the initial conception of the Social Contract.

In sum, far from becoming more compatible with what might be loosely termed 'corporatism', British trade union structure in many respects became less compatible with it. Whereas in Britain shop stewards began to wield increased influence at national level during the period of the Social Contract, in other societies such as Sweden (Korpi, 1979) and West Germany (Streeck, 1982), the influence of local activists had diminished as 'corporatist' arrangements developed. One other factor is significant: in Britain affiliated unions constitutionally play a major role in the Labour Party, whereas in many 'corporatist' societies they do not do so, relationships being maintained on a more informal basis. The British pattern, it can be argued, leads to volatility in Labour Party policy: in opposition, it is extremely dependent upon union support, and this fact is recognized in the contents of the manifesto; when in power a Labour Government faces new sets of pressures and at the same time derives its legitimacy and power primarily from the electorate. Therefore, as in the Social Contract era, a tension developed between the Labour Party in power and the unions. This was exacerbated by the traditional union emphasis upon 'free collective bargaining' which is inimical to a primary commitment to political strategies (Currie, 1979). The behaviour of Labour Governments may in turn encourage this approach.

The second way in which the developments outlined in preceding chapters were important at the national level was economic. While it would be wrong to see shop stewards and trade unions as the sole, or even possibly the primary factor, in the poor international performance of the British economy, they were significant. As chapter 4 showed, reformism was associated with a further worsening of the state of the economy relative to other countries. Conditions became less and less favourable to the achievement of the goals of the Social Contract: the economy did not perform sufficiently well to make it easy (or easier) to combine welfare and efficiency (as conventionally defined) goals. As a result, the rift between government and trade unions increased, while union members became less and less convinced of the virtues of the Social Contract.

Third, and more speculatively, developments at workplace level had an electoral significance. This was so indirectly because of the way in which they were associated with declining economic performance and with the failure to introduce the full Social Contract package: and, of course, the electoral impact of the failure of the Social Contract to lead to any major increase in the economic well-being of the average union member/voter was exacerbated by the expectations which it had built up. The 'winter of discontent', when the number of days lost through strike action mushroomed, raised serious doubts about the credibility of a Labour Government—trade union 'contract' and, possibly, about the existence of any 'easy' route to widespread affluence. In addition, and most speculatively, the failure of the Social Contract strengthened the severe doubts among union members and others about the legitimacy of intimate relationships between union leaders and the government. Not only did such a mode of policy determination go against the 'myth' of the sovereignty of the electorate, but in addition it went against the long-standing traditions of local democracy in which British trade unionism is firmly embedded. And, of course, in many respects that tradition may have been strengthened by the growth of shop steward organization over the preceding years.

The Conservative Government came to power in the late 1970s in part because it was able to tap the underlying aspirations and suspicions of the electorate, including many trade union members, at both substantive and procedural levels. The new government was able to turn back the moves towards 'corporatist' relationships with the trade unions; it was able to embark upon a series of legal initiatives designed to check and shape union power; and it attempted to resuscitate the economy through an evangelical espousal of monetarist policies and of 'rolling back' the state. Both the latter, and particularly monetarism, could only be effective if union power was reduced and if a major change of attitudes occurred.

The general state of the international economy, compounded by the long-term trend in British competitiveness and by government policy, has had major effects as far as labour relations are concerned. Unemployment grew, according to official statistics, from about 5 per cent in the late 1970s to about 13 per cent in early 1983. Redundancies involving ten or more workers confirmed as due to occur totalled nearly 1.75 million between 1979 and the end of June 1983: from 1980 the annual rate was well over double that in the late 1970s. In manufacturing, employment fell from 7.1 million in June 1978 to 5.4 million in June 1983, a reduction of 25 per cent.

This had implications for the level of union membership, which fell from 12.2 million in 1979 to only 10.5 million at the beginning of 1983. Moreover, while some unions — notably the RCN and NALGO (white-collar, public sector) — have experienced a steady increase in membership, other unions have experienced dramatic falls. Between 1979 and 1981, for example, the NUTGW lost 30 per cent of its members, the TGWU lost a fifth, the Engineering Section of the AUEW lost 16 per cent and the NUGMW 10 per cent. This has led some commentators to talk about the decimation of union membership: but, at least at plant level, in 'Donovan-type' situations, subsequent chapters will argue that this is far from the case.

It is certainly true that these developments are inducing changes in the approach of trade unions. At national level, for example, the depression has accelerated a long-term trend of the growing significance of white-collar and 'non-traditional' groups in overall union membership. This, along with depression, the results of the 1983 General Election and the approach of the government, has permitted, or is permitting, both a change in the way in which the General Council of the TUC is selected (which, at least for the present, makes it more 'right wing') and signs of a 'realism' on the part of the TUC which induces it to seek marginal ameliorations through talking with Government rather than steadfastly refusing to deal with it. At the time of writing, it is too early even to speculate on whether or not these moves are the first steps towards a more 'businesslike' form of unionism and a greater readiness to deal with any political party (and hence a weakening of links with the Labour Party), or whether a new joint union—Labour Party strategy will develop.

While there is undoubtedly a new 'realism' at shop-floor level, it does not follow that shop steward organizations are now a thing of the past, at least as far as workplace control is concerned. It is certainly true that shop stewards and trade unions have been unable to prevent the massive rise in unemployment and redundancies. But given the scale of the reduction in output and, as indicated by international manning and productivity comparisons, the 'slack' which existed in British manufacturing, what is perhaps surprising is that the reduction in employment has not been even greater. Moreover, the sectionalism of shop steward organizations, which has been noted in previous chapters, is likely to make it particularly difficult to resist closures and redundancies. In this sense, the changed situation has merely served to highlight a longstanding weakness of British shop steward and union organization — a weakness of which many were only too fully aware much earlier (some union leaders, for example, were in favour not only of the Social Contract but also worker directors as a means to rectify this weakness).

However, official statistics suggest that shop stewards and trade unions may still wield a significant degree of influence. For example, despite the fact that manufacturing output declined by 15 per cent after 1978, the ratio of the fall in employment/fall in output in manufacturing is lower for the period from 1978 to the first half of 1983 (1.47) than it was for the period 1973—8 (1.74).

Second, despite an absolute fall in union density to about 50.6 per cent, it is still higher than it was in the early 1970s. Moreover, this relative stability is all the more striking when it is compared with what happened to union membership in the inter-war period. Then, union density fell from 45.2 per cent in 1920 to 30.2 per cent in 1923 and continued to decline to a low of 22.6 per cent in 1933 (Bain and Price, 1980: although it should be noted that unemployment increased more rapidly in the inter-war period).

Third, despite the shift in the balance of power, real earnings increased for those still in work, suggesting a degree of insulation of many plants from larger economic forces. Between 1973 and 1978, average weekly earnings had risen by 117 per cent while prices rose by 109 per cent. Between 1978 and June 1983, earnings rose by over 90 per cent and prices by 69 per cent, a faster rise in real earnings than in the earlier period. In manufacturing (the focus of subsequent chapters) hourly earnings of manual workers rose by 85 per cent for men and 79 per cent for women. In addition, industrial and commercial profits as a proportion of value-added have not increased relative to the 1978 figure (excluding North Sea oil operations).

Fourth, despite what would appear at first sight to be a dramatic shift in the balance of power within industry, output per worker in manufacturing increased more slowly between 1978 and 1983 than it had done in the previous decade. It is true that over the last few years there has been a fall in output which may make increased productivity more difficult; on the other hand, it has presumably served to reduce union and worker resistance to changes in working practices. Moreover, in 1983, official statistics indicate a considerable increase in productivity; but how far this trend will continue over the cycle is open to question.

Fifth, it is useful to look at the level of strike activity. Table 5.1 shows that the number of strikes recorded has fallen significantly since 1979, although it should be remembered that official statistics are particularly unreliable on this matter (Brown, 1981). Even when we confine our

TABLE 5.1   STRIKES, 1965—83

	Number	Workers involved ('000)	Days lost ('000)	
1965	2354	868	2925	
1966	1937	530	2398	
1967	2116	731	2787	average
1968	2378	2255	4690	= 5551
1969	3116	1654	6846	
1970	3906	1793	10980	
1971	2228	1171	13551	
1972	2497	1722	23909	
1973	2873	1513	7197	
1974	2922	1622	14750	
1975	2282	789	6012	
1976	2016	666	3284	
1977	2703	1155	10142	
1978	2471	1001	9405	
1979	2080	4583	29474	
1980	1330	830	11964	
1981	1338	1499 average	4266	average
1982	1528	2101 = 1242	5313	= 6318
1983	1255	538	3728*	

*includes POEU 'political' dispute

attention to the period 1980—3, and take an average of that period, we find that only in the 'winter of discontent' (1979) was the number of workers involved in strikes higher in the late seventies. In six of the years between 1965 and 1979, the number of days lost through strikes was lower than the average for 1980—3. Of particular interest here is that this average is higher than that for the period 1965—9. Moreover, it is over 60 per cent of the average for the period 1973—8, despite the fact that unemployment has roughly tripled. Finally, it should be noted that these figures are not adjusted for the number of people employed.

It is true that the public sector has in recent years accounted for a significant proportion of the total number of workers involved and 'days lost' through strike action. However, it is not universally the case that days lost per 1,000 workers in private manufacturing have fallen substantially in the last few years. For example, taking days lost per 1,000 workers for 1979—82 as a percentage of the days lost in the period 1970—5, we find the following: motor vehicles 85 per cent; footwear 94 per cent; furniture 117 per cent and printing and publishing 100 per cent (this rather esoteric collection of industries is drawn from Edwards, 1983, p. 222; the 1979—82 figures come from *Employment Gazette*, July 1983, p. 304).

These data, then, suggest that the level and significance of shop steward activity in many companies may still be considerable. Unfortunately, the existing data are inadequate to provide a coherent picture for the most recent period. The most recently published survey (Daniel and Millward, 1983) was actually undertaken early in 1980, when the full impact of the recession/depression was scarcely visible: output had been rising since 1975, and only started to fall in the year of the survey; unemployment at the end of 1979 was only about half the current figure and it was only in 1980 that the rate of redundancies really accelerated; union density was increasing up to the end of 1979; and the rates of wage and price increases remained high. Invaluable though the survey is, it would — at least at first sight — be dangerous to treat it as a picture of the current pattern of industrial relations.

It also seems dangerous to rely upon the experience of the most publicized companies: the very fact that they are so well publicized suggests that they are exceptional. Moreover, the accounts of 'macho' managers reasserting control and 'knocking shop stewards into line' tend to come disproportionately from the public sector, and — within it — from companies facing severe financial problems. Managers in these situations are particularly susceptible to pressures to adopt a 'hard line' in industrial relations. And even in some of these cases it is still open to question what degree of success management has actually achieved: in Leyland — perhaps the most publicized case — not only are there signs that shop-steward organization may be regaining influence, but it is also worth noting that the company — at the time of writing — is still not profitable, while labour productivity has not surpassed the level of the late 1960s, despite massive redundancies and capital investment. Moreover, recently conducted and ongoing research on industrial relations, and discussions with managers and shop stewards and others, do not suggest that the Leylands of this world are at all typical.

Because of the dearth of data on what is happening, it was decided to undertake a survey of workplace industrial relations. The Research Committee of the Department of Social and Administrative Studies kindly made a small grant which was used for a postal survey; any larger project would have taken a long time and would have involved a lengthy process of fund-raising. Given the scale limitations, I decided to focus upon what might be termed the classic Donovan situation: that is, manual workers in large manufacturing plants, which belong to large, privately owned companies. After some investigation, a satisfactory method (as far as could be judged) was devised by which a sample of plants could be drawn. This was done in two stages: first, using the *Times 1,000*, a sample of companies mainly or significantly engaged in manufacturing was taken; all the largest companies were included, and the sampling fraction was reduced as one moved to smaller companies. Second, and again weighting by company size, I drew a sample of manufacturing plants belonging to the selected companies: this proved a lengthy process, involving the use of a variety of directories. In all, 312 plants were selected in this way. Postal questionnaires were addressed to the personnel manager in each of these plants in June 1983 and several weeks later a reminder was sent, requesting that the questionnaire be returned even if it was not completed.

By September 1983 a total of 211 questionnaires, or 68 per cent of those sent out, had been returned. These included sixty-nine refusals, five cases where the questionnaire was not applicable and six where manufacturing had ceased. An attempt was made to assess what proportion of the non-responding plants were still engaged in manufacturing: from a check on about a third of the non-respondents it is estimated that over twenty of the total non-respondents had closed down. This suggests that the 133 completed questionnaires provide a 'real' response rate of about half — very much higher than that typically achieved with postal questionnaires: I am most grateful to the many managers who evidently took considerable time and care to complete the questionnaire.

In all, the plants which cooperated in the survey account for over 2 per cent of employment in manufacturing (in mid-1983). As this suggests, and as table 5.2 shows, the plants tend to be large: over a quarter employed over 1,000 people and a similar proportion between 500 and

TABLE 5.2 FULL-TIME EMPLOYEES BY INDUSTRY (%)

Size category	Engineering and metals		Food and chemicals		Other		Total	
	Total empl.	Manual empl.	Total empl.	Manual empl.	Total empl.	Manual empl.	Total empl.	Manual empl.
Under 100	3	12	—	4	4	4	2	8
100—199	11	16	10	27	8	20	10	21
200—499	37	42	34	27	32	36	35	35
500—999	26	18	25	23	28	40	26	24
1,000 +	23	10	29	17	28	—	26	11
Not known	—	2	2	2	—	—	1	1
Total	100	100	100	100	100	100	100	100
Distribution by industry	44		37		19		100	

999. At the other extreme, only 2 per cent employed less than 100 workers. The distribution in terms of manual employment is obviously more skewed towards smaller size categories. The table also shows that engineering and metal handling account for 44 per cent of responses, and food, drink and tobacco and chemicals for 37 per cent.

The survey focused primarily upon manual workers and was designed to investigate the themes discussed in Part I. Whenever possible it asked questions which had been employed in earlier surveys in order to facilitate comparisons: such comparisons, however, are inevitably crude due to differences in sampling procedures, with the exception of one case: that of the 1978 IRRU survey. In this case, David Deaton of the IRRU kindly reweighted the 1978 survey by size and industry (and taking only subsidiary establishments) to make it comparable with the 1983 survey.

The findings need to be treated with care for a variety of reasons. First, a brief postal survey cannot hope to catch all the subtleties and complexities of industrial relations — we are using a very blunt instrument. Second, the response rate, although gratifyingly high for a postal survey, suggests that particular types of plant may be under-represented. But what might be the greatest concern in this respect — that respondents tended to come from plants which have not felt the full impact of the recession — does not appear to be the case: this is indicated by the industrial distribution of respondents and by the scale of labour force reductions in these plants (see chapter 7). Third, the questionnaires were completed by personnel managers (where they existed): while they are probably one of the best — if not the best — single sources of information on industrial relations within a plant, they were being asked to describe and assess shop-steward organization. It has to be recognized that shop stewards may have answered these questions differently. However, surveys which have interviewed both managers and stewards have not generally found major differences in the replies of the two sets of respondents to questions of the kind posed in the 1983 survey (see, for example, Daniel and Millward, 1983).

Chapters 6—8 are based almost exclusively upon the findings of the survey. Chapter 6 looks at the structure and organization of management and of shop stewards. Chapter 7 looks at various labour relations 'strategies' employed by management and chapter 8 goes on to look at steward activity and influence. Throughout we focus upon the themes which shaped Part I: that is, we look systematically at questions relating to management structure, the impact of steward bureaucracy and oligarchy, and questions of steward influence. Figures have been kept to a minimum in the more detailed discussion, but where relationships are highlighted they are almost invariably statistically significant at a 10 per cent — and generally higher — level of confidence.

6 Management and Union Organization

In chapters 2 and 3 we attempted to assess the degree and significance of changes in management and shop steward organization in the decade after Donovan. In this chapter the same themes are pursued for the current period. The first section considers the nature of management organization in relation to labour relations: as in chapter 2, emphasis is placed upon the existence and role of a personnel function, the locus of decision-making, the centrality of labour relations considerations, and structures of control. The second section outlines the formal structure of union organization in the plants surveyed, and focuses in particular upon what chapter 3 described as the key aspects of steward bureaucracy. The third and final section draws upon the survey findings to investigate more systematically than was possible in chapter 3 the question of oligarchy in shop steward organizations and the extent to which it is associated with 'bureaucracy'.

MANAGEMENT STRUCTURE AND LABOUR RELATIONS

In chapter 2 we argued that the increasing numbers of personnel specialists could best be explained in terms of an 'organizational' rather than a purely 'industrial relations' rationale. Consistent with this, it was found that such specialists were associated with primarily procedural changes, involving in particular a shift to single-employer bargaining and a centralization of decision-making. The extent to which personnel specialists were associated with a fuller recognition of labour relations considerations in management decision-making was limited, particularly outside of 'traditional' industrial relations issues. Given both the current recession and the more generally hostile environment for trade unions which has developed since 1978, a series of questions present themselves. Among them are: whether or not the existence and role of personnel specialists has changed; whether they are still associated with essentially procedural issues and centralizing tendencies; and whether 'union power' still affects management decision-making in the way it did in the late 1970s. If we adopt a simple model based upon the general state of the labour market, then it might be expected that workers would be more quiescent, with the consequence that personnel specialists would be deemed less necessary, their role would be reduced and their procedural emphasis would have changed; along with these developments, this simple model might predict that labour relations considerations would play even less of a role in management decision-making than they did in the 1970s, particularly since the threat of worker sanctions had waned.

On the other hand, if the growing numbers of personnel specialists were primarily attributable to an organizational logic, then it might be argued that, since that logic was still relevant, that is, top management still has to achieve control and direction in large corporations — then there would be little change in the distribution and role of personnel specialists. Similarly, it can be plausibly argued that managements are still likely to place considerable emphasis upon labour relations (relative, that is, to 1978) for a variety of reasons. These would include the following: attempts to use the current high levels of unemployment as a sanction on workers by threatening to replace them on any significant scale would be impracticable, risky or extremely costly; if companies are to introduce more efficient working practices then they need to 'carry' stewards and workers with them; and, third, managements might be expected not, in the main, to adopt 'macho' tactics for fear that, if and when the balance of power shifted in workers' favour, they would resort in kind. The following sections investigate the extent to which these competing accounts are supported by the survey findings.

Personnel Specialists

Table 6.1 shows that, compared with 1978, there has been no statistically significant change in the number of plants which had personnel specialists at establishment or board levels. There is, however, a decline — statistically significant at a 5 per cent level of confidence — in the number of plants where a personnel function exists above the level of the establishment. The overall picture, however, is that in these primarily large plants the personnel function remains almost as well developed as it was in 1978. In four-fifths of cases personnel managers exist at establishment level, while in about two-thirds of cases a specialist personnel function is found at a higher level and, slightly less often, on the board.

TABLE 6.1 PERSONNEL SPECIALISTS, 1983 and 1978 (%)

Plants with personnel specialists	*1983*	*1978*
At establishment level	82	87
Above establishment level	68	79
On board of directors	62	62

As in 1978, there is a strong tendency for the existence of specialists at these three levels to be closely interrelated. It is possible to build up an index of personnel bureaucracy, scoring one point for each of the types of personnel specialist distinguished above. Almost half of the establishments score the maximum on this index, 10 per cent score 2, a third score 1 and just under 10 per cent score 0. Again as in 1978, there is a fairly strong 'size effect' (table 6.2). It is particularly strong as far as personnel specialists at plant level are concerned. The size effect also operates for personnel specialists above plant level, although in these cases the impact of size of company and employment in 1978 are stronger. The latter suggests that an explanation of the existence of personnel specialists today should be, in part, of a historical nature.

Consistent with this point, the association of personnel specialists with indicators of an organization rationale and union pressure are fairly weak. Hence, for example, while foreign ownership is associated with a greater level of personnel bureaucracy it is not a particularly strong relationship. But it is stronger than the association with 'industrial relations' factors. For example, the relationship between strike action in the last two years and the presence of different types of personnel specialist is either non-existent or negligible. However, there is a close relationship between personnel and steward bureaucracy. The overall picture can best be summarized by looking at the relationship between the personnel bureaucracy index and a similar bureaucratization index for shop-steward organization. This scores 1 point for each of the following: the existence of senior stewards, of regular steward meetings, and of full-time stewards. Table 6.3 provides the relevant data — for example, half the plants which score the maximum on the personnel bureaucracy index also do so on the steward bureaucracy index. At the other extreme, over half the plants which score 0 on the former index score 0 or 1 on the steward bureaucracy index.

It would seem, therefore, that the present level of personnel bureaucracy largely reflects organizational innovation in earlier periods: in 1978 it was found that in the vast majority of establishments the personnel function had become more important over the preceding few

TABLE 6.2 PERSONNEL SPECIALISTS BY SIZE OF PLANT

	Number of employees		
Personnel specialists	*<200*	*200—499*	*500 +*
At establishment level (%)	31	76	100
Above establishment level (%)	31	51	63
At board level (%)	31	56	72

years. The 1983 survey also asked respondents whether the role of the personnel function had changed over the last five years. Given the state of the economy and the relatively high level of personnel bureaucracy (at least in numerical terms) in 1978, what is perhaps striking is that half the 1983 respondents say that the personnel function has become more important (compared with 89 per cent in 1978). Only 5 per cent (none in 1978) claim its role has decreased: where this is so the plants confront particularly acute economic problems and have reduced their labour forces dramatically over the last five years. However, it should be noted that sizeable job reductions have occurred in other plants and yet there has not, according to respondents, been a reduction in the role of the personnel function. Of greater numerical significance are plants where the personnel function has become more important in recent years: these tend to be in those sectors where 'sophisticated' steward organization tends to be relatively new — food, drink and tobacco, chemicals, and textiles and clothing. Two-thirds of respondents from these industries claim a greater role for the personnel function, compared with only two-fifths of other respondents. But once size is controlled, there is no significant variation by industry in the level of personnel bureaucracy.

TABLE 6.3 THE RELATIONSHIP BETWEEN PERSONNEL AND STEWARD BUREAUCRACY

Personnel bureaucracy score	*Steward bureaucracy score*				
	3	*2*	*1*	*0*	*Total (%)*
3	50	31	17	2	100
2	37	27	18	18	100
1	28	35	28	9	100
0	9	36	46	9	100

The Centrality of Personnel and Industrial Relations Considerations

The second aspect of management's approach to labour relations which can be investigated with the survey is the extent to which personnel and industrial relations (P & IR) factors impinge upon management policies and decision-making. The 1983 survey, like the 1978 IRRU survey, investigated the extent to which P & IR considerations entered into the formulation of decisions and policies in a number of areas. Given the length limitations of a postal questionnaire, only two areas could be investigated — major changes in production methods, and redundancies. The same wording was used in the 1983 as in the 1978 survey. Table 6.4 shows the responses to the two questions. While there has been a marginal increase in the role of P & IR considerations in decisions relating to major changes in production methods, there has been a greater decrease in their significance for decisions on redundancies. In chapter 2, we placed considerable emphasis upon the tendency for P & IR to play a smaller role in decisions which were outside of the 'traditional' areas of industrial relations. That contrast still exists, but the effect of changes over the five years is to reduce the scale of that difference — from 83 points to only 43 points.

Considering major changes in production methods first, we find that P & IR considerations are slightly more centrally involved in those industries where sophisticated shop steward organization tended to develop in the 1970s — that is, in food, drink and tobacco, chemicals and textiles and clothing (see chapter 3). However, a much stronger relationship is found with the size of the labour force, and in particular total employment (rather than manual employment or employment in 1978). P & IR considerations play a greater role in larger plants. There is

TABLE 6.4 P & IR CONSIDERATIONS IN MANAGEMENT DECISIONS, 1978 AND 1983

P & IR considerations are	*Major changes in production methods (%)*		*Redundancies (%)*	
	1978	*1983*	*1978*	*1983*
Centrally involved	5	4	41	38
Heavily involved	45	54	45	29
Consulted	37	37	12	26
Not involved at all	12	5	2	7
Total	99	100	100	100
Score (see chapter 2)	142	155	225	198

no variation in the centrality of P & IR by labour costs, the degree of integration of production or by crude indicators of trends in output or financial performance.

The existence of a 'personnel bureaucracy' is associated with a more central role for P & IR considerations. This is true if we take the overall index or any of the specialisms distinguished earlier. The strongest relationship, however, is with the presence of a specialist personnel director, and the relationship, though weaker, still holds even when size of plant is controlled for. Similarly, the centrality of P & IR considerations is related to aspects of 'steward bureaucracy': the bureaucracy index and its individual items are all associated with greater centrality. The strongest relationship, however, is with the existence of full-time stewards. Again the relationship is weakened, but still holds, when size of plant is controlled for.

The relative 'impact' of personnel directors and full-time stewards is very similar: the former are associated with an increased score of thirty-eight points, the latter thirty-five points. Moreover, they tend to have an independent impact: that is, P & IR considerations tend to be more centrally involved where there are full-time stewards even when we take separately plants with and without personnel directors, and if we compare the impact of the latter separately for plants with and without full-time stewards. However, the impact of, for example, full-time stewards tends to become slightly weaker where a personnel director exists, stronger where such a board member does not exist.

Bureaucracy on both management and union sides, then, increases the role which P & IR considerations play in decisions relating to major changes in production methods. But, as has been noted above, there tends to be a close interrelationship, if not mutual support, between these two 'bureaucracies'. The survey, however, permits us to look at how far 'independent' company and union factors impinge upon the centrality of P & IR considerations. On the company side we can assess the impact of ownership, while on the union side we can look at the exercise of sanctions.

Ownership is only weakly related to the centrality of P & IR considerations in decisions on major changes in production methods: this variation is primarily attributable to the size effect (foreign-owned plants tending to be larger). Only very weak relationships exist between the various forms of industrial action and the role of P & IR considerations, which may be due to the decline in the scale of such activity. However, a more useful indicator exists in the form of responses to questions concerning the extent to which trade unions obstruct changes in working practices. Such 'union obstruction' is associated with a greater centrality of P & IR considerations. (This relationship still exists even when the existence of personnel directors is controlled for.)

In sum, P & IR considerations tend to play a more central role in decisions on changes in production methods in large plants; greater centralization is associated with bureaucracy on both management and union sides. When we seek to assess the impact of 'independent' company and union factors, we find that 'union obstruction' plays a greater role than ownership. It should, however, be noted that 'union obstruction' tends to play a rather weaker role than personnel management and steward bureaucracy.

In the case of redundancy decisions, the centrality of P & IR considerations is generally associated with the same set of factors as in the case of major changes in production methods. Thus these considerations are more central in industries where steward organization is relatively new, and in larger plants (in terms of total employment). P & IR considerations are centrally or heavily involved in redundancy decisions in about four times as many large as small plants. Again, centrality is not related to labour costs, integrated production, relative financial performance or output trends. Nor is it related to the scale of reduction in the manual labour force over the last five years.

P & IR considerations play a more central role where there is a high level of personnel bureaucracy and where there is a high level of steward bureaucracy. All aspects of personnel management (and the bureaucracy index) are associated: the strongest relationship is with the existence of a personnel specialist at establishment level. Some features of steward bureaucracy have no significant relationship with P & IR centrality in redundancy decisions: the strongest relationship is with regular steward meetings. The impact of personnel bureaucracy is greater than that of steward bureaucracy: in 'points' terms, regular steward meetings are associated with an increased score of twenty-seven points, personnel specialists at establishment level with an increase of ninety points.

P & IR considerations are said to play a rather greater role in redundancy decisions in foreign-owned plants. While this relationship is not very strong, it is greater than those with various indicators of union power. Indeed, the latter are negligible. The organizational rationale, therefore, appears to be stronger than 'union power' pressures, but the strongest relationship is with personnel bureaucracy.

While comparisons with the findings outlined in chapter 2 are fraught with problems, given the different samples, there would appear to be both interesting similarities and differences. As in 1978, it has been found that union power — or perceived union power — has a considerable impact upon 'mainstream' management decisions, but little upon redundancy decisions. The role of personnel bureaucracy is considerable for both the issues investigated, and greater than that of steward bureaucracy, as far as redundancy is concerned. This picture is consistent with what might be expected, given the state of both product and labour markets: the impact of shop stewards relative to personnel specialists appears to have declined. But the former still exists, at least as far as ongoing manufacturing activity is concerned.

THE STRUCTURE OF MANAGEMENT CONTROL

Chapter 2 showed that the existence of personnel specialists could be seen as part of a corporate strategy to control its own affairs and to centralize key decisions. If this was indeed part of a more general 'organizational rationale', then one might expect these patterns still to hold. But in addition, the 'hard times' which many companies face now might lead to an even greater centralization of decisions as top management seek to rationalize production and cut costs. On the other hand, if worker power were to be reduced by high levels of unemployment, then it is possible that companies would decentralize control in order to maximize their ability to exploit the possibilities of increased efficiency with a quiescent workforce. In order to pursue these themes, this section considers changes in the main level at which collective bargaining is conducted, the level of local management discretion and changes in the degree of freedom enjoyed by lower level supervision. In addition it briefly considers membership of employers' associations.

The Level of Collective Bargaining

While management has a significant impact upon bargaining arrangements and while their discretion on such questions may have increased with high unemployment, trade unions and workers also play a role (see, for example, Batstone *et al.*, 1984). However, collective bargaining arrangements are discussed in this section because they form an indispensable back-cloth to the consideration of management decision-making (see chapter 2).

Table 6.5 compares the most important level of bargaining for manual workers' pay in 1978 and 1983. Two changes are significant: the decline in establishment-level bargaining and the increase in 'no bargaining'. An attempt was made to identify the characteristics of plants where respondents said no bargaining occurred. In half these cases, no trade

TABLE 6.5 MOST IMPORTANT BARGAINING LEVEL FOR MANUAL WORKERS' PAY, 1978
AND 1983 (%)

Most important level		*1978*		*1983*
Establishment		52		41
Company, above plant level		23		27
Multi-company:		19		21
region/district	1		1	
industry	14		19	
wages council	4		1	
'No bargaining'		5		11
Other		1		—
Total		100		100

union is recognized, and this is likely to be true of the corresponding cases in the 1978 survey. In three other plants which did not bargain union density was under 50 per cent, and given the overall pattern of union density (see below), it seems unlikely that union membership fell in these plants over the last five years. But there are also four plants with 100 per cent union density which, apparently, do not bargain over manual workers' pay. All of these face acute problems; they have experienced dramatic falls in output, are faring badly financially and have made massive redundancies. Nevertheless, most of these four plants still have fairly developed shop steward organizations. It may be that in some of these cases management — within the formal bargaining procedures — simply make a single and final offer. One respondent indicates that this is indeed the case.

Excluding those plants where no bargaining occurs, there is only a weak relationship between plant size and bargaining level: smaller plants are marginally more likely to engage in multi-employer bargaining. Plant bargaining is more common in 'traditional' industries, company-level bargaining being more common in the 'new' industries.

As was found in chapter 2, the level of personnel bureaucracy is closely related to bargaining level. Where 'full' personnel bureaucracy exists, only 14 per cent of plants do not engage in single-employer bargaining while, at the other extreme, half of those with no personnel specialists bargain jointly with other employers. Moreover, there is a strong tendency for the existence of personnel specialists above plant level to be associated with single-employer bargaining covering a number of plants (corporate bargaining). Ownership, however, is not strongly related to bargaining level.

The level at which pay bargaining occurs is not significantly associated with union density or the coverage of the closed shop. It is, however, strongly related to various characteristics of shop steward organization. As the number of stewards increases there is a greater probability of single-employer, and particularly corporate, bargaining. In addition, as the score on the steward bureaucracy index rises, multi-employer bargaining becomes less common. Regular steward meetings are particularly common where plant bargaining takes place, full-time stewards where corporate bargaining occurs. Overall, steward bureaucracy is rather more developed in the latter than in the former type of situation. Finally, the experience of industrial action is not significantly related to bargaining level: 'union obstruction', however, is rather more common in plants where single-employer bargaining occurs, and particularly where this takes place at plant level.

Another important aspect of bargaining arrangements is the extent to which, particularly with single-employer bargaining, all work groups and unions are included in the same set of negotiations. Unfortunately, I failed to include any questions on such 'bargaining units' in the questionnaire. However, respondents in multi-union plants were asked whether the unions negotiated jointly or separately. In three-fifths of plants with more than one union, the unions do not negotiate jointly: the extent of joint negotiation does not vary with the level of bargaining.

Joint negotiations on the part of unions is considerably more common in 'traditional' than in 'new' sectors. It does not vary significantly by size of plant, ownership or the level of personnel bureaucracy. Joint negotiation is, however, related to a number of characteristics of union organization. It is less common the larger the number of unions in the plant and, relatedly (see below), the higher the coverage of the closed shop and the greater the density of shop stewards. However, it is related to only one aspect of steward bureaucracy (which is not included in the index used elsewhere in this and the following chapter) — the frequency of meetings of stewards from the various unions is greater where joint negotiation occurs.

In sum, over the last five years there has been a slight increase in unilateral employer decisions over manual workers' pay at the expense of plant bargaining. However, single-employer bargaining is still the norm and is intimately related to personnel — and steward — bureaucracy. The extent to which joint bargaining occurs in multi-union situations is related to union characteristics rather than features of management. 'Independent' variables such as ownership and union power do not appear to have any significant influence upon bargaining arrangements, at least in this sample of relatively large plants of major companies.

Local Management Discretion

While the pattern of formal bargaining arrangements may be related to broader characteristics of management organization, it is still possible, as chapter 2 showed, for the pattern of management control to vary. In pursuing this theme, three questions, comparable with those asked in the 1978 IRRU survey, were posed in the 1983 survey concerning local management discretion. These investigated the degree of autonomy over manual workers' pay and redundancies, and what changes in local discretion had occurred over the past five years. Table 6.6 shows that there has been no statistically significant change in the overall pattern of local discretion on either of the issues investigated over the last five years: there have, however, been some marginal tendencies: discretion over pay has been reduced, and this seems consistent with the decline in plant bargaining. There has also been a small reduction in discretion over redundancies, no doubt reflecting the massive reductions in manpower across companies.

It is possible that this overall picture disguises considerable shifts within individual plants and companies. For only half the respondents claim that there has been no change in local discretion over the last five years. A third claim it has increased, and 16 per cent that it has decreased. In about two-thirds of the cases where local discretion has increased, respondents state that they now have complete or considerable discretion over manual workers' pay, while this is so in only a quarter of the plants where local discretion has been reduced (no respondents referred to changes in bargaining level, in answer to a general question concerning changes over the last five years).

TABLE 6.6 LOCAL MANAGEMENT DISCRETION, 1978 AND 1983 (%)

	Discretion over manual workers' pay		*Discretion over redundancies*	
Local discretion is	*1978*	*1983*	*1978*	*1983*
Complete	30	29	35	36
Considerable	34	29	32	29
Limited	20	24	18	25
Virtually non-existent	15	18	11	7
Other	1	—	4	4
Total	100	100	100	100

Changes in local discretion are closely related to the existence of personnel bureaucracy. Thus in those plants with high scores on the personnel bureaucracy index and which now have considerable freedom on pay there has been a sizeable 'net' increase in plants which enjoy greater discretion (that is, those declaring an increase minus those declaring a decrease), while for comparable 'non-bureaucratic' plants the 'net' figure is zero. If we consider only those plants which currently have limited levels of discretion, the impact of high personnel bureaucracy is reversed.

Not surprisingly, local discretion over manual workers' pay is closely related to bargaining level. In four out of five plants where there is plant bargaining local management have considerable discretion over pay. The proportion declines to a quarter where there is corporate bargaining. Where multi-employer bargaining occurs, the degree of local discretion is intermediate between these two extremes. It is therefore necessary to control for bargaining level in considering discretion over pay.

Once this is done, the analysis becomes rather complex, and so it is convenient to consider each bargaining level independently. In the case of plant bargaining, the level of local discretion falls where there are signs of union power. In contrast, the existence of a personnel specialist at establishment level is associated with greater local discretion under plant bargaining. In the case of corporate bargaining, the role of full-time stewards becomes particularly significant. Only 10 per cent of corporate bargaining plants with such union representatives have any significant degree of local autonomy, whereas over half the other plants bargaining at this level enjoy such freedom. Regular steward meetings are also associated with less discretion under corporate bargaining. The existence of personnel specialists both at plant and board level is also associated with greater discretion. Finally, we need to look at plants which are not involved in any form of single-employer bargaining. In these cases, signs of union power play a significant role. Where there is 100 per cent union density, local discretion diminishes and, similarly, 'union obstruction' reduces discretion. In this instance, the existence of personnel bureaucracy is associated with reduced, rather than increased, local management discretion.

The second aspect of local management discretion investigated concerned redundancies. Basically, patterns of variation are similar to those for manual workers' pay. Indeed, the levels of discretion over the two issues are closely related: nearly two-thirds of the plants with significant freedom over pay have considerable autonomy over redundancies, compared with only 6 per cent of other local managements. As in the case of manual workers' pay, discretion is related both to bargaining level and the degree of personnel bureaucracy. Union power, as indicated by the experience of lengthy strikes, is associated with less local discretion over redundancies. Finally, local freedom on this question varies by the scale of job reductions over the last five years: it is greatest where, in percentage terms, there have been large-scale cuts over this period; local discretion is rather less where no reductions have occurred and is least where only relatively small cuts in the labour force have taken place. Some caution, however, is required in interpreting the general significance of this point: the findings only relate to plants which are still in existence, and plant closures are likely to be determined centrally.

Over the last five years, then, there may have been a slight overall increase in local management discretion. Nevertheless, the general pattern is little different from that found in 1978, and bargaining level still plays an important role in shaping management freedom. It is interesting that while personnel bureaucracy is associated with more centralized formal bargaining structures, within these it is associated with greater local discretion in many cases. On the other hand, where union pressures exist to any significant degree, management decisions tend to be more centralized.

Supervisors' Discretion

The data thus lend some support to the view that local management discretion varies inversely with the level of union power and that, given high unemployment, there has been a slight tendency to greater freedom for plant management. It was decided to pursue this theme somewhat further by asking about changes in the freedom of lower levels of management. Again, two competing theses have some *a priori* plausibility. On the one hand, major processes of rationalization and cost reduction might mean that the freedom of foremen was reduced. On the other hand, they might have experienced an increase in autonomy. For during the sixties and seventies it seems that foremen's powers were reduced (see, for example, Child and Partridge, 1982) in an attempt to prevent them making *ad hoc* concessions to shop-floor pressures. If the latter were now less strong, then the pursuit of increased efficiency might have led to foremen being given back some of their traditional powers.

The survey evidence suggests that the actual trends are rather more complex than these simple hypotheses suggest. For while there have been shifts in supervisory discretion in almost half the plants, they are not uniformly in any particular direction: in nearly a quarter of plants the autonomy of foremen has grown, but it has fallen in almost one in five of plants.

These changes are related to neither size nor ownership, nor to any features of the production process, output or financial trends. They are, however, related to the existence of personnel specialists and the role of trade unionism (but not to bargaining level). Where personnel specialists exist at plant level, the discretion of foremen has tended to grow. A plausible explanation for this is that during the 1970s such personnel managers had attempted to reduce the freedom of supervision in the interests of applying 'equitable' and formal rules. In the changed circumstances of the last few years, such 'consistency' has become less important and so foremen have been allowed greater freedom. However, this freedom has occurred only under particular circumstances. Essentially, these have been where union power is relatively low. Greater discretion for foremen tends to be found where steward bureaucracy (particularly in the form of full-time stewards) is low, and more importantly, where strikes have not occurred, where the range of negotiations is lower, where steward influence over members is limited and where the unions do not prevent changes in working practices. More generally, the reason why supervisory discretion has not increased as much as might be expected is that union power does not seem to have fallen as rapidly or dramatically as the thesis outlined at the beginning of this section would suggest.

Employers' Associations

In the seventies, despite the growth of single-employer bargaining, most plants and companies maintained their membership of employers' associations. This, it was argued, was to be explained by the services, such as advice and information, which these bodies provided to management. In the context of reduced profits and weakened trade unions, it might be expected that such services would be seen as less important or central to management endeavour.

The survey findings indicate that there has indeed been a decline in membership of employers' associations. In 1978, 71 per cent of plants affiliated to such bodies: in 1983, only 57 per cent do so. What is interesting, therefore, is that employer organization may have declined more rapidly in the recession than union organization.

Membership is particularly high in engineering and printing — industries characterized by falling output and a significant degree of 'union obstruction'. The level of personnel bureaucracy is not significantly related to membership. However, as in 1978, there is only a weak (though positive) relationship between multi-employer bargaining and membership of an employers' association. It seems, then, that as Brown (1981) argues, there are deemed to be advantages other than joint negotiation in such affiliation, but they appear to be becoming less attractive.

TRADE UNION ORGANIZATION

In Part I grave doubt was cast upon the early liberal pluralist and radical analyses: both would have predicted that industrial relations would have ceased to be a 'problem' in the 1970s and, therefore, that the current recession would have been less severe than it is and/or that union organization would not be a significant constraint upon management attempts to return to profitability.

If these analyses are implausible, then three other hypotheses can be suggested concerning the fate of union organization at workplace level. The first would argue that, particularly if workplace union organization obstructed management goals in the 1970s, management would exploit the changes in the labour market to remove or reduce the institutional bases of union power. The second hypothesis would predict that management would not need to engage in any such concerted onslaught: being above all pragmatic animals, shop stewards would be only too aware of the shift in the balance of power and so would be prepared to make significant concessions in order to preserve organization. The third hypothesis argues that it is misleading to 'read off' the balance of power within the workplace directly from the general state of the labour market. While recognizing some possible validity in the second hypothesis, it would claim that workers in employment still possess considerable power for the following reasons. It is not practicable for employers to sack all their present workers and recruit totally afresh, given not only their skill requirements but also the plant-specific knowledge required of workers. If production is to continue, management has to achieve some minimal degree of commitment from the workforce which may not be won simply through coercion (see, for example, Kusterer, 1978). In a recession companies themselves are in a vulnerable position, so that, unless they are in extreme straits, it would be unwise to risk losing markets by incurring strike action even if workers were ultimately defeated. Finally, managers imbued with the culture of British industrial relations may be loath to break the habits of a lifetime, particularly when 'macho' tactics would disrupt the culture of the workplace which had been developed over a numbert of years. On this basis, then, according to the third hypothesis, managements might not challenge the structure of trade unionism, but rather try to win the cooperation of stewards and workers. While such an approach may lead to less than a technically optimum level of efficiency, it may be seen as not so risky both in the short term and the longer term: for if 'macho' tactics were to lead to renewed economic vitality, then workers might be induced to adopt similarly aggressive tactics as the balance of power turned in their favour.

Both the second and third hypotheses suggest that union organization within the workplace should have remained largely intact over the last five years, although to the extent that plants with especially strong workplace organizations have been shut down, the 'average' strength of union organization has obviously fallen — unfortunately, the nature of the survey precludes us from taking this fully into account. This section investigates how far this is indeed the case (chapter 8 tries to assess how far the power and orientation of shop stewards has changed). First, union membership and recognition, the closed shop and check-off are discussed; then we turn our attention to the characteristics of shop steward organization.

Union Membership and its Institutional Supports

Union density

Eighty-four per cent of the manual workers employed by the plants in the survey are union members. In the adjusted 1978 survey, manual union density was 87 per cent (this decline is not statistically significant). The overall picture, then, is one of continuing high levels of membership. In nearly three-fifths of plants all the manual workers are union members, and in another 11 per cent over 90 per cent of them are. At the other extreme, in only 3 per cent of plants are no manual workers in a union, and in another 12 per cent less than half of them are. Union membership is particularly high in printing and in mechanical engineering; it does not vary by ownership.

Union density increases with size, whether measured by total or manual employment currently. However, the strongest 'size effect' is found for the level of manual employment in 1978. This point is particularly worthy of note since it suggests that few employers have tried — or at any rate succeeded in any attempts — to reduce union membership over the last five years.

The level of union density is not associated with the level of personnel bureaucracy, but it is closely associated with union recognition and the existence and coverage of the closed shop. All manual workers are unionized in two-thirds of the plants where one or more unions are recognized by management, but this is so in only two of the thirteen plants which do not recognize unions. Similarly, in virtually all plants operating a 100 per cent closed shop manual union membership is total; but such high levels of union density are found in less than a fifth of other plants. The length constraints of a postal questionnaire precluded any investigation of whether high union density led to recognition and closed shops, or vice versa. In practice, the particular pattern is likely to vary between plants; although it is probable that significant levels of union density in most cases lead to recognition and closed shop arrangements which, in turn, lead to (near) total union membership.

Union recognition

In only 10 per cent of the plants which have any manual union members are trade unions unrecognized by management: the level of union density in these cases tends to be low. This indicates no significant change from 1978. Recognition is not related to ownership, but is strongly related, as in the case of union density, to levels of manual employment in 1978: nearly two-thirds of those not recognizing unions employed fewer than 200 manual workers in 1978.

Most plants with any union members recognize a number of manual unions; only 24 per cent recognize only one manual union, while 43 per cent recognize three or more. Such multi-union recognition is particularly common in printing and in vehicles, chemicals and food, drink and tobacco. Again, not surprisingly, the number of unions recognized tends to increase with size, and particularly with the number of manual workers employed in 1978. (Multi-union recognition is also more common where labour costs are high and where there is less integration of production.) Multi-union recognition (defined as recognizing three or more manual unions) is associated with a higher proportion of workers being covered by the closed shop, suggesting that the latter reflects union pressure rather than purely management initiative.

The closed shop

In 62 per cent of the plants which have any manual union members, there is a closed shop at least for some groups. This suggests an increase in the coverage of closed shops since 1978. If we take the 1978 IRRU survey data adjusted to the current size distribution of the 1983 survey, it appears that the closed shop has spread to a further 14 per cent of plants. However, this adjustment may be criticized for failing to take into account the reduction in the size of plants over the last five years.

It might be more useful, therefore, to adjust the 1978 survey by the 1978 size distribution of the 1983 survey plants. When this is done, the apparent increase in the number of plants with closed shops declines — but there still appears to have been an increase. In overall terms, 56 per cent of the manual workers in the 1983 survey were covered by a closed shop: the corresponding 1978 figures are 44 per cent (on the basis of the current size distribution of the 1983 survey) and 51 per cent (on the basis of the 1978 size distribution of the 1983 survey). This slight increase in the coverage of the closed shop is all the more striking given some decline in management support for it. In the adjusted 1978 survey, only 4 per cent of managements opposed the closed shop where it existed (this figure applies no matter how the 1978 data are reweighted), whereas the figure rises to 10 per cent in 1983. This growth of opposition appears to be part of the attempt by a minority of companies actively to reduce the role of the union (see chapter 7).

In the majority of the plants where closed shops exist, they cover all manual workers; this is so in four-fifths of cases. While closed shops are not associated with ownership, they are more common in large plants (the strongest 'size effect' is with current manual employment). Closed shops are also slightly more common where labour costs are low and where production is integrated.

The 1983 survey provides an opportunity to assess the view that closed shop arrangements, particularly since they are typically supported by management and are nowadays mainly of a post- rather than pre-entry nature, are a means for management to incorporate unions. Because of the length constraints of a postal questionnaire, respondents could not be asked about the origins or precise nature of closed shop arrangements; accordingly the discussion which follows is necessarily somewhat crude.

While the existence of total closed shops is not associated with the level of personnel bureaucracy, it is related to other features of union and steward organization. In particular, nearly half the plants with a total closed shop score the maximum on the steward bureaucracy index, while this is true of only 16 per cent of plants where the closed shop does not exist. Moreover, such relationships are found in the case of the existence of full-time stewards and regular stewards meetings, even when the size of the manual labour force is controlled for.

There is some evidence that a total closed shop is associated with steward 'oligarchy' (see the next section). While there is no significant variation in steward or senior steward tenure, the relative tenure of the latter compared with the former tends to be higher where a closed shop exists. Similarly, while there is no variation in the level of 'ordinary' steward influence over members, that of senior stewards tends to be relatively greater where a closed shop exists. Steward organization is less likely to be fragmented and there is a slightly greater probability of senior steward control where there is a closed shop. However, the relative influence of senior stewards over earnings and work organization is not greater where there is a closed shop.

While, then, steward oligarchy tends to be greater in 'procedural' terms when there is a closed shop, it is not associated with a loss of control by ordinary stewards over member interests. Indeed, they are more likely to have a significant degree of influence over, for example, work organization: this is so in nearly two-thirds of total closed shop situations, compared with slightly over a third of other plants.

Where a total closed shop exists stewards are less likely to show much sympathy with management views. It is not surprising, therefore, to find that challenges to management are more common: unions are seen as a significant check on changes in working arrangements in four times as many plants with a total closed shop as in others. Similarly, these plants are much more likely to have experienced a strike in the last two years.

Check-off

Like the closed shop, check-off — the deduction of union subscriptions from workers' pay by the employer — has been seen by some commentators as an important aspect of management's attempts to incorporate shop stewards. The theory was that the collection of dues had been a crucial opportunity for steward—member contact which no longer existed because of check-off. I have already questioned the validity of this view above and the 1983 survey provided an opportunity to check the argument more fully.

Eighty-four per cent of plants operate a check-off system. This suggests that the system has become more widespread since 1978. In that year, 72 per cent of comparable plants deducted union dues at source; or, if we adjust the 1978 survey to the 1978 size distribution of the 1983 survey, the figure is 77 per cent.

Check-off is less common in industries such as mechanical engineering and vehicles, and printing where workplace union organization has traditionally been strong. There is no variation by ownership, but it is more common in large plants. The fuller development of personnel bureaucracy is associated with the use of check-off. However, it is only very weakly related to the degree of steward bureaucracy.

At first sight, the incorporation account of check-off appears to receive some support from the data — for example, steward influence over members tends to be less and the relative influence of senior stewards is greater where there is check-off. But, once we control for industry, these variations no longer exist: in other words, they reflect the fact that check-off is less common in those industries where steward organization is of longer standing. Once this fact is allowed for, then there is no tendency for steward oligarchy to be greater or steward challenges to management to be less where check-off exists. The alternative interpretation — that check-off created or fostered weaker steward organization in particular industries — is scarcely credible if only because it ignores the history of steward organization in different industries.

Shop Steward Organization

The number of shop stewards

Only one plant where any manual workers are union members has no shop stewards. In 43 per cent of other plants there are ten or fewer stewards while, at the other extreme, a quarter of plants have 26 or more stewards. The mean number of stewards per plant was 19.4: this compares with a mean of 18 for similarly sized plants in 1978. However, if we adjust the 1978 survey to the 1978 size distribution of the 1983 survey, there has been a decline in the number of stewards, for the 1978 mean number of stewards was 23. In other words, the number of stewards has diminished but marginally less than in proportion to the fall in manual employment (clearly there are likely to be significant variations in changes in the number of stewards depending upon the precise nature of job reductions).

The number of shop stewards is strongly related to the number of workers, and this fact explains most of the variation by industry. Only 6 per cent of plants with fewer than 200 manual workers have more than ten stewards, compared with 95 per cent of those employing a manual labour force of more than 500 workers. (Given this particularly strong relationship, all subsequent cross-tabulations were controlled by size.) There is no relationship between ownership or the degree of production integration with the number of stewards. There is, however, a tendency for the number of stewards to be greater where labour costs are lower. Even when controlling the size of the manual labour force, the number of stewards is higher the greater the degree of personnel bureaucracy: single-employer bargaining is also associated with a larger number of stewards. There is a weak tendency for the number of stewards to increase with union density. A stronger relationship, however, exists with the number of unions recognized by management.

Steward density

Steward density refers to the ratio of stewards to workers. The average figure for the sample is 3.6 per 100 workers (broadly in line with the figure for 1978). In the following discussion high steward density refers to a ratio higher than 3.6; low density to a below average ratio.

High steward density is to be found in industries where steward organization is long-standing — engineering and printing. Steward density is not related to labour costs or the integration of production: it is, however, closely related to the scale of labour force reduction. Where this has been large, steward density is higher. Steward density is not significantly related to the size of the manual labour force either currently or in 1978. The degree of personnel bureaucracy is not significantly related to steward density; nor is bargaining level.

The key factors explaining high steward density relate to union membership. Density is higher where membership is 100 per cent (relatedly, steward density tends to be higher the greater the coverage of the closed shop). It is also higher the larger the number of unions in the plant, and is higher still where these negotiate jointly. Density is not significantly related to the number of stewards nor the level of steward bureaucracy.

Senior shop stewards

Senior shop stewards exist in 85 per cent of the plants in the survey. This suggests no significant change relative to 1978: if anything, they are marginally more common now than they were in comparably sized plants five years ago. Of those plants with stewards, just over a third have only one senior steward while 13 per cent have six or more. Larger plants tend to have more senior stewards — two or more of them exist in twice as many plants with more than 500 manual workers as in those with less than 200. In addition, there tend to be more senior stewards where labour costs are higher. There is a weak positive relationship between the number of senior stewards and the level of personnel bureaucracy; more senior stewards also exist where plant-level bargaining takes place. As might be expected, there are more senior stewards the larger the number of unions recognized. However, there is no significant tendency for the number of senior stewards to increase with union density or the coverage of the closed shop.

Full-time shop stewards

Thirty-five per cent of the plants in the survey have at least one full-time shop steward. This indicates no significant change since 1978: indeed, depending on how one adjusts the 1978 survey (by current or 1978 employment of the 1983 sample) there appears to be either a marginal increase or a marginal decline. However, if we look at the number of plants which have two or more full-timers, there does appear to have been a reduction: in 1983 only 11 per cent have more than one full-time steward; weighting by current employment in the 1983 survey, 16 per cent of plants in the 1978 survey had this number, while if we weight by the 1978 employment levels of the 1983 sample, one-fifth had two or more full-timers. It seems reasonable to conclude that while there has been no change in the number of plants with full-time stewards, there has been a reduction in the number of full-timers possibly in greater proportion than the reduction in employment.

Full-time stewards are almost exclusively found in plants with large manual labour forces. This strong 'size effect' explains most of the industrial variation which exists. Neither ownership nor labour costs are associated with the existence of full-timers, but they do tend to be more common in integrated plants.

The level of personnel bureaucracy is associated with the existence of full-timers. They are twice as common in plants which score the maximum on the bureaucracy index. Full-timers are especially associated with the existence of personnel specialists above the level of the plant. Relatedly, full-timers are most common where bargaining over pay takes place at company level and least common where there is multi-employer bargaining. This relationship holds even when size of manual labour force is controlled for.

The existence of full-time stewards is more likely where union density and complexity are greater. They are three times as common where there is a total closed shop; a similar pattern is found with union density, and this is true even if we control for the size of the manual labour force. They are also much more common the greater the number of unions which are recognized.

Regular steward meetings

The third aspect of steward bureaucracy is regular meetings of shop stewards: as noted in chapter 3, it is open to question how far such meetings provide a means for senior stewards to exercise control over other stewards rather than the reverse.

Table 6.7 suggests that the number of plants which have regular steward meetings has declined over the last five years. The 1978 figure is based upon the IRRU survey adjusted to the present size distribution of the 1983 survey. If we adjust to the 1978 size distribution, then the decline is even greater. However, there has been no significant increase in the proportion of plants where stewards never meet together.

Stewards meet regularly in over two-thirds of plants which employ over 500 manual workers, but in only 15 per cent of those with a manual labour force of under 200. Once size is controlled, there are no significant variations by ownership or characteristics of the production process. Also in part attributable to the 'size effect' is the relationship between this element of steward bureaucracy and the level of personnel bureaucracy: regular meetings are more common in plants which score the maximum on this index. A stronger relationship exists with bargaining level: plants which engage in single-employer pay bargaining are twice as likely as those where multi-employer bargaining occurs to have their stewards meeting regularly.

Regular steward meetings are more common in plants where union organization is more developed in terms of union density and the coverage of the closed shop. However, the strongest relationship is with the number of shop stewards, suggesting that once stewards become numerous they require formal methods of coordination. Hence plants with fewer than ten stewards are only a quarter as likely to have regular meetings as those with more than this number of stewards.

Meetings of stewards from various unions

Of those plants with more than one manual union, a third have regular *joint* shop steward meetings — that is, meetings of stewards from the various unions; however, in two-fifths of cases the stewards from the various unions never formally meet together. Comparison with the 1978 survey suggests a slight fall in the number of plants where joint shop steward meetings are held: reweighting the survey by the current size

TABLE 6.7 WHETHER MEETINGS OF STEWARDS TAKE PLACE, 1978 AND 1983 (%)

Meetings of stewards held	1978	1983
Regularly	63	51
Occasionally	28	42
Never	9	7
Total	100	100

distribution of the 1983 survey, 38 per cent of plants in 1978 had regular steward meetings. If we adjust the 1978 survey by the 1978 size distribution of the 1983 survey, the decline in regular steward meetings appears greater, for 43 per cent of the plants then held regular joint shop steward meetings.

Regular joint shop steward meetings do not vary by ownership, labour costs or the integration of the production process. They do, however, vary by the size of the manual labour force, but not in a simple and direct manner: they are most common in medium-sized plants (200—500 manual workers) and least common in small plants. There is a weak tendency for regular joint shop steward meetings to be more common the greater the degree of personnel bureaucracy: the strongest relationship is found with the presence of a personnel specialist at plant level. No relationship exists between bargaining level and the regularity or existence of joint shop steward meetings.

This form of steward contact is not related to union density or the coverage of the closed shop. Joint meetings of shop stewards from different unions are more common the larger the number of unions in the plant. Similarly, and perhaps more basically, joint meetings are more common where the various unions negotiate jointly: in less than a third of plants where this is not the case are there regular joint meetings, while in over half of those plants where the unions negotiate jointly the various stewards meet regularly.

The overall level of steward bureaucracy

The preceding discussion can best be summarized by building up an index of steward bureaucracy of the kind referred to earlier in this chapter. Table 6.8 shows that almost two in five plants have all three characteristics, scoring the maximum on the index. Just under a third of

TABLE 6.8 LEVELS OF STEWARD BUREAUCRACY

	Senior stewards	Regular meetings	Full-timers		% plants
3 characteristics	Yes	Yes	Yes		38
2 characteristics (a)	Yes	Yes	No	27⎱	32
2 characteristics (b)	Yes	No	Yes	5⎰	
1 characteristic	Yes	No	No		24
0 characteristics	No	No	No		6
Total					100

plants have two bureaucratic characteristics, full-time stewards being the least common feature. Only 6 per cent of plants have no bureaucratic features of steward organization.

Fully bureaucratic steward organizations — that is, those with all three characteristics — are found in over two-thirds of plants with more than 500 manual workers: they exist in only 7 per cent of plants with fewer than 200 workers. Even when we control for this 'size effect', there is a tendency for steward bureaucracy to be more developed where personnel bureaucracy is 'complete'. In addition, 'total' steward bureaucracy is more than twice as common where plants engage in single- rather than multi-employer bargaining and is particularly common where bargaining takes place above plant level.

Steward bureaucracy is also greater where union organization is more developed in terms of union membership and coverage of the closed shop. Stronger relationships, however, are found with the number of unions recognized. In 56 per cent of plants which recognize three or more unions, steward bureaucracy is fully developed, while this is so in less than a quarter of other plants. This pattern holds even when size is controlled for, although the relationship is much stronger in industries where steward organization is 'traditional' rather than of more recent origin. Steward bureaucracy is also much more common where the number of stewards is greater: it is fully developed in only 9 per cent of plants with fewer than ten stewards but in three-fifths of plants where there are a larger number. Again, this relationship holds even when we control for size of plant. Finally, two other features of steward organization are more common where steward bureaucracy is more developed: *joint* shop steward meetings and combine committees. For example, in half the plants where steward bureaucracy is complete stewards attend combine meetings, while this is so in about a third of other plants.

Domestic organization and the larger union

In any survey it is impossible to investigate all issues of interest, and this applies particularly to a postal questionnaire. Many of the matters relating to links between the larger union and domestic organization such as branch structures and the extent to which stewards and other union members in the plant were involved in other union bodies were not therefore investigated. Respondents were asked about only two things: the existence of meetings of stewards from various plants within the company, and the extent to which full-time officials took part in negotiations 'on major issues'.

The question used to investigate the extent to which multi-plant meetings of stewards occur ('do meetings take place between manual stewards from this establishment and stewards from other parts of the company?') has been used in other surveys and is generally interpreted as a means of identifying combine committees. In chapter 3 we queried this interpretation on the grounds that responses might equally well relate to 'official' multi-plant meetings organized by union officials (or even management). While in the 1983 survey the example of a 'combine committee' was added to the question, positive responses may still refer to other kinds of multi-plant meeting.

Meetings of stewards from the various plants within the parent company occur in 43 per cent of the plants in the survey, but in only 11 per cent of cases on a regular basis. This suggests a slight decrease since 1978: on the basis of the current size distributions of the 1983 survey, 49 per cent of plants in 1978 had 'combine' meetings (18 per cent had regular meetings); on the basis of the 1978 size distribution, the decline is even greater: 54 per cent of plants in 1978 had combine meetings, 20 per cent on a regular basis. It seems likely that such 'combines' may have collapsed in plants where particularly large-scale reductions in the manual labour force have occurred; this would be consistent with the widely recognized weaknesses of steward organization at company level.

'Combines' are not related to ownership but are more common in mechanical engineering. They tend also to be more frequently found where labour costs are higher and production is more integrated. 'Combines' exist in fewer small than large plants. The level of personnel bureaucracy is not significantly related to the existence of 'combines' although they are twice as common where bargaining is at corporate level. Multi-plant meetings of stewards are not related to union density, the coverage of the closed shop or the size of the steward body. There is a slight tendency for them to be more common where steward bureaucracy is more developed and particularly where full-time stewards exist.

The marginality of combines in practice is suggested by a number of factors. They are not related to some key indicators of 'oligarchy', those relating to tenure and the relative influence of senior stewards over earnings and work organization. Senior steward control of the steward body tends to be greater where combines exist, but the relative influence of senior stewards over members tends to be less, although steward influence with members tends to be rather greater where combines exist. This leads to some interesting questions about the extent to which 'combines' create tensions within the steward body — unfortunately we cannot trace them further with the survey data.

Furthermore, the existence of 'combines' is not significantly related to most of the indicators of steward influence; even senior steward influence is only marginally greater where combines exist. And this relationship is largely attributable to the role of corporate bargaining (and, relatedly, the more restrictive nature of formal, written agreements where 'combines' exist). Similarly, there is no significant tendency for the unions to be seen by respondents as more 'obstructive' where there are combines, nor is overall industrial action more common. In short, 'combines' do not appear to be in reality a major source of strength for shop stewards: this reflects the limitations of steward hierarchy.

Given the emphasis upon workplace organization and bargaining in recent years, there is a danger of assuming that full-time officials rarely, if ever, play a part in company industrial relations. This view is clearly incorrect: where multi-employer bargaining takes place, then full-time officials clearly play a key role; in much single-employer bargaining in the public sector the same is true; and in the private sector full-time officials may also play a leading role in single-employer bargaining. So it is not surprising to find that in answer to a question on how often full-time officials were involved in the negotiation of major issues, only 6 per cent of respondents say 'never' and almost a third say that they are 'generally' involved. Nevertheless, over the last five years there has been a slight overall reduction in the involvement of full-time officials: in only 12 per cent of plants is their involvement said to have increased, while for twice this proportion full-time official involvement has fallen. But what is most important is that, according to most respondents, the level of involvement has not changed.

The extent to which full-time officials are involved in negotiations is not significantly related to ownership or any measures of the size of the labour force. They play a more active role in those sectors in which shop steward organization is new. The role which full-time officials play is not related to the degree of personnel bureaucracy but is linked to bargaining arrangements: such officials are generally involved in major negotiations in about two-fifths of plants where bargaining occurs at corporate level or jointly with other employers, but in only a fifth of 'plant bargainers' do they generally play a role in major negotiations.

Full-time officials also appear to play a role in shaping and maintaining organization within the workplace. Thus, for example, they are more often involved in negotiations where the number of unions recognized is large. Whether this is to defend the particular interests of their individual unions and/or to foster unity between the different unions is an interesting question: the former may be more likely given the fact that full-time officials are twice as often involved where unions negotiate separately than where they do so jointly. Full-time officials also play a rather more active role where strikes have occurred in the last two years.

'OLIGARCHY': POWER AND INFLUENCE IN SHOP STEWARD ORGANIZATIONS

A key strand in the analysis of trade unions has been the extent to which an 'iron law of oligarchy' applies. This theme has until recently primarily been discussed in relation to the national level of trade unions. However, as we saw in chapter 3, with workplace reform a number of writers began to argue that shop stewards, who had previously been seen as an important check upon oligarchical tendencies, were themselves developing a form of elitism. Along with this, they were deemed to have become increasingly supportive of management rather than worker interests. Chapter 3 questioned the validity of this argument, but it was necessary to use less than ideal data. In the 1983 survey a series of questions were asked concerning patterns of influence within shop steward organizations.

Two preliminary points need to be made. The first is that the survey was addressed to personnel managers: it would have been preferable to develop objective measures of oligarchy but this is particularly difficult in a postal questionnaire. Some would argue that it is absurd to ask personnel managers about shop steward organization since they will be ignorant or biased. This criticism has some validity, but it might apply equally to asking only senior or only other stewards. The ideal is, of course, detailed investigation by the researcher, but this was not feasible in this case, and has rarely been done in any systematic manner in the past. In fact it would be unwise to dismiss the assessments of plant-level personnel managers too readily, for they are interested observers of shop steward behaviour. If they are to undertake their responsibilities at all effectively then they need to have a fairly sophisticated picture not only of the formality but also the reality and micro-politics of the shop steward organizations with which they deal. And, from my own previous research experience, I would suggest that many personnel managers do indeed have a fairly sound idea of the way in which shop stewards operate in their plants.

The second preliminary point concerns the nature of the analysis in this section. It should be emphasized that the structure of the account of the survey draws a distinction between what I have called steward bureaucracy and 'oligarchy' on the simple grounds that formal structures need not be paralleled by the realities of the distribution of power and influence. But there is a further problem. The notion of oligarchy, if it is to have any significance, involves the idea that particular groups have more power than they should 'properly' have: this was noted in chapter 1 in contrasting the use of the terms union 'government' and union 'democracy'. It is, however, difficult to identify what the 'proper' distribution of influences should be and this is particularly true when we look at the indicators of oligarchy used in this survey.

Questions were asked about a variety of dimensions of steward 'oligarchy'. The first concerned the number of years for which stewards and senior stewards had held their current posts. For it is a key element in accounts of oligarchy that the powerful can hold on to their official positions for as long as they wish. But length of tenure may be due to other factors: 'oligarchical' leaders may hold office for only a short time, simply because the post ceases to be attractive; tenure may be short because the previous incumbent recently retired or was made redundant. More fundamentally, perhaps, one might expect senior stewards to spend longer in office than other stewards simply because over time they have accumulated a great deal of expertise which is invaluable to the membership. Some would argue that such a monopoly of expertise is in itself an indication of oligarchy or that it is on the basis of this expertise that oligarchy is developed. Both these points may have some validity, but it does not automatically follow that all those who have held office for long periods are therefore oligarchs — they may maintain their positions precisely because they do serve members' interests. Here, of course, we enter into further problems: oligarchs may maintain their position by shaping the attitudes and perceptions of those who elect them or may be able to manipulate voting or declared election results. We have discussed these issues at length elsewhere (Batstone *et al.*, 1977 and 1978): all that can be said here is that it would be extremely difficult to tap these subtleties by means of a postal questionnaire.

The second aspect of oligarchy which was investigated in the survey concerned the degree of steward and senior steward influence over members. Here again there are a number of intractable problems. Most commentators on trade unions and shop stewards would expect that stewards should have influence with those they represent — the main focus of debate concerns the directions in which they should exercise that influence. Similarly, the very logic of the position of a senior steward is that he should have more influence than other stewards, if only because he plays a key coordinating and representative role.

The third dimension of oligarchy investigated concerns the role of senior stewards in relation to other stewards: that is, the extent to which they dominate and control as against simply being *primi inter pares*. Fourth, one can consider steward oligarchy in terms of the relative influence of senior and other stewards over the work experience of members: again, the problem arises of how to identify exactly what degree of senior steward control constitutes oligarchy.

The discussion, then, focuses upon four dimensions of oligarchy and seeks to discover how these aspects interrelate with each other and with other features of workplace industrial relations. Given the severe problems of identifying what degree of power constitutes 'oligarchy', I will confine myself simply to talking in terms of 'more influence' or 'higher tenure', leaving readers to judge how they would rate the variations observed.

Tenure in Office

Respondents were asked to state roughly what proportion of stewards had held their posts for four years or more, this period being taken to permit crude comparisons with earlier surveys (see chapter 3). A similar question was asked about senior stewards. The responses to these two questions give three indicators of tenure, not only of stewards and senior stewards, but also comparative tenure — that is, whether senior stewards are more or less likely than other stewards to hold office for four or more years.

Table 6.9 shows that in about three-fifths of plants less than a half of the shop stewards have been in office for four or more years; and only in a fifth of plants do three-quarters or more of the stewards have this length of tenure. Overall, senior stewards appear to have longer tenure than other stewards, but it is interesting that this is largely explained by a tendency for plants to be concentrated either in the relatively low

TABLE 6.9 DISTRIBUTION OF PLANTS BY PROPORTION OF STEWARDS AND SENIOR STEWARDS WITH FOUR OR MORE YEARS IN OFFICE (%)

Proportion with 4 or more years' tenure	*Stewards*	*Senior stewards*
Less than 25	24	27
25—49	38	23
50—74	19	5
75 +	19	45
Total	100	100

tenure or the very high tenure brackets. It is this pattern which needs to be kept in mind in the subsequent discussion of the third aspect of tenure: in 51 per cent of plants proportionately more senior than other stewards have held office for four or more years, while in just over a quarter their tenure is lower than that of other stewards.

There is a slight tendency for steward and senior steward tenure to be lower in medium-sized than in small plants; but beyond this there is no significant size effect. More important is the impact of personnel bureaucracy which increases the tenure of both types of steward. Bargaining level, however, is not significantly related to variations in steward or senior steward tenure.

Both types of tenure are slightly higher where all manual workers are union members. But the greater their density the lower the tenure of stewards. Steward bureaucracy is not associated with the tenure of stewards, although that of senior stewards is lower where regular steward meetings are held, suggesting that these may act as a check upon the development of a steward elite. Other aspects of steward bureaucracy are not associated with variations in steward tenure.

Both stewards and senior stewards also hold office longer where they have a greater impact on members' experience in the plant and earnings. But tenure does not vary significantly with the other indicators of oligarchy. Finally, steward and senior steward tenure are closely interrelated: hence in four-fifths of the plants where steward tenure is high so is that of senior stewards, while this is the case in less than a fifth of plants where few stewards have held office for four or more years.

If we turn to the third aspect of tenure, namely comparative tenure, the findings of the survey are rather different. Here there is a significant 'size effect' so that 'net' comparative tenure (of senior stewards relative to other stewards) is higher in many more large than small plants. Comparative tenure, like the other two indicators, is slightly higher where personnel bureaucracy is more developed; but unlike steward and senior tenure, it is also related to bargaining level. One might have expected comparative tenure to be greatest with corporate bargaining since the senior stewards might achieve some degree of autonomy. In fact, the reverse is the case.

Comparative tenure increases with both the size and the degree of bureaucracy of steward organization. 'Net' comparative tenure, for example, is more than twice as high where there are more than ten stewards as when their number is smaller, and an even stronger relationship exists with the number of senior stewards. But, 'net' comparative tenure is higher where there are full-time stewards.

Relatedly, comparative tenure tends to be greater where stewards as a whole have more influence over work organization and earnings. But it is not significantly associated with the other (non-tenure) indicators of oligarchy.

It might be expected that comparative tenure would be greater where formal agreements played a more restrictive role, for under these conditions senior stewards might both have a better understanding of the complexities of the agreements and play a more crucial role in negotiations. But, in fact, the reverse is the case, suggesting that under such restrictive conditions senior stewards may be subjected to greater challenges. Finally, despite the fact that where comparative tenure is higher senior stewards tend to be more sympathetic than other stewards towards management, industrial action and strikes are more common in plants where senior stewards tend to have been longer in office than other stewards.

Steward Influence over Members

Respondents were asked two main questions on this count. First, they were asked 'how much influence do stewards have over their members' and to choose between four options ranging from 'a great deal' to 'none at all'; second, they were asked whether senior stewards 'have more or less influence over workers than their own stewards'.

In two-thirds of plants respondents state that shop stewards have a 'fair amount' of influence over their members; only one in ten said they had 'not much' and only two said they had 'none at all'. In just over a fifth of plants stewards are said to have a 'great deal' of influence over the membership. (Very crude comparisons indicate that this picture of steward influence is broadly similar to that found in 1966.) In just over 55 per cent of plants senior stewards are thought to have more influence than other stewards, and in only 7 per cent are they said to have less.

Stewards are more often deemed to have a 'great deal' of influence over members in industries where they have a longer tradition, but the level of steward influence is related neither to size of plant, level of personnel bureaucracy nor bargaining level. In short, steward influence is related primarily to characteristics of union organization, and in particular to the level of steward bureaucracy and the extent to which stewards affect the life chances of members. Hence where steward bureaucracy is fully developed stewards are five times as likely to be assessed as having a 'great deal' of influence over members as in other plants: relationships of similar strength are found in the case of full-time shop stewards and regular steward meetings. Similarly, the level of steward influence is positively associated with the degree of steward and senior steward influence over both work organization and earnings. However, steward influence over members is not associated with any of the indicators of 'oligarchy' except the influence of senior stewards over members. In this case, senior and other steward influence are positively related. In other words, senior steward influence does not appear to be at the expense of the influence of other stewards.

The relative level of senior steward influence over members does not vary significantly by industry although it does tend to be slightly higher in larger plants. Again, it is associated neither with the degree of personnel bureaucracy nor bargaining level. Unlike the level of steward influence, however, it is related to basic features of union organization such as union density and the coverage of the closed shop. For example, senior stewards are said to have more influence than other stewards in almost twice as many plants where all workers are union members as in other plants. On the other hand, and again in contrast to steward influence, there is no significant relationship between greater senior steward influence and the level of steward bureaucracy.

Greater senior steward influence is, however, related to other indicators of steward 'oligarchy'. They are said to have more influence over members in four-fifths of the plants where they are seen to exert tight control over other stewards, in less than half the plants where the steward body operates collectively and in only just over a quarter of cases where stewards and work groups 'go their own way'. Similarly, senior stewards are said to have more influence over members where they have a greater influence than other stewards over work organization; but no such relationship exists concerning influence over members' earnings. Finally, greater senior steward influence is associated with a higher level of steward influence more generally, but not with the role or coverage of formal, written agreements.

The Nature of Shop Steward Organization

Respondents were asked to select from the options shown in table 6.10 which best described 'the nature of shop steward organization in this plant'. In nearly two-thirds of plants respondents say that stewards operate as a collectivity, and about a fifth choose each of the other two options. As the table shows, there is a considerable 'size effect': relatively speaking, in small plants there is little coordination among stewards, in medium-sized plants coordination tends to be of a collective nature, while in large plants senior stewards are more likely to act as a powerful coordinating force. But even in the large plants domination by senior stewards exists in less than a third of cases.

TABLE 6.10 THE NATURE OF SHOP STEWARD ORGANIZATION BY SIZE OF MANUAL
LABOUR FORCE (%)

	Size of manual labour force			
	< 200	200–499	500+	Total
Senior stewards exert tight control over other SS	13	10	29	18
SS collectively formulate an overall policy binding on them all	52	82	55	63
Individual stewards and work groups tend to 'go their own way'	35	8	16	19
Total	100	100	100	100

The way in which shop stewards operate is not significantly related to the levels of either personnel bureaucracy or bargaining. Again, it is the nature of union organization which is crucial. Hence the larger the number of trade unions recognized, the greater the tendency for stewards and work groups to act autonomously rather than collectively; such autonomy declines and senior steward domination increases the greater the coverage of the closed shop and the larger the number of stewards. The strongest relationship, however, is with the holding of regular steward meetings which provide an opportunity for stewards to coordinate their activities and, in some instances, for senior stewards to play a more central role. Stewards and work groups 'go their own way' in a third of plants where no regular steward meetings are held, but in only 7 per cent of plants where they are. Senior stewards 'exert tight control' in only 11 per cent of the former plants, but in 24 per cent of the latter. This pattern still appears even when we control for the size of the manual labour force.

As we saw in the preceding section, there is a fairly strong relationship between the pattern of steward operation and the relative influence of senior stewards over members. Similar relationships exist with the relative influence of senior stewards (compared with other stewards) over work organization and earnings. For example, where senior stewards exert tight control over other stewards they are twice as likely to be rated as having more influence than other stewards over work organization as in plants where stewards act collectively, and five times as likely to be so assessed as in plants where stewards 'go their own way'. Relatedly, senior steward influence over both work organization and members' earnings is higher where they exert tight control; however, where stewards act autonomously, senior steward influence over work organization is considerably greater than where stewards act collectively.

Relative Senior Steward Influence over Members' Life Chances

The fourth aspect of 'oligarchy' concerns the relative influence of senior as against other stewards over work organization and members' earnings. These indicators are derived by comparing respondents' ratings of senior and other stewards' influence over these two areas. In a quarter of plants senior stewards are seen to have more influence than other stewards over matters relating to the organization of work, while in 7 per cent they are thought to have less influence. Relative senior steward influence tends to be higher over members' earnings: it is rated so in 35 per cent of plants, while in only one case is the level of senior steward influence thought to be lower than that of other stewards. On these indicators, steward 'oligarchy' would appear to exist in only a minority of plants.

Greater senior steward influence is three times as common where there is plant bargaining. Greater senior steward influences over earnings is also more common in large plants, but no such relationship is found in the case of work organization. Both indicators are associated with a larger number of senior stewards and with regular steward meetings: for example, the influence of such officials is seen to be greater than that of other stewards over earnings in nearly five times as many plants with two or more senior stewards as in those with only one. Greater relative influence by senior stewards is also associated with greater absolute influence on their part. In the case of work organization, greater senior steward influence is much more common in plants where such officials have significant influence. In this case, greater relative influence is also associated with lower steward influence and a slight tendency for formal agreements to be more restrictive. Finally, relative senior steward influence over these two issues is closely interrelated: in two-thirds of plants where they are seen to have greater influence over work organization they are also seen to have greater influence over earnings, while this is so in only a quarter of other plants.

The Overall Level of 'Oligarchy'

In an attempt to develop an overall picture of the extent and significance of 'oligarchy' within shop-steward organizations an index was built up. For the reasons outlined at the beginning of this section it was decided to exclude the tenure indicators, leaving four indicators to be included: greater senior than other steward influence over members, senior stewards exerting tight control over other stewards, and relatively greater senior steward influence over earnings, and over work organization. Each of these was scored 1, giving a maximum possible score of 4. Table 6.11 shows that only 8 per cent of plants score the maximum on the index and a further 6 per cent score 3. At the other extreme, a quarter fail to score at all and over a third score only 1. Overall, then, the extent of steward 'oligarchy' would appear to be fairly limited.

In order to ensure a sufficient number to permit analysis, 'high oligarchy' plants will be defined as those scoring two or more on the index — scarcely a very demanding definition. 'High oligarchy' plants are not significantly concentrated in any particular sector nor size category. Nor are they distinguished by their level of personnel bureaucracy, although nearly half the plants engaging in plant bargaining have a high level of 'oligarchy' (only a third of other plants have).

Steward 'oligarchy' is more common in plants where union density and the closed shop are total — about half such plants score high on the 'oligarchy index', compared with about a quarter of other plants. Largely independent of these factors, and more statistically significant, is the strong association between the number of senior stewards and the degree of 'oligarchy'. Fifty-five per cent of plants with two or more stewards score high on the index, compared with only 16 per cent of other plants. Other aspects of steward bureaucracy are only weakly related to the 'oligarchy index'.

A high level of steward 'oligarchy' is related to a significant degree of influence over work organization and earnings on the part of senior stewards: for example, in half the 'high oligarchy' plants they are said to have a great deal of influence over earnings, while this is so in only a fifth of 'low oligarchy' plants. There is no significant tendency for the influence of othe stewards to be less — or greater — in high 'oligarchy' plants, although steward influence over members tends to be higher: it is said to be 'a great deal' in three-fifths of high 'oligarchy' plants, but in

TABLE 6.11 PLANT 'OLIGARCHY' INDEX SCORES

Score	% plants
4	8
3	6
2	26
1	35
0	25
Total	100

two-fifths of the remainder. Finally, the coverage and role of formal written agreements is not significantly associated with the degree of 'oligarchy'.

In sum, the simple equation of 'oligarchy' and 'bureaucracy' is misleading. The survey evidence, admittedly less than ideal but considerably more extensive than other commentators have provided, suggests that the existence of 'oligarchical' features — in the sense of a relatively significant degree of influence on the part of senior stewards — is best explained by the existence of a group of senior stewards who are able to play a coordinating role and to provide each other with support. In this respect, the survey findings indicate the utility of the sort of approach adopted in *Shop Stewards in Action* (Batstone *et al.*, 1977). And, as was argued in that study, there is no tendency — according to the survey — for 'oligarchical' organizations to be more sympathetic to management or to pose less of a challenge to them. Indeed, 'union obstruction' is rated as slightly greater in plants which score high on the 'oligarchy index'.

A Note on Non-manual Union Organization

The survey focused primarily upon manual workers. However, a number of characteristics of non-manual union organization were investigated — density, the coverage of the closed shop, the existence and number of union representatives, and the most important level of bargaining over pay.

Some non-manual workers are union members in over four-fifths of the plants in the survey; this indicates no significant decline since 1978. However, the level of union density is considerably lower than in the case of manual workers: in only 2 per cent of plants are all non-manual workers union members, and in less than half is there over 50 per cent membership. The relationship between union density and the number of non-manual workers is relatively weak; non-manual density is more strongly related to total employment. Relatedly, density tends to be considerably higher where personnel and manual steward bureaucracy are more developed. A particularly strong relationship is found with the degree of 'union obstruction' to management posed by manual workers: non-manual union density is 50 per cent or more in two-thirds of plants where such obstruction is seen to be significant but in only about a quarter of other plants.

A closed shop covering non-manual workers exists in only a fifth of the plants where non-manual union members are found. This is similar to the situation in 1978. However, it often covers a small proportion of non-manual workers — less than half in half of the plants where it operates. Even so, union density is higher where there is a closed shop.

Closed shop arrangements are more common in 'traditional' industries. They are also more common in larger plants, defined in terms of total or manual employment. The existence of a closed shop for manual workers also appears to be a precondition for similar arrangements for non-manual workers, and, relatedly, the latter is strongly associated with 'union obstruction'.

In nearly 10 per cent of plants where there are non-manual union members there are no stewards — such a lack of representation does not appear to have become significantly more common since 1978. However, in less than a fifth of plants are there more than ten non-manual stewards, and just over an additional quarter have six to ten stewards. The number of non-manual stewards is most strongly (and positively) associated with the size of the manual labour force and the number of manual stewards.

Table 6.12 shows the most important bargaining level for non-manual workers' pay. It is clear that single-employer bargaining is by far the most common. However, as in the case of manual workers, there has been a decline in establishment bargaining, as the number of plants which do not negotiate pay has risen to over a fifth (along with a slight shift to multi-employer bargaining). The pattern of bargaining for non-manual workers is intimately related to that for manual workers. And, as in the case of manual workers, corporate bargaining is more common in 'new' industries, establishment bargaining in 'traditional' sectors. Bargaining level is not significantly related to any measure of size of the labour force; it would seem, then, that non-manual union organization in the plant tends to follow, and probably depends upon, the development of manual union organization.

TABLE 6.12 THE LEVEL OF NON-MANUAL BARGAINING, 1978 AND 1983 (%)

Most important bargaining level	*1978*		*1983*	
Corporate		31		34
Establishment		44		33
Multi-employer:		8		12
industry	5		8	
region	1		2	
wages council	2		2	
No negotiations		15		21
Other		2		—
Total		100		100

7 Management's Labour Relations Policies

In this chapter we turn from the institutional or procedural aspects of workplace industrial relations to investigate the policies adopted by management and the role that shop stewards play. It is tempting, following current trends in the literature, to talk of management and union strategies. But, as a number of writers have pointed out (for example, Batstone *et al.*, 1984), there is a risk of exaggerating the coherence and consistency of management action in using the term 'strategy'. This is even more true of shop stewards, particularly viewed as a collectivity within the workplace.

One important limitation of the present discussion should be mentioned. It focuses upon the policies adopted by management and the influence stewards achieve at workplace level in plants which still exist. Now clearly this is a partial picture: we cannot hope, by means of a workplace survey, to develop an overall picture of corporate action in the current recession. The data obtained through the survey do not provide us with a picture, for example, of the extent to which rationalization has occurred throughout a company by means of total plant closures: despite sizeable reductions in manning, many of the plants in the survey may be relatively fortunate compared with others which have been totally shut down. In addition, a workplace survey cannot deal with another key issue: namely, the extent to which companies are shifting their activities abroad. It appears that a number of large companies have over the last few years increased the proportion of their total manufacturing activity in other countries at the expense of British-based production. How far such courses of action have been informed by industrial relations considerations is a question which would be worthy of investigation. Foreign manufacture may not only reduce employment but may also shift the balance of power in management's favour in existing British plants if companies are now less dependent upon the output from those plants.

The discussion of management policy in this chapter, therefore, can only cover a limited range of topics, since it focuses upon what is happening within plants which are still in existence. Moreover, the nature of the survey is such that particular trends which may be significant for the longer term but which are not as yet numerically common are not traced and identified. In particular, there has been considerable interest in the approaches adopted both by some Japanese companies in this country and by a number of electronics companies. In the electronics industry, for example, the primary means of worker representation may not be union-based and attempts are made through a variety of means to promote consensus and instil into workers an identity with the employer. The union, therefore, occupies a secondary role. These developments are not discussed in detail here, although the survey evidence indicates that many companies are developing policies which are, in many respects, not dissimilar to these strategies.

Chapter 6 suggested that only in a few cases have managements attempted to remove the institutional bases of union organization in the plant. It would seem, then, that the kinds of strategy which have been widely adopted in the USA (Kochan *et al.*, 1983) have not been employed by management in Britain on any significant scale. However, it does not follow that managements have not tried to reduce the role which the unions in practice play within the workplace. If they were successful in such endeavours, then there would be little need to engage in a frontal assault on trade unions. Similarly, if shop stewards and workers now demonstrated a new awareness of the importance of plant viability — whether due to their reduced job security, the shift in the balance of power or whatever — then it is possible that far from being an obstruction, steward organization might become a useful additional tool for management. That is, the current economic situation might have in fact achieved what reform, according to many accounts, was meant to achieve in the 1970s.

It was further suggested, however, that there was a risk of exaggerating the extent to which worker and steward power had been reduced through high unemployment: if production continues, managements still depend upon some minimal degree of cooperation. If this line of argument is pursued, then one might expect that management would seek to foster worker and union cooperation. In order to continue in production, changes in production methods and work organization will often be necessary and these require that workers accept new practices. And if the plant does confront serious problems, then local management has little reason to hesitate over revealing the true state of affairs. In such situations, therefore, one might expect management to seek to increase union involvement, with the consequence that there might be no reduction in the range of bargaining. Such involvement might be facilitated if, in the current situation, stewards and workers identify their interests more closely with those of management.

Where such attempts to foster cooperation through union involvement take place, an interesting question arises as to how far management is able to reassert control over working practices. There is, as was argued in Part I, a danger of confusing management intention and actual outcomes. It is quite possible that stewards and workers do not demonstrate any greater sympathy with management and refuse to relax their controls over working practices. And, even where they are prepared to co-operate, it does not thereby follow that they forsake all their previous controls. Indeed, it is more likely that stewards and workers will seek to make the minimum concessions to ensure plant survival and will be guided in their actions by the way in which they assess the current balance of power. In short, union involvement policies may not necessarily lead to greater cooperation, and, where they do, it does not necessarily mean either that workers forego all their controls nor that that control becomes less than it would have been if they had not cooperated to some degree with management.

The focus of the preceding discussion has been upon management policies towards the unions. But there have also been clear signs over the last decade of a growing interest among employers in developing more direct forms of communication with, and involvement of, rank-and-file employees. This has often been interpreted as an attempt to reduce the role of the unions which in many cases had built up a monopoly over particular kinds of management—worker communication. This question of how far employee involvement policies reduce the role of the unions is clearly worthy of investigation. But if, as appears to be the case, union organization is still fairly well entrenched and if, as has just been suggested, managements may have embarked upon policies of increased union involvement, then the extent to which attempts more fully to involve employees have weakened union control and influence may be considerably less than many commentators have supposed.

Particularly in the context of a major recession, however, it is not likely that managers would confine themselves to juggling with procedures: the rationale underlying the preceding comments is that employers may not only wish to put labour relations on a new basis but also to achieve particular substantive ends. As the scale of redundancies clearly shows, one major substantive policy has been the reduction of manpower, either in line with falls in output and/or as part of a more general process of rationalization. An obvious question concerns not only the scale of reductions in the labour force but how far such reductions are indeed associated with reductions in union influence and with particular labour relations policies on the part of management.

Relatedly, there has been a good deal of discussion recently concerning major changes in work organization and working practices, and in particular increased flexibility and mobility between jobs. An obvious task is to investigate the extent of such changes, how these changes have been achieved and with what consequences. However, in pursuing these themes, two points need to be kept in mind: first, changes in working practices — at least on paper — have been a common feature of manufacturing industry for many years. For example, in the IRRU survey in 1978 it was found that in almost half the plants some form of productivity bargain had been made in the recent past. Second, changes in working practices may vary widely — they may simply reflect adjustments to reduced output or they may involve the introduction of major new principles of work organization. The fact that productivity has not increased dramatically over the last five years would indicate that changes of the latter kind have either been less common than we might suppose or that they have yet to feed through into substantial changes in performance.

It should also be remembered that many British companies were not faring too well during the 1970s. Indeed, the lack of competitiveness of British industry was a factor leading to the establishment of the Donovan Commission in the mid-1960s and was a stimulus to reform more generally. Among the changes in substantive labour relations issues which were particularly widespread in the 1970s were changes in payment systems and related issues, and, as was noted in chapter 4, techniques such as job evalutation and work study were seen to be particularly significant by a number of commentators. It is, therefore, useful to see how these techniques have fared in the recession.

In this chapter an attempt is made to investigate the various themes outlined above. Unlike many surveys undertaken in the late 1970s, the 1983 survey tried to assess — albeit crudely — the extent to which various management policies affected the organization and influence of shop stewards. That is, the themes which were central to the discussion in Part I — particularly matters relating to steward bureaucracy, oligarchy, the range of steward bargaining activity and influence, and the role of formal agreements — are related to various management policies. This chapter looks first at reductions in the labour force and changes in working practices; second, at payment systems; third, at approaches to the union and, finally, at the question of employee involvement.

MANNING LEVELS AND WORKING PRACTICES

Reductions in the Labour Force

In most plants there have been significant reductions in the manual labour force since 1978: in all, the plants in the survey have reduced their manual workforce by a third over the last five years. And, in addition, about 10 per cent of the plants from the original sample have probably ceased manufacturing in the last few years. Only 11 per cent of respondents say there has been no reduction in the labour force. At the other extreme, 16 per cent have more than halved the number of manual workers they employ, and a further 34 per cent have cut the number by between a quarter and a half.

As the official statistics on employment indicate, large-scale reductions have occurred particularly in mechanical engineering and textiles and clothing. There is no significant variation in the scale of labour force reductions by ownership or by the crude available indicators of the nature of the production process or labour costs. Reductions in labour have, however, been particularly marked in plants which employed large numbers of manual workers in 1978. This is true not only in absolute, but also percentage, terms. Only 38 per cent of the plants which employed fewer than 200 manual workers in 1978 have reduced their manual employment by more than a quarter, while 61 per cent of those which employed more than 500 workers have done so. Similarly, almost a quarter of the small (in 1978) plants have not reduced the size of their workforce, compared with only 7 per cent of the largest plants.

The scale of redundancy is not related to the current level of personnel bureaucracy, despite the fact that both are associated with large plants. Two explanations of this finding are possible: the first is that plants with high levels of personnel bureaucracy have been less likely to engage in larger-scale job reductions. The second is that where big reductions are made personnel specialists as well as manual workers are made redundant. The latter explanation receives some support from the finding that rather fewer plants in the 1983 survey have a specialist IR function above plant level than is found in the adjusted 1978 survey (although there is no significant variation as far as other types of personnel specialist are concerned). Furthermore, the role of the personnel function is less likely to have grown in the last five years where large-scale manpower reductions have occurred.

Large reductions in the size of the labour force also appear to be associated with other changes within management. As one moves from situations of no labour force reduction through to situations where there have been large job cuts the centrality of P & IR considerations in redundancy decisions falls while local discretion on this issue increases (however for companies as a whole, local discretion over redundancies may have fallen as top management shut down plants in an attempt to rationalize production). More generally, while the level of local discretion has not changed (overall) in the few plants where there has been no manpower cuts, it has increased where large-scale reductions have occurred. However, while in these cases plant management may now enjoy greater autonomy, this is not the case for lower levels of management.

Consideration of shop steward organization in relation to redundancy is complicated by the fact that data are not available concerning steward bureaucracy in these plants in 1978. However, as noted in chapter 6, comparisons with the adjusted 1978 survey suggest that steward bureaucracy has tended to decline slightly, although — overall — marginally less than in proportion to the reduction in manual employment. In some respects, union organization is therefore formally stronger. Hence proportionately large manpower cuts are associated with particularly high levels of union density and coverage of the closed shop today.

However, it does seem as if large-scale job cuts impinge upon shop steward organization in other ways. Here the analysis is inevitably somewhat speculative: if, for example, a relationship exists between some aspect of steward oligarchy and large-scale job reductions we can put forward two types of account. The first would say that that aspect may have been present in 1978; the second would say that that characteristic has been brought about by or with the cut in jobs. The only way out of this problem would have been to ask all the questions posed in the survey not only about the current situation but also about 1978. This would have made the questionnaire impossibly long. However, a number of crude questions were asked about changes in steward organization over the last five years and these can be used to guide the analysis.

The level of steward influence over members does not vary significantly according to the scale of job cuts, nor does the scale or direction of changes in the degree of such influence. However, the influence of senior stewards (relative to that of other stewards) does tend to have fallen. Nevertheless, the actual level of senior steward influence over members does not vary significantly by the scale of job reductions which has occurred, although the frequency of senior steward domination of other stewards is marginally less where large job cuts have taken place (and stewards are more likely to 'go their own way'). This relationship is not, however, statistically significant. While the influence of senior stewards relative to others over earnings does not vary by the scale of manpower reductions, it is greater as far as work organization is concerned where there have been large job cuts.

The range of negotiations is higher in plants where job cuts have occurred, even though large job reductions are associated with a small 'net' reduction in the range and amount of bargaining. There has been a slight reduction in the role of formal agreements where there have been large-scale reductions, although they still tend to cover a wider range of issues than in situations where no cuts or smaller cuts in manpower have occurred. There is no significant variation in the current role which formal agreements play.

There have been marginally different patterns of change in the influence of stewards and senior stewards over earnings and work organization where large scale reductions have taken place. The influence of senior stewards over work organization is slightly less likely to have increased; and where there have been large-scale job cuts the influence of senior stewards over earnings has fallen slightly while in other plants it has increased. Similar patterns are found as far as other stewards are concerned.

In the small number of plants where there have been no job reductions, the level of steward control over wage and effort issues tends to be low. If we compare plants where job reductions have been large (over a quarter) with those where they have been smaller, no significant variation in senior steward influence over the two sides of the wage-effort bargain are found. Nor is there any variation in the level of influence of other stewards over earnings. However, in plants where job losses have been large stewards are rather less likely to have a significant degree of influence over work organization than in plants where job losses have been smaller.

Stewards in plants where there have been no job losses are more sympathetic to management, and their senior stewards are even more so. Where job losses have occurred no significant differences in the perspective taken by either stewards or senior stewards are found. Moreover, there is no significant variation in changes in steward views according to the fact or scale of job cuts.

Finally, it is possible to look at the relationship between job loss and the extent to which workers and stewards challenge management. In less than a third of the plants where there have been no job reductions do respondents believe that working practices could be made more efficient, and in only two cases are the unions seen as a significant block to changing working arrangements. In other plants where cuts in jobs were large and small more than three out of five respondents say that changes could be made to increase efficiency. And in more than two out of five cases trade unions are seen as a significant obstruction to any such endeavour. Again, there is no variation by the scale of job loss. Similar patterns are found as far as strikes and other forms of industrial action are found. For example, nearly three-quarters of the plants which have not cut their labour force have experienced no form of industrial action in the last two years. Fifty-six per cent of plants which have experienced job cuts of less than a quarter have done so, as have 62 per cent of those which have cut employment by more than a quarter.

Respondents were also asked whether they had made workers redundant in the last five years and whether such redundancies had been of a voluntary or enforced nature. Possibly due to a lack of clarity in the questionnaire, a significant minority of respondents did not provide information on the number of voluntary and enforced redundancies, and therefore it has been decided not to use these data. It is still possible, however, to look at whether or not these two methods were used (rather than at the scale of their usage). In just under 15 per cent of the plants which had reduced their manual workforce over the last five years this had been achieved without resort to any redundancies. In 84 per cent of plants some redundancies had been made on a voluntary basis, and in 64 per cent of plants some redundancies had been of a compulsory or enforced nature.

The means used to cut the size of the labour force is most strongly related to the scale of the reduction. Reductions without redundancy were virtually all in plants which had cut their labour force by little in percentage terms. Of the twenty-eight plants which had been able to cut labour by resort to voluntary but not enforced redundancy, two-thirds had reduced the number of workers by less than 25 per cent. The proportions were reversed for the sixty-one plants which had used a combination of voluntary and enforced redundancies — one-third had cut jobs by less than a quarter, two-thirds by more. Eight of the ten plants which had only used enforced redundancies had reduced the manual workforce by more than a quarter. In addition, the use of the different means of shedding labour varied by the number of manual workers employed in 1978. Small plants were rather more likely to cut labour without resort to redundancies, but were also rather more likely to use compulsory redundancies only.

The (current) level of personnel and steward bureaucracy is also related to the methods used to cut labour. Where personnel management is fully bureaucratized there is a slightly smaller tendency to resort to redundancies (although clearly the number involved is very small). The degree of steward bureaucracy is related to the use of voluntary redundancy: for example, full-time stewards are associated with more frequent resort to voluntary redundancies. Conversely, enforced redundancies were less common where full-time stewards exist.

The methods by which labour was reduced are not significantly related to other features of management: for example, to ownership, the degree of local discretion or the centrality of P & IR considerations in decisions on redundancies. But the nature of steward organization, other than 'bureaucracy', is associated with the methods used. Where stewards have a significant degree of influence over work organization, for example, there is a greater use of voluntary redundancy. The methods used, however, are not related to whether or not redundancies are currently negotiated or covered by a formal, written agreement.

In sum, reductions in the manual labour force have been widespread and have occurred on a massive scale over the last five years: they have been particularly concentrated in industries which have suffered severely in recent years and in plants which employed large numbers of manual workers in 1978. These reductions are associated with changes in both management and steward organization. In the latter case, it is probable that the degree of bureaucracy has been reduced (for example, the number of stewards has decreased) but generally not more than to keep the pattern of organization roughly comparable with that in 1978 for a given size of plant. The powers of stewards have been reduced, according to respondents, or have increased less rapidly where cuts have been large. However, this does not mean that stewards in these situations are powerless: indeed, they still have a significant role in many instances — as great as in plants which have not experienced such massive cuts in the labour force. Moreover, trade unions are still seen as a significant constraint upon management in many plants which have reduced labour on a large scale, and workers still impose sanctions upon management in these plants.

It would seem, therefore, that the major cuts in employment have occurred in plants where steward organization was especially strong. Whether this was force of necessity or strategic choice on the part of employers cannot be said from the evidence of the survey. However one intriguing question is how steward power has been reduced: this question is taken up in a later section. But for the present attention is turned to changes in working practices.

Changes in Working Practices

Since the time of Donovan there has been a great deal of discussion over the need to change working practices — through productivity bargaining, the more general reform of workplace industrial relations or the reassertion of managerial control. As was argued in Part I, it is open to doubt how many of these endeavours achieved major and long-term increases in productivity and efficiency. Moreover, in the changed economic environment of the 1980s, and with the discipline of high levels of unemployment as well as the need to adjust to falls in output, it might be expected that there has been a major drive by management to achieve new working arrangements, and that these would have achieved considerable success.

The survey confirms these expectations. In all but 14 per cent of the plants 'major' changes in working practices have been introduced in the last five years. The constraints of a postal survey precluded any detailed investigation of the nature of these changes: but they are likely to be primarily of two interrelated kinds. The first is simply the need to reorganize work in the face of redundancies and new capital equipment; the second is attempts to improve the effective utilization of labour time more generally, by increasing levels of effort and by greater flexibility. It should, however, be noted that constraints are likely to exist on how far it is possible or rational to push greater flexibility; for example, while some companies have developed 'crafticians', or super craftsmen, any large-scale move of this kind is limited by the levels of training and knowledge which are required. Greater flexibility, therefore, is likely to be focused upon less skilled jobs and to be very much 'at the margin' as far as many crafts are concerned.

The first and most obvious question to answer is why some plants have not changed working practices. In only three cases has management planned changes and then not subsequently introduced them. The main reason for not introducing changes appears to be the most obvious one — management have no need to: these plants are less likely to have had to make any sizeable reductions in the labour force (the analysis here is confined to plants which recognize unions). And, at the same time, in none of them are trade unions seen as a significant obstacle to changes in working practices: indeed, in all but two of them it is claimed that no scope exists for making working practices more efficient. (There are no significant relationships with size of plant, industry, ownership, labour costs or the risk of breakdown.) In these plants P & IR considerations play a rather less central role in decision-making and local discretion has not been increased.

In unionized plants which have not introduced changes in working practices, the union is less firmly established: union density tends to be lower and in few of them are all workers covered by a closed shop agreement. Similarly, the number of shop stewards tends to be lower as does the level of steward (and personnel) bureaucracy. The range of negotiation and the coverage of formal agreements, also tend to be lower. Stewards (and senior stewards) in plants which have not changed working practices are only half as likely as in other plants to be rated as having a significant degree of control over the organization of work.

Hence it would seem that working practices are less likely to have been changed in plants where union organization is less bureaucratic and plays less of a role. Moreover, in these plants stewards and senior stewards tend to be more sympathetic to management — for example, stewards in these plants are twice as likely as those in other plants to demonstrate some sympathy to management. Moreover, this does not appear to be due to greater changes in steward views over the last five years. (However, there is no significant difference between these and other plants in resort to industrial action over the last two years.)

The second question of interest is whether changes in working practices were the subject of negotiation with trade unions. In the case of three plants no trade unions existed, and these are excluded from the subsequent analysis. In all but 11 per cent of the other plants which introduced changes in working arrangements these were the subject of bargaining with the unions. The twelve plants where changes in working practices had not been negotiated had experienced redundancies and changes in output similar to other plants. What distinguished them was that they were more likely to be small. and to have been small (under 200 manual workers) in 1978. In other respects they were fairly similar to plants which had not introduced any changes in work practices: for example, fewer workers were members of closed shops. In particular, they were plants where steward organization was relatively under-developed (although they are not likely to score lower on the personnel bureaucracy index) — for example, in only two of them was there a full-time shop steward. Relatedly, the range of negotiation and coverage of formal agreements are below the sample average, as is the degree of steward influence over work organization. However, in these cases neither stewards nor senior stewards are any more likely than their counterparts in other plants to show greater sympathy with management, and industrial action is no less likely to have occurred. But in only one of the twelve plants is trade unionism seen as a significant obstruction to the adoption of more efficient methods of working. There is no hint in the data that these plants have sought to reduce or eradicate union organization over the last five years.

The implication of the preceding discussion is that plants where changes in working practices have taken place and where these have been the subject of negotiation are strongly organized plants in which the union continues to play a significant role and is far from giving management a free hand even after these changes have been introduced. These plants have highly bureaucratic steward organizations.

Respondents were asked how far these changes in working practices 'led to increases in efficiency and productivity'. They were asked to rate any such changes as 'major' or 'minor'. The data on the scale of change is, therefore, extremely crude and needs to be treated with considerable caution. In addition, as noted previously, the survey did not investigate the nature or scale of changes in working practices beyond specifying that they be 'major'. But as long as these caveats are kept in mind, it does seem worthwhile briefly to identify those types of situations in which 'major' increases in efficiency were deemed to have occurred.

In 71 per cent of plants these changes were said to have led to 'major increases' in productivity and efficiency and in only two cases had they led to no increase at all. Plants in which major increases in efficiency are said to have been achieved do not differ from other plants by size, by industry or by scale of job loss. Nor are major changes in productivity more likely to be associated with new capital equipment. Plants which have achieved 'major' increases are, however, likely to have lower labour costs: this could, of course, be a reflection of the changes in working practices. But it is more likely that this finding reflects the fact that in more capital-intensive production processes the impact of any given change in manning or working arrangements is likely to be that much greater.

'Major' gains in efficiency are also more likely where plants have only intermediate scores on the personnel and steward bureaucracy indices. 'Major' increases are also rather less likely where corporate-level bargaining occurs. The achievement of 'major' increases in efficiency is related to management organization and decision-making. In plants achieving such 'major' gains, P & IR considerations are more central in decisions and local discretion tends to be greater. In particular, the 'net' increase in the discretion of lower management tends to be higher.

The level of steward control over work is not significantly related to the scale of increased efficiency reported, nor is the degree of oligarchy nor the views of stewards and senior stewards. Nor is it related to changes on any of these dimensions. Again, it is not associated with such factors as the use of job evaluation or payment by results. Where 'major' increases are said to have been gained the unions are no less likely to continue to be a significant obstruction to further changes, although it is less likely that industrial action has occurred in the last two years. Finally, claimed major increases are not associated with attempts to reduce the role of the unions.

In sum, it can be stated that in many plants there have been major changes in working practices and that in the vast majority of cases these have been the subject of negotiation. The exceptions to this pattern tend to be plants where steward organization is — and probably was five years ago — less bureaucratic, with less influence over the organization of work. 'Major' increases in efficiency are claimed to have resulted from these changes in plants where the degree of bureaucracy within management and in the shop steward body is intermediate. Given the other relationships noted in this book, it seems plausible to say that in less bureaucratic situations the scope for major increases in efficiency was less, while in fully bureaucratic situations there was greater potential scope, but it was that much more difficult for management to exploit it to the full. However, as noted in the introduction to this chapter, one should not exaggerate the extent to which widespread changes in working practices are a new phenomenon. Moreover, the actual gains in productivity may be exaggerated by respondents — for example, the actual increase in productivity achieved in the last two years is not significantly higher in those plants where major gains in efficiency are said to have been achieved through changes in working practices than in others. It is true that the time periods covered by the two questions do not exactly correspond — changes in productivity were investigated for a two-year period, changes in working practices over five years: it is possible, therefore, that major gains were achieved in the period 1978—81. But a more plausible explanation might be that if it had not been for changes in working practices, productivity growth would have been even lower than it in fact was. If either of these interpretations is accepted, then it seems that management's ability to reassert control has not been as dramatic as many commentators would suppose.

PAYMENT SYSTEMS

In the discussion over the last two decades on industrial relations reform, payment systems and related issues have assumed a central position. In the 1960s in particular it was argued that piece-work systems were a major cause of industrial disputes and, accordingly, specialists recommended a change to measured day-work. In fact, as chapter 4 showed, few companies took this advice, at least for any period of time. There was, however, a significant move towards two means of controlling pay: work study — the measurement of labour input — became more common and was seen as a means whereby, among other things, payment-by-results systems might be more effectively controlled by management. The second technique which became widely used was job evaluation as a method for determining the relative pay rates of different jobs in a systematic manner. Recently it has been claimed that the use of job evaluation has become crucial to management's labour relations strategy: for, it is argued, it serves to centralize bargaining over pay and, in so doing, permits management to achieve considerable freedom in the day-to-day organization of work without resort to detailed bargaining or complex written agreements: these points were discussed in chapter 4, although on the basis of less than ideal data. Finally, in the 1970s — at least for a period — two other pay components achieved considerable interest. The first of these was attendance pay which, for some, was in reality a no-strike bonus. The second was some form of plant or company bonus: the significance of this was seen to lie in fostering worker identification with the company (or plant) and with management's goals. In short, it was the financial complement to other means of fostering employee involvement and identification. In the survey questions were asked about these various pay-related matters.

Payment by Results

Respondents were asked whether individual or group payment by results systems existed for any substantial proportion of manual workers in their plants. Table 7.1 indicates that, overall, there has been very little change in the use of payment by results (PBR) over the last five years (in contrast to the 1970s). However, there have been some changes. Hence, within the sample, there has been a slight move away from individual payment by results and a slight net shift towards group based systems. Five per cent of plants have dropped individual PBR since 1978 and only 1 per cent have introduced such a payment system. Seven per cent have introduced group-based schemes, but 3 per cent have dropped them since 1978. Overall, about one-third of plants use individual PBR and a third group PBR: one-fifth of plants use both types of PBR, 13 per cent individual PBR only, 17 per cent group PBR only and 47 per cent use neither. Individual PBR was used in five of the eight textile plants and in just under half the fifty engineering plants. There was little industrial variation in the use of group PBR.

TABLE 7.1 PAYMENT BY RESULTS, 1978 and 1983 (%)

Payment by results exists	1978	1983
Yes	58	53
No	42	47
Total	100	100

Such incentive payment systems are not particularly concentrated in any size of plant. They are, however, more common in British-owned plants: individual PBR exists in two-fifths of them, and in less than one-fifth of other plants. A similar, though rather less strong, pattern is found in the case of group-based systems. In addition, PBR tends to be found in plants where labour costs (as a proportion of total costs) tend to be higher.

Individual PBR, although not group-based systems, are less likely to exist where the level of personnel bureaucracy is high. In particular, it is twice as common where there is no personnel director. Relatedly, both types of PBR are related to bargaining level — they are most common where multi-employer bargaining occurs. Individual PBR is least common where bargaining occurs at company level; group PBR is least common where there is plant bargaining.

Steward bureaucracy is also related to the use of PBR. In particular, where there are full-time stewards individual PBR is only half as common as in other plants. A similar pattern exists as far as regular steward meetings are concerned. (It is likely, however, that the nature of the payment system has a significant impact upon steward organization.)

How does the existence of PBR affect steward activity? The classic argument, at least in the case of individual PBR, is that it tends to foster sectionalism and informality at the same time as it provides significant control for the shop floor; it is also seen to foster industrial action. While it is not possible from the survey to look at the control of individual workers under PBR, it is possible to see how incentive pay relates to the internal organization and influence of shop stewards.

The size of steward constituencies tends to be larger where there is individual PBR: in three out of five cases the average steward represents more than twenty-five people, while this is so in less than half the other plants. At the same time steward and senior steward tenure tends to be higher under this system of payment. However, while senior stewards have greater tenure than 'normal' stewards under individual PBR, in many respects, as one might expect, individual incentives tend to reduce the likelihood of a steward oligarchy. Hence in individual PBR plants senior stewards are only half as likely as in other plants to dominate and control other stewards. Similarly, the influence of senior stewards is more rarely rated higher than that of other stewards as far as work organization is concerned in individual PBR plants; the same is true in the case of earnings. However, there is no variation in either direction in senior steward influence over members.

Stewards in plants operating individual PBR systems are no more or less likely to have a significant degree of influence over their members than in other plants. While 'normal' stewards are more likely to have a greater effect upon members' earnings under individual PBR, senior stewards have rather less influence than in other plants. No variation exists, however, in the case of steward or senior steward influence over work organization. Nor is there any tendency for the number of issues negotiated to be greater or the number of issues covered by formal agreements to be smaller under individual PBR. Such formal agreements as do exist, however, impose less of a constraint upon the negotiating activity of stewards. Stewards (or senior stewards) under individual PBR are no more or less likely to adopt a worker's perspective than those in other plants.

Contrary to the wisdom of the 1960's and 1970's individual PBR is not associated with the existence of strikes or other forms of industrial action. Even more surprisingly, managers in 'individual PBR' plants are less likely to claim that working practices could be made more efficient: just over half do so compared with over two-thirds in other plants. Similarly, while just over half the respondents in other plants claim that trade unionism is a significant factor in preventing the introduction of more efficient working practices, only 30 per cent of those in plants with individual PBR do so.

Group PBR is rather less strongly related to features of steward organization. There is no variation in steward or senior steward tenure between 'group PBR' and other plants despite the fact that the size of steward constituencies tends to be larger. The tenure of senior steward compared with other stewards does, however, tend to be higher. There is no distinctive tendency for senior steward influence over earnings or work organization to be greater than that of other stewards under group PBR, or for senior stewards to have greater influence over members.

Where there is group PBR there is a greater likelihood that the stewards operate as a collectivity. At the same time, stewards under group PBR are less likely to adopt the worker's view wholeheartedly, and there is also a weak tendency for senior stewards to be more sympathetic to management's perspective than is the case in other plants. Group PBR is not associated with greater or less steward or senior steward influence over earnings or work organization; nor is it associated with the number of issues negotiated or the coverage and role of formal agreements.

Slightly fewer plants using group PBR have experienced some form of industrial action over the last two years. Consistent with this, fewer 'group PBR' respondents can identify possible improvements in working practices or see trade unionism as being a significant obstruction to changes in working practices.

However, neither type of payment by results system is associated with any of the rather crude indicators of performance employed in the questionnaire. Nor are changes in the range, amount or distribution of bargaining and control distinctive in any way in PBR plants.

Job Evaluation

In chapter 4 it was noted that job evaluation was seen by some commentators not only to have considerable significance in itself as a basis of a 'rational' wage structure, but also to be a central feature in a strategy of reducing steward control and negotiation without resort to detailed written agreements concerning work organization. In this section we investigate these arguments on the basis of the survey data.

There had been a significant growth in the use of job evaluation in the 1970s; table 7.2 suggests that over the last five years this expansion has probably slowed down as far as manual workers are concerned. By 1983 two-thirds of plants used job evaluation: sixty-one per cent had introduced it before 1978. While nearly 5 per cent had changed to job evaluation in the last five years, 3 per cent had ceased to use it.

TABLE 7.2 JOB EVALUATION, 1978 AND 1983 (%)

Job evaluation exists	1978	1983
Yes	59	66
No	41	34

Job evaluation is used more frequently in relation to manual workers in plants which are foreign-owned; it is also associated with the employment of large numbers of manual workers. Fifty-seven per cent of plants employing fewer than 200 manual workers use job evaluation: the proportion rises steadily to 76 per cent of those employing over 500.

Job evaluation is very much a strategy of personnel specialists. It is far more common where any type of such manager exists and increases with the score on the personnel bureaucracy index. And, given this strong relationship, it is not surprising to find that job evaluation is closely related to bargaining level. It is used most often in plants which engage in corporate bargaining and least often where multi-employer bargaining occurs. However, what is rather surprising is that evaluation is not related to steward bureaucracy: neither full-time shop stewards nor regular steward meetings are associated with its greater use.

The survey findings give little support to the view that job evaluation has major significance for industrial relations. In the first place, in many plants such 'rationality' in the wage structure which might derive from job evaluation is disrupted by payments from individual or group-based incentive systems. For in nearly half the plants which use job evaluation, some system of payment-by-results is also employed.

Second, if job evaluation played a key role in limiting sectional steward activity, then it seems reasonable to expect that steward oligarchy would be greater and steward control less. As has already been noted, steward bureaucracy is not greater in plants with job evaluation. When we consider the various aspects of oligarchy, the thesis receives little support. Neither stewards nor senior stewards have longer tenure in office in job evaluation plants; nor is the relative tenure of senior stewards higher. There is no greater probability that senior stewards dominate steward organization, nor less likelihood that stewards go their own way. Consistent with this, senior stewards under job evaluation are no more likely than their counterparts in other plants to have greater influence with the membership than other stewards. And, finally, the relative influence of senior stewards over work organization and earnings is not greater where there is job evaluation. In short, there is no evidence to support the view that job evaluation is associated with greater steward oligarchy.

More important, however, is the question of the degree of steward control under job evaluation and the uses to which they put it. There is a slight tendency for stewards to have less influence over members in plants with job evaluation. But there is no tendency for stewards or senior stewards to have less (or more) influence over work organization and earnings where there is job evaluation; similarly, there is no variation in the number of issues negotiated between job evaluation and other plants. Far from formal agreements playing less of a role where job evaluation exists, the reverse is the case. Moreover, formal agreements are not merely broad frameworks where there is job evaluation — they are slightly more restrictive than in other plants.

Shop stewards as a whole are no less likely to adopt the worker's point of view under job evaluation than they are in other plants. However, under job evaluation senior stewards are more likely (compared with other stewards) to be more sympathetic to management. In addition, all forms of industrial action are less common where job evaluation exists. However, while in rather fewer job evaluation plants do respondents claim that working arrangments could be made more efficient, they are more likely to see trade unionism as a significant obstruction. Moreover, there is no evidence — on the crude indicators used in the survey — of job evaluation leading to superior performance in terms of efficiency. Finally, there is no evidence of differences between 'job evaluation' and other plants concerning changes in bargaining or steward control except in one instance: the amount of bargaining is more likely to have fallen where job evaluation exists.

In overall terms, then, job evaluation appears to have a fairly limited impact — at least according to the findings of the survey. It is associated with a greater relative sympathy for management by senior stewards and less industrial action: but it is not related to greater steward oligarchy, or less steward control. (More detailed tabulations do not support the view that these findings are primarily attributable to a 'size effect'.)

Work Study

Like job evaluation, the use of work study became more widespread during the 1970s. In 1980, 70 per cent of plants used this technique for studying labour input. As is seen in table 7.3, it would appear that its use has declined over the last five years. This picture of decline receives some support from the 1983 survey itself. In 59 per cent of plants work study had been introduced prior to 1978 and still continues to be used. Six plants have introduced it in the last five years, but eight have ceased to use it. Work study is used in the majority of PBR plants but also in a third of other plants.

TABLE 7.3 USE OF WORK STUDY, 1978 AND 1983 (%)

Work study used	1978	1983
Yes	70	62
No	30	38
Total	100	100

There is no tendency for the use of work study to vary by ownership. It is, however, more frequently used in large than in small plants — only 44 per cent of plants with fewer than 200 manual workers use this technique, compared with almost three quarters of larger plants. Work study is not related to the degree of personnel bureaucracy as such, nor to the existence of such specialists above the level of the plant. But it is used more frequently where there is a personnel manager locally. Similarly, while regular steward meetings are not associated with work study, this method is more widely employed where there are full-time stewards.

Work study is not associated with any overall tendency towards steward oligarchy. The tenure of neither stewards nor senior stewards varies by the use of work study, although there is a slight tendency for the relative tenure of senior stewards (compared with other stewards) to be rather higher where work study is used. But on the other indicators of oligarchy — the relative influence of senior stewards over members, work organization and members' earnings — there is no variation between work study and other plants. There is, however, a slightly greater tendency for shop stewards to operate as a collectivity where work study is employed.

Work study does not appear to affect the actual levels of steward or senior steward influence over work organization or members' earnings. Stewards are, however, slightly more likely to have a 'great deal' of influence over members. While there is no variation in the number of issues negotiated, formal agreements do appear to play a slightly greater role where there is work study. They tend to cover rather more issues and are marginally more likely to 'limit and shape' or 'effectively preclude' steward negotiation, than in other plants.

While shop stewards in work study plants are more likely to be sympathetic to management, this was not true of senior stewards. However, despite this the unions are equally rated as an obstruction to more efficient working practices where there is work study; some form of strike action has occurred more often in work study plants.

In most respects, the performance and the rate and nature of change in work study plants is not significantly different to that of other plants. However, the range and amount of negotiation is more likely to have declined where work study is used.

In the main, then, work study does not appear to have any major impact. While it is associated with greater senior steward sympathy towards management, it is also associated with a higher level of strike action.

Company Bonuses

A rather vague question was asked in the survey concerning the payment of plant or company bonuses: it does not permit an analysis of the precise form which such payments took, but it is probable that they are primarily of a value-added nature — such bonuses became popular in the late 1970s. In 1978, 31 per cent of plants in the 1983 survey paid a bonus of some kind at plant or company level. Since then twelve plants (9 per cent) have introduced such a bonus, while six have ceased payments of this kind.

Foreign-owned plants are more likely than British-owned plants to pay plant/company bonuses; and they are also rather more common in large plants than in small ones. Their payment does not vary according to the degree of personnel or steward bureaucracy, or by any of the elements of these two indices.

The payment of plant or company bonuses only relates to the pattern of steward organization in one respect: there is a weak tendency for senior stewards (relative to other stewards) to have slightly greater influence over members' earnings than in other plants. More generally, stewards tend to have greater influence over members where these bonuses are paid, and stewards are seen to have more influence over earnings; agreements also tend to be rather more restrictive. Finally, while there is no variation in the frequency of industrial action, the payment of plant/company bonuses is associated with a slightly lower level of 'union obstruction' to changes in working practices.

Attendance Payments

There were some signs, at least for a period in the late 1970s, that companies were increasingly introducing attendance payments: these could be seen as an attempt to reduce absenteeism and/or as means of discouraging strike action. In fact, it seems that relatively few plants had introduced them by 1978: only 12 per cent had done so. Since then, three plants have ceased such payments, and in one plant attendance payments have been introduced within the last five years.

Attendance payments tend to be found in smaller plants and where personnel bureaucracy is either fully developed or non-existent. It exists primarily where bargaining occurs above the level of the plant, and where manpower reductions have been small in percentage terms.

Steward tenure is greater where attendance payments are made and steward influence over members and their earnings is greater. Stewards show greater sympathy with management and agreements tend not to play a restrictive role. The unions are less likely to block changes in working practices. It is difficult to believe that these features result from the payment of a bonus for attendance: it seems more probable that they reflect the type of plant into which this kind of payment has been introduced. However, if attendance payments were aimed at reducing strike action they appear to have met with little success — strike action is no lower in plants which pay such a bonus.

CHANGES IN MANAGEMENT'S APPROACH TO UNIONS

The discussion of union organization in chapter 6, indicates that there has been little concerted and successful onslaught upon the institutional bases of trade unionism in the workplace. However, as noted at the beginning of this chapter, managements may have fostered or endeavoured to reduce the role which shop stewards actually play. In this section we discuss the two extreme approaches — attempts to increase union involvement and moves to reduce the role of unions.

Increased Union Involvement

Some form of union-based joint consultation exists in virtually all (97 per cent) of the plants in the sample which recognize trade unions. The overall proportion of plants has not changed since 1978, although three plants have introduced such consultation, and three have dropped it in the last five years. It should be noted, however, that this was a very general question: some responses may well relate to such bodies as joint health and safety committees. For the proportion of plants which have union-based joint consultation (broadly defined) is much higher than is found in the adjusted 1978 survey, while only one or two respondents made any reference to the recent introduction of works councils or similar bodies in answer to a general question on changes in relations with stewards. Nevertheless, one can be confident that there has been no overall decline in the number of plants where joint consultation takes place between management and stewards.

A more general question was asked about changes in relations with shop stewards over the last five years. By far the most common response — 41 per cent of plants — concerned an increase in union involvement and participation (other key responses are discussed below). In two-thirds of the plants where steward involvement has increased, there have also been moves to involve employees more directly in some way.

Increases in union involvement do not vary significantly by industry or ownership, or by size of plant. Nor is such a change associated with the proportion of costs attributable to labour or with the extent to which production is integrated. Greater union involvement is more likely, however, in plants which have made a significant proportion of workers redundant and is slightly more common in plants whose performance has been fairly poor relative to the relevant industry as a whole.

Moves to increase the involvement of trade unions do not vary with the level of personnel bureaucracy; it is associated only with the existence of a personnel specialist at plant level. The overall degree of steward bureaucracy is only weakly associated with increases in union involvement. It is, however, marginally more common where plant bargaining occurs and least likely in plants involved in multi-employer bargaining.

Greater union involvement is associated with some indication of an increase in steward oligarchy. While in other plants there has been a net reduction in the influence of senior stewards, there has been a net increase in their influence where union involvement has been increased. However, there is only a marginally greater probability that senior stewards dominate other stewards, and there is no greater tendency to oligarchy on the other indicators.

An equally important question is whether or not increases in union involvement are associated with reductions or increases in steward influence. Steward influence over members has increased slightly where union involvement has increased, whereas it has fallen in other plants. However, despite these trends, there is currently no difference in the level of steward or senior steward influence with members between plants where union involvement has been increased and where it has not. The level of senior and 'other' steward influence over work organization tends to be lower where union involvement has been increased in the last five years; steward influence over earnings also tends to be lower. However, these relationships do not appear to be the result of greater union involvement — quite the reverse. For moves to increase union involvement are associated with increases, rather than reductions, in steward and senior steward influence over both work organization and earnings.

There is no tendency for the number of issues negotiated to be lower (or higher) where unions have become more involved, and, while formal agreements tend to cover a wider range of issues, they are no more likely to restrict negotiations than they are in other plants. Indeed, greater union involvement is associated with greater increases than in other plants in the range and amount of bargaining, and in the role of formal agreements.

Union influence, however, may be supportive or obstructive of management goals, and it might be expected that management initiatives to increase the involvement of the unions would be associated with greater sympathy with management on the part of stewards: in short, strategies of greater union involvement would be incorporating.

However, the survey findings indicate no tendency for stewards or senior stewards to be more sympathetic to management in such a situation, nor is there any significant tendency, relative to stewards in other plants, for them to have become more sympathetic to management over the last five years. Moreover, neither strikes nor other forms of industrial action are any less likely where union involvement has been increased, and in these plants unions are no less of an obstruction to changes in working practices than they are elsewhere. Indeed, the increases in efficiency achieved from such changes tend to be rather lower in these plants.

We have seen that in the majority of plants where unions have become more fully involved there have also been moves to increase employee involvement. It may therefore be that the impact of union involvement is rather different in situations where workers have become more fully involved and where they have not. Increases in involvement for stewards only has occurred in a relatively small number of plants in the survey and so the analysis has to be treated with some care: these plants are to be differentiated from other plants which have increased union involvement primarily by the fact that they are more likely to be in industries (such as food, drink and tobacco) where developed steward organization tends to be relatively new. Increased union involvement only is slightly more common where production is integrated and bargaining occurs at plant level. It is only weakly related to the degree of personnel bureaucracy (and inversely related to the existence of a specialist personnel function above plant level), and it is rather more common where there are full-time stewards.

In these plants the increase in the influence of senior stewards is, relatively speaking, no greater than in other plants which have increased employee involvement, and there is no greater probability that senior stewards dominate shop steward organization. On other indicators of oligarchy there is no significant variation between these and the other plants in the survey.

Trends in steward influence are no different where only union involvement has been increased compared to where it is associated with techniques of involving employees. The level of steward and senior steward influence over work organization and earnings is also similar. However, where both union and employee involvement have been increased steward (and senior steward) influence over both work organization and earnings is likely to have increased: but where only union involvement has been increased there is no tendency for influence over work organization to have grown, although both stewards and senior stewards are likely to show less sympathy to management than in the remainder of the plants in the survey. In cases where only the unions have become more fully involved, managers are no less likely than in other plants to believe working arrangements could be made more efficient but are marginally less likely to see trade unions as a major obstruction to change. How far this reflects changes over the last five years cannot be definitely ascertained from the survey: but it is worth noting that productivity gains from changes in working practices tend to be marginally less in plants where only union involvement has increased. This suggests that the lower level of union obstruction in 1983 reflects less changes in the last five years than the situation prior to 1978. Finally, there is no significant variation in industrial action between situations where only union involvement has been increased and other plants.

In general, then, increases in union involvement tend to occur in plants which have faced severe problems. It is associated with increased steward influence and with a few signs of increases in oligarchy. But the survey does not support the view that greater union involvement has made stewards more sympathetic to management or that it is associated with less union obstruction of management.

'Putting the Unions in their Place'

In attempting to assess how common attempts 'to put the unions in their place' are, the survey permits two approaches. The first focuses upon responses to the questions on changes in approaches to stewards and employees over the last five years: these indicate that 15 per cent of plants in the survey have attempted to reduce the role of shop stewards and unions. The second approach involves a systematic search of responses to identify any signs that the role or influence of shop stewards has been reduced, in terms of the range and amount of bargaining, and the level of senior and 'other' steward influence over work organization and earnings. The latter is likely to exaggerate any reduction in steward control, for it may include, among other things, shifts in the distribution of influence within shop-steward organizations. More fundamentally, it assumes that a reduction in the amount of bargaining means a reduction in union influence. While this may be a plausible assumption, it still remains only an assumption: it is conceivable that stability or a fall in the range or amount of bargaining may reflect a belief among managers that particular issues cannot be usefully pursued in the current context. Certainly discussions with some managers indicate that they are acutely conscious of constraints upon how far they would be likely to succeed in certain kinds of attempt to rationalize labour relations. In any event, this second approach suggests that rather more plants — 23 per cent — have attempted to reduce the role of the unions. However, if 15 per cent underestimates the number of 'macho' managers, 23 per cent is likely to exaggerate it.

Fortunately, in seeking to identify the situations in which these 'reductionist' approaches have been pursued, and assess their consequences, the patterns of relationships found for each of the two approaches are similar — as one would expect, since they are seeking to tap the same thing. First, attempts to reduce the role of the unions are most common in industries where steward organization is 'traditional'; and, relatedly, 'reductionist' plants have experienced severe reductions in manning associated with falls in output and poor (relatively) financial performance (although managers are rather less likely to adopt 'reductionist' policies where production is integrated).

Attempts to reduce the role of shop stewards are not strongly or simply related to the levels of personnel or steward bureaucracy. They are marginally more common where bureaucracy on both counts is intermediate, but this appears to be the result of the reductionist strategies — that is, in some cases attempts to reduce the role of the unions involve not only some weakening of steward organization but also of personnel bureaucracy. However, as was remarked in the previous chapter, such developments are not widespread.

'Reductionist' policies are associated with some other characteristics of management decision-making. P & IR considerations play a somewhat more central role in decision-making, no doubt with the wish to avoid major confrontations. But, at the same time, the role of the personnel function is rather less likely to have increased over the last five years where attempts have been made to reduce the role of the unions. 'Reductionist' strategies are also associated with increased discretion for plants and, to a lesser degree, with greater autonomy for lower levels of management.

On some counts, moves to 'put the unions in their place' appear to have been fairly limited in intent or consequence. The fact that the level of union density and the coverage of the closed shop remains high where 'reductionist' policies have been pursued suggests that in these plants union organization was particularly strong and that managements have not tried — or have tried and failed — to remove trade unions. Certainly in a small number of these cases management is opposed to the closed shop. But in other respects, such as check-off, or the right of stewards to leave their jobs and to hold meetings of members, these plants do not differ from others.

The two ways of identifying 'reductionist' strategies on the part of management are closely related. Hence if we take those plants where respondents make some explicit reference to attempting to reduce the role of the union, we find that they have experienced sizeable net reductions in the range and amount of bargaining and in the degree of steward and senior steward influence over work organization and earnings. For example, in other plants there has been a net increase in the amount of bargaining, while in situations where attempts have been made to reduce the role of the union there has been a substantial net loss. Similarly, in the latter plants there has been a net loss in steward influence over work organization but a small net increase in other plants. Attempts to reduce the role of the unions are also associated with a decline in the significance of formal written agreements, while in other plants these have assumed greater significance. In a few cases management claim that they no longer negotiate over wages.

Despite these reductions in influence, however, shop stewards still maintain a significant role. There is no significant variation between 'reductionist' and other plants in the number of issues negotiated or in the current level of steward and senior steward influence over work organization and earnings. Industrial action is no less common. The findings about union obstruction of changes in working practices vary according to the definition of 'reductionism' used. If we take plants where respondents make explicit reference to such a strategy, then there is no variation in the level of union obstruction. If we take the looser definition, then 'union obstructionism' does appear to be lower where 'reductionist' strategies have been pursued. However, the available indicators do not suggest any markedly superior performance from plants where attempts have been made to reduce the role of the union: indeed, on some indicators they are inferior. But these findings are difficult to interpret: if reductionist strategies had not been pursued, it could be argued, the level of performance in these plants would have been even lower.

A further question of some interest concerns the ways in which 'reductionist' strategies affect shop steward organization. It has already been suggested that in some cases it has probably led to a lower level of steward bureaucracy. Moreover, there are some signs that it has reduced the level of steward 'oligarchy': while the various dimensions of steward and senior steward tenure do not vary significantly between 'reductionist' and other plants, the level of senior steward influence over members has been significantly reduced. Moreover, in very few 'reductionist' plants are senior stewards seen to dominate the steward body, while this is so in a fifth of other plants. And, possibly consistent with a reduction in regular steward meetings, in 'reductionist' situations the stewards are slightly more often seen to 'go their own way'. In addition, the relative influence of senior compared with other stewards over earnings tends to be less where managements have attempted to reduce the role of the union. However, there is no significant variation as far as work organization is concerned.

If we turn to relations between stewards and members, the survey evidence again indicates that stewards have lost a good deal more influence where management has tried to reduce their role. However, despite this, there is no tendency for the present, actual level of steward (or senior steward) influence over members to be lower in 'reductionist' plants. Finally, stewards and senior stewards are not more likely to demonstrate any less sympathy to managements which have attempted to reduce their role, nor have their attitudes changed in any distinctive manner.

In sum, it appears that in about a fifth of the plants in the survey management has made some attempt to reduce the role of the union. Such a strategy seems to have occurred in plants which have confronted particularly acute problems in the depression and where steward organization was especially strong. The strategy does not appear generally to have involved successful attempts to reduce such union facilities as check-off, although in a few cases it is likely that attempts were made to reduce the level of steward bureaucracy. The main focus of managerial endeavour has been to reduce steward influence over the wage effort bargain, although only in a minority of cases do respondents state that they do not negotiate over manual workers' wages. These attempts appear to have reduced the level of steward control from its previously very high levels. But it is not the case that such control has been eradicated — it now stands at the level found in other plants. At the same time, while the degree of steward oligarchy has been reduced and now appears — at least on some counts — to be lower than average where managements have tried to reduce the role of the unions, and while steward influence over members has also fallen, it is still the case that that influence is currently no less than the average for the sample as a whole.

EMPLOYEE INVOLVEMENT

For a number of years there has been a growth of interest in strategies directed at employee involvement. This can be related to a number of more general developments. First, some would argue, employee commitment to corporate goals is especially important with particular kinds of production system: unless workers are alert and use their initiative, productivity will be low or major breakdowns will occur. From this kind of 'new working class' thesis, one might argue that employee involvement strategies might have a second aim: they constitute one among an armoury of tactics which management uses to create and maintain an 'internal state', based upon some form of isolation from wider market forces. Second, it is possible to argue that employee involvement strategies are a logical development, given certain conditions, of events in the 1970s. This argument could contain a number of themes: when Donovan-style reformism failed to develop a stable form of accommodation acceptable to management within the workplace one might expect management to seek a greater legitimacy for its position and policies through greater involvement of both stewards and workers. Moreover, such moves were strengthened by union dissatisfaction with workplace reform, and the trend towards greater union involvement in policy-making at the level of the state. Out of these developments in the 1970s it appeared possible — at least at one point in time — that trade unions would achieve a right to parity representation on the boards of large private companies. Although this possibility quickly faded, it was sufficient to stimulate a variety of moves on the part of many companies first to extend union-based systems of consultation and subsequently to direct their efforts increasingly towards employees as well as, or instead of, their representatives. This steady shift from 'industrial democracy' to 'participation' and 'involvement' was stimulated by a third factor — the changing economic and political environment. At the political level, the change of government meant that there were few prospects for any legal or moral support for a shift in the balance of power in favour of the unions. More than this, the government's message was one of reducing union power and fostering a unitarist perspective within the company. At the same time, the deterioration in the economy and in the fortunes of many companies meant that there was a need to change working practices and reduce labour. While these clearly reduced union power, in many instances worker and union opposition might seriously obstruct the achievement of profitability. And, at the same time, companies which were making losses had a strong incentive to highlight their problems to workers (if not shareholders), and to seek their cooperation in overcoming them. Hence not only was there greater disclosure of information, but also moves towards tapping worker skills and knowledge more fully. In short, changes in the political and economic context strengthened the other two trends noted above.

In this section, employee involvement strategies are discussed on the basis of the survey findings. We first look at the extent to which respondents claim that they have tried to increase employee involvement over the last five years. In the remainder of the section particular systems of employee involvement are considered. Throughout the discussion a number of themes will be central: the first concerns the type of situation in which employee involvement exists or has been recently introduced. Second, an attempt is made to relate the use of various employee involvement strategies to the distribution of power within shop steward organizations, focusing upon the various indicators of oligarchy used in earlier chapters. Third, the level of steward control over the labour process and the extent to which trade unions challenge management is considered. Fourth, some comments are made concerning the relationship between employee involvement and plant performance: this, however, is a particularly difficult task. For not only were the indicators of performance used in the survey crude, but in addition it is even more difficult in this than in other cases to be sure about the direction of causality. In addition, the particular form of employee involvement under consideration may not in fact be the 'real' explanation for a particular level of performance, but simply be operating as an indicator of some more important variable. The small numbers involved often preclude more detailed analysis of the survey findings to check such possibilities.

In sum, then, the discussion focuses upon three interrelated themes: the conditions under which management seeks to promote employee involvement; secondly, and to a lesser degree, with what results; thirdly, and a key intermediate factor, shop steward organization. For it has often been claimed that the aim of employee involvement strategies is in fact to bypass the stewards, and hence that it is a step towards reducing the trade union role. And, even if this is not the primary aim of management, it does not follow that it will not occur. Against this view, however, it is possible to pose an alternative hypothesis. If, during the 1970s, shop stewards had become oligarchical and incorporated into management, then it might be expected that they might confront serious problems in controlling some groups of members in the current situation. If this were so, then moves to increase employee involvement might well have the aim, or at least the effect, of strengthening steward control and making the role of the union more, rather than less, central in the workplace. For steward 'incorporation' would be matched by employee incorporation. From another perspective, one might substitute the term 'realism' or 'pragmatism' for 'incorporation'. But whatever the term used, there still exists the basic question of how increased employee involvement relates to the operation and influence of shop steward organization.

Changes in Employee Involvement

Respondents were asked whether management had changed its approach to employee relations in the last five years. Only a third say that no change has occurred. By far the most common change identified concerns attempts to increase employee involvement: this was so in 47 per cent of cases. No other response is so frqeuently given — the next most common being increased professionalism or strategic thinking in management (14 per cent of plants) and management adopting a firm line (9 per cent of plants).

Greater employee involvement is slightly more common in British- than in foreign-owned plants and tends to have occurred in plants which are larger. It is more common — consistent with the third argument put forward at the beginning of this chapter — where output has failed to increase in recent years and where redundancies have occurred. Increased employee involvement is more common where labour costs are high, but does not appear to be related to the degree of integration of the major production process, suggesting little support for the first thesis outlined in the introduction to this section.

Greater employee involvement is more common where personnel bureaucracy is more developed. It is also related to all the individual aspects of personnel bureaucracy investigated, and in particular to the existence of a specialist personnel function above the level of the plant. Employee involvement strategies of a recent kind are also related to steward bureaucracy: they are most common in plants which score only three out of four on the steward bureaucracy index. Increased employee involvement is not related to bargaining level in any significant manner.

Only two of the seven indicators of oligarchy are related to increased employee involvement: first, stewards are more likely to 'go their own way' rather than act as a collectivity where employee involvement has recently been increased, although at the same time senior stewards are rather more likely to have greater influence than other stewards over work organization. The latter appears to reflect the impact of greater employee involvement (or related changes), for respondents in these plants are more likely to claim that the role of senior stewards in relation to work organization has increased over the last five years. However, there is no variation with respect to changes in senior steward influence over earnings, or to changes in the role of other stewards. This provides some support for the incorporation thesis outlined above. None the less, if we consider the current levels of control which stewards and senior stewards have over work organization and earnings, there is no variation by the recent introduction of employee involvement techniques. Neither does the range of issues negotiated nor the coverage and role of formal, written agreements vary. But contrary to the incorporation thesis, neither stewards nor senior stewards are more likely to demonstrate sympathy with management where worker involvement has been increased, nor to have achieved greater (or less) influence over the membership than in other plants.

It seems more likely, overall (for exceptions see below), that managements have been attempting to use a variety of techniques to win worker and steward cooperation where steward organization is strong and market or other pressures have forced management to take a series of harsh decisions. Thus where employee involvement has been increased, the range and amount of bargaining has also grown, although at the same time attempts have been made to give formal, written agreements a more central role. And in this context it is worth noting that in over half the plants where employee involvement has been increased, shop stewards have also become more fully involved.

Despite attempts to increase employee involvement, there is no greater tendency to achieve greater productivity gains from changes in working practices. It is possible that over the last five years employee involvement strategies have led to fewer union challenges to management in individual plants, but currently such opposition tends to be greater overall. Hence trade unionism is seen as a big or fairly big factor preventing changes in working practices in almost twice as many plants where employee involvement has been increased as in others. And, similarly, all forms of industrial action tend to be higher: for example, while two-thirds of 'new worker involvement' plants have experienced some form of industrial action over the last two years, only 47 per cent of other plants have done so.

However, it was noted above that in a slight majority of cases greater worker involvement was associated with increased involvement on the part of shop stewards. The obvious question, therefore, is what happens when employee involvement alone is increased. There is a slight tendency for this approach to be more common in smaller plants, although there is no significant variation by ownership. It is marginally more common where the personnel bureaucracy is well-developed, but is not related to the current level of steward bureaucracy. More important is the position in which the plant or company finds itself: in particular, it seems that increased employee involvement alone is common where, even after the adoption of this strategy, trade unions continue to challenge management: in these plants trade unions are more likely to be seen as blocking changes in working practices and strike action is more common.

Increasing the involvement only of employees, then, appears to be part of a strategy aimed at reducing the role and influence of stewards. Indeed, when asked about changes in approach over the last five years, four times as many of the respondents in these plants as in others made some specific reference to reducing the role of the unions. Certainly there are some signs that increased involvement on the part of employees alone has reduced the role of stewards: in these plants there has been a sizeable 'net' fall in the amount of bargaining which takes place; in addition, senior stewards are more likely to have lost influence over work organization and stewards over earnings (but there is no greater likelihood that the latter have lost influence over work organization, or the former over earnings). In these plants, it is also more likely for stewards to have less influence over members now than they had five years ago, and for the level of influence of senior stewards also to have fallen.

Nevertheless, where the involvement of employees only has been introduced, stewards are less likely to have become more sympathetic to management — indeed, they continue to be more committed, or to have become more committed, to a purely worker perspective. And they are still no less likely than stewards in other plants to have a significant degree of influence over their members. Moreover, both stewards and senior stewards continue to have a greater degree of influence over work organization than do stewards in other plants.

It would seem, then, that attempts to increase the involvement of employees, but not that of stewards, is common in plants which, on the one hand, have faced serious economic problems and, on the other, have confronted a high level of steward control. In certain respects it appears that management has succeeded in reducing steward influence — this has been noted at a number of points above. But what is perhaps most striking is that, despite particularly adverse trends in output over recent years, 'employee involvement only' plants are more likely than others to have achieved productivity gains relative to output. On the other hand, steward control still remains greater than it is in most plants, and the level of union challenge to management remains relatively high.

In the remainder of this section, particular types of employee strategy are considered: quality circles, autonomous work groups, briefing groups, employee reports and non-union based forms of consultation. The various forms of employee involvement which are of a direct and personal nature — briefing groups, quality circles and autonomous work groups — tend not to be strongly associated with each other, but one can usefully talk in terms of 'direct employee techniques'; the use of such methods is related to the use of employee reports, both individually and as a cluster. However, they are not related to the use of non-union-based consultation, except in the case of autonomous work groups. As will become clear in subsequent pages, these various strategies constitute important features of increased employee involvement over the last five years. But it is equally clear that they do not exhaust the techniques management has used to this end.

Quality Circles

One of the techniques which has caused considerable interest over the last few years is quality circles, which provide workers with an opportunity to put forward proposals concerning production and related issues. Its significance is seen to lie in three areas: first, it draws upon and uses for management purposes the detailed knowledge and skills of those immediately involved in the production process; second, it may thereby foster worker identity with management goals and interests; and third, it may thereby reduce worker and union controls and may even weaken the role of the union within the workplace.

Only three plants had operated quality circles before 1978. But over the last five years a significant minority of plants have introduced them, so that 19 per cent operate quality circles for manual workers in 1983. They are particularly widespread in engineering and appear to be common in plants which confronted serious problems — notably large-scale redundancies — in the past. They are rare in plants employing fewer than 200 workers, and are not concentrated in British or foreign-owned firms. Two-thirds of the plants which have quality circles also use payment by results (primarily of an individual kind).

There is no tendency for quality circles to be associated with the level of personnel bureaucracy nor with the existence of any particular kind of personnel specialist. They are not found more or less frequently where there are full-time stewards. They do tend to be rather more common where stewards do not hold regular meetings. The use of quality circles is not significantly related to bargaining level.

Quality circles do not appear to be strongly related to the internal operation of shop-steward organizations: tenure of senior and other stewards does not vary, nor does the relative influence of senior stewards over members or over work organization. The facts that senior stewards are less likely to have greater influence over members' earnings and that they are less likely to dominate other stewards again largely reflect the impact of individual PBR. However, steward influence over members tends to be greater rather than smaller with quality circles.

It might be thought that this rather surprising finding reflects the newness of quality circles and the traditions of the plants in which they operate. However, the survey evidence is somewhat mixed on this point.

There is no tendency for steward influence over members to have fallen more in 'quality circle' situations than in others; on the other hand, member influence over stewards is more likely to have risen.

While there are no variations between 'quality circle' and other plants in the actual level of steward and senior steward influence over work organization or members' earnings, and while the amount of negotiation is rather more likely to have fallen, respondents in quality circle plants claim that the influence of senior and other stewards over the organization of work has increased more than in other plants. One possible explanation for this is that quality circles, or the factors associated with them, encourage greater sympathy with management on the part of stewards, both directly and indirectly through membership pressure. This possibility is supported by two pieces of evidence: first, in almost twice as many quality circle plants as in others it is claimed that stewards have become more sympathetic to management over the last five years; second, while there is no tendency for strike action to be less common where there are quality circles, other forms of industrial action are. Stewards in particular tend to be more sympathetic to management where quality circles exist. Nevertheless, 'union obstruction' is no less in quality circle plants, and there is no sign of 'superior' performance from the data gathered in the survey.

Autonomous Work Groups

If quality circles are the 'in thing' of the 1980s, autonomous work groups enjoyed an equal status in the 1970s for broadly similar reasons. They are, however, significantly different in a key respect: whereas in the quality circle management retains control over the implementation of ideas and work organization, workers — at least to some degree — enjoy greater discretion under a system of autonomous work groups.

Autonomous work groups exist in a fifth of the plants surveyed. In 10 per cent of plants they had been introduced before 1978, and in an equal number of instances they have been introduced more recently. Their use is not related to size of plant but is slightly more common in foreign-owned plants. Autonomous work groups are, however, more common where personnel bureaucracy is well-developed: they are related to the index as a whole and to each of its constituent elements. Consistent with this relationship, autonomous work groups are related to bargaining level: they are found most often in plants engaged in corporate-level bargaining. However, features of steward bureaucracy are not associated with the existence of autonomous work groups.

The actual levels of steward and senior steward tenure are not related to the existence of autonomous work groups, although the comparative tenure of senior stewards tends to be rather higher. And at the same time there is a weak tendency for senior stewards to have more influence than other stewards over members (this may be more attributable to corporate bargaining). However, senior steward influence over the steward body, work organization and members' earnings does not vary according to the existence of autonomous work groups.

Turning to the question of steward control, there is a slight tendency for stewards to have greater, rather than less, influence over members where there are autonomous works groups, and at the same time senior stewards tend to have greater influence over work organization. But there is no tendency for other stewards to have more influence, nor for any type of steward to have a greater impact on earnings. Possibly related to the more significant role of senior stewards is the perhaps surprising fact that where there are autonomous work groups formal agreements tend to cover more issues and to play a slightly more restrictive role as far as bargaining by stewards is concerned.

Stewards tend to show rather more sympathy with management where there are autonomous work groups and senior stewards tend to be even more sympathetic. Consistent with this, industrial action and strikes tend to be considerably less common, although 'union obstruction' is only slightly less likely to be found, according to respondents, where there are autonomous work groups. Despite this greater steward cooperation, the crude indicators available in the survey do not suggest that performance and productivity tend to be superior in these plants.

Briefing Groups

Briefing groups, whose function is to communicate and explain information relating to company plans and performance, exist in 63 per cent of the plants in the survey. In two out of five plants they were introduced prior to 1978. Since then almost a quarter of plants have introduced them, and only one plant has stopped a system of briefing groups.

Briefing groups are most widely used in large plants: they exist in 84 per cent of those which employ more than 500 workers, but in only 43 per cent of those with fewer than 200. There is no variation by ownership. They are found more often in plants which score high on personnel and steward bureaucracy (although they are not related to bargaining level). Three-quarters of plants with a maximum score on personnel specialists have them. Similarly, in nearly four-fifths of plants with full-time stewards there are briefing groups, but in only half of other plants.

None of the indicators of steward oligarchy is related to briefing groups, nor are any of the indicators of steward power and influence. However, it should perhaps be emphasized that steward control does not appear to have been reduced through the introduction of briefing groups. There is no greater tendency than in other plants for the level of steward influence over issues or for the range or amount of bargaining to have changed. And while stewards have become rather more sympathetic to management's position where briefing groups exist, lengthy strikes (that is, of a day or more) have been more common in these plants (although this is in large part explained by the size effect).

Employee Reports

Over the last decade or so there has been considerable discussion concerning the disclosure of company information. At least in the late 1970s, much of this focused upon more company data being given to trade unions for negotiating purposes. However, a growing number of employers began to provide more (although still fairly restricted) information directly to workers, with the intent of fostering commitment to management goals. Briefing groups are a particularly 'intensive' approach of this kind. Employee reports are slightly more common, existing in just over three-quarters of plants, and in nearly half of all plants they existed prior to 1978. Only four plants have stopped employee reports in the last five years.

Employee reports are more common in large plants. There is no variation in their use between foreign- and British-owned plants. Both personnel and steward bureaucracy are strongly related to these reports: they exist in nearly all the plants which score the maximum on the personnel bureaucracy index but in only about three-fifths of other plants. Similarly, reports to employees are more common where stewards meet together regularly.

Only two aspects of steward oligarchy are related to employee reports: senior steward tenure tends to be rather lower, and shop stewards are rather more likely to 'go their own way'. They are not associated with any aspects of steward control or influence or with industrial action or union obstruction. However, according to respondents, stewards in plants with employee reports are rather more likely to have become more sympathetic to management over the last five years. At the same time, member influence over stewards is rather more likely to have increased (and steward influence over members decreased) where there are employee reports. It seems unlikely, however, that these relationships are attributable to employee reports in and of themselves; rather, such reports may be indicative of broader management strategy or the situation the plant confronts.

Non-union-based Consultation

A third of plants have some form of non-union-based joint consultation. Most of these systems existed prior to 1978: only seven plants have introduced non-union consultation over the last five years, and five have ceased such schemes. As might be expected, this type of consultation is common in the few plants which recognize no manual unions. However, nearly a third of plants which recognize unions also have employee consultation. Small plants are more likely to consult employees. There is no tendency for worker consultation to vary by ownership.

Despite the relative concentration of employee consultation in smaller plants, there is no inverse relationship between the levels of personnel bureaucracy (or any of its constituent elements) and such consultation. It is, however, inversely related to steward bureaucracy: it is also less likely where bargaining occurs at plant level.

Steward and senior steward tenure are rather higher where employee consultation exists: but there are no other significant relationships with aspects of steward oligarchy. However, in plants where management directly consults employees senior and other stewards have less influence over earnings and work organization, while the range of negotiation is lower. Moreover, the level of steward influence over members tends to be lower, and is more likely to have fallen over the last five years in employee consultation plants. The role of formal agreements is also more likely to have declined.

While other stewards show no more or less sympathy to management than in other plants, senior stewards are less likely than other stewards in these plants to be sympathetic to management. However, steward challenges to management — in the form of obstructionism or industrial action — are less likely where non-union consultation exists (even in unionized plants).

'Direct' Employee Involvement

Earlier in this discussion the notion of 'direct' employee involvement strategies was used to refer to quality circles, autonomous work groups and briefing groups. While they differ from each other in significant respects, they all constitute means whereby employees are directly involved rather than through their representatives or merely receiving a document. It seems useful, by way of a partial summary to the foregoing, briefly to discuss these techniques of direct involvement together.

In all, nearly three-quarters of the plants in the survey use some type of direct employee involvement strategy. Such techniques are particularly common in large plants; moreover, they are to be found more frequently not in those industries in which shop-steward organization tends to be new, but in its more traditional locales such as engineering. The relative size of labour costs is not related to the use of direct employee strategies, but they are rather more likely in situations where production is integrated. But this relationship is so weak that it can scarcely be seen to give much support to 'new working-class' hypotheses of the kind mentioned at the beginning of this section. More plausible is the thesis that these techniques largely reflect an attempt by management to gain worker cooperation in the context of serious economic problems. One other factor is worthy of particular note: these techniques of employee involvement are nearly twice as common where PBR exists. This is of particular interest, for it indicates that in many cases the 'efficacy' of these strategies may be dependent upon their association with techniques which are the antithesis of human relations.

Direct employee strategies are to be found more, rather than less, frequently where industrial relations are more bureaucratic. Thus they are found in over four-fifths of plants which score the maximum on the index of personnel bureaucracy, and the proportion falls steadily to only a quarter in plants where no personnel specialists exist. A broadly similar pattern is found in the case of steward bureaucracy. Given these associations, it comes as no surprise that these strategies are most common where there is corporate bargaining, less common with plant bargaining and least often found where multi-employer bargaining occurs.

However, the survey evidence provides no direct support for the view that these techniques are associated with a reduction in steward influence and control. First, they are not significantly related to attempts directly to reduce union control. Second, there are no significant relationships between these strategies and the level of influence which stewards and senior stewards have over members, or work organization and the range and amount of bargaining. Nor does the survey evidence indicate that these techniques are associated with any different pattern of change in steward powers than is found in other plants. And, while union obstruction and industrial action are fractionally lower in plants which use direct employee involvement techniques, these relationships are not statistically significant. Indicators of plant performance — for example, productivity gains from changes in working practices — do not vary significantly.

In sum, there are hints that direct employee involvement strategies have a marginal impact: and this appears all the more credible when the traditional strength of worker and steward controls in the 'traditional' industries, in which these techniques are most common, is taken into account. Responses to questions concerning changes in steward influence lend support to this view. It seems safest, therefore, to state that direct employee strategies have been used in situations which may be least favourable to them; while they may have played some role in gaining worker support for management policies, this — to say the least — has not transformed the situation in these plants in any major way. It should again be emphasized that the survey data are less than ideal for measuring the complexities of changes in strategies and their impact.

However, one reason for this limited impact is that in many instances increased employee involvement (of all kinds) is often associated with moves to greater steward participation. It is only where these two approaches are *not* associated that the survey suggests employee involvement has much impact. And in these cases employee involvement is often part of a direct and conscious attempt to reduce the role of the unions within the workplace.

8 Bargaining and Steward Activity

The previous chapter investigated a variety of management labour policies, seeking to identify under what kinds of condition they were employed and with what effects. Attention focused, in particular, upon how bargaining and the influence of shop stewards was related to the different kinds of policy. In this chapter we look directly at the range of bargaining and levels of steward influence: that is, an attempt is made to assess for 1983 many of the issues raised for earlier periods in chapter 4. There we found that the data for the 'decade after Donovan' were less than ideal for an investigation of these issues since surveys in the late 1970s tended to adopt a primarily procedural emphasis. In the 1983 survey a number of questions were asked not only about the range of bargaining and the coverage of formal agreements but also the extent to which shop stewards affected aspects of the labour process.

More specifically, this chapter is divided into two main sections. The first focuses upon the range of steward bargaining and the coverage and role of formal agreements. The second investigates the influence of shop stewards over the wage—effort bargain and the ways in which they seek to use that influence.

BARGAINING AND FORMAL AGREEMENTS

The Role of Bargaining

As was noted in Part I, certain reformists and 'hardline' radicals argued that the range of bargaining would be reduced with the implementation of Donovan-type proposals. It was seen that this did not generally appear to be the case. However, given high levels of unemployment, it might be expected that employers would now be able to reduce both the range and amount of bargaining, insisting either upon their 'prerogatives' or upon formal agreements being strictly applied.

Against this viewpoint, it can be argued that the range of bargaining may have remained constant or even increased. Two scenarios of this kind are possible. The first is based on the view that, despite high unemployment, those who still have jobs also still have a significant degree of power: it is unlikely that an employer would try to sack a workforce which obstructed its wishes and recruit totally afresh. In addition, managements depend upon a certain degree of day-to-day cooperation if they are to achieve a satisfactory level and quality of production. Many managers will also be loath to adopt 'macho' tactics for fear that, if and when the situation of the company improves, workers will use their relatively more advantageous position to the full. The second scenario is not necessarily inconsistent with the first. It argues that employers, stewards and workers, are aware of the realities of the balance of power. Stewards and workers recognize that in the current situation they have to make certain concessions if employment is to be maintained. Employers seek to change working arrangements in order to increase or maintain efficiency, and — wishing to maintain some form of relationship with the unions — therefore expand the range and amount of bargaining. In this process of negotiation stewards are certainly likely to make 'concessions', if only because they have little choice. But in agreeing to some management proposals they achieve two significant things: they maintain union organization and influence within the plant and, relatedly, they impose a check upon how far management shifts the wage—effort bargain to its advantage.

When we look at the survey data, it appears that few employers have reduced bargaining activity, although with certain notable exceptions which were discussed in the previous chapter. In half the plants respondents say that there has been no change in either the range or amount of bargaining over the last five years; and a quarter claim that bargaining has increased and a fifth that it has been reduced.

The range of bargaining was investigated more fully by asking respondents whether stewards negotiated particular issues — these concerned the pace of work, manning levels, transfers between jobs, the subcontracting of work, discipline and dismissal, and redundancy. It should be noted that the question asked was 'tough' relative to that used in some previous surveys: it did not ask whether stewards 'ever' negotiated these issues, nor did it ask whether they negotiated 'matters relating to' them.

Table 8.1 shows the extent to which stewards negotiated this list of issues. At first sight, it would appear that the range of steward bargaining has been reduced since 1980. Daniel and Millward, for example, reported considerably higher levels of negotiation over manning and redeployment

TABLE 8.1 RANGE OF ISSUES NEGOTIATED BY STEWARDS

	% of plants where stewards negotiate
Pace of work	21
Manning levels	39
Transfers between jobs	45
Contracting work out	27
Redundancy	75
Discipline and dismissal	70

by manual stewards at establishment level in manufacturing (1983, p. 199). They found that in 66 per cent of plants there was establishment-level bargaining over 'manning' and in 77 per cent there was such bargaining over redeployment. Some fall would be consistent with the finding that in a significant minority of plants respondents claim there has been a reduction in the range of bargaining over recent years.

On the other hand, some caution is required in explaining the whole of the variation between the two surveys in this way. First, there is no variation in the proportion of plants where redundancy is the subject of negotiation. Second, the 1980 survey question was rather more biased towards the assumption that negotiation did occur on particular issues. Third, it asked about any form of negotiation rather than negotiation by shop stewards: it is therefore possible that in some plants in the 1983 survey negotiations occurred but were conducted by full-time officials. As was noted in chapter 5, in over a quarter of the plants in the 1983 survey respondents say that full-time officials generally take part in negotiations on major issues, and in a further three-fifths that they occasionally do so. Fourth, the exact issues investigated in the two surveys differed: the 1980 survey, for example, asked about 'redeployment' rather than 'transfers between jobs' and about 'manning' rather than 'manning levels'. Furthermore, the 1983 survey distinguished between manning and pace of work, although in practice these are generally interrelated. If we combine positive responses to these two questions, then we find that in 45 per cent of plants effort levels are the subject of negotiation. On the other hand, the 1983 survey included a large proportion of large plants, and in both surveys the range of negotiation was greater the larger the size of the manual labour force.

Finally, the 1983 survey also suggests that the range of bargaining may not have fallen dramatically. As was noted above, over a quarter of respondents claim that the range of bargaining has increased, while less than a fifth say it has fallen. The precise nature of these changes was not investigated. But one explanation which is consistent with the various findings of the 1983 survey and with the contrast with the 1980 survey is that in those plants where the range of bargaining has fallen stewards formerly negotiated a wide range of issues, whereas a greater range of bargaining is found where stewards, both now and in the past, tend to negotiate fewer issues. That is, while the comparison between the two surveys exaggerates the decline in areas of bargaining, a fall probably has occurred largely because in a number of formerly very strongly organized plants a hard-pressed management has been able to reduce the range of steward influence and control somewhat. While this does not 'show up' if we consider the number of issues negotiated, a pattern emerges when we consider only 'work process' issues. For in those plants where 'macho' tactics have been adopted and where union density is 100 per cent (the vast majority of them) such issues are only half as likely to be negotiated as in comparable plants where such tactics have not been adopted.

It is also possible to make crude comparisons of the 1983 survey with the 1966 workplace industrial relations survey which reports the extent of negotiation 'as standard practice' on particular issues. When this is done, there appears to have been a dramatic increase in the extent to which redundancy and discipline and dismissal are the subjects of negotiation; the extent of negotiation over manning and transfers also appears to have increased; the number of plants where the pace of work is the subject of bargaining is broadly comparable.

I should emphasize again that comparisons of this kind are extremely crude and have to be treated with considerable caution. It appears probable that the range of bargaining has indeed fallen over the last few years as far as matters relating to the organization of work are concerned, although the comparison between the 1980 and 1983 surveys may exaggerate this trend. However, the comparison with the 1966 survey would suggest that the range of bargaining is probably considerably higher than it was in the pre-Donovan era.

The number of issues negotiated is higher in plants in sectors where shop steward organizations is 'traditional', that is, engineering and printing. In addition, the range of negotiation increases with the size of the manual labour force, although a high level of personnel bureaucracy is associated with a lower range of negotiation. The existence of personnel specialists above the level of the plant is the major factor explaining this pattern; it would, therefore, seem to reflect the more general centralization of issues associated with personnel management found in this and the 1978 survey. This association of personnel bureaucracy with a smaller range of negotiation is much weaker in industries where shop steward organization has a longer tradition.

The range of bargaining increases where union organization is more developed: for example, it is a good deal higher where a 100 per cent closed shop exists. In addition, steward bureaucracy is associated with a wider range of bargaining: here, the role of the full-time steward is particularly significant. This is so even when we consider only plants with total coverage of the closed shop.

Here, then, personnel and steward bureaucracy appear to have opposite effects, the former reducing and the latter increasing the range of negotiations. Hence four-fifths of plants with full-time stewards but with an 'incomplete' personnel bureaucracy, negotiate three or more issues compared with three-fifths of plants where both full-timers and a fully developed personnel bureaucracy exist. Just under three-fifths of plants with neither of these features negotiate a wide range of issues, while in only a quarter of the plants with a 'full' personnel bureaucracy but no full-time stewards does bargaining cover three or more of the issues investigated.

Because of the association of steward bureaucracy with a wider range of bargaining, the 'bureaucratization' thesis would lead one to expect that in plants of this kind there would be clear signs of a steward oligarchy and a higher level of cooperation between stewards and management. But this is not the case: while stewards are seen to have more influence over their members in plants where a larger range of issues are negotiated, none of the indicators of oligarchy vary significantly. Similarly, neither stewards nor senior stewards demonstrate any greater sympathy with management in plants where the range of bargaining is greater. And management is twice as likely to see the unions as a significant check on the introduction of more efficient working practices in plants with a larger range of bargaining as in other plants. In addition, both steward and senior steward influence over work organization and earnings are rated considerably higher in plants where more issues are the subject of negotiation.

However, a consideration of the number of issues negotiated does not necessarily tell us much about the types of situation in which stewards bargain over matters directly relating to the work process as such. An analysis of plants in which negotiations take place on such issues was therefore undertaken: more specifically, analyses were made of plants where the negotiation of effort (that is, of manning and/or pace of work) takes place, where transfers and subcontracting are the subject of bargaining. Negotiation of these three areas overlaps considerably and therefore they can conveniently be discussed together. As noted above, in 45 per cent of plants stewards negotiate manning levels and/or the pace of work. In nearly three-fifths of plants effort, transfers and/or subcontracting are the subject of negotiation on the part of shop stewards.

Negotiation of the work process does not vary significantly by industry, although it does tend to be higher where labour accounts for a high proportion of total costs. Only in the case of the negotiation of subcontracting is there any significant 'size effect'.

While personnel bureaucracy is associated with a lower range of bargaining overall, it is not associated with less negotiation of effort or subcontracting: negotiation of transfers between jobs does, however, tend to be rather less common where personnel bureaucracy is more developed. Relatedly, bargaining over transfers and subcontracting, but not effort, is more likely where the main level for bargaining over pay is the plant.

The negotiation of the work process is considerably more common where union organization is more developed. High union density, 100 per cent closed shops and the recognition of a larger number of unions are all associated with negotiation of the work process. In addition, negotiation of the work process is more common where steward bureaucracy is more developed. This relationship between steward bureaucracy and negotiation of the work process is weak in plants where union membership is less than 100 per cent; but it is strong where union density is total. In other words, given high levels of membership, steward bureaucracy appears to extend and confirm union influence.

As in the case of the more general question of the range of bargaining, negotiation of the work process is associated with greater steward influence over members but is not associated with the indicators of 'oligarchy'. There is a slight tendency, however, for stewards to act more autonomously where they bargain over effort and transfers. In addition, both steward and senior steward influence over work organization and earnings is rated considerably higher where negotiations over the work process occur, suggesting that such bargaining is more than a charade. Stewards and senior stewards are no more sympathetic to management where they bargain over the work process, and the unions are seen as a considerably greater check upon management in these situations.

In sum, then, the range of negotiation tends to be greater where union membership is higher and where steward bureaucracy is more developed. This is also true as far as negotiations of the work process is concerned. Personnel bureaucracy tends to reduce the overall range of bargaining but does not significantly affect the negotiation of effort. A wider range of bargaining is not associated with any greater tendency towards steward oligarchy but does constitute a significant means of steward influence which imposes a check upon management freedom. There does appear to have been some reduction in negotiation over 'work process' issues in the last few years, however, which is primarily concentrated in plants where managements have adopted concerted attempts to reduce the role of the union.

The Scope and Role of Formal Written Agreements

In Part I it was suggested that, far from constraining negotiation, formal written agreements in the decade after Donovan in practice often encouraged and facilitated negotiation by both stewards and senior stewards. However, the evidence available was less than ideal since previous surveys had not investigated this relationship systematically; it was, therefore, necessary to rely upon interpreting case studies. In the 1983 survey, however, a number of questions were asked about the coverage of such agreements and the role which they played in relation to negotiations by stewards.

Related to this is the issue of whether and how the role of formal written agreements has changed as unemployment has increased. A number of alternative developments appear plausible. If formal, written agreements had in fact played the role generally attributed to them in the 1970s — that is, providing a base for relative management autonomy — then there seems little reason to expect their role to have changed over the last five years. On the other hand, if my earlier account of the 1970s is correct, then a number of possibilities seem plausible. The first is that managements would seek to remove the constraints agreements imposed upon them by getting rid of them. This account would seem broadly consistent with the argument put forward by Sisson and Brown (1983) that managements have avoided detailed formal agreements on work organization issues. Alternatively, it might be argued that, whereas with full employment stewards could exploit, manipulate or ignore such agreements, management is now in the position to require that such behaviour cease, so that agreements would now assume a more central role. It is, however, also necessary to take into account steward strategy: if their power has been reduced and if, as I have argued, formal agreements in practice often established particular steward rights, then it might be expected that they would try to impose constraints upon management by making increasing resort to such agreements. That is, whereas in the past they may in practice have treated agreements in a somewhat cavalier fashion and thereby achieved considerable influence, they would now treat them more seriously in an attempt to preserve a degree of influence. In other words, I am suggesting that stewards might seek to use the 'stickiness' of formal agreements, which reflect the balance of power at the time that they were signed, rather than the current balance of power.

The overall picture, according to respondents, appears to conform with my thesis. In less than half the plants respondents say there has been no change in the role of formal, written agreements. In less than one in ten plants has their role decreased over the last five years, while in nearly two-fifths it has increased over the same period. In the minority of cases where formal agreements have become less important, managements have adopted a concerted strategy of reducing the role of union, (see chapter 7).

There is, however, the question of the precise coverage of formal, written agreements. Respondents were asked whether 'formal written agreements — other than general procedure agreements' covered the same list of issues that was used to investigate the range of bargaining. Table 8.2 shows the responses: the vast majority of plants have formal,

TABLE 8.2 RANGE OF ISSUES COVERED BY FORMAL, WRITTEN AGREEMENTS

	% of plants where issues covered by agreement
Pace of work	18
Manning levels	26
Transfers between jobs	48
Contracting work out	17
Redundancy	70
Discipline and dismissal	83

written agreements dealing with redundancy and discipline and dismissal. Comparisons with the 1973 workplace survey (1975, p. 28) suggests a dramatic increase in agreements of these kinds over the last decade. Slightly less than half the plants have formal agreements concerning transfers between jobs, but again, it would seem that there has been a dramatic increase in agreements of this kind in the last ten years. Formal agreements on individual 'work process' issues, however, continue to be relatively rare, although there appears to have been some increase since 1973. However, this picture is misleading in some respects: for if we ask whether any specific formal written agreements cover effort (manning plus pace of work) then we find that this is the case in two-fifths of plants. It would seem, then, that formal, written agreements relating to work organization are relatively common.

Formal written agreements cover more issues in larger plants. They also tend to cover more issues in industries where steward organization is more traditional and in foreign-owned plants. The coverage of agreements is weakly but inversely related to the level of personnel bureaucracy. Formal, written agreements, however, cover three or more issues in three-fifths of plants where plant-level bargaining occurs, in less than half where corporate bargaining takes place, and in only one-third of other plants.

The coverage of agreements is not significantly related to such aspects of union organization as density, coverage of the closed shop or the number of unions which are recognized. They do, however, cover more issues where full-time stewards exist (but this relationship is to be largely explained by the 'size effect'). The coverage of agreements is not significantly related to other aspects of steward bureaucracy.

According to some radical commentators, a greater role for formal, written agreements would not only be associated with steward bureaucracy but also steward oligarchy. We have just seen that the former is not the case once we control for size of plant. Nor is the latter supported by the findings of the survey: none of the available indicators of oligarchy are significantly associated with the number of issues covered by formal, written agreements. Moreover, far from being more sympathetic to management, stewards are seen to be more firmly committed to workers' interests where the coverage of agreements is greater while senior stewards are not more likely to be sympathetic to management than other stewards in such situations.

The wider coverage of formal, written agreements does not appear to be a substitute for steward negotiation. Rather, the two are intimately related: negotiation occurs on issues in over two-thirds of the cases where they are covered by formal, written agreements, but in only 13 per cent of other cases. Not surprisingly, therefore, steward and senior steward influence over the organization of work is likely to be seen as greater where agreements cover a larger number of issues. Similarly, union 'obstructionism' is seen to be considerably more important where the number of issues covered by formal, written agreements is greater.

As we saw in Part I, much of the debate on the role of formal, written agreements has centred on their impact upon work organization. Agreements cover some aspects of the work process in the majority of plants. If we look more carefully at the situations in which such agreements exist a number of interesting points arise. The first of these is that agreements relating to effort are not subject to the 'size effect', although those relating to job transfers and subcontracting are. Second, work process agreements are more common in foreign-owned plants and in industries where steward organization is traditional. Third, while the overall coverage of formal agreements is inversely (although weakly) related to the degree of personnel bureaucracy, no such associations exist in the case of 'work process' agreements. Fourth, agreements concerning transfers and subcontracting are more common where union density and the coverage of the closed shop are greater, but this is not true of agreements on pace and manning. Fifth, written agreements on work process issues are more common where steward bureaucracy is more developed but are not systematically related to indicators of steward oligarchy. Both steward and senior steward influence over work organization and earnings tend to be greater where agreements deal with work process matters while union obstructionism is also rated considerably higher in these situations.

The role of formal, written agreements was investigated further in the survey by asking respondents to choose from a list of options that which best described 'the role of formal, written agreements in this establishment in relation to negotiations by shop stewards'. Table 8.3 shows that the majority of respondents see agreements as considerably more than simply a broad framework, and that in nearly half of the plants respondents say that they impose some form of restriction on negotiations by shop stewards (options (d) and (e)).

Agreements are seen to impose a greater restriction on steward negotiation in large plants: they are described as restrictive in only a third of plants employing under 200 manual workers, but in 62 per cent of those with over 500. Restrictive agreements are only marginally more common where the level of personnel bureaucracy is high, and this relationship disappears once we control for size. Where bargaining over pay takes place at plant or company level, agreements tend to impose a greater restraint upon negotiations.

Agreements are more frequently described as restrictive where there is a 100 per cent closed shop. But there is no relationship between the index of steward bureaucracy and the role of agreements. While the

TABLE 8.3 THE ROLE OF FORMAL, WRITTEN AGREEMENTS

Agreements	%
(a)　Do not exist/play a negligible role	2
(b)　Provide a broad framework with considerable scope for negotiations	14
(c)　Provide a set of rules over which a good deal of negotiation occurs	36
(d)　Provide a detailed set of rules which limit and shape negotiations	42
(e)　Effectively preclude negotiations	6
Total	100

latter is not related to the presence of a full-time steward, there is a tendency for the holding of steward meetings on a regular basis to be associated with a more restrictive role for agreements.

Where agreements are described as restraining or precluding negotiations, the tenure of senior stewards relative to that of other stewards tends to be considerably lower. This is contrary to what the 'hard-line' radical thesis might lead one to expect, as are the facts that no other indicators of oligarchy are related to the role agreements play, and neither are steward and senior steward views. Finally, it seems possible that when agreements are described as 'restrictive' this need not mean that stewards have less influence over the life chances of their members: neither the number of issues which stewards negotiate nor union obstructionism nor industrial action are any lower where agreements are deemed to be restrictive. Similarly, senior steward influence over work organization and both senior and other steward influence over earnings are not rated lower where agreements are described as restricting bargaining: the influence of 'other' stewards on work organization is however, deemed to be less significant.

THE SIGNIFICANCE OF SHOP STEWARD ACTIVITY

Steward Influence over the Wage—Effort Bargain

A basic question in the analysis of workplace industrial relations concerns the extent to which stewards achieve influence over the wages and work experience of their members. However, as was shown in chapter 1, commentators define influence in different ways: for some, steward influence exists largely and primarily where they successfully challenge management. From this perspective, the interest in the influence achieved by stewards relates to notions of 'the frontier of control' between capital and labour. For others, greater emphasis is placed upon the compatibility of the interests of workers and employers. Hence steward influence — and, relatedly, the promotion of worker interests — need not rest solely upon challenging management: power is not zero-sum. It is true that in recent years the difference between these two approaches has been somewhat modified, but it still exists.

Clearly, the precise way in which influence is defined affects the types of hypothesis put forward concerning the way in which the economic recession and high unemployment affect steward influence. Obviously, if a 'zero-sum' conception of power is used, then steward influence is more likely to be seen as having fallen over the last few years. However, it has been suggested at a number of points in the preceding pages that, for a variety of reasons, stewards may have lost less influence than might at first sight be supposed. And the findings of the previous chapter — notably attempts to increase union involvement — suggest that influence may not have fallen; this might be true even if we adopt a contestatary model, since union involvement strategies seem to have led to relatively few concrete results. It is, of course, true that stewards have 'conceded' job reductions and changes in working practices, but this is far from new: and, as noted in chapter 5, what seems striking is how far worker organization appears to have maintained its role over the last five years.

It is, however, difficult to develop, particularly through a brief postal questionnaire, objective indicators of steward influence. In the survey, therefore, a series of questions were asked which simply tapped respondents' assessments of the level of steward influence. Such all-too-common escapism, leaving the definition of complex concepts to respondents, is far from ideal. Not only does the question of the 'accuracy' of respondents' views arise (a theme touched upon elsewhere in Part II), but also — and more fundamentally — how exactly respondents defined the concept of influence. An answer can, at least in part, be given to this question by comparing responses on steward influence with those relating to indications of steward challenges to management. Such comparisons suggest that for many respondents steward influence is more than a procedural rubber-stamping of management wishes and involves a significant degree of challenge to them. Hence there is a strong association between assessments of steward influence and 'union obstructionism': in four-fifths of plants where stewards are said to have a great deal of influence over the organization of work, for example, unions are seen to be a significant check upon the introduction of more efficient working practices — such obstructionism is seen to exist in only a third of other plants. This, it could be objected, merely reflects a certain consistency in the attitudes of respondents, and tells one more about their approach to the unions than anything else. I have some sympathy with this view — hence my normal preference for detailed and systematic study — but it does not thereby follow that there is not an important relationship between attitudes and reality such that these attitudes cannot be used as an approximation to the 'real' situation (the significance of assessments of union 'obstructionism' is discussed below).

We can glean a better idea of the utility of respondents' assessments of steward influence by seeing how they relate to more 'objective' phenomena: in particular, industrial action and productivity trends. Again, neither are ideal 'tests' — workers may be defeated in strikes, while if sufficiently powerful they may have no need actually to engage in any form of industrial action. With these cautions in mind, we can look at the relationship between respondents' assessments of steward influence and industrial action. We find the two are closely associated: for example, two in five of the plants where stewards are said to have a 'great deal' of influence over work organization have had three or more strikes over the last two years (a particularly 'tough' test — see below), compared with only one in twenty other plants.

Again, changes in productivity over the last two years are clearly affected by a large variety of factors, not least output trends. While there is no tendency for trends in output to be significantly different in plants where stewards have a 'great deal' of influence, slightly fewer of them have experienced increases in productivity. Only two in five have done so, compared with three in five other plants.

To put it at its most tentative, while assessments of stewards' influence have to be treated with considerable caution, it would seem that they do bear some relationship to the 'real' levels of influence they enjoy. Hence they seem a useful guide relative to sheer prejudice or vacuous theorizing. It, therefore, seems worthwhile to investigate the 'sources' of steward influence, albeit with a suitable dosage of doubt.

Influence over work organization

Respondents were asked to assess 'how important for determining the way in which work is organized on the shop floor here are negotiations by (i) senior stewards, (ii) "other" stewards?' The responses are shown in table 8.4. It can be seen that senior stewards are believed to have

TABLE 8.4 STEWARD INFLUENCE OVER WORK ORGANIZATION

	Senior stewards (%)	Other stewards (%)
Very important	25	14
Fairly important	38	39
Not very important	21	24
Unimportant	16	23
Total	100	100

somewhat greater influence than other stewards, although the variation is far from dramatic. Moreover, assessments of senior and other steward influence tend to be closely interrelated. Hence in nine out of ten cases where senior stewards are believed to have a significant degree of influence so also are other stewards; where the influence of senior stewards is said to be relatively small, the same is said in about two-thirds of cases of the influence of other stewards. Senior steward influence does not, then, appear to be at the expense of the role which other stewards play.

About two-thirds of the respondents claim that the degree of senior and other steward influence over work organization has not changed over the last five years: and where changes have occurred, then steward influence is more likely, according to respondents, to have increased than fallen.

There is a slight tendency for steward and senior steward influence to be seen as greater the larger the number of manual workers employed. The role of stewards is also seen to be rather greater in more 'traditional' industries. Steward influence tends to be slightly higher where personnel bureaucracy is more developed.

However, the level of steward influence is most strongly related to various features of union organization. First, the role which both stewards and senior stewards play in the organization of work is intimately related to the cluster of membership characteristics — union density, coverage of the closed shop and the number of unions which are recognized. For example, the impact of stewards upon work organization is deemed to be twice as high in plants where three or more unions are recognized: and variations of a similar scale are found with 100 per cent union density and closed shop coverage. In addition, and in large part independent of these correlations, the level of steward bureaucracy is related to the impact of both kinds of steward: in particular, their role in relation to work organization is greater where there are full-time stewards. In over two-thirds of plants where full-timers are found, normal stewards are said to play a significant part in determining work arrangements while this is so in only two-fifths of plants where there is no full-timer.

Where senior steward influence over work organization is greater, 'oligarchy' also tends to be higher. The tenure of both types of steward increases, and senior stewards are more likely to have spent longer in office than other stewards. Similarly, senior steward influence over members is seen to be greater than that of other stewards twice as often where the former's influence over work organization is said to be significant than where it is not. In addition, greater senior steward influence over work organization is associated with a slightly greater probability, not only that other stewards will be closely controlled by senior stewards, but also that they will act autonomously. Relationships between the influence of other stewards and 'oligarchy' are rare, the one exception being that where their influence over work organization is low the relative influence of senior stewards tends to be rather higher. Despite some relationship between 'oligarchy' and senior steward influence, there is a slight tendency for strike action to be more common where senior stewards are said to have considerable influence over work organization.

Finally, a significant steward role in relation to members' earnings is twice as common where they play a similar role in relation to working arrangements. Moreover, there is a slight tendency for stewards to have more impact on work organization where the coverage of formal, written agreements is greater: steward influence is not lower where agreements are said to impose constraints upon negotiation.

Influence over members' earnings

Respondents were asked to assess senior and other steward influence over members' earnings using a question similar to that used concerning work organization. And, as on that issue, there is a close relationship between the assessments of influence of the two types of steward — where the impact of senior stewards is seen to be greater, so also is that of other stewards.

Table 8.5 shows that in over half the plants senior stewards are seen to have a significant degree of influence over members' earnings: steward influence is rated rather less highly. In only a fifth of plants are senior stewards said to have no influence at all; in nearly a third other stewards are said to lack influence on members' earnings.

The impact of senior stewards is seen as greater in 'traditional' industries, in foreign-owned plants, and where the production process is more integrated: these relationships are relatively strong so that, for example, in almost twice as many integrated as non-integrated production processes senior stewards are said to have 'a great deal' of influence over earnings. Senior stewards are also said to have more influence over earnings in large plants, although this is not the case with other stewards — but this might be explained, at least in part, by the

TABLE 8.5 STEWARD INFLUENCE OVER MEMBERS' EARNINGS

	Senior stewards *(%)*	*Other stewards* *(%)*
A great deal	31	12
A fair amount	26	25
Not much	22	31
Not at all	21	32
Total	100	100

nature of the payment systems used (see chapter 7). Senior and other steward influence over earnings is higher where plants engage in single employer bargaining: hence, for example, senior stewards are said to have 'a great deal' of influence in nearly three times as many of these plants as elsewhere. Similar, though weaker, relationships are found between bargaining level and the role which other stewards play in relation to earnings. Relatedly, both kinds of steward have a greater impact where personnel bureaucracy is more fully developed.

The role of senior stewards in relation to earnings is greater where union density and the coverage of the closed shop are total: they are seen to have 'a great deal' of influence, for example, in twice as many plants with 100 per cent union membership as in other plants. But the relationship between union density and the influence of other stewards is only half as strong. Where steward bureaucracy is more developed the greater tends to be the role of senior stewards in relation to earnings: for example, in just under half the plants with full-timers senior stewards are said to have 'a great deal' of influence, while this is so in only a fifth of other plants. There is also a weaker tendency for the role of other stewards to increase with steward bureaucracy, but with one notable and significant exception: for where there are two or more senior stewards the impact of other stewards on earnings is considerably lower: in only a quarter of these plants are they said to have significant influence compared with a half of other plants. However, limitations upon steward influence over earnings are not related to the coverage or role of formal agreements.

The influence of stewards over members' earnings is related to only one aspect of steward 'oligarchy' — the tenure of senior stewards tends to be greater where steward influence is greater. Stronger relationships between 'oligarchy' indicators and senior steward influence exist: in particular, domination of the steward body by senior stewards is twice as common where the latter are said to have a great deal of influence over earnings, although such domination is still found in only a third of plants. Overall, half the plants where senior steward influence over earnings is said to be considerable score high on the 'oligarchy' index (see chapter 6) compared with only a fifth of other plants. Moreover, strike action is also more common where senior stewards have a great deal of influence over members' earnings.

Steward Orientations

The question of the exact meaning of steward influence raises the question of the way in which stewards use that influence, and this is likely to be shaped by their perspectives. For some writers so-called 'influence' is a sham, particularly where steward bureaucracy and oligarchy exist; for stewards — and particularly senior stewards — will be more sympathetic to management and less committed to member interests. In earlier sections of this volume we have already questioned a number of the key linkages in this argument: we have raised doubts, for example, over the strength of any simple link between bureaucracy and oligarchy, and drawing upon a variety of sources we have questioned the link between these factors and steward views. The 1983 survey provides an opportunity to look at these questions more directly. Again, we need to caution readers that we are taking the assessments of personnel managers; but this problem has been discussed at length in previous sections and so the relevant considerations need not be repeated here.

Respondents were asked 'whose point of view are manual stewards most inclined to take — management's or workers'?' This question had been asked in previous workplace surveys. In the 1973 survey, for example, three-fifths of those giving a definite answer said stewards adopted the workers' view; the remainder said they adopted a '50—50' approach (Parker, 1975, p. 64). In only one plant in 1983 was it claimed that stewards took management's view. In just over half the plants they were seen to be committed solely to workers' interests and in the other half they were said to adopt a '50—50' approach. While strict comparisons with earlier surveys are not possible, it seems that stewards may have become more sympathetic to management over the last decade. The view that stewards have shifted their approach in this way is also supported by the responses to the question 'over the last five years, have stewards become more or less sympathetic to management's views?' In half the plants it is claimed that they had become more sympathetic while in only one in ten plants had they become less sympathetic.

A third question posed was whether or not senior stewards are 'more or less sympathetic to management's views than other stewards'. In half the plants they are said to be more sympathetic. The relative sympathy of senior stewards is not related significantly to the actual nature of stewards' views.

There is no strong and unilinear relationship between stewards' views and the size of the manual labour force, although senior stewards tend to be more sympathetic to management than other stewards as the size of plant increases. Interestingly, senior stewards are not more aware of managerial interests where personnel bureaucracy is more developed: but stewards are less sympathetic to management and more firmly committed to workers' views where elements of personnel bureaucracy, notably personnel directors, exist. However, while there is no significant relationship between bargaining level and steward views, senior stewards are relatively more sympathetic to management where plants engage in single-employer bargaining.

Where union organization is more strongly based there is a tendency for stewards to be more firmly committed to workers' views. On the other hand, senior stewards tend to be more sympathetic to management where union organization is more developed. Again, it is difficult to interpret this finding, but certainly it does not mean that senior stewards are simply 'management lackeys'. To say that senior stewards are more sympathetic to management relative to stewards who are firmly committed to workers' views does not mean that they take management's view or even that they necessarily adopt a '50—50' approach.

The nature of steward views is not significantly related to the level of steward bureaucracy: however, senior stewards do tend to be more sympathetic to management where the degree of steward bureaucracy is greater. Most of this variation, however, is accounted for by the size effect.

The views of 'normal' stewards vary significantly with only one indicator of 'oligarchy': they tend to show greater sympathy with management where senior stewards dominate other stewards. However, no such relationship exists in the case of senior stewards' views. The latter tend to show slightly more sympathy to management than other stewards where their influence over members tends to be relatively greater and where they tend to have been longer in office than other stewards.

If we look at the relationship between steward views and the level of influence and the range of negotiation, no significant associations are found, and the same is true of senior stewards' views. However, there is a relationship between stewards' attitudes and the coverage of formal, written agreements: where they cover three or more of the issues investigated stewards are said to be more committed to a worker perspective. But no relationship exists between the coverage and role of formal agreements and the views of senior stewards. Finally, it is perhaps worth mentioning that the unions are seen as a significant check on changes in working practices in twice as many plants where stewards are said to be committed to workers' views than where they adopt a '50—50' approach; industrial action is also more common in the former plants. The fact that there is no relationship between these factors and the relative view of senior stewards counsels caution in interpreting the exact significance of the latter.

The Steward Challenge

In this section we have so far considered the degree of influence exerted by stewards and the views which inform that influence. The next task is to examine how far steward influence obstructs management policy.

Again, the problem of indicators confronts us. The basic question posed here embodies all the problems of conception and of the questionnaire method which have been discussed in earlier sections. In the survey, two types of indicator were used: the first was industrial action, the problems of which are well known. The second was a question which was used in the 1966 survey.

'Union obstruction'

In 1966 managers were asked whether there were any ways in which the organization and arrangement of work in the plant could be improved if they were free to arrange their labour force as they wished. Where managers felt this was possible, they were asked what percentage of working hours could be saved, and about the significance of trade unionism as a factor 'preventing you from arranging your labour as you would wish'. In 1966 about half the managers interviewed (64 per cent of those in large plants) believed that working practices could be made more efficient; just under a third of those who felt able to specify potential savings put the figure at 11 per cent or more; and just under half thought that trade unionism was a big or fairly big factor in preventing more efficient working practices (Government Social Survey, 1968, p. 90).

In 1983, using the same questions, 62 per cent of managers feel that working practices could be improved, 44 per cent claiming potential savings of 11 per cent or more. 73 per cent of managers who see the possibility of greater efficiency say that trade unionism is a big or fairly big factor in preventing changes in working practices.

The first problem is obviously what exactly this question is tapping — is it anything more than a reflection of management prejudice? In many large companies, fairly careful calculations are made of potential labour savings and this would suggest that, if prejudiced, at least responses are likely to be carefully estimated prejudices. However, the assessment of union 'obstructionism' might be seen as more open to question. Certainly one cannot ignore the tendency to engage in union 'scapegoating'; but, as was suggested in chapter 4, manning levels tend to be considerably higher in Britain than in many other countries, largely due to craft demarcations. And recent changes in working practices seem only to have marginally changed the situation. Furthermore, industrial action is higher where union 'obstructionism' is seen to be significant. In short, it seems plausible to suggest that the assessment of union 'obstructionism' is rather more than simple management prejudice, even though it is less than an ideal measure of steward challenge (see also Wenban-Smith, 1982).

There is a slight tendency for significant union 'obstructionism' to increase with the size of the manual labour force. While it does not vary according to the level of personnel bureaucracy, it is considerably higher where single-employer bargaining occurs.

High levels of union organization, in terms of union density, coverage of the closed shop and the number of unions recognized, are strongly associated with significant union 'obstructionism'. Similarly, that other presumed plank of steward incorporation — steward bureaucracy — is also closely associated with a significant union check upon management. For example, in three-fifths of plants where there are full-time stewards the unions are seen to play a significant role in this respect, while this is so in a third of other plants. If we control for the union organization variables just discussed, then we find that the impact of steward bureaucracy is relatively small in plants where, for example, there is not 100 per cent union membership. But where union density is total, then significant union 'obstructionism' is still closely related to high levels of steward bureaucracy. Union obstructionism is also greater in plants which score higher on the steward 'oligarchy' index.

Industrial action

In line with the 1978 IRRU survey, respondents were asked about the frequency of various forms of industrial action over the last two years: the types investigated were strikes of less than a whole day or shift, longer strikes and other forms of industrial action such as overtime bans and go-slows. Table 8.6 shows the findings from the survey and also the corresponding data from the 'Deaton-adjusted' IRRU survey.

It can be seen that fewer plants in 1983 than in 1978 had experienced some form of industrial action, although the difference is not as great as might be expected. The greatest difference appears to be in the number of 'lengthy' strikes, these declining from 46 per cent of plants to only 27 per cent. This is of interest since it is only lengthier strikes which tend to be included in national statistics so that these may exaggerate the decline in strike action. Furthermore, this finding raises questions over the conventional wisdom that strikes tend to be fewer and longer in a depression. It would seem that workers may over the last five years have resorted to more 'subtle' forms of industrial sanction rather than the high risk tactics of the lengthy strike — hence in only 3 per cent of plants have there been four or more strikes of more than a day or shift duration in the last two years, while about three times this proportion have experienced an equal number of short strikes or other forms of industrial action; in all, a fifth of plants have experienced four or more cases of industrial action over the last two years and a slightly smaller percentage have experienced two or three.

The experience of industrial action does not vary significantly, in any of the forms distinguished above, by industry or ownership. There is, however, a significant 'size effect': industrial action is significantly more common in larger plants. This pattern is found in the case of each type of industrial action investigated. In part related to the 'size effect' is a tendency for strike action to be more common where production is integrated. This suggests that workers are aware of their strategic power in these situations and are prepared to use it.

The level of personnel bureaucracy is only weakly — though positively — related to the experience of industrial action. The same is true concerning each type of personnel specialist distinguished, and of corporate bargaining. What appears to be more important than actual bargaining level is the level at which management decisions on pay are made. Thus less than half the plants where local management have 'considerable discretion' or 'complete freedom' over manual workers' pay have experienced some form of industrial action in the last two years, compared with nearly three-quarters of plants where local

TABLE 8.6 FORMS AND FREQUENCY OF INDUSTRIAL ACTION

	Percentage of plants				
	Strikes (less than 1 day)	*Strikes (1 or more days)*	*All strikes*	*Other ind. action*	*All ind. action*
Adjusted 1978 survey					
Yes	29	46	51	N/A	71
No	71	54	49	N/A	29
1983 survey					
Yes — once	7	16	14	15	20
— twice	3	6	8	6	10
— three times	1	2	2	6	7
— four or more	9	3	12	10	20
No	80	73	64	63	43
Total	100	100	100	100	100

managers have little freedom on this matter. And, of course, personnel specialists are associated with constraints of this kind being imposed on local management.

Industrial action of all kinds is more common where union organization, such as union density, the number of unions recognized and the coverage of the closed shop, is more developed. Hence, for example, only a third of plants with incomplete closed shops have experienced some form of industrial action in the last two years, while three-quarters of those with a total closed shop have done so. This relationship still exists even when such variables as size of plant are controlled for.

Steward bureaucracy is also closely related to the experience of industrial action. All forms of industrial action, except strikes of more than a day's duration, are considerably more common where steward bureaucracy is fully developed. Both regular steward meetings and full-time stewards are strongly related to industrial action. These relationships exist even when we control for the other strong associations discussed previously.

Industrial action is no less common in plants which score high on the steward 'oligarchy' index. Indeed, when one considers individual indicators of 'oligarchy', such relationships as are found with industrial action are positive. For example, strikes are slightly more common where senior stewards have held office longer than other stewards; and short strikes are most common where senior stewards dominate other stewards, less common where stewards operate collectively and least common where they tend to go their own way.

Industrial action is also associated with greater steward activity. In particular it is more common, in all its forms, the greater the level of steward influence over the organization of work. Overall, industrial action is more common where the range of negotiation is greater, but this is primarily attributable to a strong relationship between this variable and non-strike forms of industrial action. Conversely, steward influence over earnings is related to the experience of strikes, but not to other forms of industrial action. The coverage of formal, written agreements is not significantly related to industrial action, but there is a tendency for strikes — mainly those of a shift or more — to be more common where agreements are said to impose greater restrictions upon negotiation by shop stewards.

In this chapter it has been shown that the range of bargaining is still significant, although it has declined somewhat over the last five years largely due to the adoption of 'macho' tactics by a minority of managers. Formal agreements similarly cover a fairly wide range of issues, but do not appear to be associated either with lower levels of negotiation or with reduced steward influence. The latter also remains relatively high and is associated with a considerable level of 'union obstruction'. However, industrial action, particularly resort to lengthy strikes, has decreased over the last five years, while stewards tend to have become more sympathetic to management. The various features of steward activity were found to be related to a variety of factors: in the main, the findings give little support to the arguments commonly espoused in the 1970s concerning 'reformist' strategies. The case I put forward in Part I concerning the decade after Donovan, therefore, receives considerable support from the evidence in the more recent period. This is true not only concerning steward influence but also features of reform discussed in the earlier chapters in Part II.

The findings of the survey have to be treated with some caution, for reasons outlined at various points in preceding pages. In addition, in the interests of brevity, certain variables were omitted from the investigation which have subsequently been shown to be significant, notably the proportion of women employed and skill levels (Daniel and Millward, 1983): however, these factors operate in large part through the variables investigated here, although they may also explain associations such as those between various aspects of union and steward structures and action on the one hand, and 'traditional' and 'new' sectors on the other. Nevertheless, the survey findings seem to be useful for at least two reasons. First, they have permitted a rather more systematic analysis of many issues central to an understanding of industrial relations than has been undertaken in the past. Second, they provide an up-to-date account of the state of workplace industrial relations in large plants in the private manufacturing sector.

9 Conclusions

The purpose of this book has been to assess the impact of 'reforms' in workplace industrial relations in the decade after Donovan, and of changes since that date. I do not mean to summarize the details of the argument at any length in this final chapter — this has already been done at appropriate points in the course of the argument. The aim here is rather to relate the detailed findings of the main body of the book to the various approaches to industrial relations outlined in chapter 1. Some of these approaches, in particular, cannot be satisfactorily assessed solely on the basis of an analysis of workplace 'industrial relations': we need to extend our perspective to the level of society as a whole. This is the task undertaken in the second section of the chapter. The final section brings these various elements together and seeks to draw out lessons for future analysis.

FRAMES OF REFERENCE AND REALITY

In chapter 1 three broad approaches to the analysis of industrial relations were identified, along with a number of 'sub-variations'. The first approach, constituting the 'official' rationale for workplace reform from the late 1960s, was the liberal pluralist. The clearest expression of this view is to be found in the Report of the Donovan Commission; it was subsequently modified in a number of ways in the light of experience with reform (for the latest 'modification', see Durcan *et al.*, 1983, pp. 409 – 12). The second was the unitarist frame of reference, which has played a more significant role in state policy over the last five years or so. And the third was a more radical approach which, in a variety of ways, emphasized the need to locate the analysis of industrial relations within a wider perspective.

Part I was shaped largely by the arguments of Donovan and related theses put forward by some members of the radical school. The crucial points are to be found in chapter 4. There it was argued that the overall 'outputs' from industrial relations — in terms of productivity, earnings, strikes and related matters — provided little support for the more simple liberal pluralist model. We reached similar conclusions on the basis of a more detailed consideration of various changes in the procedures and substance of industrial relations.

It would, of course, be wrong to attribute events in the decade after Donovan solely to the failure of reform. Indeed, many liberal pluralists would now argue that their earlier analyses placed too much emphasis upon specifically 'industrial relations' factors in explaining the sorry plight of the British economy. But it does not follow from this that industrial relations played an insignificant role: for example, if it were possible to attribute 'causal weightings' one might say that industrial relations accounted for a fifth of the low competitiveness of British industry. If reform had fulfilled the aspirations of its architects, then the course of the British economy over the last fifteen years would have been dramatically different. In fact, of course, it is extremely difficult to attribute such weightings: for example, if management strategies more generally were less than ideal and reformism also contained serious internal weaknesses, then the cumulative impact of these two factors might be greater than the impact of each in isolation. In addition, the nature of British industrial relations can be seen as both a partial cause and a partial effect of other characteristics of British industry.

Similarly, the British and the international economies have suffered a series of shocks over the last fifteen years (although those who emphasize these facts tend also to underplay a number of distinct advantages — such as North Sea Oil — which at one time were seen as tremendous boosts to the British economy). These have clearly made it that much more difficult to achieve the goals to which many commentators and participants have aspired. But it is less than satisfactory to argue that it is solely because of these shocks and crises that the reformist model failed to work. For, in the first place, many countries have managed to ride these shocks far better than Britain. Second, reformism was meant to be able to overcome the 'problems' of the British economy. It is true that at the time of Donovan these were less severe than they subsequently became, but if the liberal pluralist analysis and prescription had been as robust as was initially thought, one might have expected a better 'showing'. In short, shocks and crises, important though they were, are not in and of themselves a satisfactory explanation of the failure of reformism.

The thrust of the argument in Part I was that there were serious problems inherent in the Donovan analysis. At least in the context of

British industrial relations, the expansion of 'formal' rules of both a procedural and substantive kind did not lead to an increase in managerial freedom over the use of labour. There were a number of reasons for this. First, these rules and agreements often encouraged the expansion of workplace union organization and built up expectations of influence on the part of workers and shop stewards. When, for whatever reason, workers objected to management actions they were, therefore, more able than they had been in the past to challenge those actions. Second, in order to achieve joint agreement over new rules, managements often extended rather than reduced the union role, and their formal recognition of that role. Thus agreements could in fact reduce rather than increase managerial prerogative. Third, the explicit statement of rules increased their visibility: it was now easier for groups to challenge management actions which were not consistent with the rules. Relatedly, the rules could be subjected to a variety of interpretations. Fourth, rules are general by their very nature but have to be applied to specific situations. This provides considerable scope for negotiation over which rules should be applied (for often a variety of rules may potentially apply to any particular issue) and their precise interpretation. This point is particularly important where the new 'formal' rules are introduced into a situation previously governed by a complex of understandings, custom and practice and *ad hoc* rules, where a profusion of people have been accustomed to creating and interpreting such understandings (see, for example, Batstone *et al.,* 1978, pp. 52—3 on the 'career' of agreements). Fifth, and relatedly, new 'formal' rules do not exist in a vacuum: they have to be applied to ongoing social situations which are characterized to varying degrees by understandings about the 'normal way of doing things'. To the extent that the new rules challenge these conventions, then far from leading to a new 'normative order', they may foster the very situation which they are designed to avoid — some form of anomie. For the new rules may challenge and cast doubt upon the legitimacy of old practices without themselves becoming fully internalized by actors. Accordingly, a situation may develop in which there is a profusion of rules, all of which have some degree of legitimacy as 'vocabularies of motive'. Actors may be able to exploit this profusion of rules along with concepts of fairness and justice. Sixth, not only may conflict arise between old and new rules, but also between various new rules. Batstone *et al.* (1984) detail at length the conflicts experienced in one case of attempts to reform industrial relations; for example, the desire to achieve a rational pattern of differentials between groups conflicted with the principle of performance-related payments. Seventh, the new rules often embodied particular conceptions of workers and of the wage—

effort bargain: in Fox's (1974) terms, they frequently implied that workers were not to be trusted and that they were essentially economistic. The embodiment of this view in rules implied that management was trying to regulate more closely the two sides of the wage—effort bargain. Particularly given the growth in worker organization, it is scarcely surprising that workers should reciprocate in kind, their actions demonstrating an increased 'bargaining awareness'. Finally, the rhetoric of reform, in terms of workers sharing in the prosperity which would follow, along with the sizeable payments made to 'buy out' old practices and 'buy in' the new rules, almost certainly expanded worker expectations of the pay increases that were possible.

Along with these more detailed problems, the reformist case underestimated two things, as later studies within the liberal pluralist tradition (for example, McCarthy and Ellis, 1974) have recognized. First, Donovan underestimated the extent to which there could be a conflict of interest between employer and employee, even when both were represented by 'reasonable men'. Second, the initial reformist case did not take sufficient account of either 'external shocks' involving the need for continual change or the scale of rising worker expectations. In other words, it was open to question how far any meaningful and mutually acceptable 'normative order' could be created through reformist strategies.

Related to these two criticisms is the emphasis upon procedure on the part of liberal pluralists, at least in the past. The logic for this emphasis was two-fold: first, if interests could be accommodated in principle but not in practice, then a plausible explanation could be that the structures for negotiation were not conducive to key representatives of the different parties getting together in any meaningful way. Second, underlying the liberal pluralist analysis was what seems a reasonable argument: procedure agreements are more important than substantive agreements because the latter are likely to require frequent alteration in the face of changes in markets, technologies, expectations and so forth. Procedure agreements could provide means by which these substantive changes might be more easily achieved. The logic of Donovan, therefore, was that the 1960s was one of those relatively rare times when procedures had to be changed to recognize shifts in the distribution of power within trade unions. This argument, however, confronted a number of problems which were insufficiently recognized.

The view that procedural arrangements should assume primacy had no explanation of why the parties should conform to the requirements of procedure. In chapter 1 we saw not only that this had been a key point of criticism of the reformist case, but also that liberal pluralists themselves appeared somewhat uncertain about it. Trying to persuade actors of the need to conform to procedure seemed to contradict key tenets of liberal pluralism itself. And an argument couched in terms of enlightened self-interest does not just raise questions about the nature of interests and the perception of their interests on the part of actors; it might equally point to the need to breach procedures under particular circumstances. These problems confronted both reformist analyses of industrial relations, and also many other accounts of the institutionalization of conflict, notably that of Dahrendorf (1959). His account of the efficacy of institutionalization is based upon an ideal type which has, at least in the British case, limited utility in understanding the real world. For he specifies three conditions 'for effective regulation': the parties 'have to recognize the necessity and reality of the conflict situation and, in this sense, the fundamental justice of the cause of the opponent' (p. 225): second, interest groups must be organized: and third, 'the opposing parties have to agree on certain formal rules of the game that provide the framework of their relations' (p. 226). It is not immediately obvious why the recognition of conflict should lead — in any sense — to the recognition of 'the fundamental justice of the cause of the opponent', and it is clear that it frequently does not (see, for example, Fox, 1974, pp. 297—313). Further, even if it did, it does not follow that conflict will be reduced. Interest groups may exist, but a necessary, though insufficient, condition for Dahrendorf's model to apply is that those who are involved in the detailed operation of institutional arrangements should have a very great degree of control over the interest groups they represent. Third, it is open to question how far the formal rules of the game will be the guiding light for the parties or their representatives; this is particularly true if the substantive gains achieved through procedural conformity are limited.

The logic of the liberal pluralist case was, of course, that since there was scope for positive-sum accommodation between conflicting interests, then substantive outcomes from procedural conformity would serve further to cement commitment to the institutions of joint regulation. But this tended to be assumed rather than systematically analysed: and this, in turn, can be related to the tendency to isolate a primarily procedural analysis of industrial relations from broader issues. As we have remarked before, liberal pluralists later recognized the limitations of this account. Durcan *et al.* have recently argued: 'by concentrating on the necessity of having adequate procedural arrangements, the [Donovan] report tended to play down the significance of substantive terms and the difficulties involved in achieving substantive agreements which are acceptable to all parties' (1983, p. 411). Extending this argument, one might add that Donovan underestimated the problems of what might be termed a 'revolution of rising expectations' deriving from institutionalization — a point of which Durkheim was only too fully aware.

Rather than taking an *a priori* approach to the analysis of institutional arrangements, which tends to abstract them from their social location, it seems more useful to see them as both a reflection of the balance of power and as something which may, in turn, shift that balance and affect the ways in which people seek to pursue their interests. Such an approach is consistent with the points made in the preceding discussion. For example, it can cater for the possibility that institutions, by recognizing workers' interests, may increase rather than reduce conflict as workers' expectations are boosted, as procedures facilitate the pursuit of demands and as a proliferation of rules develops which may be exploited.

There are, of course, many admissions in more recent writing within the liberal pluralist tradition that the Donovan-type model was too simple. But no one within this tradition has developed a more satisfactory or coherent analysis. Some writers, such as Clegg (1979), recognize that things are rather more complex than Donovan suggested but still maintain that the basic analysis is fruitful. McCarthy and Ellis (1974) go rather further and point to the need for ongoing and deeper negotiation and for a variety of supportive policies on the part of the state. In some respects, then, they may be seen as moving towards the more radical end of the pluralist spectrum. For others, such as Purcell (1981), there seems to be little left except pessimism and an appeal for 'trust'.

And yet it would be unwise to dismiss totally the insights of the liberal pluralist tradition. In particular, the emphasis in much of their work on coordination and centralization is consistent with a wide range of more recent work within a political economy tradition. In effect, the Donovan Report constituted an appeal for management at plant or company level to act as the 'encompassing organization' that it really was; the moves recommended for the development of more coordinated forms of shop steward organization are of a similar kind. The recommendations of Donovan would, therefore, be consistent with the arguments put forward by Olson concerning the way in which the shape of interest groups affects economic growth (1982; see also Mueller, 1983 and Moe, 1980). And, again consistent with Olson, the reform of industrial relations can be seen as an endeavour to overcome problems of 'institutional sclerosis'. If Olson's arguments are valid at the level of society, why should they not apply equally at plant or company level?

If we turn our attention away from Britain towards the experience of other countries, similar points emerge. For in many countries, institutional arrangements and formal agreements of both a procedural and substantive nature do not appear to have the same effects as they do in Britain. This dichotomy is considered more fully in the next section.

For the moment, we can simply note that a number of explanations appear to merit some initial credence: the first is that in these societies the nature of specific procedural and substantive rules may be different; second, it may be that interests are organized in ways which constrain the exploitation of rules; third, underlying economic, social and political conditions may be more favourable in some way; and fourth, the role of the state may be significantly different.

One of the arguments which has been widely put forward in international studies is, of course, that the way in which interests are organized is different in countries such as Sweden or Germany (see the next section). But, as we have seen, a key element of the Donovan analysis focused precisely on this point. And in chapter 3 it was argued that the extent to which workplace reform led to a more coordinated or centralized pattern of shop steward organization has often been grossly exaggerated; the survey findings discussed in Part II supported this contention. It may, therefore, be the case that if reform had actually led to the 'bureaucratization of the rank-and-file', then the Donovan prescriptions might have met with a greater degree of success.

The question that arises is why reform failed to transform shop steward organization. A number of reasons can be suggested: in some cases, it would seem that reformism simply lacked the weight to change firmly entrenched patterns of behaviour. Rather than the reformist measures changing the stewards, the stewards changed the reformist measures. Along with this it is not clear why, given their traditional orientations, stewards or workers should necessarily have wanted to transform their organization. And, particularly where steward density increased and where 'bureaucratization' was partial in formal terms and possibly even less in real terms, developments in steward organization in the 1970s may have exacerbated problems of steward coordination as power shifted even more from external full-time officials to the steward collectivity and as stewards became constrained by the sectional demands of their members.

Chapter 2 suggested that organizational constraints upon reformism were also to be found on the management side, albeit in a rather different form. Management attempted to achieve greater coordination and control as far as labour relations were concerned. But in the face of strong sectional pressures on the part of stewards and workers, they found there were limits to how far such formal coordination could be maintained alongside coherence in management's substantive strategies. Moreover, it has been argued that the nature of coordination and of a more conscious attempt at strategy on the part of management were not such as to facilitate the achievement of management's goals. For they were largely of a procedural kind which both fostered and frustrated steward expectations, while at the same time they involved no significant change in the extent to which labour relations considerations intruded into general management thinking on key issues. In short, changes tended to be more in form than in substance, and this was because changes in industrial relations management reflected broader organizational changes which, in turn, flowed from the traditional priorities of British management (see also Blackler and Brown, 1980).

It was also noted in chapter 2 that British managements tended to be less qualified than their counterparts in other countries, and that control structures placed less emphasis upon technical and production issues. If this is so, then it seems plausible to suggest that a crucial set of factors in understanding the 'problem' of British industrial relations may relate to technical failures of design and organization of production. Such failures might be expected to lead to industrial relations 'problems' for at least two reasons: first, design errors may make managements particularly dependent upon worker cooperation if satisfactory finished products are to be made, with the consequence that small work groups achieve a great deal of power. Second, if there are continual breakdowns or shortages of components then potentially contentious issues relating to labour flexibility and mobility are likely to be considerably more common than if production were better organized. Certainly it is possible to cite examples which support these suggestions, although what general credibility such arguments have is difficult to assess. But they do seem worthy of more detailed research. And, if they are of general importance, then a major means of 'improving' industrial relations would seem to be to improve the organization of the production process.

These points suggest that, even though the main thrust of the Donovan analysis was flawed, its failure was also attributable to the fact that the organizational changes required were not achieved either in degree or in kind. That this was so in itself indicates weaknesses in the Donovan analysis which, after all, laid claim to being a practical blue-print: it was argued that management, once they realized the gains to be achieved from reform, would wholeheartedly espouse it. In the event it was clear that Donovan had failed to take sufficient account of the 'micro-politics' and interests of management (cf. Batstone *et al.,* 1984). And, of course, not dissimilar points arise as far as trade union and worker interests are concerned. In short, the problems noted in chapter 1 concerning the nature of interests, along with a failure to pay sufficient attention to the social processes involved in the formulation and pursuit of policies, meant that the liberal pluralist approach was much more difficult to put into practice than its architects had expected.

The Radical Analysis of Reformism

If these problems affect the liberal pluralist analysis, they apply even more strongly to much of the radical case, at least in its Marxian versions. For many of the writers within this school of thought argued strongly that reformism would incorporate shop stewards without providing any substantial, longer-term gains for workers. In contrast, liberal pluralists had argued that such incorporation would at least bring substantial benefits to workers and their unions. In other words, the Marxian radicals rather than the liberal pluralists — at least in this respect — should properly be classed as the institutionalists *par excellence*. This is particularly ironic, not to say contradictory, in view of their insistence on the fundamental conflict of interest between capital and labour and, accordingly, the need for a major social transformation as a precondition of 'order'.

In chapter 1 a number of related problems in this type of radical analysis were expounded. If workers were 'essentially' radical, how could a few incorporated stewards or full-time officials really hold them back from playing their true historical role? There were, it was shown, severe problems in the identification of workers' 'real' interests, particularly in analyzing a particular, concrete situation rather than dealing with abstractions (cf. Hindess, 1981). Similarly, the Marxian radical analysis, while it places extraordinary emphasis upon the internal negotiation of order within trade unions which transforms means into ends, has typically ignored the corresponding social processes within management. As a result, we are provided with a picture of a disorderly, conflict-riven trade union movement confronted by an omniscient 'capital' — a reified concept deriving from an *a priori* logic or a too ready acceptance (and partial reinterpretation) of the early claims of liberal pluralists on the wonders of reform. These problems have been confounded by a failure to treat the available evidence with sufficient care and attention. In short, at least as far as the analysis of workplace industrial relations is concerned, Marxian radicals have compounded the weaknesses of the liberal pluralist approach by seeking to reinterpret its claims within a framework of inequality and all pervasive conflict — the overall frame of reference and the more detailed claims do not sit easily with each other. For example, having criticized the pluralist frame of reference for expecting workers to conform to agreements, a number of Marxian writers have gone on to claim that they — or their representatives — do precisely this. At the least, therefore, Marxian writers need to specify more clearly, coherently and carefully the links between their general frame of reference, on which they place so much reliance, and the specific situations which they seek to analyze (cf. Goldthorpe, 1972). It is, of course, the case that there have developed other Marxian approaches to the analysis of production relations, although they have not been developed systematically in relation to labour relations. These are considered below.

The radical pluralists' analyses of workplace reform stand up better when confronted with actual experience. Writers such as Fox and Goldthorpe argued that there was little reason to believe that reformism would lead to 'better' industrial relations: it was not clear, they argued, why workers should forego their relatively successful pursuit of sectional interests in the cause of orderly industrial relations. Fox further developed his argument in his analysis of trust relations, which is broadly consistent with the preceding chapters. But, invaluable though Fox's analysis is, it is open to question how far labour relations can be analysed primarily in terms of trust and, relatedly, how far some meaningful form of accommodation can be achieved if management adopts a 'high trust' approach towards workers. For there is a good deal of evidence to suggest that those groups who enjoy considerable discretion and autonomy — notably professional and craft workers — may exact a not insignificant price for their 'responsibility'. And, of course, the appearance of 'trust' may reflect the strategies and sanctions of the groups apparently trusted rather than the initiatives of management (see, for example, Turner, 1962; Blumberg, 1969). The radical pluralist, however, also emphasizes broader structural preconditions for the establishment of normative order; and a good proportion of recent writing has attempted to develop this theme by the study of international variations in such things as industrial conflict, economic growth, inflation and unemployment. It is, therefore, inappropriate to assess radical analyses exclusively on the basis of workplace industrial relations. Accordingly the next section seeks briefly to evaluate those approaches which seek to employ a societal framework.

Finally, some comment should be made concerning the new wave of radical work in the area of the labour process; this focuses upon the way in which the capitalist seeks to achieve control over workers in the pursuit of profit. Although the seminal work in the area chose not to consider the issue of worker resistance (Braverman, 1974) a good deal of more recent work within this tradition has made it a central theme (for example, Edwards, 1979; Friedman, 1977; Burawoy, 1979). This school of thought might, therefore, be expected to have a clear relevance to the analysis of workplace industrial relations. In practice, this can scarcely be said to be the case. Edwards, for example, makes worker resistance the key factor in explaining changes in management control strategies, but pays scant attention to the possibility of ongoing resistance or to the role of union organization. Nor does he pay much attention to the way in which unions may play a major role in the formulation of rules which obstruct management — this theme has been discussed at greater length in *Consent and Efficiency* (Batstone *et al.,* 1984). Burawoy similarly discounts the significance of worker resistance and manipulation of rules, claiming that it simply constitutes a diversionary game. While this may be so in the plant he studied, his account fails to prove this to be the case and cannot easily be generalized. Moreover, his data might equally well be explained by some form of liberal pluralist analysis which stressed fractional bargaining between workers and foremen unbeknown to higher management. Both of these studies pay scant attention to the ways in which market forces may impose pressures upon 'monopoly capital' to restrict bargaining or to achieve greater flexibility through the reduction of rules.

Friedman in his study of Britain pays rather more attention to worker resistance and the role that shop stewards play. Hence, he argues, management has increasingly adopted towards 'privileged workers' 'Responsible Autonomy' strategies aimed at harnessing 'the adaptability of labour power by giving workers leeway and encouraging them to adapt to changing situations beneficial to the firm' (1977, p. 78). Included in such strategies, and of considerable significance, Friedman argues, is the 'increased use of techniques to co-opt worker organizations'. Responsible Autonomy, therefore, includes a wide range of techniques which do not necessarily vary together (as he seems to realize) and hence the concept is in danger of becoming just a sponge. What is important is that he is aware of 'contradictions' in managerial strategy and the problems which may be posed by 'Responsible Autonomy' for the achievement of flexibility. However, these points — and the relevant issues concerning the degree of success of cooption — are not developed in any coherent way.

Perhaps more fundamentally, once analyses of this kind become less abstract and are forced to recognize the complexities of the real world, it is not clear how they vary from some pre-Braverman and non-Marxian studies — notably Baldamus (1961) and Etzioni (1961) — in terms of the general problems posed, nor in terms of key issues for analysis. Hence a concern with the nature of management strategy is to be found within organization theory and 'mainstream' industrial relations, as a number of recent reviewers have pointed out (for example, Wood, 1980; Purcell, 1983). The same is true as far as the nature, strength and sources of worker resistance and patterns of industrial relations are concerned (see, for example, Clegg, 1979 and Zeitlin, 1984): indeed, labour process writers might do well to consider some of the classic non-Marxian studies in this area, for example, Turner (1967) and Sayles (1959).

Edwards and Scullion's recent study of industrial conflict (1982) gives rise to similar problems. The extent to which their detailed analysis in fact derives from a specifically Marxian starting-point is open to doubt: while many non-Marxians might hesitate to use the term 'labour process', few would baulk at the idea of looking at 'the way in which activities are constituted as aspects of conflict by different forms of organization of the labour process' (p. 277). Edwards and Scullion, for example, seek to differentiate between their approach and that of Batstone *et al.* (1977, 1978), arguing that the latter fail to take account of structural factors. A number of points can be raised in Batstone *et al.*'s defence. First, the Edwards and Scullion argument is factually incorrect (see Batstone *et al.*, 1977, pp. 131—53; 1978, pp. 27—44). Second, Batstone *et al.* provide a more satisfactory analysis of the relationship between 'structure' and 'action' than simply claiming that the success of worker strategy 'depends ultimately on management's willingness to treat as structural those aspects of the situation on which they depend' (see, for example, Batstone *et al.*, 1977, pp. 217—19). Indeed, a great deal of the analysis is couched precisely in terms of the interaction between 'structure' and 'action' and of the constraints imposed upon choice (see, for example, 1977, p. 263). But such constraints, in the forms both of the feasibility of courses of action and of whether the costs and uncertainties of such actions are outweighed by possible rewards, apply both to workers and managers, albeit within a larger structure biased in management's favour. This point becomes particularly important once we take into account the specific interests of particular managers and the micro-politics of management decision-making. Third, Edwards and Scullion claim that Batstone *et al.* 'slip' from the question 'of strikes as an objective element of class relations to their role in fostering class consciousness' and that 'notions of structure and the effort bargain' have to be brought in 'at the end of the discussion and in a passing reference' (pp. 281—2). On the former point, Edwards and Scullion appear to be unable to distinguish between the physical proximity of statements and endeavours to make distinctions. The latter point misunderstands the focus of Batstone *et al.*'s analysis of strikes — namely, 'the mobilization of strike action' (p. 1) which, they recognize, needs to be located within a broader context (chapters 1 and 16). In addition, the discussion of 'vocabularies' shaping strike action highlights the centrality of notions of the wage—effort bargain (1978, pp. 45—62). Finally, Edwards and Scullion note that Batstone *et al.* 'confront problems such as imputing real interests to workers' and make great play — with little result — of the studies' 'idealist problematic': but Batstone *et al.* explicitly recognize this point, while Edwards and Scullion also admit that 'we do not claim to have solved such problems.' Nor is it evident that their 'clear framework' adds anything; indeed, they go on to state that the insights deriving from this 'clear framework' 'are well-known and require no detailed repetition here'. In short, while I applaud Edwards and Scullion's study, it is by no means clear that they provide a framework which is superior to or indeed significantly different from, that of Batstone *et al.*, particularly once the differences in the specific subjects of interest are taken into account.

The point of this discussion of the labour process is not, however, to criticize Marxian writings for failing to be truly Marxist: it is, rather, to argue that the extent to which they have made useful contributions — beyond increasing interest in the issue — to the understanding of the 'labour process' is as yet rather limited. (Indeed, much of the argument has failed to provide even a convincing logical case: for example, if one is to argue — as Braverman (1974) does — that there has been a progressive and general degradation of work, it is not sufficient, particularly when using less than satisfactory concepts and evidence, to point to this process occurring within particular occupations without taking account in the general argument of shifts within the occupational structure.) However, it should also be said that, particularly in the case of recent developments, few writers of any school have gone far beyond restatements of the need to study, for example, management strategy (for example, Wood, 1980; Purcell, 1983) — a theme stressed ten years ago by many (for example, Bain and Clegg, 1973). One of the few non-historical studies to go beyond exhortation, repetition or *a priori* and reified argument is Batstone *et al.* (1984).

The Unitary Approach and the Role of Market Forces

From the unitary perspective, reformism was seen to exacerbate the very trends which underlay the decline in the British economy: it fostered union power which had challenged managerial prerogative, smothered entrepreneurial spirit and obstructed the workings of the market from which the welfare of all sprang. Moreover, there was no guarantee — indeed, little likelihood — that the extension of union power would lead to a greater sense of 'responsibility', so that agreements would be kept and employees would realize the need to accept the workings of the market system. However, while the unitarist predictions of the effects of reformism may receive some support from the evidence outlined in Part I, it does not follow that it is a satisfactory analysis.

Since 1979 the government has espoused policies consistent with a unitary frame of reference: it has sought to remove a number of restrictions upon the working of the market mechanism and upon private enterprise, it has tried to constrain union power and make it more accountable both through legislation and its market-oriented policies, and it has favoured moves to foster direct, rather than union-mediated, relationships between employer and employee. The findings outlined in Part II are, therefore, of greater relevance to an assessment of the unitary approach.

It must first be re-emphasized that the findings of the 1983 survey have to be treated with some caution: despite the fact that it covered a not insignificant proportion of the manufacturing labour force, it included a relatively small number of plants and was conducted through a postal questionnaire which was necessarily rather crude. Nevertheless, given the lack of alternative data, it is the best we have. Moreover, the findings are broadly consistent with 'macro' data relating to earnings, productivity, industrial conflict and union density.

A consideration of the unitary approach can best be pursued under three main heads: the workings of the market, the role of legislation and strategies of involvement.

The basic argument concerning the operation of the market mechanism is simple. Those who can best meet the demands of consumers will prosper, those who cannot will suffer. Market signals will reward those who are efficient and give warning signals to the less efficient, stimulating them to change their ways or go out of business. Signals from the product market will pass through to the labour market. Any firm which does not meet the standards required by the market will be less able to pay the going market rate for labour and will, through its own decisions or those of workers, reduce its labour force. Workers who obstruct adequate responses to market signals will similarly suffer. The consequent increase in the proportion of workers seeking work will tend to reduce wages and the bargaining power of workers, thereby facilitating recovery — employers can reduce costs and become more competitive both through paying lower wages and through utilizing labour more effectively. On this analysis, therefore, the dramatic increase in unemployment over the last five years should have led to a reduction in real wages, greater cooperation and increased productivity.

In fact, this does not appear to have been the case in certain key respects. As was shown in chapter 6, real earnings have risen faster and productivity more slowly since 1978 than they had done in the earlier 1970s. And while in a number of respects strike action has declined, the annual average worker involvement in strikes since 1980 has been higher than in many years in the last two decades. 'Days lost' through strikes have fallen relative to most years in the 1970s, but still exceed the average for the late 1960s. Moreover, a not dissimilar pattern emerges from the inter-war period of high unemployment: real earnings rose between 1923 and 1937 (Glynn and Shaw, 1981, p. 123): between 1922 and 1939 total productivity rose by only about 1 per cent per year (admittedly an increase on the 1900—13 annual average); the number of strikes fell in the inter-war period (1922—38 relative to 1900—13), but the number of workers involved in strikes did not (even if 1926 is excluded), nor did the number of 'days lost'. The inter-war data are particularly relevant since they cover a much longer period and union density plummeted. Despite these facts, the extent to which high unemployment achieved the successes implied by the market model was extremely limited.

The survey evidence suggests that in many plants stewards have become rather more cooperative, but this is not to say that they now accept a unitary perspective. Changes in working practices have occurred, but the 'macro' data on productivity would suggest that these have been insufficient even to maintain the rate of productivity growth of the decade after Donovan. In some cases, managements have reduced the influence of shop stewards (although merely down to the 'average' level) but only, it would seem, when plants have been in particularly dire straits. Overall, then, up to the present what is striking is not the efficacy of market forces, but their limited effect upon those plants which survive. Moreover, while market forces have hit some formerly powerful groups of workers severely, they have affected other similar groups relatively little; and, equally, they have hit many workers — for example, in small firms where entrepreneurs lack liquidity and suffer from reductions in orders by large firms — who have posed little challenge to managerial prerogative.

The obvious problem is how to account for these rigidities in the labour market. Two broad types of explanation are required: one relating to the strategies of employers, the other to those of workers and unions. If we take the latter, then a number of reasons for labour market rigidities appear to be plausible. Trade union organization in Britain is very sectional, and it has been argued in this volume that this pattern has not changed significantly since the time of Donovan. Union structure is, therefore, biased against the adoption of policies which relate to (potential) workers as a broad collectivity: it cannot trade jobs and earnings in the way in which more centralized unions might. The same would appear to be the case even when we focus attention purely upon the company level: indeed, the survey evidence suggests that the very channel through which they might be able to act collectively at this level — the 'combine committee' — has been one of the features of steward organization most susceptible to decline. Second, and relatedly, British trade unions have often been prepared to 'trade' increased earnings for jobs: in the inter-war period, for example, Glynn and Shaw argue that 'the official trade union attitude . . . was that wages were to be held at all costs, and attempts to impose reductions were to be strenuously resisted' (1981, p. 123) and, to this end, they were in fact prepared to accept increased unemployment which they saw as a 'political' problem. Currently, this approach on the part of the unions is encouraged by employer strategies of offering sizeable redundancy payments for those who volunteer; in other words, potential resistance to redundancy is sidestepped with the consequence that union organization is less endangered or weakened than it might otherwise be. Third, while some plants may be hard hit by the recession, others are not, so that workers who impose severe constraints on managerial prerogative may not experience any real threat to their power or be induced to cooperate more with the employer. Fourth, the sectional nature of shop steward organization means that it exerts considerable influence over the day-to-day process of production and is intimately tied to the work groups and interests which develop from that process. As a consequence it is difficult (as preceding chapters have shown) to induce change: if production continues, then steward organization is likely to maintain its strength and its sectionalism.

The role the unions can play is, of course, in part dependent upon the approach employers adopt. The market model rests, in reality, upon the assumption that increased unemployment shifts the balance of power in favour of the employer. But this tends to ignore the relationship between product and labour markets. If employers do not receive signals from the product market that there is a need for change, then there is less incentive for them to seek to exploit the fact of increased unemployment. If they do receive such signals then the logic of the market would suggest that their position is also being weakened. In such a situation — at least until the brink of bankruptcy is reached — employers are in a difficult position. For if they adopt 'macho' tactics they may well encounter concerted worker and union opposition which further weakens the firm's position in a competitive product market. They, therefore, have an incentive to win the cooperation of the unions and the workforce in making possibly somewhat marginal changes rather than adopting a high-risk strategy. On this argument, the pragmatic employer will only seek fully to exploit the state of the labour market when he has nothing to lose.

A number of other factors are also relevant to understanding employer strategy. The market model, at least in its cruder forms, operates on the assumption that current and potential employees are interchangeable in the short term: it is only on this assumption of a daily or frequent auction of jobs that one can talk about high levels of flexibility. But in practice this is clearly not the case. In the first place, the transaction costs involved would be prohibitive and continuous auctions could lead to considerable uncertainty (cf. Williamson, 1975). This is particularly important, given the trends towards long-term planning of production, and the complexities of integrated production processes. Second, such an auction would only be attractive to an employer if he or she could be sure that each day workers with the requisite skills would be available. This assumption is especially open to question once we recognize the importance of 'tacit' skills, familiarity with specific machines and the importance in many instances of patterns of group working which can only be built up over time. Third, such an auction assumes that workers act individualistically, but in the kinds of plants with which this volume has been primarily concerned this is clearly not the case. Hence auctions can only occur if collective organization has first been removed or severely weakened, and this has clearly not been achieved. Fourth, the attempt to remove collective organization would involve a major reversal of corporate policies since at least the time of Donovan. Such moves would be difficult not only because of worker opposition and the severe risks of exacerbating a situation of 'normative disorder', but also because of questions relating to the extent to which management would be capable of successfully implementing such policies both in the short and longer term. In the short term there would be problems of organization and administration; in the longer term there would be severe risks that, in the event of an upturn in company fortunes, workers would similarly fully and wholeheartedly apply the logic of the market. Fifth, and relatedly, larger employers for a number of years have sought to develop some form of internal labour market. While the significance of career progression for manual workers in British plants has tended to be exaggerated, it is nevertheless the case that many employers have sought to select 'responsible' workers who would stay with the firm, and they have also pursued a number of other policies consistent with this — the creation of what Burawoy (1979) has termed the internal state. A reversal of this approach would be extremely difficult; indeed, the survey suggests that employers have in recent years sought to strengthen the identification of remaining workers with the firm, a theme to which we return below. Sixth, if the arguments put forward in chapter 2 concerning the history and nature of British management are correct, then it would seem that the extent to which British employers would be capable of pursuing a more market-sensitive industrial relations strategy are limited, even if we ignore the vested interests of managers themselves. Seventh, any major changes in working practices would in many cases require significant reorganization of plant and at the same time major investment in training (particularly since 'overmanning' in Britain relative to other countries tends to be concentrated in skilled maintenance areas). While the scale of this 'problem' may in part be reduced by new and more reliable equipment, it is nevertheless the case that retraining is likely to be a long-term process and one which involves major confrontations with powerful unions. And, ironically, marginal reductions in craft demarcations may serve to give them a more secure future.

There are, of course, other techniques open to the employer. An increasingly common argument is that large employers seek to overcome rigidities by exploiting the secondary labour market. This view reverses the logic of conventional dual labour market theory; it involves arguing that there are features of the present situation which induce employers to adopt a new strategy aimed at increasing flexibility in the future (there is some evidence that this is happening in some Japanese companies). The available systematic data relating to the last five years or so in manufacturing give little support to this view at least at a general level. Home-based work of a manufacturing nature has fallen, as has part-time work. There has been a steady trend towards the sub-contracting of industrial catering (and possibly cleaning) for many years — but largely to other large employers. More generally, subcontracting has always been a common feature in manufacturing (Friedman, 1977, pp. 118—19), although the number of subcontractors in the car industry, for example, is declining. The one area in manufacturing (other than catering) where there is fairly reliable evidence to date of increased subcontracting is the maintenance of new technology but this is not generally economically rational and is a reflection of union power preventing the training-up of employees. It may well be that secondary labour market strategies are becoming more common — but we need firmer evidence than we have had to date on this issue.

Other strategies open to the employer include changes in location of operations with the aim of finding a more cooperative workforce. But such moves are likely — except in the very long term — to be extremely costly, not least in terms of capital outlay. Moreover, a number of studies suggest that the gains in productivity achieved tend to be attributable to the newness of plant (for example, McKersie and Klein, 1982; see also Fothergill and Gudgin, 1982) while there is no guarantee that 'green labour' will remain quiescent (see, for example, Dubois,

1976). The major thrust of relocation policies may be, and indeed appears to be, to shift operations away from Britain.

This discussion of market forces is, of course, largely speculative and is not intended to suggest that they have had no impact upon workplace industrial relations. But hopefully they do provide the beginnings of an explanation for the findings of the 1983 survey which, as we have seen, are broadly consistent with a variety of macro-economic indicators. On the basis of these arguments, then, the working through of market forces is likely to be an extremely painful and lengthy process, the results of which may be politically unacceptable and/or economically catastrophic. For change will occur largely through the demise of many parts of British industry. A major reduction of union power, then, if it occurs at all, will take place through a shift in the industrial and occupational distribution. This assumes that those employed in growth sectors will not achieve the same degree of control as those in declining sectors — quite an assumption.

The logic of recent industrial relations legislation is, of course, to reduce labour market rigidities through the imposition of constraints upon union action. At the time of writing it is difficult to assess how effective this approach will be. The 1983 survey evidence, perhaps unsurprisingly, indicates that so far it has had little impact. This is consistent with the experience of the 1971 Act (Weekes *et al.,* 1975). It is beyond the scope of this volume — and the competence of its author — to pontificate at all usefully upon the probable impact of legislation, but a few comments can be made. First, some elements of the (proposed) legislation concerning election of representatives, ballots over closed shops and for strikes could radicalize unions, while the risks for 'official' unions if they engage in unlawful actions could give further freedom and tacit support to shop stewards. Second, and more basically, the question arises of how far and in what way new laws will be integrated into ongoing patterns of labour relations. The thrust of much of the argument presented here is that one reason for the relative failure of reform concerned the problem of developing formal, written rules which could actually shape shop-floor practice in the way planned by management. Workers and their representatives, along with managers, might attribute greater priority to other sets of rules, often of a more private nature, and/or might seek to evade, manipulate and exploit the new rules. If this is true of agreements and rules created within the company, then such behaviour seems even more likely when rules are externally imposed. In other words, it is open to question how far employers will seek to use the law, and, if they do, it seems probable that workers and their representatives will seek to evade and manipulate it (as in France — see

Batstone, 1978). The shape of the new legislation does, of course, stack the cards against traditional patterns of union organization and, accordingly, may afford some advantage to employers who are prepared to accept a 'souring' of industrial relations in an attempt to achieve a new basis of 'order'. There have certainly been a few well-publicized cases of such endeavours, but the 1983 survey suggests that few employers (as yet at least) are prepared to adopt such a high-risk strategy. In part, this appears to be because they believe it is essential to develop and maintain some form of agreed accommodation with their workers and unions, if only for fear of inducing concerted collective opposition if the balance of power changes. Moreover, even in the present situation, we have suggested that a number of factors provide workers with not insignificant power resources which can be used against management and which cannot easily be tamed or controlled through legislation. That is, a crucial question relates to the compatibility of legal regulation and the dominant patterns of labour relations and of the production process (see, for example, Kochan *et al.,* 1983 on the recent American experience; on the impact of legislation, see Henry, 1983).

The third theme within the unitarist frame of reference concerns strategies of employee involvement. We noted in Part II that many companies have in recent years introduced schemes aimed at fostering worker cooperation with, and commitment to, the company. Again, it should be emphasized that the survey questions on this issue were extremely crude so that the data have to be interpreted with some care, but the overall picture suggests that (so far) the impact of such techniques has been somewhat limited. This might in part be attributable to the fact that in the main they have been associated with similar moves as far as shop stewards are concerned. Where they have not been, then the signs are that they are associated with some reduction in steward control: but this may be more directly attributable to the market position of the plants concerned and/or concerted attempts to reduce the role of the unions.

Direct employee involvement strategies come up against a number of problems. First, it is by no means certain that such strategies — particularly where they are of a marginal nature (see, for example, Fox, 1974) — will be favourably received by workers (for example, Turner and Lawrence, 1967). Second, where they are, then such techniques may build up the workers' expectations about their ability and right to influence management in such a way that they begin to challenge further areas of managerial prerogative (see, for example, Elden, 1977; Gustavsen and Hunnius, 1981). Third, where direct employee involvement techniques involve giving workers greater autonomy or control over aspects of the production process, this new-found power might be wielded against management. Fourth, the interests which workers develop in the specific organizational arrangements associated with those techniques may impose serious constraints upon future management options. Fifth, greater communication may exacerbate conflict by giving workers prior knowledge of managerial intentions which challenge their interests. Sixth, it is open to question how effective these techniques can be unless they are supported by a broader set of consistent strategies and arrangements. For example, in the Japanese case the success of such methods as quality circles is in large part attributable to broader factors relating to patterns of work organization, payment systems and welfare provision, and the assumption of long-term job security. This suggests that a major transformation of work organization would be necessary in Britain if employee involvement was to achieve any significant degree of success. In particular, the Japanese case indicates that employee involvement requires a greater isolation of workers from market forces — that is, it conflicts with attempts to remove labour market rigidities, at least in the primary sector. Flexibility is therefore achieved in two main ways: first, by mobility within the company, and second, by a large secondary labour market where strategies of employee involvement are not a key characteristic. In short, employee involvement implies a strong element of duality in the labour market.

POLITICAL ECONOMY AND SOCIETAL ANALYSIS

All the main approaches to industrial relations rest upon conceptions of the nature of the wider society, although the extent to which these are made explicit and used in the analysis of specific issues varies. For radical pluralists, in particular, recent analyses have emphasized broader trends in society and societal variations to explain both particular features of industrial relations, notably industrial conflict, and phenomena — such as inflation, unemployment and economic growth — which are often seen as intimately related to industrial relations factors. It is not my intention here to provide a general review of this literature; rather, by taking two well-known and widely respected analyses within this tradition, I shall simply try to assess the strengths and weaknesses of this type of approach. The first of these is Goldthorpe's sociological account of inflation; the second is Korpi and Shalev's analysis of international variations in industrial conflict.

A Sociological Analysis of Inflation

Goldthorpe begins his analysis of inflation with a critique of economic theories on the grounds that they fail to take any account of the way in which inflationary pressures are built into the structure of society. Writing in 1978, he argues that 'the current inflation derives ultimately from changes in the forms of social stratification, giving rise to more intense and more equally-matched social conflict than hitherto' (p. 210). In this way, what economists treat as 'error, ignorance or unreason' can be seen 'as a response by actors which is in accord with the logic of their situation'. More specifically, Goldthorpe identifies three factors leading to inflationary pressure 'in the case of present-day Britain', although he clearly sees them to be of relevance to other advanced Western societies. These are (i) the decay of the status order; (ii) the realization of citizenship; and (iii) the emergence of a '"mature" working class' (p. 196).

Goldthorpe's analysis can be criticized on a number of grounds: first, it is open to question how far the factors to which he alludes can be seen as explaining inflation in any consistent and coherent fashion; second, they can neither explain the precise timing of inflation in Britain nor why inflation rates should vary so greatly between societies; third, his account pays scant attention to specifically economic variables; fourth, Goldthorpe takes no account of the role of institutional arrangements; and fifth, the kinds of factor to which he refers may be more usefully developed in relation to the key locale of class relations — the workplace.

Turning to the first of these themes, a number of weaknesses can be detected in Goldthorpe's argument. First, it is unclear whether he defines traditional status orders as being exclusively 'pre-industrial': the fact that he refers to the work of Plowman *et al.* (1962) suggests that he does not. Accordingly, he has to recognize the fact that industrialization can create 'interactional' status systems, as has been widely noted in the case of 'traditional proletarian' workers (see, for example, Lockwood, 1966). Similarly, there is a risk of exaggerating the extent to which consensus over status criteria and rankings existed in the past (as between various craft groups, for example; Maitland's argument that Goldthorpe's analysis is flawed because of the evidence of consensus over the broad structure of society in Britain (1983) largely misses the point. For what are significant are not views of the broader structure of society but disagreements on relativities and differentials among contiguous groups; see, for example, Willman, 1982). Moreover, it is far from evident that traditional proletarian groups are not at the forefront of demands for wage increases which are inflationary.

Similar problems arise if we look at Goldthorpe's discussion of the significance of citizenship rights. It is perfectly correct to point to tensions between citizenship and class, but it does not follow that these tensions become manifest. Indeed, what is striking is how little 'citizenship rights' have entered into industry: the rights introduced by legislation have not been particularly strong, while those to which Goldthorpe refers (p. 213) in practice have limited significance and often postdate the rise in the inflation rate. Goldthorpe also refers (p. 203) to the debate on industrial democracy surrounding Bullock, but what is striking about such ideas is that they received so little active support from workers and unions. In this context, it is also worth noting that after the Second World War, whilst applauding the welfare state, the unions espoused Morrisonian principles for nationalized industries which effectively denied industrial citizenship (Currie, 1979). Finally, the relationship between 'full political citizenship' and 'industrial citizenship' defined in terms of 'independent trade unions and collective bargaining' is considerably more complicated than Goldthorpe suggests: it is difficult to find any clear relationship between the various Reform Acts and the introduction of the welfare state, on the one hand, and union density and the coverage of collective bargaining on the other. One reason for this is that industrial pressure was a factor in the development of 'political citizenship'.

Goldthorpe goes on to argue that notions of citizenship impose constraints 'on governments seeking to pursue standard deflationary policies' since they are associated with normative expectations of employment; if unemployment rises, therefore, one might expect concerted, class-based opposition. It is certainly true that many believed this to be the case in the 1960s and early 1970s. But the point scarcely needs expanding: in the present situation of high unemployment, the re-election of a government committed to deflationary policies and the reduction of industrial citizenship, and a singular lack of concerted class action, Goldthorpe's argument receives little support from the experience of recent years. Two of the several reasons for this are worth mentioning in the present context. The first is that one aspect of 'industrial citizenship' — redundancy payments — was designed to facilitate terminations of employment (Fryer, 1973), while the welfare state may also serve to reduce opposition to unemployment (see, for example, Glynn and Shaw, 1981); the second is that the very sectionalism which leads to inflation itself poses a major obstruction to any form of concerted class action. Some writers have even cast doubt upon how far the strength of workers, deriving from full employment, can in fact be attributed to the establishment of the welfare state (Smith, 1981).

The third factor identified by Goldthorpe as leading to inflationary pressures is the emergence of a mature working class which has enjoyed continuous citizenship rights so that 'the existence of trade unions and of a labour movement is an established fact of life, and for whom, moreover, trade unionism . . . is the normal mode of action by which conditions of work and standards of living are to be defended and as much as possible improved' (p. 207). This argument is less than convincing for a number of reasons. First, it ignores the fact that inflationary wage increases are not the sole prerogative of the working class (defined as manual workers): particularly with the growth of white-collar unions, such increases are also to be found in the case of clerical and other non-manual groups. Second, working-class maturity might be expected to be more common in 'traditional' industries where interactional status orders exist: hence Goldthorpe's first and third factors are likely to be in conflict. Third, he provides little evidence to support his thesis of the effects of working-class maturity. In fact there are a number of reasons for questioning it. Members of the 'mature' working class may well have kin who have been upwardly socially mobile and may have aspirations for such mobility for their children. Similarly, it is open to question how far members of this 'mature' working class are union members and how far their parents were. Manual union density is still only about 50 per cent (and tends to be lower among less skilled groups where members of the mature working class are likely to be concentrated); for much of the inter-war period, manual union density was less than 25 per cent. The number of members of the mature working class who have been brought up in a tradition of trade unionism is, therefore, likely to be relatively small, at least overall (that is, such traditions may be concentrated in particular industries — those of a traditional proletarian nature where interactional status orders still exist). Goldthorpe recognizes this fact, it seems, for he qualifies his argument on the normality of trade union action by stating 'even if with little involvement on the part of the majority' (p. 207) in trade unions. This argument — particularly given current levels of union density — seems somewhat confused. A more credible argument might be that one only requires a minority of workers/employees to be able to establish inflationary wage increases, and then market forces will require that the wages of other groups follow, at least to some degree. But if this argument is espoused, then doubts are raised over the significance of the other elements of working-class maturity on which Goldthorpe places such great emphasis.

The second broad type of criticism of Goldthorpe's sociological account of inflation concerns its inability to explain either the timing of the increase in the rate of inflation in Britain and its subsequent decline or variations in inflation between societies. It should be said that Goldthorpe's paper is of an exploratory nature and is clearly, therefore, not to be seen as the last word on the subject. But inflation began to 'take off' in Britain in the late 1960s/early 1970s, and reached double figures in 1974. What features of Goldthorpe's model can explain this? Even the addition of more classic economic variables to his model would not appear to be able to deal with this question: in other words, the model is excessively vague. Perhaps more importantly, how could Goldthorpe's factors account for the fall in inflation over the last few years? No traditional status order has been re-established, mobility out of the working class has not increased so that trends towards 'maturity' have been reversed, while at least the key features of citizenship still exist. Relatedly, it would seem that Goldthorpe seeks to develop a model which is applicable to all developed capitalist societies but which at the same time explains why inflationary pressures should be so great in Britain. But if we look at the rate of inflation in OECD countries (let alone less developed societies, many of whom experience massive rates of inflation) we find that between 1960 and 1980 about half of them had inflation rates very similar to that of Britain. Many of these did not have mature working classes, with few workers engaged in agriculture; for example, Italy and Ireland had rates of inflation comparable with Britain. Less developed and mature societies — Iceland, Spain, Portugal and Turkey — had considerably higher increases in prices over the period.

The third type of criticism which can be made of Goldthorpe's account of inflation is the fact that he pays remarkably little attention to the structure of the economy. Smith, for example, has pointed to the susceptibility of Britain to the export of inflation from the USA (1981). But, in addition, one might point to problems specific to the industrial structure of Britain: the disadvantages of being the first to industrialize and the continuity of productive capacity in terms of ageing capital equipment, and the traditions of management and work organization which mean that in certain respects Britain is less 'developed' than many less 'mature' economies such as Germany (and in this sense may be comparable with societies such as Italy, Spain and Portugal). Such factors may be important in explaining why inflationary pressures could not be absorbed and handled by increasing productivity (cf. Gilbert, 1981).

The fourth strand of criticism concerns Goldthorpe's failure to consider the way in which institutional arrangements can play a role in reducing or accommodating inflationary pressures. This theme has received considerable attention in recent years, particularly in relation to the establishment of incomes policies. Such policies, which under particular conditions can reduce the rate of inflation, are more viable in the long term, it would seem, where unions are more centralized (see, for example, Headey, 1972). Moreover, the logic of Olson's argument on the shape of interest groups would suggest that united and centralized union movements would take more account of the implications of their wage demands for inflation than would more fractionalized union movements (for arguments along these lines, see Cameron, 1982; Tarantelli, 1983). Similar themes are considered in the next section and so need not be expanded here.

Finally, and relatedly, it is possible that some processes of the kind Goldthorpe describes may be more important within the workplace than they are outside of it. That is, in his account of inflation, as with the concept of orientation to work, Goldthorpe is in danger of emphasizing non-workplace factors at the expense of workplace factors. The arguments put forward earlier in this volume suggest that the decay of the status order within the plant may be of crucial significance in explaining inflation. This is not to revert to the Fox and Flanders thesis (see chapter 1), but rather to point to the impact of reformist measures, such as productivity bargaining. These tended to increase workers' notions of the kinds of pay increase which were possible and introduced additional pay principles, which conflicted both with each other and with traditional principles and could therefore be exploited: in short, reform created, or exacerbated, normative disorder. Similarly, reformism extended what might very loosely be termed citizenship rights in that it stimulated the establishment and recognition of workplace union organization and this facilitated worker exploitation of the contradictions of reformism just noted. This line of argument would suggest that it was not only, or even primarily, a mature working class brought up in a culture of trade unionism which was crucial, but the fact that management and state initiatives defined trade unionism as normal, legitimate and proper.

I do not mean to claim that reformism was the sole or even primary factor in inflation, nor that factors beyond the workplace were unimportant. Most obviously, the role of the state was relevant: in addition to its encouragement of reformism and its role as a major employer (see, for example, Batstone, *et al.,* 1984), its role in the move towards bilateral or 'corporatist' arrangements was also significant. The introduction of incomes policies, for example, encouraged wider comparisons, disrupted traditional differentials still further and built up powerful 'heads of steam' which 'blew' as soon as restraints on wages were removed (or which broke through incomes policies). 'Corporatist' arrangements — given reformism and union structure — gave the unions new 'legitimacy' and fuelled expectations. And because of the way in which corporatist dealings, in practice, if not in original intent, tended to work against the interest of (at least) key, powerful groups of workers, it is scarcely surprising that they were induced to take their fate into their own hands.

In short, an analysis undertaken solely at the level of society seems less than satisfactory: it needs to be integrated with the analysis of the workplace. This weakness is particularly ironic given the insistence of radicals upon the centrality of class, defined in terms of relationships of production, or as Goldthorpe puts it, in terms of individuals' 'market situation — their chances of obtaining given levels of income, their degree of security of employment, their prospects of economic advancement; and . . . their work situation — their position in relation to systems of authority and control within the organization of production' (p. 197).

International Variations in Industrial Conflict

Korpi and Shalev seek to develop a class-based analysis of international variations in industrial conflict, which centres upon the extent to which workers are able to pursue their goals through political rather than industrial means. The first stage of their argument, therefore, is to demonstrate the superiority of their class analysis over the pluralist or institutional approach. To this end they evaluate the work of Clegg (1976) and of Ross and Hartman (1960) on international variations in strike activity.

Korpi and Shalev (1979) and Shalev (1980) criticize Clegg's contention that differences in strike patterns are to be accounted for by variations in the institutions of collective bargaining (1976) on a number of grounds. First, they claim that Clegg underplays the significance of class. It is certainly correct to say that Clegg makes no use of the concept or term 'class', but that does not in and of itself prove the superiority of a class analysis. Second, Korpi and Shalev claim that Clegg tends to assume a long-term trend towards industrial peace: while American liberal pluralists may have argued this in the past, Clegg — as far as I am aware — never has. Third, Korpi and Shalev argue that institutional arrangements should not be given the centrality which Clegg affords them, but should rather be seen as merely reflections of broader social forces and as able to play only a marginal independent role. While it is certainly true that Clegg focuses upon institutional arrangements, he does recognize that his analysis is partial, in that it is confined to the relationship between strike action and collective bargaining, and that his argument raises the further question of how particular institutional arrangements develop. And, on the latter point, Clegg suggests — although he does not develop the point — that the organization and strategies of both employers and the state are crucial. It is also worth noting that Korpi and Shalev confront similar problems in explaining union structures and the role which 'leftist' parties play (see, for example, Shalev, 1980: Shalev and Korpi, 1980). Fourth, Korpi and Shalev seek to support their criticism of an institutionalist approach by taking the case of Sweden. Institutional innovations were introduced, they argue, in the early twentieth century but did not lead to a decline in strike activity. The strike level only fell, they say, when the Social Democrats came to power in the 1930s. But Korpi's own argument is subject to four weaknesses: Clegg (the architect of Donovan) would not wish to argue that any type of institutional arrangement leads to industrial peace: indeed his analysis of strikes is based upon variations in the *nature* of institutions: Korpi's critique contradicts his own theory which states that the strike rate will only fall after many years of stable 'socialist' government: the Swedish strike rate fell very rapidly after the election of the Social Democrats; it also began to fall prior to Social Democratic government and this could be attributed to such institutional innovations as a labour court; finally, a key factor in explaining the further decline in strikes after the Social Democrats came to power was new institutional arrangements, particularly the Basic Agreement of 1938. The strike pattern in Sweden is therefore not inconsistent with Clegg's thesis (see Anderman, 1983).

The second object of Korpi and Shalev's attack is the work of Ross and Hartman (1960). Shalev (1980) seeks to damn their work by faint praise and finds them guilty by association. He argues that they form part of the institutionalist school of thought and, while noting that they take some account of political factors, claims that they pay excessive attention to institutional arrangements and the micro-politics of trade unions. The latter criticism is open to question: Ross and Hartman stressed not only organizational stability, leadership conflicts and the status of union—management relationships, but also the importance of 'labor political activity' ('labor parties and labor governments have contributed towards the relinquishment of the strike by providing a political alternative' — p. 68) and the role of the state ('the instrumentalities of the state are more powerful than the apparatus of collective bargaining' — p. 58; this point is footnoted in Korpi's latest account of his argument — 1983, p. 256). Moreover, as is argued below, one weakness of the Korpi—Shalev analysis is that they pay insufficient attention to 'non-political' factors. It is, of course, correct that Ross and Hartman believed that there was a general tendency for strikes to wither away: with the advantage of experience since their work was published, it requires little theoretical sophistication to point to the error of this contention. But two points are worth noting here. First, Ross and Hartman control strike data not by the size of the labour force but by the level of union membership. This can have a dramatic effect upon the direction of trends in strike activity: for example, union member involvement in strikes in Japan was almost halved in the late 1940s and early 1950s relative to the inter-war period, whereas worker involvement in strikes increased eighteen-fold over the same period. Second, it can be argued that the failure of strikes to 'wither away' can be explained by the kinds of factor which are embodied in Ross and Hartman's analysis.

Having, at least to their own satisfaction, dismissed pluralist studies, Korpi and Shalev go on to develop a 'political' analysis which is founded upon the contention that 'industrial conflict is something more than an incident of the collective bargaining process' (Shalev, 1980, p. 31). The sphere of production is the fundamental source of class position and leads inevitably to inequality and conflict. That conflict is political in nature and has wider political implications since it shapes wider social arrangements and the broader distribution of power. However, the balance of power can be shifted somewhat in workers' favour through collective organization, which can act as a check upon the power deriving from the control of capital. The exact distribution of power is seen to be significant both in itself and because of the way in which it shapes expectations.

Working-class power will be stronger under particular conditions: where union density is high; where unions are industry-based, integrated and centralized; where there is strong electoral support for united leftist parties; and where there is close cooperation between these parties and the union movement. If the working class is strongly organized in this way, Korpi and Shalev argue, it can acquire control over political institutions: it can, therefore, both check the exploitation of the state by capital and at the same time use political means to achieve its own ends. That is, demands arising from the production process will be channelled into the political sphere, and in consequence the level of strike action falls.

In support of this thesis, Korpi and Shalev have produced analyses of industrial conflict between 1900 and 1976 for eighteen OECD countries, relating strike patterns to features of union organization, electoral support for left parties and the representation of such parties in the cabinet, and data relating to social policy and inequality. Put at its most simple, the thesis they develop is that in those countries where there was a high level of working-class mobilization whereby workers achieved political influence, governments adopted a variety of social policies which met working-class demands with the consequence that the level of strike action fell in the post-war period relative to 1900–38.

A variety of serious empirical and analytical weaknesses mar Korpi and Shalev's analysis. First, their argument is developed on the basis of a five-fold categorization of the countries studied in terms of the level of working-class mobilization and the degree of leftist political representation. The fact that this produces some amazing bedfellows in each category (Edwards, 1983, p. 465) would be acceptable if it were not for the arbitrary manner of classifying some countries (that is, using their criteria, one could legitimately shift many of the countries into different categories) and that the categorization does not in fact lead to an adequate account of strike activity.

Second, it should be stressed that the focus of their analysis in fact becomes the level of strike activity in the period 1946–76, taken as a whole. They do not even attempt to check their broader claims systematically by looking at aspects of social policy and inequality in the inter-war period. Moreover, their arbitrary periodization obscures significant shifts in strike trends within particular countries: in this sense, their explicandum can be seen as an artificial construction (cf. Cronin, 1979 and Shalev, 1983). It is, of course, the case that the period surrounding the Second World War was one in which significant changes in strike patterns and industrial relations occurred in many countries. If this is used as the legitimation for the periodization employed, then it seems rather surprising that the war and its aftermath — for example, in terms of fostering major union reorganization, the setting up of new institutional arrangements, the commitment in some cases to cooperation between unions, employers and the state in the name of reconstruction, and so on — are not made more central to the analysis (cf. Ross and Hartman, 1960). A recognition of the impact of the war would seem to be a useful means of explaining strike patterns in a number of countries which clearly puzzle Korpi and Shalev.

Third, many of their indicators are less than satisfactory. As we have seen, they list a variety of features of union organization as being relevant to an understanding of working-class mobilization, but in their empirical analysis they consider only union density and political and religious divisions. They do not even consider the significance of occupational divisions which, of course, are significant in such countries as Sweden (see, for example, Hart and von Otter, 1976; for a more careful study of unions, Visser, 1983; the question of union organization is taken up more fully below). Similarly, many of their indicators of social policy are less than adequate: for example, their data on 'redistributive effects of government budgets' — which is central to their argument (Korpi, 1983, p. 179) — relates only to a few years in the 1960s, but is used to 'explain' industrial conflict between 1946 and 1976. It might also be noted in this context that they place considerable emphasis upon social policies and taxation in relation to individuals; they have nothing to say specifically about company taxation or subsidy or about wage/profit ratios. This is a rather surprising omission for an analysis based upon the conflict between capital and labour.

Fourth, and most fundamentally, their empirical data do not support their argument, so that Korpi and Shalev are forced to make significant modifications to their theory. For while their general argument is basically informed by Scandinavian — and specifically Swedish — experience, low levels of strike action are also to be found in countries where unions are less strong and united and where support for left-wing parties is relatively weak, notably Germany, the Netherlands and Switzerland. Moreover, their general argument might lead one to expect low levels of strike action in countries where there is 'low mobilization' and exclusion from political control, whereas in practice these countries have particularly high levels of strike action. For they take no account of the meaning or exact distribution of union membership. In the case of Germany, the Netherlands and Switzerland, Korpi and Shalev confront particular difficulty since these countries demonstrate the kinds of political 'output' which their theory predicts but have not had leftist governments over the bulk of the post-war period: in other words, they are forced to recognize that there may well be factors other than class solidarity which explain industrial peace. Religious division is not in itself a sufficient explanation, for the proportion of Catholics in these countries is very similar to the proportion in the USA and Canada, both of which have high strike levels. Korpi therefore reverts to a discussion of ethnic and territorial cleavages, relations between the church and the state, and so on, in the eighteen countries investigated — all in just over three pages (1983, pp. 26—9, and cf. Korpi's critique of Edwards, 1983, p. 76). Despite this, Korpi concludes in this latest attempt to deal with this problem that

> developments in the three religiously divided European countries . . . indicate, however, that there are also other ways of reducing industrial conflict than by a division of governmental and economic powers between capital and labour. The situation would appear to

be the result of a long historical development, where conflicts based on religion and class have crossed each other. (1983, p. 182)

The unsatisfactory attempts to explain the origins of particular union structures and political parties (Shalev, 1980; Korpi and Shalev, 1979; Korpi, 1983, pp. 26—9), therefore, indicate that Korpi and Shalev's analysis confronts problems not entirely dissimilar to those of Clegg, that is, explaining the social forces which lead to particular organizational and institutional arrangements.

Fifth, Korpi and Shalev's argument rests upon the ways in which government action can substitute for industrial action as a means of achieving working-class goals. Yet many of the features they consider give less than robust support to their thesis. Accordingly, they end up emphasizing the importance of two variables: the redistributive effects of government budgets (the weaknesses of the data used here have already been noted) and the level of unemployment. But even here they encounter problems: they shift the focus from strike involvement and duration to days lost; and they seek to explain very large variations in strike levels by what (for the period they investigate) are remarkably small variations in the redistributive effects of budgets and unemployment. The last point raises the question of whether these variables are acting as proxies for something else, which has more direct relevance to the interests of powerful work groups and interests (see below).

Sixth, while in their general model Korpi and Shalev include 'economic performance' and 'international context' (for example, Korpi, 1983, p. 169) they in fact only make use of these variables to explain in a rather casual manner findings which give little support to their argument (for example, Korpi, 1983, pp. 177—8). They similarly pay scant attention to the way in which levels of welfare expenditure and of unemployment might be affected by the age distribution of a society and changes in the size of the working population (cf. Wilensky, 1975).

More fundamentally, Korpi and Shalev's analysis is not consistent with their proclaimed starting-point, namely, a Marxian conception of class and class conflict within a capitalist society. This is so in three key respects. First, as Edwards (1983) has argued at length, they pay scant attention to the nature of the state within a capitalist society. They ignore the extent to which — if for no other reason than the need to protect its sources of revenue — the action of the state is constrained by the need to maintain the viability of private industry. This is particularly ironic given the fact that Korpi is so aware of the centrality of this point in his discussion of Swedish experience (1978) and the way in which, as he recognizes, the rights of private capital are currently the subject of heated debate in Sweden. However, in his discussion of international variations in industrial conflict his only references to this point concern Sweden, for example: 'Business interests, however, were able — often with great success — to make the Social Democratic government remember the acknowledgement made by Ernst Wigforss in 1938 of the necessity of maintaining favourable conditions for private enterprise' (1983, p. 173). Consistent with this, Korpi and Shalev do not consider such questions as the scale of public ownership or the importance of the state as an employer (cf. Batstone *et al.,* 1984).

The second conceptual weakness of the Korpi and Shalev approach is the scant attention paid to the strength of the employers and their degree of organization. This might be explicable if the point just made had been more satisfactorily handled. However, the unity of employers and the precise strategies which they adopt — for example, seeking to impose constraints upon the role of the union within the workplace — would seem likely to affect both union structure and the scale of industrial conflict. Korpi, in his latest repetition of the 'theory', does mention employers' associations but sees them simply as responses to union pressure: 'it is the threat from a strong and unified union movement which is most effective in inducing employers to organize' (1983, p. 258). This is unsatisfactory on at least two counts: while the catalyst for employer organization may often be union organization, it is not clear that unions have either to be strong or unified before they induce employer organization; in addition, Korpi does not take into account the ways in which, once organized, employers' associations may affect the level and nature of union organization (although, ironically, in seeking to explain American 'exceptionalism', Shalev and Korpi (1980) do point to the significance of employer strategy).

The third and most fundamental weakness is that Korpi and Shalev start from a position which stresses conflict deriving from the production process and then scarcely mention it again. But if a class analysis were to be followed through more fully, then one would expect greater attention to be paid to the way in which political action served to reduce issues of conflict at the point of production or shaped the resolution of conflict in such a way as to reduce resort to industrial action. The kinds of political 'output' to which Korpi and Shalev refer do not appear to be sufficient explanations. Their analysis cannot explain, for example, why skilled, secure and powerful workers should be prepared to forego imposing sanctions upon their employer as a means of promoting their interests. To argue that they do so because of state commitments to low unemployment and a marginal redistribution of income seems insufficient in itself. This is particularly so since such groups were not likely to become unemployed (at least in the period 1946—76), while redistribution policies might well involve them in a net loss of personal income. More fundamentally, such political policies do not in and of themselves resolve questions relating to conflicts of authority and distribution at workplace level.

That such worker pressures exist is evident. For example, between 1953 and 1965 wage drift accounted for 52 per cent of the increase in earnings in Sweden and for 22 per cent in Austria (both societies which 'fit' the Korpi—Shalev thesis) compared with only 19.5 per cent in Britain (UN, 1967, ch. 3, pp. 32—3). Similarly Carlson notes of Sweden that

> Those groups who had the best qualifications to ask for higher wages were often able to get these locally while consciously refraining centrally . . . This way there was a wage drift in Sweden . . . which strongly aggravated a planned wage policy. The wage drift is nothing new as such, it stems from the structure of collective agreements. Most collective agreements in Sweden are based on minimum wages and in principle a higher wage is expected than the stated one. This expected additional part is an individual one, that can become subject to local negotiations. Another element influencing the wage drift is the presence of piece-work . . . As an average more than 70 per cent of all working hours in industry are paid on a piece-work basis. (1969, p. 85)

Moreover, Korpi himself has detailed at considerable length the scale of piece-work negotiation — and unofficial workplace stoppages — in Sweden (1978, 1981). Relatedly, questions of the degree of local drift and of the conflicting interests of different groups have been important sources of tension within the Swedish Confederation of Trade Unions (LO) and between it and the other union federations in Sweden (see, for example, Fulcher, 1976). Worker dissatisfaction is also suggested by the high rates of absenteeism and turnover in Sweden (see, for example, NEDO, 1973).

A class analysis would also indicate the need to investigate questions of managerial prerogative and the organization of work. For much of the post-war period Article 32 of the Swedish Employers' Confederation (SAF) meant that 'collective agreements that give employees any influence over the right to direct and allot work cannot theoretically be signed by SAF member companies'. While such management freedom has been steadily whittled away, 'the unions have nonetheless failed to bring about any real change, either in form or content, in the power relationships prevailing at places of employment' (Forsebäch, 1976, pp. 50—1: for an interesting study of union endeavours to achieve some control, see de Geer, 1982). While Forsebäch probably underestimates the degree of union constraints on employer discretion (particularly from the 1970s onwards), arguments such as his do at least require some attention in a Marxian analysis of industrial conflict: the question of industrial bargaining, and its relationship to political action should be at the centre of the analysis. In his discussion of international variations in industrial conflict, the nearest Korpi gets to this is a remarkably evolutionary model in which, with growing strength, workers 'will be able to act on a wider basis than on the level of the plant' (1983, p. 176).

In short, a number of questions need more careful consideration: whether, for example, in societies with low levels of strike action, the degree of 'inherent' or 'perceived' conflict is lower at the workplace; whether workplace issues are dealt with in some distinctive manner; and whether some form of constraint is imposed upon the recourse to sanctions by workers.

One factor of relevance to these questions concerns union structure. As Korpi and Shalev note, it is far more difficult to develop a class or politically oriented approach where trade unions are divided: that is, where particular sectional interests have some form of organizational embodiment. The analysis of the origins of different union structures is, therefore, of considerable importance, particularly since these tend to shape the way in which — in changed circumstances — worker interests are defined and pursued. It is not enough simply to look at formal structures: for example, a single union or federation may in fact be riven by political, religious or occupational divisions (hence Ross and Hartman's emphasis upon factions and so on), while — as in the Netherlands — formally separate union federations may cooperate closely. In the latter case it may be possible for the union movement to achieve stable political influence no matter which party is in power.

Where unions are more united and centralized they take on the character of 'encompassing organizations' and, other things being equal (a very wide condition covering matters such as the precise strategies pursued by unions and others), one might expect union leaders to take more account of the way in which union 'gains' may impose costs upon their members as, for example, consumers. This line of argument leads to the interesting conclusion that the more a strong union movement assumes a class character, the less militant it is likely to be. And this may be particularly true if the union is associated with a political party (as Ross and Hartman noted). Korpi's own work (1978) on Sweden recognizes this; indeed he emphasizes the significance of the historic compromise in which the unions recognized the need to cooperate with employers in the drive for efficiency. To a significant degree, therefore, they ceded workplace control to the employer and accepted, until recently, the legitimacy of private capital.

The obvious question (raised earlier) is how union leaders were able to control workers at the place of work in order to conform to this commitment. One factor may be concerted attempts to socialize union members, and particularly activists, in the union ideology (see, for example, Lewin, 1980, on Swedish unions). But, in addition, a centralized structure permits union leaders to exert a degree of control over members — by definition. This theme is, of course, widely recognized in the literature on union democracy (and by Ross and Hartman). And such control by the leadership may receive support from employers and the state where the leadership is 'realistic' and 'responsible' (see, for example, Pizzorno, 1978; Sabel, 1983; Batstone *et al.,* 1984 on the internal union tensions involved in such situations). Again, Korpi's own work on Sweden highlights the importance of these oligarchical tendencies: he details the way in which LO leaders gradually reduced the influence and autonomy of local union activists (1978; see also Streeck, 1982, for an account of similar tendencies in German trade unions).

Once we recognize these possibilities and the potential conflict between national and local/sectional interests within trade unions then there is clearly a need to look at union structure and organization more carefully. Yet within the 'political economy' and 'corporatist' studies of variations between societies we find a rather casual approach to the study of union structure. Schmitter (1981), for example, uses an index of union centralization and unity as a measure of 'societal corporatism'; the scoring of different unions on indicators of centralization and so on is often done by drawing upon previous less than satisfactory works (notably Headey, 1971). But even when these indices cover only eighteen or fewer countries, the degree of correlation between them can be alarmingly low (see, for example, Tarantelli, 1983, p. 67). Furthermore, in many studies the centralization of bargaining is part of the indicator of union centralization — ironically, therefore, when writers expatiate upon the relationship between political action by centralized unions or corporatist arrangements and strike action, they may be simply supporting a version of Clegg's thesis (1976). Indeed, there is a remarkably strong relationship between days lost through strikes and the degree of union and bargaining centralization. (Relatedly, Cameron (1982) recently found stronger relationships between changes in strike activity and features of union structure than with leftist parties' representation in cabinets.)

In particular, it seems necessary to look more carefully at the relationship between workplace activity and the larger union. When this is done, it becomes strikingly apparent that societies with relatively centralized unions tend to establish rights and procedures — either through legislation or centralized agreements — both nationally and at workplace level as a result of some form of 'historic compromise'. For example, the extent to which workplace representation and procedures are formalized tends to be high. Italy and France also score high on the IDE (1980) index of formalization, but such formalization does not relate to the right to strike (Anderman, 1983) nor does it reflect any historic compromise so that it is used in a Machiavellian manner (see Batstone, 1978; Berger and Piore, 1980; cf. the discussion in chapter 4 above). Germany may be deemed consistent with this argument, given both the formal importance of industry and regional bargaining, the dominance of IG Metall in the DGB (see Leminsky, quoted in Clark *et al.,* 1981), and the way in which workplace representation was intimately related to the (re)construction of West German society — that is, it constituted part of a historic compromise. In other words, one hypothesis worthy of more careful consideration concerns the way in which centralized unions or union—state relationships may, as part of some meaningful compromise, establish sets of rights of representation at the workplace: through these, workers may to some degree pursue their sectional interests, and possibly impose some constraints upon the employer, without resort to strike action.

What is important is not only that such formalization establishes rights, but also that constraints upon workplace activity exist. Where union density is relatively low, workplace representation is typically not union-based. This, along with a 'peace obligation', imposes constraints upon workplace activism and its formal influence upon union policy. Where union density is higher, workplace representation is union-based but the union activist is subjected to tight union control. Under these conditions, low levels of strike action are typical. The exception to this pattern is Belgium, where shop stewards are relatively autonomous and appear to have a good deal of influence in the larger union (see, for example, Carew, 1976), and here the level of strike action is higher (see also Cameron, 1982 on the relationship between the existence of works councils before 1965 and strike activity since that date).

Other aspects of the workplace should be taken into account, in particular, the extent to which there are systematic variations in the way in which work is organized, and whether these relate to 'historic compromises' or forms of workplace representation. One intriguing possibility here concerns the scale and nature of training (and the role which unions, employers and the state have played in its development). This theme has recently been raised in a number of studies. Maurice, Sellier and Silvestre (1982), in a comparative study of France and Germany, have shown how levels of conflict are related to the nature and bases of hierarchy and job content, and these in turn are related to the structure of education and training. Pursuing this theme, Marsden (1981) has suggested that craft training in Britain fosters the notion of job control on the part of workers: it, therefore, reflects and reinforces the pattern of labour relations. Such studies, along with the work of Gallie (1984), highlight the complex interaction between the workplace and broader societal factors. When we consider the main OECD countries, there does appear to be a relationship between education and training and days lost through strikes: in those countries where a higher proportion of those leaving school go directly into some form of training, the number of days lost through strikes tends to be lower. And, of course, the importance of skill acquisition applies not only to manual workers but also to other groups, notably management. Hence, as Maurice *et al.* and others have pointed out, there are significant differences in the extent and nature of qualifications among managers in different countries. This theme takes us back to the discussion in chapter 2.

A further aspect worth considering is the way in which 'historic compromises' and their output in the form of institutional regulation induce managements to pay greater attention to worker interests and industrial relations considerations in the formulation of policy, thereby reducing the potential for conflict in the workplace, and more generally. A number of studies suggest that this may be the case (for example, Jacobs *et al.,* 1978). It is worth adding in this context that many liberal pluralist writers place considerable emphasis upon substantive factors in their analyses of industrial conflict (see, for example, the discussion of individual industry strike patterns in Durcan *et al.,* 1983).

In sum, then, Korpi and Shalev's account of international variations in industrial conflict is less than satisfactory on both empirical and conceptual grounds. It fails to follow through the logic of a class analysis and to take sufficient account of possible conflicts deriving from the production process. In this respect it shares the same weaknesses as Goldthorpe. Relatedly, it fails to pay sufficient attention to sectional interests and conflicts — Korpi and Shalev do not look at the problems and the tensions of 'class action'. A number of tentative hypotheses have been put forward which might overcome these weaknesses; they relate to alleviation of conflict and its accommodation at workplace level, and union structure as a form of control. (The utility of such an approach is suggested by the problems confronted in Sweden when attempts were made to reduce and further constrain workplace activity.) In other words, if 'institutional' analyses are incomplete, so also are those based on a 'political economy' tradition: Ross and Hartman's conceptual framework, therefore, seems more useful than Korpi and Shalev would suggest. I hope to develop the themes outlined here in a future publication.

The Structuring of Work and Rewards: the Japanese Case

It is clear then that we need to pay attention to the nature of interests at the workplace. This may lead on to the analysis of variations in industrial conflict and industrial relations within societies. Such investigations, and related questions of variations in industrial structure (cf. Ingham, 1974), might serve to foster further doubts about the utility of the approach adopted by Korpi and Shalev. For example, in Japan, which is about midway in the strike league of the main OECD countries, a major proportion of the 'days lost' through strikes is accounted for by the public sector and medium-sized firms. In contrast, at least since the late 1950s, strikes have been relatively rare in the primary, private sector of large firms. And in these companies the pattern of industrial relations appears to impose few constraints upon productivity growth. It seems useful, therefore, to develop some of the themes of the preceding section by looking more fully at the case of Japan.

The nature of labour relations in the large private Japanese firm is often seen to be attributable to job security, seniority-based payment systems and enterprise unionism. These factors, on closer inspection, are less than adequate as an explanation of a pattern of labour relations which permits peaceful and high economic growth. First, these features also existed in the immediate post-war period of high industrial conflict and less impressive economic performance: it is not evident in the general account why their role should have changed. Second, these three features of labour relations are most strongly present in the public sector, much of which enjoys neither the industrial peace nor the productivity record of the Japanese economy as a whole; at the same time, unionism and job security are not characteristic of the small firm sector (see Shigeyoshi, 1982; Kato, 1980). Third, the types of variable adduced in any explanation of Japanese labour relations must also be able to account for the pattern of labour relations in other societies. It is not self-evident that company-based forms of worker collectivity, life-time employment or seniority-based pay lead in other societies to peaceful, high-productivity industries: note, for example, British shop stewards as a form of enterprise unionism, the growth of strike action among public sector workers with jobs for life and among white-collar workers with service-related pay in other countries (see more generally, Shirai 1983).

A more adequate explanation of the pattern of labour relations in the primary private sector can be developed on the basis of three key variables. The first of these is the degree of mobility within the company. Such mobility takes three forms: first, workers are frqeuently transferred from one plant to another (in large companies, it would seem that 5 per cent or more of the labour force may be moved to another plant in any one year). Second, most companies operate a 'career' system whereby even blue-collar workers may experience significant changes in their formal job designation every few years. Third, in part under the guise of training for this career route, workers may be frequently shifted between tasks on a monthly or even weekly basis.

Such a pattern of mobility can be seen as conducive to economic efficiency and low conflict in a number of respects (compare the discussion of training in the previous section). Most obviously, it permits management a very high level of flexibility in its allocation of labour, so that it can adjust rapidly to changing circumstances and reduce idle working time. It may also widen workers' perspectives and increase their understanding of the ways in which particular tasks relate to the wider production process. At the same time, high levels of mobility (along with the nature of the payment system) mean that work group solidarity is likely to be weaker and, to the extent that it exists, is likely to focus upon more stable members of the group, notably foremen. Finally, notions of 'job territory', which are a precondition of worker attempts to achieve control over jobs in opposition to management, are less likely to develop where there is high job mobility.

Nevertheless, it might be expected that workers would object to a system of labour allocation and work organization which can present them with considerable uncertainty to say the least. It is here, I would suggest, that the second factor — the 'merit' system — assumes major significance. By 'merit', I mean the extent to which the pay and conditions of workers are subject to managerial discretion. In contrast to the European notion of wages as a reward for work done, in Japan wages can more accurately be described as a reward for loyalty and commitment to the company. Most obviously, an important component of pay relates to length of service: even by the age of thirty, men who have always worked for the same large company since leaving high school may expect to earn about 20 per cent more than workers with a similar educational background who have worked elsewhere for a number of years. But, in addition, the cumulative effects of differential merit assessments upon earnings both directly through annual increments and indirectly through promotion can be substantial. Hence analysis of payment systems and of wage survey data from a number of companies suggests that the basic earnings of forty-year-old blue-collar workers with identical years of service and educational backgrounds may vary in some cases by as much as 40 or 50 per cent. In seeking to explain these variations, it is necessary to look more closely at the criteria by which merit is determined. Here the notion of ability is in stark contrast to that applied to Western blue-collar workers. For in Japan, 'ability' goes far beyond a simple notion of the technical competence required to undertake a particular set of tasks adequately. It frequently includes assessments of ability to improve task design, of understanding the context of the job in terms of corporate priorities, leadership qualities, and most importantly, a heavy emphasis upon factors such as obedience, cooperation and reliability.

A payment system based upon such criteria is clearly consistent with, and supportive of, the pattern of labour utilization discussed above. Most obviously, many job changes are defined as 'promotion' up the career hierarchy. How meaningful such career hierarchies are in skill and responsibility terms is open to question: clearly, in some cases, years of experience do lead to the growth of skill. But in many sectors of mass production, the difference in skill between different blue-collar jobs must be marginal. And, in some companies at least, managements have quite consciously created these 'mock' career structures in order to promote mobility and worker cooperation.

The merit system facilitates mobility and cooperation in other ways. For example, a worker who is unprepared to change jobs or move between plants is clearly not demonstrating commitment to the company, and this may be reflected in merit assessments. More generally, the nature of the reward system fosters a pattern of worker behaviour which supports, rather than challenges, managerial goals. For example, a major factor in the rapid expansion of quality circles seems to be the way in which participation in them became incorporated into the assessment of merit: pressures of this kind, along with growing managerial 'guidance' of such groups, appear to have increased over recent years (see also Saburabayashi, 1983).

It is open to question how far these attempts to foster worker identity with corporate goals succeed in normative rather than instrumental terms. Official Japanese surveys, for example, consistently indicate that worker dissatisfaction is significantly higher than in Western countries (see, for example, Prime Minister's Office, 1981). How, then, can one explain the combination of internal dissatisfaction and the external appearance of cooperation?

Crucial in this respect is the fact that *all* the major companies employ broadly similar patterns of work organization and payment systems. To express dissatisfaction by moving jobs is not likely to improve a worker's lot significantly and will involve a considerable financial cost through lost seniority and merit pay. Given this, it is surprising how many workers voluntarily quit their jobs even if they have worked for a long time in a large firm (see, for example, Ministry of Labour, 1982; Foreign Press Center, 1982, p. 86).

There is one important situation in which it is economically rational for a worker to leave the large firm — if he receives low merit ratings (in some companies, it seems that a 'black mark' against a worker sticks with him for life). In such circumstances his pay may well be higher even in the secondary sector of small firms than if he stays with his present employer. To the extent that poorly rated workers adopt such economically rational behaviour, the potential for conflict within the large firm is correspondingly reduced.

In recent years managements have sought to strengthen worker support for the system of labour control further by fostering worker involvement in the process of merit assessment, and by making it more systematic. This is particularly striking, for it means that in many large Japanese companies the detail of company records on the personal characteristics of blue-collar workers compares with the records kept in British firms only on management (see, more generally, Amaya, 1983).

Such a comparison with Britain raises the third factor — the role of unions. For what is so striking in comparison with Britain is that the unions largely accept both the legitimacy of the managerial determination of individual merit and the right of management to investigate in such detail the personal views of the worker. More generally, the union intrudes into the workplace to a very limited degree, and management appears very jealous of its prerogative. The major constraint upon management appears to concern overtime; but union influence on this issue rests upon the law, while in practice collective agreements tend to be sufficiently flexible to permit additional overtime — albeit with union consent — in order to meet production targets at times of crisis. Controls over mobility, except for some 'welfare' aspects of inter-plant moves, are virtually non-existent; union influence over the job — beyond essentially 'consensual' issues concerning safety and training — is strikingly low. And, most symbolic of all, management's unilaterally determined merit payments are included as part of the collectively negotiated annual increase. In 1983, for example, the regular (or periodical) wage increase — which is largely based on merit assessment — accounted for nearly half the total wage rise; and, in addition, the amount that workers actually receive from the negotiated 'base up' component of wage increases is also affected by merit assessment.

The monitoring role of the union in the private sector focuses upon two features: first, unions typically emphasize that they would seek to influence features such as work pace, merit payments and mobility if they were to become particularly onerous for workers. But, at the same time, factors such as the pay and career structures foster an identity of worker (and hence union) and corporate interests so that unions may argue that workers should be prepared to undergo hardships in the interests of corporate success. Second, the unions in effect exchange detailed workplace control for some involvement in the broader corporate planning process: the opportunity to learn of, and possibly comment upon, those plans. How much influence they actually achieve — indeed should have — appears to be a growing matter of contention. Survey evidence also suggests that the range and depth of consultation varies significantly — more radical unions are given access to fewer issues by management possibly because they insist upon a greater depth of influence (Shimabukuro, 1982).

Why do the unions in Japan accept this role? Two factors appear to be important. The first is an historical one: in much of the private sector, alternative unions which were more sympathetic to management were developed in the 1950s with management support to challenge the predominance of unions less prepared to accept the exertion of managerial prerogative in the workplace. Second, and relatedly, union structure mirrors the company hierarchy and organization. The union includes within its membership manual workers, white-collar workers, and even university graduates, and frequently foremen. These potential sources of division are further exacerbated by the divisions associated with the merit and career systems. In many situations, therefore, involvement in grievances over day-to-day work organization could put the union in an invidious position, having to support one union member — say, a semi-skilled production worker — against another, such as the foreman. Moreover, in many countries members of higher occupational status assume key leadership positions within the unions, particularly if this is favoured by management. In the Japanese case this means that foremen and university graduates — future managers — are over-represented in key posts in the unions. The opportunities for opposition to management are thereby further reduced.

If this argument is correct, then the less peaceful and productive record of major parts of the public sector should be explicable by the lack of the three characteristics I have listed. And this does appear to be so: workers and unions enjoy a mugh higher degree of job control in areas such as the postal service; strict seniority rather than merit is the principle for promotion and pay increases; while the major unions are insistent upon being involved in the detailed organization of work. Moreover, union opposition is encouraged in the public sector by constraints upon the legal right to strike, for strike action often leads to disciplinary action and dismissal.

The pattern of labour relations in large private firms has been associated with a dramatic improvement in the well-being of workers, particularly those with 'regular' status within large firms. Real hourly earnings rose by more than 5 per cent per year on average between 1960 and 1980. This has undoubtedly further strengthened the legitimacy of the system. But between 1973 and 1980 the rate of increase of real earnings per hour in Japanese manufacturing industry was only half the rate found in the major OECD countries, despite the fact that Japanese productivity grew more than twice as fast. At the same time, the share of profits in GDP is considerably above the average for the major OECD countries.

Moreover, the system of labour relations appears to be rather like a house of cards: the system requires of workers a very high level of trust — or the appearance of trust — in management. If such 'trust' is broken, then the consequences could be dramatic. Certainly managements seem to be acutely and increasingly aware of this fact. The implication of seniority and merit-related pay is job security, the priority of many unions. And in a number of sectors such security can no longer be provided, particularly after the flexibility of temporary and subcontract labour has been exhausted. Along with this, the slow-down in growth and the ageing of the labour force (see, for example, Yashiro *et al.,* 1982; Economic Planning Agency, 1983) suggest that many companies will be confronted with very dramatic increases in labour costs over the next decade or so: on the current pattern of wages, an increase in the average age of workers in a company from twenty-seven to forty-seven years of age would increase wage costs by about two-thirds, as well as blocking career structures. In such a situation there are clearly strong pressures on management to try to change the 'rules of the game', and there are signs that some companies are trying to do this. But how such a breach of long-term commitments to workers — that is, devaluing their investments in their companies — is possible without leading to concerted worker and even union opposition is open to question. If such a reaction were to develop, the current labour relations arrangements could work in reverse, forming a vicious circle of conflict spurred on by worker feelings of moral indignation and a sense of managerial betrayal.

This pattern of labour relations has often been seen to have particular historical and cultural origins. A few, inevitably crude, points are worth making on this. The pattern of work organization and the nature of the payment system derive from Japanese attempts at rapid industrialization through the importing of foreign technology. This was associated with a shortage of relevant skills with the result that employers were loath to train new recruits fully for fear that they would then exploit their strengthened market position; this, and the attempt to exclude trade unionism, led to both seniority and merit payments (see, for example, Okayamu, 1983; Taira, 1970; Levine and Kawada, 1980). However, this pattern received a severe shock with the defeat of the Japanese in the Second World War and subsequent American occupation. The Americans encouraged the growth of trade unionism at the same time as they initially sought to check the power of the traditional entrepreneurial elite. Union membership grew rapidly, although there was considerable debate as to the structure — centralized and powerful federations or enterprise unionism — the union movement should adopt. The latter option was chosen, if only because the workplace was the obvious unit of organization of attempts to reconstruct a decimated economy and obtain the means of subsistence. Another significant choice by unions was the decision to accept key elements of the traditional payment system; hence they sought to reduce employer discretion in the form of merit payments and to establish a system of age- and seniority-related payments (see Farley, 1950; Levine, 1965).

The policy of the American occupying forces began to change as the unions showed signs of growing radicalism and as the Korean War developed. Favour was more and more shown to employers rather than the unions, and stricter economic policies were adopted. American techniques of management were introduced, and employers became prepared to endure long strikes in order to reassert their control, after which, in many cases, they encouraged the growth of more moderate unions (similar moves are now being made in parts of the public sector). Subsequently, employers sought to develop a specifically Japanese style of management: in practice this involved the resurrection of techniques employed before the Second World War along with elements of Western management practice. Japanese tradition was, therefore, selectively interpreted and developed (see Cole, 1980; and more generally on labour relations Levine, 1965; Okochi, 1958; Ayuswara, 1966).

The Japanese primary private sector thus highlights the way in which strategies develop over time and choices are made. At the same time, it indicates the importance of the interaction between the organization of work and industrial relations, and cautions against over-simple recipes for industrial relations. Moreover, in this instance, 'peaceful' industrial relations are not attributable to union influence upon the state nor to 'welfare'-oriented policies on the part of the state. Trade union unity and centralization at national level do not appear to be a necessary precondition of industrial peace: such a structure at company level, with an associated strict control over shop-floor union activity, appears under certain conditions — outlined above — to play a similar role.

The large private Japanese company, despite superficial similarities between enterprise unions and shop steward organization, also provides an interesting contrast with Britain. First, management tends to be expert in matters of relevance to the firm, production issues are considered in detail by senior managers, and industrial and labour relations issues appear to figure importantly in management decision-making. Second, union organization is centralized in the company in contrast to the continued sectionalism of British shop steward organization. Third, the union plays a relatively small role in day-to-day issues; the pattern of work organization is of a kind which makes any form of sectional collective activity difficult. Japan also exemplifies a situation similar to that of Britain in much of the public sector (where similar sorts of policy to those considered in Britain are the subject of serious discussion). The experience of Japan, therefore, provides a good deal of support for the types of argument put forward in earlier sections.

This final chapter has ranged widely and raised many themes. In conclusion, therefore, it is useful to draw the various strands together and relate them back to the arguments outlined in chapter 1. It has been shown, first, that none of the three frames of reference — at least as they are currently promulgated — provides a very satisfactory analysis of workplace industrial relations in Britain over the last two decades. Second, we have identified a variety of weaknesses in the fundamental starting-point of these approaches. Third, we have suggested that there is no *a priori* reason for believing that one particular frame of reference is at present clearly superior in its analytical bite to any other. Examples can be found of 'peaceful' industrial relations in societies or sectors which conform, relatively speaking, to the preconditions outlined by each perspective (a point accepted, for example, by radical writers in their thesis of rank-and-file bureaucratization, and more general theories of incorporation and oligarchy). This suggests that what are often regarded as the starting-points of analyses in terms of assumptions should more properly be seen, at least in part, as matters for empirical analysis. And it follows from this that there are key sets of questions which have scarcely been posed, let alone answered — for example, we should be asking not so much whether, but under what conditions, particular kinds of strategy and action have a particular outcome. Fourth, and relatedly, a series of questions arises concerning the very concept of 'order' around which analyses centre. In the main, 'order' would seem to refer to the existence of industrial peace (and possibly consensus) along with industrial efficiency (although variously defined) and the satisfaction of certain interests (the precise nature of which is a matter of considerable disagreement). The time period we are considering when we define 'order' is also relevant, but normally receives relatively little careful consideration. It is true that both radical and unitarist writers argue that prescriptions contrary to their model can succeed only in the short or medium term. But there needs to be more careful consideration of the ways in which patterns of labour relations develop over time. Change may reflect not only the strategies of the parties, the balance of power and existing organizational arrangements; 'external' shocks, such as war, may also play a significant role. Factors which currently provide the bases of 'order' may under different circumstances foster 'disorder'. Of equal interest is the way in which factors which at one point in time are conducive of 'order', may, as their 'logics' develop and as they lead to changes in the nature of production and society, come actively to foster 'disorder' — for once-dormant contradictions may become central and stir up major conflicts, as we have seen (cf. Lindblom, 1951). These points do, however, highlight the need to take account of the interaction between broader management structure and 'strategy', worker and union structure and goals, and the way in which both the production process and the larger society are organized, and change. That is, the analysis of industrial or labour relations has to take into account the way in which interests and their pursuit are shaped by organization, the specific nature of the 'labour process' and broader social forces and, in turn, how those interests and the way in which they are promoted and defended impinge upon the industrial and social structure.

Given this perspective, perhaps one of the most striking points to come out of the discussion is how little hard, reliable and relevant data are available. Another is how little developed are the theories of industrial and labour relations. These two weaknesses are intimately related: the limitations of theory have led to a failure to collect relevant data; that lack of data has, in turn, meant that theoretical notions have been insufficiently subjected to rigorous empirical test. There is, then, a crying need to rectify these weaknesses. Such a task is not only important for the cause of academic improvement, it also has great relevance to those directly involved in industrial relations. While the interests of the parties clearly differ, they all need an adequate understanding if they are to adopt optimal policies. In this sense, there should be no disjunction between 'theory' and 'practice'. In other respects, that separation is vital if real understanding is to be achieved and adequate theory developed.

References

Aaronovitch, S. (1981). 'The relative decline of the UK', in S. Aaronovitch *et al.* (eds), *The Political Economy of British Capitalism,* London: McGraw-Hill.

Aaronovitch, S. and M. Sawyer (1975). *Big Business: Theoretical and Empirical Aspects of Concentration and Mergers in the UK,* London: Macmillan.

Abercrombie, N., S. Millard, and B. Turner (1980). *The Dominant Ideology Thesis,* London: Allen & Unwin.

Ahlström, G. (1980). *Engineers and Industrial Growth,* London: Croom Helm.

Allsopp, C. J. (1979). 'Economic Growth', in D. Morris (ed.), *The Economic System in the UK,* Oxford: Oxford University Press.

Amaya, T. (1983). *Human Resources Development in Industry,* Japanese Industrial Relations Series No.10, Tokyo: Japan Institute of Labour.

Anderman, S. (1983). 'Legally enforceable peace obligations, trade union mediation and workshop industrial action', *Economic and Industrial Democracy,* 4 (4): 501—18.

Armstrong, P., J. Goodman and J. Hyman (1981). *Ideology and Shop-Floor Industrial Relations,* London: Croom Helm.

Ayuswara, I. F. (1966). *A History of Labour in Modern Japan,* Honolulu: East-West Center Press.

Bacon R. and W. Eltis (1974). *Britain's Economic Problem,* London: Macmillan.

Bain, G. and H. Clegg (1973). 'A strategy for industrial relations research in Great Britain', *British Journal of Industrial Relations,* 12 (1): 91—113.

Bain, G. and R. Price (1980). *Profiles of Union Growth,* Oxford: Blackwell.

Baldamus, W. (1961). *Efficiency and Effort,* London: Tavistock.

Ball, J. and N. Skeoch (1981). 'Interplant comparisons of productivity and earnings', Government Economic Service Working Paper no. 38, Department of Employment.

Barratt-Brown, M., K. Coates and T. Topham (1975). 'Workers' control versus "revolutionary" theory', in R. Miliband and J. Saville (eds), *The Socialist Register,* London: Merlin Press.

Batstone, E. (1978). *Arm's length bargaining: workplace industrial relations in France',* mimeo.

Batstone, E. (1979). 'Recurrent education and industrial democracy', duplicated paper prepared for OECD.

Batstone, E., I. Boraston and S. Frenkel (1977). *Shop Stewards in Action,* Oxford: Blackwell.

Batstone, E., I. Boraston and S. Frenkel (1978). *The Social Organization of Strikes,* Oxford: Blackwell.

Batstone, E., A. Ferner and M. Terry (1983). *Unions on the Board*, Oxford: Blackwell.

Batstone, E., A. Ferner and M. Terry (1984). *Consent and Efficiency*, Oxford: Blackwell.

Beaumont, P. and D. Deaton (1980). 'Personnel management in the management hierachy: a model and results for manufacturing in Britain', *Management Decision* (Winter).

Beaumont, P. and D. Deaton (1981). 'The extent and determinants of joint consultative arrangements in Britain', *Journal of Management Studies*, 18 (1): 49—71.

Berger, S. and M. Piore (1980). *Dualism and Discontinuity in Industrial Societies*, Cambridge: Cambridge University Press.

Beynon, H. (1973). *Working for Ford*, Harmondsworth: Penguin.

Blackler, F. and C. Brown (1980). *Whatever Happened to Shell's New Philosophy of Management?*, Farnborough: Saxon House.

Blumberg. A. S. (1969). 'The Practice of Law as a Confidence Game' in V. Aubert (ed.), *Sociology of Law*, Harmondsworth: Penguin.

Bowey, A. *et al.* (1982). *Effects of Incentive Payment Systems: United Kingdom 1977—80*, Department of Employment Research Paper No. 36, London: HMSO.

Brannen, P. *et al.* (1976). *The Worker Directors*, London: Hutchinson.

Braverman, H. (1974). *Labor and Monopoly Capital*, New York: Monthly Review Press.

British Institute of Management (BIM) (1972). *The Board of Directors*, Management Survey Report No. 10, London: BIM.

British Institute of Management (BIM) (1976). *Incentive Payment Systems*, London: BIM.

Brown, C. J. and T. Sherriff (1979). 'Deindustrialization: a background paper', National Institute of Economic Research.

Brown, G. (1973). *Sabotage*, Nottingham: Spokesman.

Brown, W. (1973). *Piecework Bargaining*, London: Heinemann.

Brown, W. (1974). 'Productive of Change', *New Society*, 30 (632), 14 November 420—1

Brown W. and K. Sisson (1975). 'The use of comparisons in workplace wage determination', *British Journal of Industrial Relations*, 13: 23—53.

Brown, W., R. Ebsworth and M. Terry (1978). 'Factors shaping shop steward organization in Britain', *British Journal of Industrial Relations*, 16: 139—59.

Brown, W. (ed.) (1981). *The Changing Contours of British Industrial Relations*. Oxford: Blackwell.

Burawoy, M. (1979). *Manufacturing Consent*, Chicago: University of Chicago Press.

Cameron, D. (1982). 'Social democracy, corporatism and labour quiescence: the representation of economic interest in advanced capitalist society', paper to Conference on Representation and the State, Stanford University.

Cameron, Lord (1957). *Report of a Court of Enquiry into the Causes and Circumstances of a Dispute at Briggs Motor Bodies Limited, Dagenham*, Cmnd 131, London: HMSO.

Campaign Against a Criminal Trespass Law (1979). *Whose 'Law and Order'?*, London: CACTL.

Carew, A. (1976). *Democracy and Government in European Trade Unions*, London: Allen and Unwin.

Carlson, B. (1969). *Trade Unions in Sweden,* Stockhold: Tidens.

Carrington, J. and G. Edwards (1979). *Financing Industrial Investment,* London: Macmillan.

Caves, R. (1980). 'Productivity differences among industries', in R. Caves and L. Krause (eds), *Britain's Economic Performance,* Washington: Brookings Institution.

Caves, R. and L. Krause (1980). 'Introduction and summary', in R. Caves and L. Krause (eds), *Britain's Economic Performance,* Washington: Brookings Institution.

Central Policy Review Staff (CPRS) (1975). *The Future of the British Car Industry,* London: HMSO.

Chandler, A. D. and H. Daems (1974). 'The rise of managerial capitalism and its impact on investment strategy', Working Paper, European Institute for Advanced Studies in Management, Brussels.

Channon, D. (1973). *The Strategy and Structure of British Enterprise,* Cambridge: Harvard University Press.

Chapman, D. (1970). 'Seebohm Rowntree and factory welfare', in A. Tillett *et al.* (eds), *Management Thinkers,* Harmondsworth: Penguin.

Chemicals Economic Development Committee (1978). *Chemicals Manpower in Europe,* London: NEDC.

Child, J. and A. Keiser (1979). 'Organization and managerial roles in British and West German companies', in C. J. Lammers and D. J. Hickson (eds), *Organizations Alike and Unlike,* London: Routledge & Kegan Paul.

Child, J. and B. Partridge (1982). *Lost Managers,* Cambridge: Cambridge University Press.

Clack, G. (1967). *Industrial Relations in a British Car Factory,* Cambridge: Cambridge University Press.

Clark, J. *et al.* (1980). *Trade Unions National Politics and Economic Management,* London: Anglo-German Foundation.

Clarke, R. *et al.* (1972). *Workers' Participation in Management in Britain,* London: Heinemann.

Clegg, H. A. (1970). *The System of Industrial Relations in Great Britain,* Oxford: Blackwell.

Clegg, H. A. (1975). 'Pluralism in industrial relations', *British Journal of Industrial Relations,* 13: 309—16.

Clegg, H. A. (1976). *Trade Unionism under Collective Bargaining,* Oxford: Blackwell.

Clegg, H. A., A. Killick and R. Adams (1961). *Trade Union Officers,* Oxford: Blackwell.

Clements, L. (1976). ' Wage payment systems and work groups' frames of reference', *Industrial Relations Journal,* 7 (1), 40—9.

Cliff, T. (1970). *The Employers' Offensive,* London: Pluto Press.

Cole, R. E. (1980). *Work, Mobility and Participation,* Berkeley: University of California Press.

Commission on Industrial Relations (CIR) (1971). *Facilities Afforded to Shop Stewards,* Report No. 17, London: HMSO.

Commission on Industrial Relations (CIR) (1973). *Industrial Relations at Establishment Level,* London: HMSO.

Conboy, B. (1976). *Pay at Work,* London: Arrow.

Cowling, K. (1982). *Monopoly Capitalism,* London: Macmillan.

Cressey, P. and J. MacInness (1982). 'The modern enterprise, shop-floor organization and the structure of control', *International Yearbook of Organization Studies 1981*: 271–302.

Crichton, A. (1968). *Personnel Management in Context,* London: Batsford.

Cronin, J. (1979). *Industrial Conflict in Modern Britain,* London: Croom Helm.

Croucher, C. (1982). *Engineers at War 1939–1945,* London: Merlin Press.

Crozier, M. (1964). *The Bureaucratic Phenomenon,* London: Tavistock.

Currie, R. (1979). *Industrial Politics,* Oxford: Clarendon Press.

Dahrendorf, R. (1959). *Class and Class Conflict in an Industrial Society,* London: Routledge & Kegan Paul.

Daniel, W. W. (1976). *Wage Determination in Industry,* London: Political and Economic Planning.

Daniel, W. W. and N. MacIntosh (1973). *The Right to Manage?* London: MacDonald.

Daniel, W. W. and E. Stilgoe (1978). *The Impact of Employment Protection Laws,* London: Policy Studies Institute.

Daniel, W. W. and N. Millward (1983). *Workplace Industrial Relations in Britain,* London: Heinemann.

Deaton, D. (1983). 'Management & industrial relations', duplicated paper.

Deaton, D. and P. Beaumont (1980). 'The determinants of bargaining structure: some large-scale evidence for Britain', *British Journal of Industrial Relations,* 18: 202–16.

Department of Employment (D of E) (1971). *The Reform of Collective Bargaining at Plant and Company Level,* Manpower Paper No. 5, London: HMSO.

Derber, M. (1955). *Labor–Management Relations at the Plant Level under Industry-Wide Bargaining,* Chicago: University of Illinois Press.

Donovan (1968). Royal Commission on Trade Unions and Employers' Associations, *Report,* Cmnd. 3623, London: HMSO.

Dryburgh, G. D. M. (1972). 'The man in the middle', *Personnel Management,* May.

Dubois, P. (1976). 'Les formes de lutte dans les usines nouvelles', in Groupe de Sociologie du Travail, CNRS — Université de Paris VII (ed.), *Décentralisation Industrielle et Relations de Travail,* Paris: La Documentation Française.

Dubois, P. and D. Monjardet (1978). *La Division du Travail dans l'Industrie: Etude de Cas Anglais et Français,* Paris: Groupe de Sociologie du Travail.

Durcan, J., W. E. J. McCarthy and G. Redman (1983). *Strikes in Post-war Britain, 1946–73,* London: Hutchinson.

Durkheim, E. (1893). *The Division of Labour in Society,* Glencoe: Free Press (1964).

Eaton, J. and C. Gill (1981). *The Trade Union Directory,* London: Pluto Press.

Economic Planning Agency (1983). *Japan in the Year 2000,* Tokyo: Japan Times.

Edwardes, M. (1983). *Back from the Brink,* London: Collins.

Edwards, P. (1983). 'The political economy of industrial conflict: Britain and the United States', *Economic and Industrial Democracy,* 4 (4): 461–99.

Edwards, P. (1983). 'The pattern of collective industrial action', in G. Bain (ed.), *Industrial Relations in Britain,* Oxford: Blackwell.

Edwards, P. and H. Scullion (1982). *The Social Organization of Industrial Conflict,* Oxford: Blackwell.

Edwards, R. (1979). *Contested Terrain*, London: Heinemann.

Elden, M. (1977). 'Political Efficacy at Work', paper to seminar on social change and organization development, Inter-University Centre, Dubrovnik.

Elliott, D. and R. Elliott (1976). *The Control of Technology*, London: Wykeham.

Elliott, I. and A. Hughes (1976). 'Capital and labour: their growth, distribution and productivity', in M. Panic (ed.), *The UK and West German Manufacturing Industry 1954—72*, London: HMSO.

Employment Gazette, various issues.

England, J. (1981). 'Shop Stewards in Transport House', *Industrial Relations Journal*, 12(5): 16—29.

Etzioni, A. (1961). *A Comparative Analysis of Complex Organizations*, New York: Free Press.

Farley, M. (1950). *Aspects of Japan's Labor Problems*, New York: J. Day.

Fidler, J. (1981). *The British Business Elite*, London: Routledge & Kegan Paul.

Flanders, A. (1964). *The Fawley Productivity Agreements*, London: Faber and Faber.

Flanders, A. (1970). *Management and Unions*, London: Faber and Faber.

Foreign Press Center (1982). *Facts and Figures of Japan*, Tokyo: Foreign Press Center.

Forsebäch, L. (1976). *Industrial Relations and Employment in Sweden*, Stockholm: The Swedish Institute.

Fothergill, S. and G. Gudgin (1982). *Unequal Growth*, London: Heinemann.

Fox, A. (1973). 'Industrial relations: a social critique of pluralist ideology', in J. Child (ed.), *Man and Organization*, London: Allen and Unwin: 185—234.

Fox, A. (1974). *Beyond Contract: Work, Power and Trust Relations*, London: Faber and Faber.

Fox, A. and A. Flanders (1970). 'The reform of collective bargaining: from Donovan to Durkheim', in A. Flanders, *Management and Unions*, London: Faber and Faber.

Friedman, A. L. (1977). *Industry and Labour*, London: Macmillan.

Fryer, R. (1973). 'Redundancy, values and public policy', *Industrial Relations Journal*, 4 (2): 2—19.

Fryer, R., A. Fairclough and T. Manson (1974). *Organization and Change in the National Union of Public Employees*, London: NUPE.

Fryer, R., A. Fairclough and T. Manson (1978). 'Facilities for female shop stewards: the Employment Protection Act and collective agreements', *British Journal of Industrial Relations*, 16, 160—74.

Fulcher, J. (1976). 'Class conflict: joint regulation and its decline', in R. Scase (ed.), *Readings in the Swedish Class Structure*, Oxford: Pergamon.

Gallie, D. (1978). *In Search of the New Working Class*, Cambridge: Cambridge University Press.

Gallie, D. (1984). *Social Inequality and Class Radicalism in France and Britain*, Cambridge: Cambridge University Press.

De Geer, H. (1982). *Job Studies and Industrial Relations*, Stockholm: Almquist and Wicksell International.

Gilbert, M. (1981). 'A sociological model of inflation', *Sociology* 15 (2): 185—209.

Gill, C., R. Morris and J. Eaton (1977). 'Managerial control and collective bargaining', *Personnel Review*, 6 (4): 51—7.

Gill, C., R. Morris and J. Eaton (1978). *Industrial Relations in the Chemical Industry,* Farnborough: Saxon House.

Glasgow University Media Group (1976). *Bad News,* Vol. 1, London: Routledge and Kegan Paul.

Glynn, S. and S. Shaw (1981). 'Wage Bargaining and Unemployment', *Political Quarterly* 52 (1): 115—26.

Goldthorpe, J. (1964). 'Social stratification in industrial society', in *The Development of Industrial Societies,* Sociological Review Monograph No. 8.

Goldthorpe, J. (1972). 'Class, status and party in Modern Britain: some recent interpretations, Marxist and Marxisant', *Archives Européens de Sociologie* 12 (2): 342—72.

Goldthorpe, J. (1977). 'Industrial relations in Great Britain: a critique of reformism', in T. Clarke and L. Clements (eds), *Trade Unions under Capitalism,* London: Fontana.

Goldthorpe, J. (1978). 'The current inflation: towards a sociological account', in F. Hirsch and J. Goldthorpe (eds), *The Political Economy of Inflation,* London: Martin Robertson.

Goodman, J. and T. Whittingham (1973). *Shop Stewards,* London: Pan.

Government Social Survey (1968). *Workplace Industrial Relations,* London: HMSO.

Gustavsen, B. and G. Hunnius (1981). *New Patterns of Work Reform,* Oslo: Universitetsforlaget.

Hannah, L. and J. Kay (1977). *Concentration in Modern Industry,* London: Macmillan.

Hansard (1970). *Parliamentary Reports,* 14 December.

Hart, H. and C. Von Otter (1976). 'The determination of wage structures in manufacturing industry', in R. Scase (ed.), *Readings in the Swedish Class Structure,* Oxford: Pergamon.

Hawes, W. and D. Smith (1981). 'Employee involvement outside manufacturing', *Employment Gazette* 89 (6): 265—71.

Hawkins, K. (1972). 'Productivity bargaining: a reassessment', *Industrial Relations,* Spring: 10—34.

Headey, B. (1970). 'Trade unions and national wages policies', *Journal of Politics* 32: 407—39.

Heath, R. H. (1969). 'The national power loading agreement in the coal industry and some aspects of workers' control', K. Coates *et al.* (eds), *Trade Union Register,* London: Merlin.

Heller, F. *et al.* (1981). *What do the British want from participation and industrial democracy?* London: Anglo-German Foundation.

Henry, S. (1983). *Private Justice,* London: Routledge & Kegan Paul.

Herding, R. (1972). *Job Control and Union Structure,* Rotterdam: Rotterdam University Press.

Hickson, D. and G. Mallory (1981). 'Scope for choice in strategic decision-making and the trade union role', in A. Thomson and M. Warner (eds), *The Behavioural Sciences and Industrial Relations,* Aldershot: Gower.

Higgs, P. (1969). 'The convenor', in R. Fraser (ed.), *Work,* Vol. 2, Harmondsworth: Penguin.

Hobsbawm, E. J. (1969). *Industry and Empire,* Harmondsworth: Penguin.

Hopwood, A. (1973). *An Accounting System and Managerial Behaviour,* London: Saxon House.

Hopwood, A. (1974). *Accounting and Human Behaviour*, London: Accountancy Age.

Horovitz, J. H. (1980). *Top Management Control in Europe*, London: Macmillan.

Hyman, R. (1974). 'Workers' control and revolutionary theory', in R. Miliband and J. Saville (eds), *The Socialist Register*, London: Merlin Press.

Hyman, R. (1975). *Industrial Relations: A Marxist Introduction*, London: Macmillan.

Hyman, R. (1977). *Strikes*, London: Fontana.

Hyman, R. (1978). 'Pluralism, procedural consensus and collective bargaining', *British Journal of Industrial Relations* 13: 16—40.

Hyman, R. (1979). 'The politics of workplace trade unionism', *Capital and Class*, 8: 54—67.

Hyman, R. and A. Elger (1981). 'Job controls, the employers' offensive and alternative strategies', *Capital and Class*, 15: 115—49.

Incomes Data Services (IDS) (1978). *Productivity Bargaining*, Study 162, London: IDS.

Incomes Data Services (IDS) (1979). *Productivity Schemes*, Study 186, London: IDS.

Incomes Data Services (IDS) (1981). *Productivity Improvements*, Study 245, London: IDS.

Industrial Democracy in Europe (IDE) International Research Group (1981). *Industrial Democracy in Europe*, Oxford: Clarendon Press.

Ingham, G. (1974). *Strikes and Industrial Conflict*, London: Macmillan.

Inman, P. (1957). *Labour in the Munitions Industries*, London: HMSO.

Institute for Workers' Control (IWC) Motors Group (1978). *A Workers' Enquiry into the Motor Industry*, London: CSE.

Jacobs, E. *et al.* (1978). *The Approach to Industrial Change*, London: Anglo-German Foundation.

Jamieson, I. (1980). *Capitalism and Culture: A Comparative Analysis of British and American Manufacturing Organizations*, Farnborough: Gower.

Jefferys, J. (1946). *The Story of the Engineers 1800—1945*, London: Lawrence and Wishart.

Jefferys, S. (1979). 'Striking into the '80s: modern British trade unionism, its limits and potential', *International Socialism*, 5: 1—52.

Jessop, B. (1980). 'The transformation of the state in post-war Britain', in R. Scase (ed.), *The State in Western Europe*, London: Croom Helm.

Jones, D. T. (1976). 'Output, employment and labour productivity in Europe since 1955', *National Institute Economic Review*, 77.

Kahn-Freund, O. (1979). *Labour Relations: Heritage and Adjustment*, Oxford: Oxford University Press.

Kaldor, N. (1966). *Causes of the Slow Rate of Growth of the United Kingdom*, Cambridge: Cambridge University Press.

Kaldor, N. (1975). 'Economic growth and the Verdoorn Law', *Economic Journal*, 35 (December).

Kato, Y. (1980). *Pattern of Labour Use in Japan*, duplicated paper.

Kilpatrick, A. and T. Lawson (1980). 'On the nature of industrial decline in the UK', *Cambridge Journal of Economics*, 4, 85—102.

Knight, I. B. (1979). *Company Organization and Worker Participation*, London: HMSO.

Kochan, T., R. McKersie and P. Cappelli (1983). *Strategic Choice and Industrial Relations Theory and Practice,* duplicated paper.

Korpi, W. (1979). *The Working Class in Welfare Capitalism,* London: Routledge and Kegan Paul.

Korpi, W. (1981). 'Unofficial Strikes in Sweden', *British Journal of Industrial Relations,* 19, 66—86.

Korpi, W. (1983). *The Democratic Class Struggle,* London: Routledge & Kegan Paul.

Korpi, W. and M. Shalev (1979). 'Strikes, industrial relations and class conflict in capitalist societies', *British Journal of Sociology,* 30, 164—87.

Kusterer, K. (1978). *Know-How on the Job,* Boulder, Colorado: Westview.

Legge, K. and M. Exley (1975). 'Authority, ambiguity and adaptation. The personnel specialist's dilemma', *Industrial Relations Journal,* 6 (3): 51—65.

Leijsne, F. (1980). 'Workplace bargaining and trade union power', *Industrial Relations Journal,* 11 (2), 58—69.

Lerner, S. (1969). *Breakaway Unions and the Small Trade Union,* London: Allen and Unwin.

Levine, S. (1965). 'Labor markets and collective bargaining in Japan', in W. W. Lockwood (ed.), *The State and Economic Enterprise in Japan,* Princeton: Princeton University Press.

Levine, S. B. and H. Kawada (1980). *Human Resources in Japanese Industrial Development,* Princeton: Princeton University Press.

Lewin, L. (1980). *Governing Trade Unions in Sweden,* Cambridge: Harvard University Press.

Lilja, K. (1983). *Workers' Workplace Organizations,* Helsinki: Helsinki School of Economics.

Lindblom, C. E. (1949). *Unions and Capitalism,* New Haven: Yale University Press.

Lloyds, P. A. (1976). *Incentive Payment Systems,* Management Survey Report 34, London: British Institute of Management.

Lockwood, D. (1966). 'Sources of variation in working-class images of society', *Sociological Review,* 14, 249—67.

Lukes, S. (1974). *Power: A Radical View,* London: Macmillan.

Lupton, T. and A. Bowey (1974). *Wages and Salaries,* Harmondsworth: Penguin.

McCarthy, W. E. J. (1966). *The Role of Shop Stewards in British Industrial Relations,* Royal Commission on Trade Unions and Employers' Associations Research Paper No. 1, London: HMSO.

McCarthy, W. E. J. and S. R. Parker (1968). *Shop Stewards and Workshop Relations,* Royal Commission on Trade Unions and Employers' Associations Research Paper No. 10, London: HMSO.

McCarthy, W. E. J. and N. Ellis (1973). *Management by Agreement,* London: Hutchinson.

McKersie, R. and L. Hunter (1973). *Pay, Productivity and Collective Bargaining,* London: Macmillan.

McKersie, R. and J. Klein (1982). *Productivity: The Industrial Relations Connection,* Working Paper, Sloan School of Management, MIT.

Maddison, A. (1979). 'The long run dynamics of productivity growth', in W. Beckerman (ed.), *Slow Growth in Britain,* Oxford: Clarendon Press.

Maitland, I. (1983). *The Causes of Industrial Disorder,* London: Routledge and Kegan Paul.

Mallory, G. *et al.* (1983). 'Implanted decision-making: American-owned firms in Britain', *Journal of Management Studies*, 20 (2): 191—212.

Manson, T. (1977). 'Management, the professions and the unions: a social analysis of change in the National Health Service', in M. Stacey *et al.* (eds), *Health and the Division of Labour*, London: Croom Helm.

Marriott, R. (1957). *Incentive Payment Systems: a Review of Research and Opinions*, London: Staples Press.

Marsden, D. (1981). 'Industrial democracy, job regulation and internal labour markets', in H. Diefenbacker and H. Nutzinger (eds), *Mitbestimmung*, Frankfurt: Campus.

Marsh, A. (1966). *Disputes Procedures in British Industry*, Royal Commission on Trade Unions and Employers' Associations Research Paper, No. 2 (Part I), London: HMSO.

Marsh, A. (1971). 'The staffing of industrial relations management in the engineering industry', *Industrial Relations Journal* 2 (2): 14—23.

Marsh, A. (1973). *Managers and Shop Stewards*, London: IPM.

Marsh, A. (1982). *Employee Relations Policy and Decision Making*, Aldershot: Gower.

Marsh, A. (1983). 'Communication in Trade Unions', duplicated paper.

Marsh, A. and E. Coker (1963). 'Shop steward organization in the engineering industry', *British Journal of Industrial Relations* I: 170—90.

Marsh, A., E. Evans and P. Garcia (1971). *Workplace Industrial Relations in Engineering*, London: Kogan Page.

Martin, R. (1980). *The Sociology of Power*, London: Routledge and Kegan Paul.

Martin, R. (1981). *New Technology and Industrial Relations in Fleet Street*, Oxford: Clarendon Press.

Maurice, M., J. Sellier and J. Silvestre (1982). *Politique d'Education et Organisation Industrielle*, Paris: PUF.

Meeks, G. (1977). *Disappointing Marriage: A Study of the Gains from Merger*, Cambridge: Cambridge University Press.

Melman, S. (1958). *Decision-Making and Productivity*, Oxford: Blackwell.

Merkle, J. (1980). *Management and Ideology*, Berkeley: University of California Press.

Miller, F. B. and M. A. Coghill (1964). 'Sex and the personnel manager', *Industrial and Labour Relations Review*, 18, 32—44.

Ministry of Labour (1982). *Year Book of Labour Statistics 1981*, Japan: Ministry of Labour.

Moe, T. M. (1980). *The Organization of Interests*, Chicago: University of Chicago Press.

Monopolies and Mergers Commission (1980). *British Railways Board: London and South East Commuter Services*, London: HMSO.

Monopolies and Mergers Commission (1981a). *Central Electricity Generating Board*, London: HMSO.

Monopolies and Mergers Commission (1981b). *Severn-Trent Water Authority, East Worcestershire Waterworks Company and the South Staffordshire Waterworks Company*, London: HMSO.

Mothé, D. (1973). *Le Métier de Militant*, Paris: Seuil.

Moulding, T. and M. Moynagh (1982). 'Pay bargaining in Britain: too many players in a game of leapfrog?', *Personnel Management*, 14 (4): 38—41.

Mueller, D. C. (1983). *The Political Economy of Growth*, New Haven: Yale University Press.

National Economic Development Council (1965). *Investment in Machine Tools*, London: HMSO.

National Board for Prices and Incomes (NBPI) (1968). *Job Evaluation*, Report 83, Cmnd. 3772, London: HMSO.

National Board for Prices and Incomes (NBPI) (1969). *Productivity Agreements*, Report 123, Cmnd. 4136, London: HMSO.

Newbould, G. D. (1970). *Management and Merger Activity*, Liverpool: Guthstead.

Nichols, T. and H. Beynon (1977). *Living with Capitalism*, London: Routledge and Kegan Paul.

Nicholson, N. (1976). 'The role of the shop steward: an empirical case study', *Industrial Relations Journal*, 7: 15—26.

Nightingale, M. (1980). 'UK productivity dealing in the 1960s', in T. Nichols (ed.), *Capital and Labour*, Glasgow: Fontana.

Niven, M. M. (1961). *Personnel Management 1913-1963*, London: Institute of Personnel Management.

Office of Manpower Economics (OME) (1973). *Measured Day Work*, London: HMSO.

Ogden, S. (1981).'The reform of collective bargaining: a managerial revolution?', *Industrial Relations Journal*, 12 (5): 30—42.

Okayama, R. (1983). 'Japanese employer labour policy: the heavy engineering industry, 1900-1930', in H. Gospel and C. Littler (eds), *Managerial Strategies and Industrial Relations*, London: Heinemann.

Okochi, K. (1958). *Labor in Modern Japan*, Tokyo: Science Council of Japan, Economic Series, No. 18.

Olson, M. (1982). *The Rise and Decline of Nations*, New Haven: Yale University Press.

Organization for Economic Cooperation and Development (OECD) (1982). *Historical Statistics 1960—1980*, Paris: OECD.

Parker, S. (1974). *Workplace Industrial Relations, 1972*, London: HMSO.

Parker, S. (1975). *Workplace Industrial Relations, 1973*, London: HMSO.

Pedler, M. (1973). 'Shop stewards as leaders', *Industrial Relations Journal*, 4, 43—60.

Pfeffer, R. (1979). *Working for Capitalism*, New York: Columbia University Press.

Phelps Brown, H. (1977). 'What is the British predicament?' *Three Banks Review*, December, 3—29.

Phelps Brown, H. (1983). *The Origins of Trade Union Power*, Oxford: Clarendon Press.

Piven, F. and R. Cloward (1977). *Poor People's Movements*, New York: Pantheon.

Pizzorno, A. (1978). 'Political exchange and collective identity in industrial conflict', in C. Crouch and A. Pizzorno (eds), *The Resurgence of Class Conflict in Western Europe since 1968*, Vol. 2, London: Macmillan.

Plowman, D., W. Minchinton and M. Stacey (1962). 'Local social status in England and Wales', *Sociological Review*, 10.

Prais, S. J. (1976). *The Evolution of Giant Firms in Britain*, London: Cambridge University Press.

Prais, S. J. (1980). 'Comment', in R. Caves and L. Krause (eds), *Britain's Economic Performance*, Washington: Brookings Exhibition.

Prais, S. J. (1981). *Productivity and Industrial Structure*, Cambridge: Cambridge University Press.

Prais, S. J. (1981). 'Vocational qualifications of the labour force in Britain and Germany', *National Institute Economic Review*, 98; 47—59.

Pratten, C. F. (1976). *Labour Productivity Differentials Within International Companies*, Cambridge: Cambridge University Press.

Pratten, C. F. and L. A. Atkinson (1976). 'The Use of Manpower in British Manufacturing Industry', *Department of Employment Gazette*, 84; 571—6.

Price Commission (1978a). *Metal Box Ltd — Open Top Food and Beverage Cans and Aerosol Cans*, Report No. 3, London: HMSO.

Price Commission (1978b). *Imperial Tobacco—Cigarettes and Cigarillos*, Report No. 26, London: HMSO.

Price Commission (1978c). *Air Products Ltd — Merchant Industrial Gases*, Report No. 28, London: HMSO.

Price Commission (1979a). *BOC Ltd — Compressed Permanent Gases and Dissolved Acetylene sold in Cylinders, Cylinder Rentals and Fixed Charges*, London: HMSO.

Price Commission (1979b). *Perkins Engine Company — Diesel, Gasoline, Reconditioned and 'Short' Engines*, Report No. 34, London: HMSO.

Price Commission (1979c). *The Rugby Portland Cement Company Ltd — Cement*, Report No. 35, London: HMSO.

Price Commission (1979d). *United Biscuits (UK) Ltd — Biscuits, Crisps, Nuts and Savoury Snacks*, Report No. 36, London: HMSO.

Price Commission (1979e). *BP Oil Ltd — Oil and Petroleum Products*, Report No. 37, London: HMSO.

Price Commission (1979f). *Esso Petroleum Company Ltd — Oil and Petroleum Products*, Report No. 38, London: HMSO.

Price Commission (1979g). *Bass Ltd — Wholesale Prices of Beer and Prices in Managed Houses*, Report No. 39, London: HMSO.

Price Commission (1979h). *Whitbread and Company Ltd — Wholesale Prices and Prices in Managed Houses of Beer, Wines, Spirits, Soft Drinks and Ciders*, Report No. 40, London: HMSO.

Price Commission (1979i). *Area Electricity Boards — Electricity Prices and Certain Allied Charges*, Report No. 42, London: HMSO.

Price Commission (1979j). *British Gas Corporation — Gas Prices and Allied Charges*, Report No. 43, London: HMSO.

Price Commission (1979k). *Shell UK Oil — Oil and Petroleum Products*, Report No. 44, London: HMSO.

Prime Minister's Office (1981). *Kinro ishiki chosa*, Tokyo: Prime Minister's Office.

Pryke, R. (1981). *The Nationalized Industries*, Oxford: Martin Robertson.

Purcell, J. (1979). 'The lessons of the Commission on Industrial Relations', *Industrial Relations Journal*, 14 (2).

Purcell, J. (1981). *Good Industrial Relations: Theory and Practice*, London: Macmillan.

Purcell, J. (1983). 'The management of industrial relations in the modern corporation: agenda for research', *British Journal of Industrial Relations*, 21 (1).

Purcell, J. and Sisson, K. (1983). 'Strategies and practice in the management of industrial relations', in G. Bain (ed.), *Industrial Relations in Britain*, Oxford: Blackwell.

Robertson, A. (n.d.) *Management and Finance: A Study in Financial Control Techniques*, London: Hallam Press.

Roeber, J. (1975). *Social Change at Work*, London: Duckworth.

Ross, A. and P. Hartman (1960). *Changing Patterns of Industrial Conflict*, New York: Wiley.

Sabel, C. (1981). 'The internal politics of trade unions', in S. Berger (ed.), *Organizing Interests in Western Europe*, Cambridge: Cambridge University Press.

Saburabayashi, M. (1983). 'Wage administration in Japan', East Asian Institute Occasional Paper 2, Free University of Berlin.

Sayles, L. R. (1959). *The Behaviour of Industrial Work Groups*, New York: Wiley and Sons.

Sayles, L. R. (1984). *Managerial Behaviour*, New York: McGraw Hill.

Shalev, M. (1980). 'Industrial relations theory and the comparative study of industrial relations and industrial conflict', *British Journal of Industrial Relations*, 18 (1), 26—43.

Shalev, M. (1983). 'Strikes and the crisis: industrial conflict and unemployment in the western nations', *Economic and Industrial Democracy* 4 (4): 417—60.

Shalev, M. and W. Korpi (1980). 'Working class mobilization and American exceptionalism', *Economic and Industrial Democracy* 1 (1): 31—61.

Shigeyoshi, T. (1982). 'The structure of the Japanese labour market', paper to the Japan-Federal Republic of Germany Symposium, Tohoku University.

Shimabukuro, Y. (1982). *Consensus Management in Japanese Industry*. Tokyo: ISS Inc.

Shirai, T. (ed.) (1983) *Contemporary Industrial Relations in Japan*, Madison: University of Wisconsin Press.

Sisson, K. and W. Brown (1983). 'Industrial relations in the private sector: Donovan revisited', in G. Bain (ed.), *Industrial Relations in Britain*, Oxford: Blackwell.

Smith, A. D., D. Mitchens and S. Davies (1982). *International Industrial Productivity*, Cambridge: Cambridge University Press.

Smith, L. T. *et al.* (1978). *Strikes in Britain*, Department of Employment Manpower Papers, 15, London: HMSO.

Smith, M. (1981). 'Accounting for inflation in Britain', *British Journal of Sociology*, 33 (3): 301—29.

Somerton (1977). *Trade Unions and Industrial Relations in Local Government*. Studies for Trade Unionists, 3, 11, London: Workers' Educational Association.

Steer, P. and J. Cable (1978). 'Internal organization and profit: an empirical analysis of large UK companies', *Journal of Industrial Economics*.

Stettner, N. (1969). *Productivity Bargaining and Industrial Change*, Oxford: Pergamon.

Storey, J. (1980). *The Challenge to Management Control*, London: Kegan Paye.

Streeck, W. (1982). 'Organizational consequences of neo-corporatist cooperation in West German labour unions', in G. Lehmbruch and P. C. Schmitter (eds), *Patterns of Corporatist Policy-Making*, London: Sage.

Supple, B. (1973). 'The state and the industrial revolution 1700—1914', in C. M. Cipolla (ed.), *The Industrial Revolution*, London: Fontana.

Taira, K. (1970). *Economic Development and the Labor Market in Japan*, New York: Columbia University Press.

Tarantelli, E. (1983). 'The regulation of inflation in western countries and the degree of neo-corporatism', paper given at European University Institute.

Taylor, R. (1982). *Workers and the New Depression*, London: Macmillan.

Terry, M. (1977). 'The inevitable growth of informality', *British Journal of Industrial Relations*, 25 (1).

Terry, M. (1978). 'Shop stewards: the emergence of a lay elite?', IRRU Discussion Paper.

Terry, M. (1979). 'The emergence of a lay elite?', *Sociologie du Travail*, 21: 380—96.

Terry, M. (1982). 'Organizing a fragmented workforce: shop stewards in local government', *British Journal of Industrial Relations*, 20: 1—19.

Terry, M. (1983). 'Shop steward development and managerial strategies', in G. Bain (ed.), *Industrial Relations in Britain*, Oxford: Blackwell.

Thomason, G. (1976). *A Textbook of Personnel Management*, London: Institute of Personnel Management.

Tolliday, S. and J. Zeitlin (1982). 'Shop-floor bargaining, contract unionism and job control: an Anglo-American comparison', paper given to AHA Convention, Washington.

Topham, T. (1969). 'Productivity bargaining', in K. Coates, T. Topham and M. Barratt-Brown (eds), *Trade Union Register*, London: Merlin Press.

Totsuka, H. (1981). 'A case study on the transition from piecework to measured daywork in BLMC', *Annals of the Institute of Social Science*, University of Tokyo, 22: 5—41.

Trades Union Congress (TUC) (1975). *General Council's Report*. London: TUC.

Trades Union Congress (TUC) (1979). *General Council's Report*. London: TUC.

Tricker, R. I. (1967). *The Accountant in Management*, London: Batsford.

Turner, A. and Lawrence, P. (1967). *Industrial Jobs and the Worker*, Cambridge: Harvard University Press.

Turner, H. A. (1962). *Trade Union Growth, Structure and Policy*, London: Allen and Unwin.

Turner, H. A. (1968). 'The Royal Commission's Research Papers', *British Journal of Industrial Relations*, 6 (3): 346—59.

Turner, H. A., G. Clack and G. Roberts (1967). *Labour Relations in the Motor Industry*, London: Allen and Unwin.

Turner, H. A., G. Roberts and D. Roberts (1977). *Management Characteristics and Labour Conflict*, Cambridge: Cambridge University Press.

TUSIU (1976). *Workers' Occupations and the North-East Experience*, Newcastle: TUSIU.

Undy, R. *et al.* (1981). *Change in Trade Unions*, London, Hutchinson.

United Nations (1967). *Incomes in Post-war Europe*, Geneva: United Nations.

Visser, J. (1983). 'The unification and centralization of the trade union movement: a comparison of ten countries', paper given at European University Institute.

Wainright, H. and D. Elliott (1981). *The Lucas Plan*, London: Allison and Busby.

Watson, T. J. (1977). *The Personnel Managers: A Study in the Sociology of*

Work and Employment, London: Routledge & Kegan Paul.

Weekes, B. *et al.* (1975). *Industrial Relations and the Limits of Law,* Oxford: Blackwell.

Wenban-Smith, G. (1982). 'Factors influencing recent productivity growth—report on a survey of companies', *National Institute Economic Review,* 101: 57—66.

Wenban-Smith, G. (1981). 'A study of the movements of productivity in individual industries in the United Kingdom 1968—79', *National Institute Economic Review,* 97.

White, M. (1981). *Payment Systems in Britain,* Aldershot: Gower.

Wiener, M. J. (1982). *English Culture and the Decline of the Industrial Spirit 1850—1980,* Cambridge: Cambridge University Press.

Wilders, M. and S. Parker (1975). 'Changes in workplace industrial relations 1966—72', *British Journal of Industrial Relations,* 13 (1).

Wilensky, H. (1975). *The Welfare State and Equality: The Roots of Public Expenditures,* Berkeley: University of California Press.

Williams, K. (1983). 'Introduction', in K. Williams, *et al., Why are the British so Bad at Manufacturing?,* London: Routledge & Kegan Paul.

Williams, K. *et al.* (1983). *Why are the British so Bad at Manufacturing?.* London: Routledge & Kegan Paul.

Williamson, O. E. (1975). *Markets and Hierarchies,* New York: Free Press.

Willman, P. (1980). 'Leadership and trade union principles', *Industrial Relations Journal,* 11 (4): 39—49.

Willman, P. (1982). *Fairness, Collective Bargaining and Incomes Policy,* Oxford: Clarendon Press.

Winch, G. (1981). 'Shop steward tenure and workplace organization', *Industrial Relations Journal,* 11 (4), 50—62.

Winkler, J. (1974). 'The ghost at the bargaining table: directors and industrial relations', *British Journal of Industrial Relations,* 12 (2): 191—212.

Wood, S. (1980). 'Corporate strategies and organizational studies', *International Yearbook of Organization Studies,* 1980: 52—71.

Wragg, R. and J. Robertson (1977). *Post-war Trends in Employment, Productivity, Output, Labour Costs and Prices by Industry in the United Kingdom,* Department of Employment Research Paper 3, London: HMSO.

Wright-Mills, C. (1948). *The New Men of Power: America's Labor Leaders,* New York: Harcourt Brace.

Yashiro, N. *et al.* (1982). *Japan's Rapidly Aging Population,* Tokyo: Foreign Press Center.

Zeitlin, J. (1980). 'The emergence of shop steward organization and job control in the British car industry: a review essay', *History Workshop,* 10: 119—37.

Zeitlin, J. (1982). 'Trade unions and job control: a critique of "rank and filism" ', paper to Conference of the Society for the Study of Labour History, Birkbeck, London, 27 November.

Zeitlin, J. (1984). 'Shop-floor bargaining and the state: a contradictory relationship', in S. Tolliday and J. Zeitlin (eds), *Shop-floor Bargaining and the State: Historical and Comparative Perspectives,* Cambridge: Cambridge University Press.

Index